The Fortune
Whitecross Street
Finsbury Fields
The Curtain
Shoreditch
Cripplegate
Moorfields
Moorgate
Mountjoy's house
London Wall
Bishopsgate
St. Olave's
Bull Inn
Bishopsgate Street
St. Helen's
Aldgate
Cheapside
Threadneedle Street
Cornhill
Leadenhall Street
Watling Street
Lombard Street
Cross Keys Inn
Gracechurch St.
Fenchurch Street
Canon St.
East-cheap
Thames Street
Tower Street
Thames Street
River
London Bridge
The Globe
St. Saviour's
Bridgegate
Tower

Also by the Author

BOOKS

Shakespeare's Poetics

The War Against Poetry

An Essential Shakespeare

The Dark Ages and the Age of Gold

The Language of Adam

A Mingled Yarn: The Life of R. P. Blackmur

The Three Romes

Young Shakespeare

EDITIONS

The Court of Venus

The Court of Virtue

King Lear

Oscar Wilde

Drama of the English Renaissance
(with Norman Rabkin)

All's Well That Ends Well

Shakespeare The Later Years

Shakespeare The Later Years

Russell Fraser

COLUMBIA UNIVERSITY PRESS *New York*

Columbia University Press
New York Oxford

Library of Congress Cataloging-in-Publication Data

Fraser, Russell A.
Shakespeare, the later years / Russell Fraser.
p. cm.
Includes bibliographical references and index.
ISBN 0-231-06766-6
1. Shakespeare, William, 1564–1616. 2. Dramatists, English—Early modern, 1500–700—Biography. I. Title.
PR2894.F66 1991
822.3'3—dc20 91-31956
CIP

Casebound editions of Columbia University Press books are Smyth-sewn and printed on permanent and durable acid-free paper.

The map printed on the endpapers was drawn by Kathleen Vonte and appeared in Hazelton Spencer's *The Art and Life of William Shakespeare* (Harcourt Brace, 1940). It is reprinted here with thanks.

FRONTISPIECE AND JACKET
Derived from but modifying the familiar Chandos Portrait, this likeness furnished a shop sign for Jacob Tonson, proprietor of the Shakespeare's Head in the Strand, 1710–20. Folger Shakespeare Library. A grant from the Rackham School of the University of Michigan contributed to the cost of the jacket.

Printed in the United States of America

c 10 9 8 7 6 5 4 3 2 1

For Nat McGrane
Who shows his back above
the element he lives in

Contents

PREFACE XI

1. *Two-Headed Janus* 1

2. *The Revolution of the Times* 34

3. *Sailing to Illyria* 65

4. *Fools of Nature* 101

5. *Treason in the Blood* 134

6. *The Wine of Life* 160

7. *Bravest at the Last* 188

8. *Unpathed Waters, Undreamed Shores* 216

9. *Journeys' End* 247

NOTES 281

INDEX 369

Illustrations follow page 114

Preface

THIS BOOK continues and completes the biography I began with *Young Shakespeare* (1988). Like its predecessor, it means to run the life and work together, clarifying one in terms of the other. Shakespeare's work seeks to stand on its own, true of any credentialed artist's, and saying where it comes from or what it reflects needs reserve and a large dose of tact. Less forthcoming than Henry James, he left no notebooks intimating connections. A few supers in the plays were known to him in person, like Marian Hacket, the fat alewife of Wincot, and that Paolo Marco Lucchese who ran a restaurant in St. Olave's parish, London, and is summoned by the Duke in *Othello*. His first version of Polonius, identified by some with Queen Elizabeth's minister Burghley, is only made-up "Corambis," however. As a rule, the more life affects him, the less he lets on. But the personal life, though he buries it deep, participates in his art, an energizing presence.

Energizing doesn't always mean troubled. Whatever the subject, Shakespeare's art is happy, "the unseen good old man" behind the arras converting grief and vexation to profit. His handling of everyday business, emotionally neutral, is like that. Living much in the world, he takes frequent notice of "current events," working a sea-change on his material. For example, Bottom's "lion among ladies" in *A Midsummer Night's Dream*. In August 1594, James VI of Scotland, later England's King, baptized a son. The allegorical pageant that went with the ceremony should have featured a lion drawing a cart. But you couldn't bring in a fearful beast like a lion, so James's courtiers used a blackamoor instead. This tale of Scottish naivete, going the rounds in London, came to Shakespeare's ears and he gave it scope in his play.

On other events of the period, personal to him or too risky to accommodate, Shakespeare is silent. His silences are often speaking silences, however, and what he doesn't address in so many words turns up in his fictions, lively but encrusted. The Gunpowder Plot, the Midland riots of 1607, and the death of his only son are examples.

A dramatic writer, Shakespeare almost never speaks in his own voice, letting recurrent words or phrases do the talking for him. This technique, like leitmotifs in music, needs highlighting, and I cite his recurrences in notes at the back of the book. Because he seems to me the best gloss on his own work, I quote him often to point the argument, not to adorn the tale. I don't always identify quotations as such, and where their source isn't obvious I give it in the notes. My reading of *As You Like It* being "new," I have published it separately (as "Shakespeare's Book of Genesis" in *Comparative Drama,* Summer 1991).

I have a point of view, sometimes different from the received one, and don't hesitate to assert it. The portrait of Shakespeare that emerges in these pages won't meet everyone's agreement. So with my treatment of matter-of-fact, for instance, the order the plays were written in. Befitting my subject, I have done my best to be scrupulous, and hope at a minimum that readers will call tenable what I put for true.

Downplaying the work in favor of the life would make the going easier. Shakespeare's life is only worth recording, though, because of the plays and poems that came from it, and I have tried to do them justice, not at great length but sufficient. This obligates readers to know something of Shakespeare's text, less a burden than a gift, and in any case not to be shirked.

Needing help, I have had the luck to find it. Robert Weisbuch, a source of wit in others, helped me say better what I meant to say. Friends who know their Shakespeare—John Russell Brown, William Ingram, and Alvin Kernan—gave me the benefit of their learning and intelligence. Though my wife Mary Zwiep had her own work to do, precluding much attention to mine, her presence made a difference.

Russell Fraser
Ann Arbor, 1991

Shakespeare The Later Years

1

Two-Headed Janus

REHEARSALS and out-of-town tryouts were over and in 1594, when this curtain goes up, Shakespeare stood before his public fully fledged. Though only thirty that year, he thought his days past the best. Sonnets, mostly youthful work, picture him "as I am now," crushed by time's hand or "beated and chopped" with age. For this precocious old man, the world-weariness has its share of literary posing. But his people on the average lived shorter lives than we do and "haggish age" stole on them early.

London when he lived there was a pesthouse, Stratford too. Country air carried death, like the air they breathed in cities. Sanitation mocked itself and his contemporaries sickened from typhus, dysentery, and bubonic plague. His brothers and sisters, seven in all, dropped off one by one, only Joan surviving past middle age. He himself died at fifty-two. Poverty waited at the lane's end, especially in the nineties, a time of worsening inflation. Some of his acquaintance, like Tom Nashe, went to debtors' prison and came out to die in straits. Many didn't have enough to eat or what they ate wasn't good for them. The Irish of their day, they were often "cup-shotten." If tradition has it right, a drinking bout finished off Shakespeare. Politics, a subtler scourge, afflicted high and low. One of his fellow playwrights, Thomas Kyd, felt the scourge. A caution to the rest, he fell foul of the thought police. Loyalty today was disloyalty tomorrow and the up-and-down wore them "out of act" or strength.

But "old," meaning decrepit, also means the real thing, veritable Shakespeare. Romeo, an "old" murderer, is practiced in killing, and Shakespeare at thirty, old or expert in craft, towered over the others, satellites to his pole star. Naturally, he made a target for envious gossip. Robert Greene, a jealous rival, seeking to account for Shakespeare's ascendancy, compared him to the provident ant. Greene himself was a grasshopper, fiddling the summer out, but his reading, though partial, includes a piece of truth. Shakespeare, his poet's eye "in a fine frenzy rolling," had a cold eye when this was wanted.

As success stories go, his seems unlikely. Late in the 1580s he had come up from Stratford, penniless and anonymous. He left behind a wife who had snared him at eighteen, also three children, doubtful assets. The Shakespeare family's fortunes had to be entered on the debit side too. John Shakespeare saw to that. Once Stratford's bailiff, he was well along on the road to the poorhouse. Shakespeare's father liked to litigate and hoped something would turn up. His mother, one of the Ardens, an ancient name in Warwickshire, had her name to console her. For Shakespeare, starting out, the auspices weren't good. But this through-and-through professional showed them how the career belongs to the talents and by 1592 had ten plays to his credit. Some brought in record returns.

Like a scenario for one of these plays, Shakespeare's story has its checks and reversals. Plague broke out in London in 1592, closing the theaters, his livelihood, for almost two years. Actors like Will Kempe, the time's famous comic, and Edward Alleyn, its great tragedian, fled the city, going on tour. If Shakespeare went with them, his travels were abridged. Plague destroyed some acting companies, Pembroke's Men among them, and likely young Shakespeare belonged to this fellowship. "As for my Lord Pembroke's," Henslowe the theater manager wrote Alleyn, his son-in-law, "they are all at home and have been this five or six weeks, for they cannot save their charges [expenses] with travel . . . and were fain to pawn their apparel." Evidently the playbooks went the way of the apparel and certain plays of Shakespeare's, once the property of Pembroke's Men, turn up later in the repertory of a rival company.

But Fortune had better things in mind for this playwright. When plague slackened in the spring of 1594, London's theaters reopened, the companies returned, and Shakespeare got back in harness. Though Alleyn's company, the Admiral's Men, dominated his theater world, other companies competed for popular favor. Shakespeare the apprentice didn't mind which one he wrote for. In June, Strange's Men performed two plays of his at Newington Butts, south of the Thames. Before the year was out, the company lost its patron but found a new one, Lord Hunsdon, High Chamberlain of England. In 1594 Shakespeare entered Hunsdon's service. He remained with this company for the rest of his career.

Pleasing the multitude, he pleased the cognoscenti too. His first attempt at comedy, farce mixed with other things and perfection of its kind, enlivened the Christmas revels in 1594 at the largest of the Inns of Court, London's law schools. This same December he received a higher accolade, performance before the Queen in her palace at Greenwich. By then pirate publishers had snapped up three of his plays, an index of their growing appeal. The first was *Titus Andronicus,* dismaying to Bardolaters but a rousing success with the crowd.

A snobbish view held that plays were insubstantial pageants, here today, gone tomorrow. Shakespeare may have concurred (the best in that kind were shadows). But poetry appealed to the ages. "I have built a monument more lasting than bronze," said Horace, one of his teachers. The pupil hoped to emulate the teacher and by 1594 his skill as a poet was widely acclaimed. Not long after, a contemporary hailed him as the modern Catullus. His two famous poems of the early 1590s, *Venus and Adonis* and *The Rape of Lucrece,* established his credentials as a serious writer, also helping feather his nest. Each carried a dedication to Henry Wriothesley, the Earl of Southampton, a young notability at Court. He was Shakespeare's patron, perhaps for some years the "master-mistress" of his passion. A patron was expected to reward the poets who flattered him and likely Southampton did this. One way or another, young Shakespeare built a stake.

In 1594 he "staked down," as in their card game of primero. Formerly a hireling in theater, he bought a partnership in his business enterprise, the Chamberlain's Men. A "composition" or deed in return for his bond entitled him to share in the company's proceeds. The "sharer" was an actor too, known for kingly roles and old man's roles. It takes a special kind of young actor to play old men successfully, and Shakespeare's facility says something of the man he was.

With all this, he found time to write plays. For roughly twenty years, he served his company as its "ordinary poet," i.e., principal writer, turning out the wares others brought to market. "Make it new," his fellows said, their eye on the box office. That he did, supplying whatever was called for: "tragedy, comedy, history, pastoral, pastoral-comical," etc. Polonius, reciting these different genres or kinds, meant to distinguish one from another. But Shakespeare wasn't simon pure and most of his plays make a hodgepodge.

Like the "singing men" or clerks who rejoiced the hearts of English in the older time, he absorbed himself in his function. Some of his fellows, previewing modern times, lived lives of notoriety, not he. Peele, a hellion, became the subject of a popular jest book. Lodge, before respectability overtook him, made a freebooting voyage to the New World. Jonson was "rare" Ben, toper and bullyboy. Shakespeare, self-effacing, kept his head down. On this side, he looks backward to his medieval forebears, most of them names in the catalog, little more. If you want to make their acquaintance you must listen to their music, true for Shakespeare too.

Medieval men, deferring to the ancients, called themselves dwarfs who stood on the shoulders of giants. That way, they saw farther. This giant of modern times stood on the shoulders of the proximate past. His first tutors who were also his competitors did him good service, notably Lyly and the "University Wits," Marlowe, trailed by others. Anonymous playwrights in the generation before him gave him sketches for his Jew of Venice, Romeo and Juliet, and Oberon, king of the fairies. A quick study, he outpaced all his teachers. But if he was sui generis, the greatest maker in "the tide of times," he was also his time's product. For him the past is prologue when the sinews of his art were developed. This past that intimates the future is young Shakespeare's story. It ends in 1594.

The competition had scattered, another way of explaining Shakespeare's early preeminence. Lyly, his first master, once all the rage for "Euphuistic" comedy, fell silent in the nineties except for begging letters. Greene, his envenomed rival, died in 1592, detractors said of a surfeit of Rhenish wine and pickled herring. Kyd went soon after, like Greene still in his thirties. Marlowe, the greatest of Shakespeare's early contemporaries, caught an assassin's dagger in 1593. He was twenty-nine.

Shakespeare, learning his trade from these playwrights, didn't forget them. In the miraculous years to come, he paid tribute to Kyd in *Hamlet* and Lodge in *As You Like It,* imitations with a difference. Toward the end of his career, writing *The Winter's Tale,* he reached back in memory to Greene. He never stopped learning, from others, not least from himself. But by 1594 his apprenticeship was over, and this year he struck out on his own.

MOVING into the city proper from lower-class Shoreditch, he took lodgings in St. Helen's parish, Bishopsgate, on the northern perimeter of London Wall. Playdays, he walked out along Shoreditch High Street to the Theater and Curtain. These first public playhouses, erected in the 1570s, stood in open fields outside the city. Each day they changed their bill of fare, and providing a new one kept Shakespeare busy. He left no calling cards in Bishopsgate but remembered this early residence in plays.

Not the only entertainer in his neighborhood, he shared the spotlight with famous Ned Alleyn. Two years Shakespeare's junior, Alleyn grew up in St. Botolph's parish on the bank of London Ditch. Nashe called him the modern Roscius, after a celebrated Roman actor. But he had no rivals, ancient or modern. "Others speak," Jonson said in a poetical tribute, "only thou dost act." Among his star roles was that of Barrabas in Marlowe's *Jew of Malta,* a great triumph of the typecaster's art. This play stimulated Shakespeare when he saw it at the Rose on Bankside. Later, though, writing *The Merchant of Venice,* he found it wouldn't do as a model. The energy, unexampled in Marlowe, seemed amazing, but typecasting was never for him.

When plague closed the theaters, Alleyn's company disbanded, some members quitting London for a Continental tour. Alleyn, joining Strange's company, went into the provinces. As in our modern despotic states, he needed permission to do this. Bureaucracy, a storehouse of paper, has its uses, and the warrant licensing his travels names the actors who went with him, all, subsequently, Shakespeare's fellows in the Chamberlain's Men.

Barnstorming in the country, Alleyn wrote letters home, making it easy for posterity to track him. The letters, thick with life, show an amiable man and affectionate husband. Plague is on his mind, and he wants his Joan to throw water "before your door" every night "and have in your windows good store of rue and herb of grace." But his "Mouse" doesn't write him. "Send me of your domestical matters," he tells her, "as how your distilled water proves, or this, or that, or anything what you will. And Jug, I pray you, let my orange-tawny stockings of woolen be dyed a very good black against I come home to wear in the winter." Reproachfully, he notes no word of his garden. His wife ought to remember "that all that bed which was parsley in the month of September, you sow it with spinach, for then is the time." Later Henslowe wrote Alleyn that the spinach bed was sown.

Shakespeare posted no letters in plague time. He had his poems to write or perhaps his Anne couldn't read. By the late spring of 1594, his company, back in London, was looking for a theater to play in. The men who had traveled with Alleyn provided a nucleus of experienced performers and Shakespeare provided the plays. Starring was a newcomer, young Richard Burbage. Art crowded out life when Burbage played *Richard III*. An anecdotist in Shakespeare's time recalled the guide who showed him round the battlefield where this tragedy ends:

> For when he would have said King Richard died
> And called "a horse, a horse!" he "Burbage" cried.

The future in drama ran through Shakespeare and Burbage but Alleyn stood in the path. Reorganizing the Admiral's Men with himself as leader and Henslowe as business manager, he preempted the Rose, Henslowe's theater. The Chamberlain's Men, after a brief interlude at Newington Butts, found a welcome in Bishopsgate at the Crosskeys Inn. One of Shakespeare's way stations, this hostelry stood on Gracechurch or Gracious Street, i.e., Bishopsgate Street going south. Strange's Men, precursor of the Chamberlain's, had played it five years before, defying a prohibition of the Lord Mayor "in a very contemptuous manner." In 1594 they were still persona non grata but their new name, a talisman, worked wonders.

Hunsdon, whose livery they wore, had a seat on the Queen's Privy Council. On October 8, he warned the Mayor off, "after my hearty commendations." His actors (in "the service of Her Majesty if need so require") used to play at the Crosskeys in winter. The plague had put a stop to this but now the danger was past and he wrote "to require and pray your Lordship . . . to permit and suffer them so to do." The mailed fist in the not-so-velvet glove, this letter cleared the way for the Chamberlain's Men. Looking forward to the summer season, they secured a second playhouse, James Burbage's Theater in Shoreditch. Until the Globe opened in 1599, they played both locations, convenient for Shakespeare. His lodging in St. Helen's put him roughly halfway between.

Sometimes custom beckoned or necessity decided and the actors went elsewhere, to East Anglia the summer after this, two years later to Sussex and Kent. When trouble over the ground lease put the Theater off limits, they adjourned to the Curtain below Holywell Lane. Romeo won his first "plaudities" there. In the early winter of 1594, a special occasion brought them to Gray's Inn. The date was December 28 and the occasion the second night of Christmas revels. Shakespeare's *Comedy of Errors* made the centerpiece for this.

A "Prince of Purpoole" presided over the revels, his name recalling Portpool Lane, east of the law school. Like Philostrate in *A Midsummer Night's Dream,* he helped the barristers beguile the hours "between our after-supper and bedtime." This was easier said than done. Students from the Inner Temple, true-blue "Senecans" who sniffed at popular plays, headed the list of the invited. Their kind of play was *Gorboduc,* a lugubrious tragedy where nothing much happens, produced by these Templars two years before Shakespeare was born.

Shakespeare's play promised livelier things, and Gray's Inn got ready for a big turnout. Scaffolds or bleachers were set up in the hall, facing an improvised platform. But the crowd kept coming, like Romeo and his fellow masquers, gate crashers at Capulet's ball. People looking for "convenient room" didn't find it, "so exceeding great" were the numbers. Mostly highborn, they dispensed with good manners. Some clambered up on stage, including gentlewomen, privileged by their sex. Before the play went on at midnight, the Templars withdrew, much discontented. A jocular reporter said the night ended "in nothing but confusion and errors, whereupon it was ever afterwards called *The Night of Errors.*" Later, a mock-inquest on the throngs and tumults complained of the presence of professional actors, base fellows from Shoreditch. Shakespeare remembered the barristers, full of "saws and modern instances," i.e., commonplace or slight.

Things went better at Court. Standing high with the Queen, his company played before her thirty-two times in her last decade. Shakespeare knew how to please, and in the same period performances by all the rival companies combined totaled only thirty-three. The theater season at Court took in the twelve days of Christmas. It opened on St. Stephen's Day (December 26), ending on Twelfth Night, the Feast of the Epiphany (January 6). Sometimes plays were performed on Candlemas Day (February 2), and always on Shrove Sunday or Tuesday. Courtiers and Queen gave a loose to their spirits on these movable feasts, before the austerities of Lent. On Shrove Sunday 1605, King James and his Scottish courtiers witnessed a performance of Shakespeare's *Merchant of Venice.* This was carrying coals to Newcastle, though, and most, drunk as lords, didn't need a play to divert them.

A Master of the Revels, one of the Queen's household, appointed the plays. In earlier days he organized them himself, and a poignant little story in the Revels' Accounts shows him stage-managing a group of boy actors "whiles they learned their parts and gestures meet for the masque." This was at Shrovetide 1574, kept by the

Queen in her palace at Hampton Court. The boys went up river by wherry from Paul's Wharf, followed by a barge with their costumes. Back in London on Ash Wednesday, "sick and cold and hungry," they received their reward, a shilling apiece.

By Shakespeare's day, the Master of the Revels, no longer directing plays, chose the ones he wanted from a list of "abridgments," not synopses, entertainments that whiled away the time. Professional companies mounted these entertainments, meant to solace the Queen. She was in her sixties the first time Shakespeare played before her, an aging beauty who wouldn't look in the mirror. Under the wig the red hair had faded, but a flaming temper still went with this and the Master chose what he hoped would keep her in temper. He was Edmund Tilney, on the job by then for fifteen years. When he died in 1610 his nephew George Buck replaced him, and these two men between them read all of Shakespeare's plays.

Reading, they had one eye for pleasure, the other for what might give offense. Over the years this second function took priority, and censorship became the important business of the Revels. A royal proclamation, dated the second year of Elizabeth's reign, instructed playwrights not to intrude in "matters of religion or governance of the estate of the commonweal." Mayors and J.P.s were supposed to enforce this, a burden London's City Fathers shouldered cheerfully. They thought it meant the end of their bugaboo, the stage.

But politics decreed otherwise. Middle-class and Puritan-leaning, the City vied for power with the Crown. Until civil war erupted, a generation after Shakespeare's death, this power struggle was fought with symbols, not bullets. The stage, patronized by the Crown, made a symbol, and London's Corporation tried to suppress it. In 1581, however, Privy Council, willing to mortify the City, transferred the censorship to the Master of the Revels. Though a bureaucrat, he was no ideologue and the players counted their blessings. Puritans, despising players, said they were rogues, counterfeits, and puppets, but Hamlet, a skeptical observer in the seats of power, called them the time's chronicles. He said it was better to have a bad epitaph than their ill report while you lived.

At first Tilney confined his surveillance to Court plays. Gradually, however, he took the whole of London's theater for his province. Some plays he "allowed" but sent others to the cutting room, meaning to obliterate "all profaneness, oaths, ribaldry, and matters reflecting upon piety and the present government." King James fumed about oaths and in 1606 forbade them by statute. Elizabeth, known for her sulphurous tongue, cared more for matters of state. Tilney strove to please both. He got a handsome fee for each play he corrected and perhaps Shakespeare grudged it. But his plays, "perused and licensed" by the Master, mostly came through unscathed, and only the Deposition Scene in *Richard II* caught the censor's attention. Was Shakespeare his own censor, forestalling trouble? More likely, he worked out a modus vivendi, satisfying Caesar but pleasing himself.

Clerkenwell, north of Newgate, housed the Revels Office. In the former Hospital of St. John of Jerusalem, more spoils of the Dissolution, the Master enjoyed the perquisites of power, a suite of thirteen rooms plus a "convenient garden." In the "great chamber" he sat in judgment on rehearsals, sorting wheat from chaff. For Shakespeare's success story, luck goes with skill, and Tilney must have had a keen eye.

Plays, a social product, cost money. Rehearsals at the Revels Office went on at night, daylight hours being reserved for plays in the playhouse. This meant torches and candles for the hall, money for the "dishes" or sconces that held them, money for the chandler too. One year's bill from Shrovetide to Shrovetide has him getting 5 pounds, 15 shillings, and 5 pence. In winter, rushes on the floor and fires in the hearth kept the actors from freezing. Four thousand sticks of wood and two loads of coal fueled the fires.

When Shakespeare's company came out to Clerkenwell, they brought some of their costumes and properties with them. Tilney, who paid the charges for freight, loaned them much of what they needed, yellow cotton to line "the monarch's gown," armor for knightly combatants, "vizards" for masquers, "apt houses made of canvas" and framed and painted in Clerkenwell, "necessaries for hunters," and a "device for thunder and lightning." In Shakespeare's plays the thunder rolls often, and the hunters, hallooing each other, rouse the sleeping lovers in *A Midsummer Night's Dream.*

Piled up in the office, all this stuff collected dust. Elaborate airings, "spring cleaning," got rid of the dust, the Master footing the bill. When time pressed, his artisans worked into the night. For this they got overtime pay, double wages. Once the office laid out money for bread and cheese "to serve the plasterers that wrought all the night and might not be spared nor trusted to go abroad to supper." Shakespeare's paymasters jibbed at these expenses, and Burghley the High Treasurer, stingy like the Queen, looked over Tilney's shoulder. Money, critical for Shakespeare's fortunes, was only the second most important thing, however. In the next reign the royal purse strings were loosened, but the Stuarts' more lavish treatment of the theater didn't insure a better product.

Rehearsals finishing up, players and equipment departed for Court, likely by boat on the Thames. The Court was where the Queen was, at Greenwich downriver, Whitehall in Westminster, or Nonsuch and Richmond in Surrey. In March 1603 her long reign ended at Richmond, and Shakespeare and the others entertained her in her palace there, seven weeks before she died. Mostly the Chamberlain's Men played at Whitehall, closer to home. But the Queen's Court Calendar shows them coming and going from one palace to another, tiring-houses (changing rooms) for Shakespeare.

Windsor was the oldest palace, begun by the Conqueror, Hampton Court the largest. Henry VIII, bluff King Hal to his subjects, played indoor tennis at Hampton Court, betting on himself and mostly losing. At tennis, if you struck your ball "into the hazard," a hole in the wall, your opponent couldn't return it. Shakespeare's Henry V, bandying the crown of France, hopes to do this. Magnificent but not self-proclaiming, Hampton Court, like Jonson's Penshurst, wasn't "built to envious show." Standing over quiet water west and south of the city, it epitomized the Tudor monarchy, saying what it was and wasn't. Despotic enough, it wasn't Leviathan, and Shakespeare's Queen, though delighting in show, didn't need specious trappings, "the divine right of kings." In the Base Court the dark gray brick contrasted with the paler red, making diaper patterns, finely wrought but simple. Later, a taste for Byzantinism grew on the age and the Royal Apartments, drearily grand, imitated the Sun King's palace at Versailles.

Performances at Court, iridescent with color but fortified with substance, took their cue from the Queen. Artificial light illuminated the "theater," a rectangular hall much like Shakespeare's private theater, Blackfriars. Going to the play was a social occasion, and the hall at first was the dining hall. Trenchers and scraps and orts were cleared away after dinner and the tables tilted up or pushed to one side. "Turn the tables up," Capulet tells the servants, overseeing his own entertainment. Now they were ready and the revels began.

But the theater, a time for letting go, was also a formal occasion. When Shakespeare played at Court, the Queen's dais stood at one end of the hall, making this a presence chamber. At the other was the stage, backed by painted scenes "that smack of geometry." Tilney and his artisans furnished these scenes-in-perspective. Actors wore a forest of feathers, guards, decked out like Swiss guards, patrolled by the doors, and all the officers from Clerkenwell, seated before the play began, hoped to look splendid in their ceremonial robes. Entering at the last possible moment, the Queen outshone them all.

For the play itself the rule was simplicity, befitting matter of consequence. Most plays at Court got along without realistic settings. In Shakespeare's first texts, changes of locality aren't specified much, so properties were few and scenes didn't have to be shifted. The army of stagehands needed by the Victorian theater wasn't needed by him. No text of Shakespeare's published in his lifetime is divided into acts or scenes, an omission that gave employment to editors in time to come. Onstage action in his early comedies occurs in an open place against a permanent background. *Love's Labor's Lost,* presented before the Queen at Christmas 1598, has a single mise-en-scène, the King of Navarre's park, "yonder coppice" (a tree or two), perhaps a stand for shooting deer. Up in Clerkenwell, they got it ready.

Some changes of scene there were but handled with a minimum of fuss. When the actors moved from station to station within the open place, uncreating Shakespeare demolished the walls that might have got in their way. You see him doing this in his first tragedies, like *Romeo and Juliet,* work of 1594. Quitting the street for Capulet's "house," Romeo and friends don't enter the house but clap on their "vizards" and "march about the stage." Pretending not to notice, "servingmen come forth with napkins" and mime their preparations for the masked ball within. This annuls place or rather relocates it, transposing outside to inside.

Romeo and Juliet, not designed for the Court, had its first performance in a public theater, probably true of *A Midsummer Night's Dream.* Some think this comedy first performed at a grand wedding with the Queen in attendance, and when James came in it was put on at Court, like *Othello, King Lear,* and *Macbeth.* Except in magnitude, however, these plays are all of a piece, suggesting a like taste across the social spectrum. This community in taste and interest, enduring for a little while, sponsored conventions. Some were metaphysical, and unlike modern artists, Yeats, for example, Shakespeare didn't need to create his own cosmos. There it was, all filled out with hierarchies, animal, vegetable, and mineral, social, political, and sexual. The lion was the king of beasts, the cedar king of trees, and the man was the head of the woman. Not that Shakespeare believed all they told him. For this uncommon playwright, convention functioned partly as an irritant. If he meant to take his own way, he needed a norm or standard to depart from. For genius, this is the chief use of convention.

Depending on shared assumptions, his stagecraft freed him from the trammels of logistics. In *A Midsummer Night's Dream* action begins in Athens but progresses to the moonlit wood, "a league without the town." This might have taxed Shakespeare's resources. The Queen and her playwright both accepted a convention, though, the foreshortening of distance. When the hero, like Romeo, had to travel from one city to another, he walked offstage and on again. A canvas backdrop, conventional too, suggested these different locations. What happened in them, however, was something new beneath the sun, no less than a revolution in theater.

Literalists in theater appealed to the belief that depends on the eye, not the ear. Setting the scene, they spelled it out on placards, like Kyd's hero in *The Spanish Tragedy.* Preparing a Court play, he tells his assistant to hang up the title. "Our scene is Rhodes." In Shakespeare, dialogue, "the viewless wings of poesy," brought them to Rhodes or wherever. Romeo, lately of Verona, finds the poison he is looking for "in Mantua, / Here." Some at Elizabeth's Court weren't appeased by this, supposing that "the stage should always represent but one place." Sidney, a neo-classical critic, mocked "Shakespeare" and company for having "Asia of the one side and Afric of the other, and so many other underkingdoms that the player, when he cometh in, must ever begin with telling where he is." Though generally not so barefaced, Shakespeare doesn't mind telling us, and his "wide and universal theater" mostly ignores the "unities" except for one pervasive unity, a theme worth a hearing.

The Revels Accounts notice "great curtains" in Court plays. They weren't drop curtains, though, and at Court and elsewhere the stage lay open to the eye throughout the performance. Sans intermission, one scene shaded into the next. Most performances in the theater after Shakespeare obscure this. Looking for Romeo outside Capulet's orchard, his companions look in vain. Pointless, they tell each other, "to seek him here that means not to be found." Ending 2.1, these sensible men go off to bed. The front curtain rattles down and stagehands concealed behind it wheel out the orchard. Spectators yawn or get up from their seats. Then—but the spell is broken—2.2 begins. Romeo, alone, utters his poignant-risible aside: "He jests at scars that never felt a wound." This line encapsulates the play but doesn't stand by itself, and Romeo is realized only when you set him against his friends and rivals. We want the chime of the couplet, "wound" rhyming with "found." The interval between the scenes that aren't really separate scenes loses this for us, however. In *Romeo and Juliet,* as Shakespeare wrote it, action, a combustible progress, never pauses. Fire and powder, Friar Laurence says, "kiss" as they consume. Not kindling much himself, he shakes his head at this.

A BIFOLD PERSONALITY, "two distincts, division none," organizes Shakespeare's Bishopsgate plays. *Romeo and Juliet* and *A Midsummer Night's Dream,* opposing faces of a single coin, present the same image but from different points of view. Probably Shakespeare wrote both in 1594, within a few months of each other. Next year he turned to *The Merchant of Venice,* a hybrid that skirts disaster, modulates to sweet sadness, and ends with an off-color joke. All three plays, exotic on the surface, tell of life in faraway places, sunny Italy, sometimes overcast, or Athens and environs before history began. The real venue is London, though, the streets and places Shakespeare knew. The time is the present, his and ours, i.e., timeless, and the business the working out of man's fate.

Romeo and Juliet is Shakespeare's first great play. Later his style tautened and he looked deeper into the life of things, but generations of theatergoers will tell you that he never bettered this early tragedy. Much risk attends it and audacity describes the risk-taker. Irony, an urbane man's defense against the charge of sentimentalizing, might have been his refuge. It often is when wise old age looks back at youth. But Shakespeare, older than his lovers, is their partisan and faithful annalist, and his rendering of the real romantic thing is unalloyed. "O, she doth teach the torches to burn bright!" But this isn't *La Dame aux Camellias,* and hyperbole, though cherished, doesn't preclude tender amusement. Shakespeare's heroine has her share of feminine wiles. "What is yond gentleman? . . . What's he that now is going out of door? . . . What's he that follows there, that would not dance?" Beating around the bush, she lights at last on Romeo. This is the one, "my only love."

Shakespeare's distinguishing trope or figure, "oxymoron," mixes things that shouldn't mix, right for a play where love rises from what it hates. "Earth" or mortality presents the hated thing, both the mother of beauty and its executioner, "womb" and "tomb" together. Not Juliet's foot nor any lover's will wear out "the everlasting flint." At first they don't know this. Youth, invincibly hopeful, "gapes" to be age's heir, and April in its finery treads on the heel of winter. But the seasons revolving, "limping winter" has the victory over youth and spring alike, and the lightning which announces the advent of either is swallowed in darkness before a man can say "it lightens." This apparition is more piercing because it doesn't last.

Sentimentality gaining on the age, Shakespeare's remorseless vision began to seem unfeeling and a Restoration playwright turned *Romeo and Juliet* into domestic tragedy. His friendlier version warms the heart but the heart is contracted and the eye sees less than it used to. Society reduces to a plaster mock-up and the young lovers to the boy and girl next door. Shakespeare's *Romeo and Juliet,* deeply personal as all attest, is first of all social. The death of the lovers makes a great crack but isn't the whole story, and he doesn't begin with them but with a quarrel in the streets. "Ancient," he calls it, also a "mutiny," with all this implies for harmony in other days, now fractured. Brawling servants, not masterless but men of two "households," are joined by their masters, then by citizens with clubs, always on the prowl in Shakespeare's London. At last the Prince enters to part this bloody fray. The head of society, he speaks for its interest. In Shakespeare's tragedies, this interest transcends the heroes and villains, not petty, only circumscribed. (Curious how the circumscribing, "gored state" or "ranged empire," adds a cubit to their stature.) In the denouement, the world they inhabit and decimate for a while with their loving and hating is soldered up again and goes on without them.

Shakespeare's dramaturgy, a house of many mansions, predicts and accommodates most who come later, and an opera by Verdi is potential in his play. Beginning in 1.5 when the young lovers fall in love at first sight, it ends in 5.3 with a vivid drop curtain: "Stabs herself and falls on Romeo's body." But Shakespeare at this point, powerful though not conclusive, possibly "sensational," still has a long way to go. Where there was dissonance, he wants subsidence. Also, he wants to put things in perspective. His absorbing tale of young love, not sufficient in itself, needs its codicil, "a glooming peace." It needs clarifying too, and he wants us to know "how these things came about." The Friar, in an epilogue, satisfies this need, putting before us what he calls "the form of death." This form is both luminous and a configuration but doesn't rationalize the shocking thing it confronts.

Though Shakespeare's play vindicates life, that isn't any help to the lovers. Thwarted in their "intents," they die before their prime, and "never was a story of more woe" than this one. But *Romeo and Juliet* makes us happy. "The exchange of joy" is its burden—literally, Shakespeare sings it—and the sorrow that follows can't countervail this. "Triumphant" is his word for Juliet's grave, a "lantern" or cupola filled with the light of her beauty. Spendthrift Shakespeare, niggardly in life perhaps, in art something else, speaks in his heroine, known for largesse. His bounty is as boundless as the sea.

At the end we get a setoff, personality—panache—opposing our endemic fate. Leaving it to the audience to assign value, Shakespeare tilts the balance, though, as in Juliet's last apostrophe before she takes her life. "O happy dagger!" Who would do this enormous thing? Not the others. Prosaic men and women, the others have their expedients. E.g., Friar Laurence:

> Come, I'll dispose of thee
> Among a sisterhood of holy nuns.

Saws and sayings rise easily to this good old man's lips. "Wisely and slow. They stumble that run fast." In this copybook wisdom, real experience participates. But banal diction undercuts it, too much clarity suffuses it, and in the event the "commission" of the Friar's years and art is revoked. He mustn't speak of what he doesn't feel.

Bidding the night come, Juliet remembers Phaeton, the reckless young man who drives the sun god's horses to destruction. Moralists like the Friar read Shakespeare's tragedy under the aspect of this cautionary fable. Bringing order out of chaos, they hark back to the storytellers Shakespeare consulted for the source of his play. The tale of Romeo and Juliet, one of them said, furnished "good examples, the best to be followed and the worst to be avoided." A narrative poem of the sixties, Shakespeare's immediate source, tells how the lovers disobeyed their parents, "thralling themselves to unhonest desire." Bitten by lust they hasten to death, and have only themselves to blame. This view of art as the means to an end, conventional in Shakespeare's time, gives him his point of departure.

Some critics in our time, itching with the same rational impulse, want it understood that character is fate. In this tragedy, however, some bitter consequence hangs in the stars and much that goes wrong is only "misadventured." Though the popular consensus ratifies Shakespeare's triumph, these critics dispute it, saying how his play isn't tragic but pathetic. (Later, getting into his stride, Shakespeare is supposed to have managed these things better.) Plot, his tragedy undressed, seems to support this diminishing view of *Romeo and Juliet*. A web of "accidental judgments" and "purposes mistook" (like *Hamlet,* to which it relates as a first essay), it bears witness to the presence of "a greater power than we can contradict." But this overmastering power isn't to be confused with fate à la Grecque. No President of the Immortals bends over the action, running our weary bark on the rocks. The hero, a pilot but not "traded" or experienced, does this himself. That isn't his fault, however, only his nature, where nature and character aren't quite the same. Character is: choleric, sanguine, melancholic, etc., showing a different mix from one man to another. But our nature is inescapably tragic.

Saying one thing in terms of another, Shakespeare has a metaphor for man's tragic fate. This is "judicial astrology," the primacy of the heavens. A medieval hangover, it no longer got the suffrage of thoughtful men in his time, and he himself was no "sectary astronomical." His metaphor still quickens for us, however, suggesting that freedom in last things is illusion. No man has power "to tell of good or evil luck" and Romeo, "fortune's fool," is only exemplary. His characterization looks forward to King Lear, "the natural fool of fortune."

"Wedded to calamity," Shakespeare's hero takes the measure of an unmade grave. This is the mouth of outrage we hear of in the last act but it yawns from the beginning and reason doesn't help to evade it. The misadventures that beset the hero are sufficiently causal, though, it being in the nature of youth and life to mean well and do ill. Paris, casually slaughtered (like the quarry of the slain in the last act of *Hamlet*), is a version of Romeo, both written down "in sour misfortune's book." For each of these young men, sprung from the fatal loins of our first parents, "casual" and "causal" mean the same.

Glancing at husbandry, his old "correlative," Shakespeare antedates moral judgment. Cankered Romeo is like a bud bit with "an envious worm." Juliet, not yet "ripe," will turn fourteen, they say, "on Lammas Eve," harvest time, when the hot blood is stirring. "Loaf-mass," some called it. At Mass on the feast day they consecrated bread made from the first-ripe wheat, giving thanks for the harvest soon to be gathered. Another tradition, deriving Lammas from "lamb" and "Mass," says that the feast remembers old times when lambs made a sacrificial tribute. Both meanings work for Shakespeare. In his tale of star-crossed lovers, "quick bright things come to confusion." Juliet has her brief incandescence—Romeo too—then the fire goes out, snuffed by old folks.

Shakespeare, declining to point the moral, has his characters do this for him. Sometimes, juxtaposing them, he lets their pairing stand for comment. Rosaline, only sugar and spice, helps define Juliet, profoundly herself. Paris and the other young men do this for Romeo.

"Old" Romeo, accosted by the "man of wax," salutes his rival as "boy," the contemptuous epithet Tybalt applies to the callow hero we first encounter. In the meantime, the hero has sloughed what he was. Now he is ready to die.

Both the meddling Friar who means all for the best and the death-dealing apothecary who sells Romeo poison help him on his way. Each, culling simples, is a medicine man but neither is efficient for good. This parallel comments on the Friar's homilies, intended to decipher the riddle of experience. Sorting out his poor compounds, he generalizes from their double nature:

> Two such opposèd kings encamp them still
> In man as well as herbs, grace and rude will;
> And where the worser is predominant,
> Full soon the canker death eats up that plant.

These facile rhymes remember the old spirit war between reason and will.

But Shakespeare adjusts the conventional opposition. Standing in for reason, a weak reed when all is said, grace comes into the lists. This might augur the happy ending and in fact the whimsical dispensing of grace is our one chance for salvation. In *Romeo and Juliet,* however, the competition is aborted or grace is withheld. It always is in Shakespeare's tragedies where the gods, who might be merciful, decline to "make them honors / Of men's impossibilities." Shakespeare means that these all-powerful gods won't do for us what we can't do of ourselves. In his comedies, our radical incapacity is even more naked but the playwright, inclined to pity, takes a hand.

FROM VERY OLD TIMES, long before Shakespeare's, London's principal churches had their famous schools, Paul's, Westminster, a third attached to St. Savior's in Southwark. On feast days learned clerks from these schools got together to argue, bringing with them their "enthymemes," syllogisms, etc. This was entertainment, not a bad model for plays. Disputants argued for either/or propositions, lifted from somebody's commonplace book. Forecasting Shakespeare the storyteller, they gave first place to "disposing" this material, moving the ink blots around until they made a composition. Sincerity didn't come into it except as the heat of argument let them know what they believed.

Shakespeare's entertainments recall these old debates. Assessing the facts but aware that they sponsor different conclusions, he wrote that way in sonnets, speaking on either side of the question. Pro vs. contra poems, they honor the given, following where it leads. This analytical poet is notably scrupulous, another and a better word for sincere, and sometimes where the given leads him is where he hadn't thought to go. In 1594, having put period to *Romeo and Juliet,* he resumed the dialectical method and wrote *A Midsummer Night's Dream.* His complementary play, verging on parody, makes jest of earnest. But unlike the old disputants he testifies against himself, blurring the line between either/or, and this comedy is "tragical" too.

Readers who read his two plays back to back will be aware how one mirrors the other. "Crossed" lovers not allowed to choose for themselves, Lysander and Hermia reflect the tragic plight of Romeo and Juliet. Helena's beauty "engilds the night," Juliet's also, and each being lovelorn, "dry sorrow," much sighing, drinks their blood. Lookalikes on the surface, Shakespeare's characters belong to different genres and ought to go their separate ways. But Shakespeare, scrutinizing his material or you could say disposing it, discovers genuine likenesses he hadn't seen before. Some are disconcerting. Lysander, a fickle hero willing to change a raven for a dove, is uncomfortably like Romeo, singling forth his "snowy dove trooping with crows." Romeo, loving "at first sight," looks like Titania, and Montague and Capulet, shaking hands at the end, have their uncanny resemblance to Bottom. "The wall is down that parted their fathers," Shakespeare's hopeful comic says.

Romantic love, exalted in *Romeo and Juliet,* becomes a theme for laughter in *A Midsummer Night's Dream,* and Shakespeare or his mouthpiece gives higher marks to the abstinent life. At the same time, though, this blessed life is "barren," something you have to endure. Mewed up in a nunnery where the sun never shines, single women chant "faint hymns to the cold fruitless moon." "Cold" comes up again in connection with a "fair vestal," presumably the Virgin Queen. Shakespeare, intending praise, says she is "fancy-free," an ambiguous tribute.

Whether we are chaste or carnal, we appear to be manipulated, as by "Dian's bud" or "Cupid's flower." The supposed domination of the stars enforces this conclusion, and for Shakespeare's characters, in comedy, possibly in tragedy, praise or blame seem off the point. Bottom, one version of the artist, wants an epilogue to rationalize the up and down of Shakespeare's story but Theseus declines to hear it. No excuse is needed, says this devotee of reason, evidently converted at the end of the play, "for when the players are all dead, there need none to be blamed." A haunting line, close to the heart of Shakespeare's psychology, it ought to be bracketed by silence.

Some think Shakespeare's play a tissue of moonshine, purged of "mortal grossness." It has this side, caught by Mendelssohn's music and promoted by teachers in schoolrooms. But the moon is an archer whose silver bow, "new-bent," is marking us down, and Shakespeare's bawdy humor, aggressively earthbound, pushes romantic love hard. Snout, a tinker, presents Wall in the play-within-the-play and Pyramus and Thisbe, canonized by old poets, not this one, echo Romeo and Juliet, coarsening their story. Shakespeare's comic lovers kiss through Wall's hole or rather that is what she kisses, "not thy lips at all." Full of themselves and looking down from a high place, they think they are playing their tragedy straight. Much is undreamt-of in their philosophy, though, and this vulgar reprise is both cruel and just.

But parody it isn't. Lysander could tell them:

> The course of true love never did run smooth. . . .
> Or, if there were a sympathy in choice,
> War, death, or sickness did lay siege to it,
> Making it momentany as a sound,
> Swift as a shadow, short as any dream,
> Brief as the lightning in the collied night.

"Momentany" is momentary, gone before you know it. "Collied" is blackened, like a collier mining coal, and in Shakespeare's comedy-plus-other-things, "the jaws of darkness" devour young love.

Titania's votaress-friend, big with child and promising fruition, belongs to festive comedy where happy endings are assured. Being mortal, though, she dies of her burden. In his prayerful ending, hoping for the best and interdicting the worst, Shakespeare makes room for the blots of Nature's hand, mole, harelip, and scar. Parody, if it wants to keep the medium intact, will leave all this alone.

Sexual violence, not a theme for laughter, stalks the edges of the play. Rape ("enforced chastity") is there between the lines, and the flower that does the damage is "purple with love's wound." Already, before the play proper gets going, Theseus, hunting a wife, has wooed her with his sword. As it nears the end we hear about the Centaurs, drunken guests at the wedding, and the hot-eyed Bacchanals who dismember the poet Orpheus. An Athenian eunuch, plucking his harp, sings the battle between the Centaurs and the Lapiths. This artist-singer is Shakespeare, fancy-free where his players do what they have to. No doubt their involuntariness is comic. Anyway, Shakespeare's Puck has a laugh at their expense. But his superiority comes partly from deprivation, and only disembodied spirit or the neutered man can say what fools these mortals be.

Comic but not burlesque, *A Midsummer Night's Dream* relates to *Romeo and Juliet* the way one energy opposes another. Shakespeare's paired opposites have their abundant value but don't suggest a hierarchy of values. Parody, a judgmental art and circumscribing in its tendency, engages Shakespeare from the beginning, but his imagination, once roused, prefers earnest to jest. *A Midsummer Night's Dream,* apparently "weak and idle," grows to something of great constancy as he ponders the given, following darkness like a dream.

"Comedies," said his fellow playwright Heywood, "begin in trouble and end in peace." Shakespeare's illustrates the rule, except that the peace, not smoothing things out, takes the trouble in. The "revels and new jollity" that enliven the ending salute a sexual triumph, playing with fire. Dissension between lovers spawns a "progeny of evils" in the beginning, and "no night is now with hymn or carol blest." In the end, reversing this, blessings are ventured and the issue of the bride-bed is in prospect. Hopeful auditors like Duke Theseus lay this change-for-the-better to cool reason's ascendancy. Reason isn't much honored in Shakespeare's comedy, however, and the ending is happy as days "steep themselves in night."

A journey, literal but implicative, gives him his story line. Stephen Gosson, one of the poet-haters and a clergyman in Bishopsgate, spoke his contempt for these peregrination-stories where the amorous hero, "passing from country to country for the love of his lady," meets many a brown-paper monster. "What learn you by that?" The monsters Shakespeare's lovers encounter on their journey aren't made in Clerkenwell, though, and that is part of the answer to the question.

Quitting Athens, the abode of reason, they "seek new friends and stranger companies." Convention, liking the tried and true, takes a dim view of this, and its wisdom is asserted strongly in the opening scene. "To you your father should be as a god." Shakespeare, no scoffer, attends closely to this speech of the Duke's, meant to admonish a headstrong young woman, it might be Capulet's daughter. The same Shakespeare, a generation later, came down hard on his own daughter for making a match he didn't approve of. But the playwright, less blinkered than the heavy father, sees that convention's account of things is partial. Hermia's irate father, an Old Pantaloon, isn't superior to sexual love, only past it. Oberon calls himself Titania's lord but he and she know better, and though the Duke, like Verona's Prince, is everyone's lord, his young subjects aren't paying attention. What convention misses or hopes to sweep behind the door is the coercive power of the triple Hecate, chaste goddess in heaven, on earth a skillful huntress, but queen of the underground too.

The lover and the poet, laid asleep in reason, acknowledge her authority. Calling his own "epistemology" in question, this poet adds the lunatic. His story of the night is an "exposition of sleep," and a fool is his expounder. Bottom, Shakespeare calls him, the core or skein of thread on which the weaver's yarn is wound. Transported or "translated" like a poet in his singing robes, he has his rare vision, the gain of sleep and dream. An affront to reason and scary in its comprehensiveness, Bottom's Dream is bottomless, "past the wit of man to say what dream it was." But the play enacts its content, plot being the dress of thought, and what the dreamer apprehends is the music of discord.

Confusion is this music's burden but works out to conjunction. Other images present it, the tangled chain, for instance, figuring disorder where nothing is impaired. Rolling like sweet thunder, this concord-discord music has an analog in the baying of Theseus' hounds. Grotesque in appearance but matched in mouth like bells, they make a mutual cry, no music more tunable. Modern panegyrists of unreason like this shrilling music. Rational men, "Apollonian," stop their ears against it. Shakespeare, belonging to neither camp, participates in both, and his comedy is patched with sadness. Outside the pale and lost, his lovers find themselves, so beget a happy ending, but what they find doesn't make them stand taller.

Night creatures, mostly sinister, live in Shakespeare's dark wood, a short list including bats, hooting owls, spiders, lizards, beetles, bears, and "boar with bristled hair," also a snake in the grass. Hermia can't free herself from this "crawling serpent." Though the fairies stand sentinel, fending off evil, their banning prayer isn't answered, and Titania, awakening, finds her vile love near. "Enthralled," she doesn't think him too hairy. The "changeling" boy she won't part with isn't too young. Oberon, not minding that the sex is wrong, has his eye on this lovely boy too.

"Best to call them generally," not separately, says Bottom, making no distinction between man and man. Lysander and Hermia, recalling Romeo and Juliet, take their oath that love won't alter. Bedswerving is the norm, though, and for every true man a million fail. The Fairy King and Queen, like Theseus and Hippolyta, have their shady past that doesn't bear looking into. For the young lovers, the past is prologue. As he errs or wanders, "doting" on her, she does the same, drawn to him by "adamant," a lodestone. A horse beguiled by a filly isn't much different.

Winding things up, Shakespeare sees to it that "the man shall have his mare again." But his ending, though concessive, is disturbingly brusque, and his play, if it really made a pièce d'occasion, must have seemed a little chilly to the members of the wedding. Perhaps like Duke Theseus, suspending disbelief for an anguishing hour, they counted on the technician to bring up the lights in Act V. The fairies for their mischief-making don't need night's help, however, and the persons of the play don't need a magic potion. In the radical case, they "peep" with their own fool's eyes. For this, they never had to leave Athens.

Still at it when they turn up next in *The Merchant of Venice,* they forfeit "the right of voluntary choosing." The song Bassanio hears when choice is thrust upon him suggests where love comes from. Not from the heart or head, "it is engendered in the eyes," displaced, in the idiom of a later time, from below. Young lovers, if they understood this, might see the wisdom of obeying their parents.

A proverb, encapsulating a corner of the play, puts the theme neatly. "To say the truth, reason and love keep little company together nowadays." Bottom, who speaks this truth, adds, however, "the more the pity." Mingling with the laughter, this adds a new dimension to Shakespeare's comedy of errors. Not for the first or last time, generic distinctions blur, and in this comedy the moon, looking down with a watery eye, weeps for human frailty. Like heroes in tragedy, we can't control our fate, a "vain boast" to think so. Perhaps for happy endings that is just as well, and in comedy the playwright, knowing better than his characters, acts on what he knows. But the ending, owing much to beneficent Shakespeare, isn't wholly thanks to him.

Lamenting the fall of greatness, his tragedies record the weakness of strength. In the major comedies, beginning with this one, tears are always in the offing but the frailty they acknowledge is cause for satisfaction too. Vindicating the flesh, Shakespeare's comedies record the strength of weakness. A line is dinning in his ear: "We shall not all sleep, but we shall all be changed." Listening for clues in this text from Corinthians, he hears the passive voice and makes it sovereign for comedy. Sleep is death, St. Paul thinks, and the change he intends is when we put off the flesh. In Shakespeare's dream play, sleep nips them into waking. All are changed, but not from flesh to spirit. Love, however "momentany," lives in the flesh, famous or disgraceful for a thousand permutations.

ESTABLISHED in Bishopsgate in the mid–1590s, perhaps by 1594, Shakespeare kept his nose to the grindstone. But matters of state, intersecting with his private life, help set him before us. Toward the end of Elizabeth's reign, the burden of the long Spanish war forced her to look for additional income. She found it in the form of Subsidies, taxing her subjects on the annual value of their lands or personal goods. These taxes drank deep and Shakespeare took evasive action.

Commissioners, assisted by underlings, exacted the Subsidy from every county and city in the kingdom. Shakespeare's England, said a self-serving analogist, was like a hive of honeybees. "Civil citizens," kneading the honey, brought it home "with merry march" to their emperor. All looked askance at "the lazy yawning drone." This version of how things were is only poetry, though, and Elizabethans, an unruly people, swerved whenever possible from the prescribed course of conduct. Keeping them in line, an army of bureaucrats taught "the act of order" to the peopled kingdom.

In Bishopsgate, this job fell to seven constables, seven scavengers, a beadle, and two tax collectors. The tax collectors were Thomas Symons, skinner, and Ferdinando Clutterbook, draper. Servants of the Lord High Treasurer, they reported delinquents to the Exchequer. Clutterbook was found money, Shakespeare considered, "an old man, sir, and his wits are not so blunt as, God help, I would desire they were." The office of the Exchequer, located in Westminster, took its name from the checkered cloth where accountants in other days paid out the money that supported the royal household. Shakespeare's highway robbers in *Henry IV,* Part One covet this money, on its way to the King's Exchequer or rather "to the King's tavern." Falstaff says this, prompted by his creator, a delinquent on the tax rolls.

In October 1596, Shakespeare, domiciled in the parish of St. Helen's, failed to meet his tax assessment, five shillings. A year later the Petty Collectors for Bishopsgate ward report him still in arrears. Parliament in the meantime having granted a new subsidy, his debt increased to thirteen shillings, fourpence. He didn't meet this assessment either and the Sheriff of Surrey was instructed to collect it. (By then, a step ahead of them, he had moved across the Thames.)

When local officialdom was doing its best to recover his taxes, Shakespeare was buying up property elsewhere. The purchase of his Stratford mansion, New Place, dates from these years. Also he bought grain and hoarded it against a rise in prices. An acquaintance says he had his eye on "some odd yard-land or other in Shottery or near about us." His biographers assume that he discharged his debt, though this isn't recorded. But he took his time about it and the commissioners entered his name on the Pipe Roll, the annual survey of the royal revenue. This entry offers clues for posterity to guess at. Was he a dilatory Shakespeare, his head in the clouds? closefisted? cunning? Possibly all the above.

His new address in Bishopsgate, more prestigious than disreputable Shoreditch, says that he was on the way up. Pleasure gardens adorned this well-to-do quarter, also many fair "tenements," the usual quota of taverns and inns, and "large built houses for merchants." John Stow, a neighbor in Bishopsgate, noted the inns, Bull, Angel, and Dolphin, some doing duty as theaters. At the Bull a pre-Shakespearean "Merchant of Venice" showed "the bloody minds of usurers." This might have offended the merchants in the houses but they didn't patronize the stage.

Usury, "a vice most odious and detestable," was forbidden by a nostalgic statute that looked back to the Middle Ages. In that simpler time, none took "a breed for barren metal of his friend." Lawgivers in Shakespeare's time penalized moneylenders with loss of their capital as well as the interest, also threatening imprisonment and fine. Many, however, flew by the nets of the law. Shylock the usurer owes part of his existence to this sociopolitical matter-of-fact.

First, though, it bears on John Shakespeare, the poet's father. Convicted moneylender and a leather merchant who dealt illegally in wool, he was summoned four times to appear before the Exchequer. This happened in the 1570s when Shakespeare was a boy. Later, youthful memory stirring, he wrote the play described by his first printer as *The Merchant of Venice,* otherwise "The Jew of Venice." Antonio was the Merchant, Shylock the Jew, but usurer and merchant had something in common and as the play ends, each is excluded from the comic round.

London's Lord Mayors, prominent merchants, lived in Crosby Place, still a Bishopsgate landmark. Shakespeare's Richard III plots a coup d'état in this fifteenth-century mansion. Though villainous, he supported a company of players, anathema to the Lord Mayor. The Mayor's identity changed every year but he was always a tradesman, generally a mercer, and whatever his name no friend to Shakespeare.

Cater-cornered across Bishopsgate Street, the brick and timber house, "most spacious of all thereabout," belonged to Sir Thomas Gresham. This premier capitalist built the Royal Exchange, modeled on the Bourse at Antwerp. The "pawn" above the exchange accommodated a hundred shops, and merchants thronged the piazza, summoned to business by a bell at noon, again at six in the evening. Crowning the bell tower was Gresham's crest, the grasshopper, a whimsical emblem for this single-minded man. Shakespeare, poet and playwright but alert to business, combined in himself the grasshopper and ant. His emblem is "two-headed Janus," the god they swear by in *The Merchant of Venice*.

Probably he lived in one of the tenements carved from the Benedictine nunnery, St. Helen's. On Sundays he attended service in the old priory church, known for its tombs and monuments as the "Westminster Abbey of the City." A "Fastolf," he noted, lay in one of these tombs. Going to church wasn't an option and no one missed Easter Communion. Parishioners like Shakespeare, given a metal token, handed it over at the communion table. Churchwardens kept track of this.

Until King Henry turned them out, Black Nuns lived in the priory, in Shakespeare's time a common hall for the company of Leathersellers. London's livery companies replaced the old guilds, like Stratford's Guild of the Holy Cross, famous for charity. The superseding of the past by an energetic present is among Shakespeare's stories, familiar to him from boyhood. In his century, witness to the biggest transfer of land since the Conquest, many prospered while others went to the wall. Shakespeare, rehearsing the implications of this, makes an unsympathetic reporter. Where were the good old days when service sweat for duty, "not for meed"? "Meed" is reward, and Shakespeare, who deplored it, angled for it too. In Stratford, the priests' "College," his town's chief private dwelling, became the residence of the local moneylender. Another parvenu, "subtle, covetous, and crafty," got title to New Place before Shakespeare moved in. Like Shakespeare subsequently, the parvenu was gentry.

This shift in tenure and status worked a hardship on poor folk. But the poor are always with us, as Shakespeare learned in church, and the halls of the companies, forty-nine in the city, stood for the capital that nourished his plays. Elizabethans had more money than their medieval forebears, consequential for Shakespeare. In fifteenth-century England, noisy with York and Lancaster's "long jars," his plays wouldn't have come to fruition.

The past, though giving way rapidly, lived on in Bishopsgate, a quickening presence. Outside the Wall in Spitalfields, men digging clay to make bricks turned up the burial urns of Romans and the bones of old Britons and Saxons. Forty years since, said Stow, easy stiles opened on the pleasant fields, now "pestered" with buildings and alleys. "Freeman" of the Merchant Tailors' Company and London's best chronicler, Stow is buried in St. Andrew Undershaft, Leadenhall Street. Pious like Shakespeare and no whit less scrupulous, he said he had attempted the discovery of "my native soil and country." The odd name of his church recalls the long shaft or Maypole that once overlooked the church steeple. Suggesting a giant phallus, it went up every May Day, an ancient festival still observed by Shakespeare's lovers in *A Midsummer Night's Dream*. Reform coming to Bishopsgate, preachers at Paul's Cross denounced the maypole, however, and parishioners sawed it up and burned it.

West of the fields was Bedlam, a hospital for "distracted people," fifty or sixty of them. Shakespeare's neighbors found mad folk amusing, and St. Mary of Bethlehem ranked among the sights of his London. Madness, a moral failure, meant diabolic possession. Whipping out the offending Adam, keepers flogged their charges, starved them, or shut them up in solitary confinement. Fettered with chains, they lay "in hideous darkness." Malvolio, madder than he thinks, gets this treatment in *Twelfth Night*. Some, disconcerted by Shakespeare's sangfroid, insist that this comic figure is tragic. Later, in *King Lear,* a skeptical Shakespeare recalls how Bedlam beggars stuck pins in their arms, enforcing charity from poor villages and farms in the country.

The streets of Shakespeare's parish, where new "commodity" rubbed elbows with the old ways, read him lessons in history. Coming home from Shoreditch, he passed Winchester House inside the Wall. This rich man's house rose on the foundations of an old monastery, built by Austin Friars. Before Shakespeare was born, mourners brought the headless corpse of Buckingham to the church choir. In *Henry VIII* Shakespeare wrote the last hour of his long weary life. After the Dissolution, the spoils of the friary went to William Paulet, first Marquis of Winchester. He sold the church monuments, stripped the lead from the roof, and turned the choir into a coalhouse. Lord High Treasurer under three successive rulers, Protestant, Catholic, and Protestant again, this supple man ran the Exchequer. How did he survive the revolution of the times? "By being a willow and not an oak," he said.

South of Winchester House, on the corner of Threadneedle and Bishopsgate streets, the church of St. Martin Outwich "had of old time a fair well." Stow remarked the two buckets, "so fastened that the drawing up of the one let down the other." Shakespeare's Richard II picks a simile from this. His golden crown was like a deep well that owned two buckets,

> The emptier ever dancing in the air,
> The other down, unseen and full of water.

That was process, devoid of point and recurring like the life of the times. But Shakespeare's play intermits it. Bolingbroke, strong where Richard is weak, puts his hand on the balance and the up-and-down is stayed. Shakespeare, who admired Bolingbroke, a man of action, had doubts about him too. Finding out right with wrong, he cuts his way to the throne. However, as they tell him, "it may not be."

Bishopsgate Street under different names bisected Shakespeare's neighborhood, beginning at London Bridge and running through the battlemented arch in the Wall. Two wickets flanked the gate, not what it used to be. Hansa merchants, wealthy Germans, proposed to repair it, but "through suit of our English merchants" their privileges were canceled and the work broken off. Local jingoes, men of the mercers' company, applauded.

Resentment of the foreigner comes up often in Shakespeare, in this respect not much different from his fellows. When a German count and his entourage visited England in 1592, he made a note in his tables. Being German they were comic, and he works them for a laugh in *The Merry Wives of Windsor.* Frenchmen were foppish and likely diseased. A colony of them lived in his district, on the edge of the ditch that ran with London's Wall. As he might have expected, these inhabitants of "Petty France" polluted the ditch with "unsavory things." Sometime afterward, however, Shakespeare, presumed "chauvinist," moved in with a French Huguenot family.

Jews were comic and/or monstrous, like the old gargoyles. One was Dr. Roderigo Lopez, a Portuguese refugee, in Shakespeare's time the Queen's physician. Xenophobia, boiling up against immigrants in 1593, focused the next year on this Lopez. Though an old man, he was Jewish, so predatory, and contemporaries knew him as Lopus or Wolf. In the hue and cry against him, Shakespeare played a part.

The Earl of Essex, Elizabeth's favorite and bad eminence to Shakespeare's patron Southampton, accused Lopez of seeking to poison the Queen. King Philip paid him to do this, said Essex, presiding over the trial. (Probably Lopez took the money but double-crossed his Spanish employer.) Convicted of treason, he was hanged, drawn, and quartered, June 7, 1594. Addressing the crowd, he protested his innocence, saying that he loved the Queen "as well as he loved Jesus Christ." This, coming from a Jew, "made no small laughter in the standers-by." An unfriendly witness, Shakespeare remembered Lopez in *The Merchant of Venice*. Shylock is this wicked man, reincarnate. His currish spirit governed a wolf hanged for human slaughter. But Shylock, a monster, gets the play's best lines.

Facing both ways, Shakespeare is an otter, Falstaff's word for Mistress Quickly. Why an otter, Sir John? "Why, she's neither fish nor flesh. / A man knows not where to have her." But the otter, a third thing, has its integrity, and Shakespeare, though one of a kind, invites description. His art, much like his person, makes a true-to-life concord of "ravening lamb" and "dove-feathered raven." These are images for Romeo who tempers extremities, Shakespeare too. The magnanimities he utters tell of the man. But so does the cut of his doublet, conforming to the fashion of the times. Decidedly highbrow, he was much in key with common folk and didn't write down but wrote from shared conviction, one reason so many flocked to hear him. A good "de casibus" man, critical of self-seekers who set their foot on Fortune's hill, he had a large bump of ambition himself. Devoting much pity to "poor naked wretches," he drew the line at some, and his plays are inflected by the prejudice of the man who wrote them. Moral in his understanding of conduct, sometimes moralizing, he didn't turn the other cheek and bromides don't suffice him. "What stronger breastplate than a heart untainted!" A weakling says this, not true in the event.

Reflecting in his pieties and antipathies alike his "native soil and country," he puts you in mind of some political leaders, the Queen being one, who lead because they know how to follow. Greater than all of them, he made life better, rivaling "Nature's own shape of bud, bird, branch, or berry." But this bettering is esthetic, not social. Some, even among the artists, care less for art than social justice, diminishing one in defense of the other. It wouldn't have occurred to Shakespeare to do this. Perhaps as a man, not as a maker, he falls short of the great spendthrifts like Latimer and More. God-bitten men, they threw away their dearest thing, a trifle. You don't imagine

Shakespeare going to the stake or the block. Surprisingly, though, the prudent man was disinterested, a virtue rarer than heroism. Like his Merchant of Venice, he held the world "but as the world," both this one and the world over yonder.

WHILE SHAKESPEARE labored his plays in Bishopsgate, his family back in Stratford coped with disaster. At summer's end in 1594, fire ran through town, again on the same day a year later. It burned two hundred buildings, mostly dwelling places, and left four hundred people homeless. In September 1595, Hamnet or Hamlet Sadler, for whom Shakespeare named his son, lost his house on the High Street. Stratford Town Council, appealing for help to the country, sent out its leading citizens to solicit contributions. Richard Quiney, Shakespeare's schoolfellow, was one of the solicitors.

The fires and their aftermath go unmentioned by Shakespeare, absentee husband and father. In these years, however, his older daughter verged on womanhood. Younger than Susanna, "ladies of esteem" in Juliet's Verona were already mothers. If this daughter's prospects in a doubtful time set him thinking, he didn't let on. But *The Merchant of Venice,* a product of the time, pays attention to fathers and daughters. Portia, left fatherless, stands for sacrifice, she says, virgin tribute to a monster from the sea.

Assimilating the matter of everyday life, Shakespeare elevates it to a higher power. This process transforms his relation with Southampton, an important presence in his play though not visibly there and never mentioned except in dedications to the narrative poems. In October 1595, Shakespeare's patron turned twenty-two and buried a stepfather. Meaning to be his own man, he pursued a new friend, golden-haired Elizabeth Vernon. Court gossip chronicles Southampton's amour and later it brought him low, but in 1595 he was still Fortune's darling. His eye, a rival poet said, crowned "the most victorious pen," presumably this poet's, not Shakespeare's. On November 17, honoring the Queen's birthday, he ran at tilt in Westminster, "valiant in arms, gentle, and debonair." "Gentle" means in blood, not manners, a distinction Shakespeare keeps before him in *The Merchant of Venice.*

This notorious play still awaits its fit audience. Some, embarrassed for Shakespeare, regret his anti-Jewish diatribe; others, coming to the rescue, suppose a closet anti-Christian making reparations. Shakespeare isn't pro or anti, though, and his play looks away from life to romance, Italianate and other. The hero isn't Southampton, the heroine isn't Mistress Vernon, and the melancholy merchant who doesn't know why he's sad isn't Shakespeare. But Shakespeare knows what sadness is and the play gives it houseroom. Whatever ails his merchant, it rubs off on Portia, weary of the world when we meet her first. World weariness oppresses minor characters too. Gratiano, a jolly chatterbox, has his weeping philosopher side and thinks that first times are the best times. Lovers burn with desire until they get their way. After that, things stale.

Even at the end when moonlight gilds the stage, they are talking of love's disasters, personated by luckless Thisbe, the witch Medea, etc. Moonstruck like other lovers, the Moon sleeps with Endymion but this flesh-and-blood shepherd eludes her in death. Medea, her name a byword for horror, is the one who helps Jason achieve the Golden Fleece. But the fleece is Portia's emblem and what has she to do with horror? Shakespeare's glamorous heroine has her beauty called in question, the sunny locks that adorn her entrapping men's hearts like gnats in cobwebs. This specious beauty, taken perhaps from a dead woman's skull, reels in Bassanio, like Hercules a rescuer of maidens. But Hercules himself makes a doubtful champion and many cowards wear his beard on their chins.

Doubt, pervasive in the play, seems the right mode for estimating things. Truth isn't itself but veiled by ornament, the beguiling shore to a dangerous sea. Shakespeare's characters, looking out to sea, don't spot the dangers coming on. Most are "sand-blind" (nearsighted) like old Father Gobbo, and "varnish" or "garnish" gets their assent. Some of this is funny as when clothes make the man, and fathers don't know their children or husbands their wives. But tainted pleas in law, "seasoned with a gracious voice," obscure evil intentions, no laughing matter. Observations like this surface often in *The Merchant of Venice*.

An unhappy Shakespeare stands behind his story but the buried life, aired out and put for sale, doesn't fester. Getting rid of ghosts, he makes them work for him. What might have shown as free-floating anxiety, signaling his own distress, hitches on to his surrogates, showing as theater. E.g., appearance and how it fools us, a poignant concern of his. Forecasting Othello, his black prince has "the complexion of a devil" but under the skin belies what he looks like. To find his truth, you have to "make incision." The caskets, whited sepulchres or the opposite of this, have their complexion too, but pickers and choosers won't want to be facile in saying what it means. Opening the silver casket, Aragon, a facile suitor, confronts a blinking idiot. In the clear air of heaven, true and false look like themselves and facility is approved. On earth, no vice so "simple" (unmixed) but it assumes the mark of virtue. The fallout of experience, this survey of how things are gives Shakespeare a theme.

Inspecting depression, his or somebody else's, he runs it through plot, his patented filtration system. Readers of the play, Shakespeare's characters too, wonder about Antonio, a "tainted wether of the flock" who can't isolate his sickness. He doesn't lack for money, has hopeful ventures at sea, and the pangs of despised love don't afflict him. At least, he spurns the suggestion. Some modern directors, looking for a new twist to spruce up their tired classic, have him cast longing eyes at his handsome young friend. This is reductive where the play is aggrandizing, and Antonio's torment, if it begins with Shakespeare's, takes on a life of its own. Shakespeare's play, not an imperfect artifact in search of a motive, dramatizes the absence of motive. Antonio is sad because he isn't merry and his unhappiness, falling like rain from heaven, has no source either he or we can point to.

Raising the ante as the play proceeds, Shakespeare suggests that people are like that. Diminishing for character, a compulsive psychology is going around and Portia's vagrant suitors have caught it. One, gloomy like Antonio, "hears merry tales and smiles not." But Nature in her time has framed many like this, men who never smile or laugh without cause "like parrots at a bagpiper." Unexpectedly, Shylock is one of these men. Why he wants his pound of flesh is a mystery, not least to him, and groping for reasons he thinks of the bagpipe. Some, when they hear it "sing i' the nose," can't contain their urine. That is how it is with Shylock, an incontinent Jew to a melancholy Christian.

Inborn bias or "affection," a radical limiting, governs for Shakespeare's dramatis personae, perhaps in the world outside the play. People in his comedies, bound hand and foot, don't say much for man the measure of all things. Shakespeare's psychology has implications for tragedy too, and across the footlights they must have stirred uneasily.

The persons of the play, consulting their wit, lose when they do this. How things turn out depends on chance or fortune, not wishing or willing, and the more forthcoming they are, the more entoiled. Even Hercules, the type of the forthcoming man, shrinks to our level when he rolls the dice. A lottery determines Portia's fate, and being human and self-willed she murmurs against it. "Hanging and wiving goes by destiny," though. Fortune, our presiding deity, drops manna on some, and this is how they don't starve. Mercy is like that, not forced or biddable but a gratuity, dropping like rain.

Some of Shakespeare's characters rack their brains or gird up their loins, and only a misanthrope will deny them their crooked grandeur. Shylock takes as a text Jacob's meditated cunning when he tricks a partner and gets the spotted lambs. "This was a way to thrive." But Antonio reproves him. "This was a venture, sir, that Jacob served for." So Heaven is ordinant, the plot discovering this, bad news to men who climb the ladder and fight with the angel. Shakespeare's heroes acknowledge their limited role, his villains dispute it, a way to tell them apart.

The Merchant of Venice ends on an upbeat but shrouded in mystery, almost impudent in its refusal to say how these things came about. Antonio's lost ships find safe harbor and Portia, though she has the details, won't produce them. The Caskets Scene (3.2), a high point for happiness but notably iffy, looks to the ending. Shakespeare's hero is fortunate, so wins the lady. Fortune isn't in his pocket, though, and if this goddess proves "a good wench" after all, that isn't because she hearkens to suggestion. Bassanio, like Hercules, has to take his chances. But he isn't herculean and what he doesn't do allows the happy ending. Skeptical where most are credulous, he doesn't believe his eyes. In the leaden casket, dull, gross, and obscure to sense, he finds the "summary" of his fortune:

> "You that choose not by the view,
> Chance as fair, and choose as true!"

Favored characters in Shakespeare are like him. They have a saying, "God sort all."

Shylock, however, stands on his own two feet. This villain loves his wife, and though devoid of pity, knows about pain. Modern-day friends of his, reading the past through the lens of the present, detect the persecuted member of a "minority." (This gives him reasons.) But Shakespeare, though generous, is pitiless too, and the ending leaves the villain in the dust. That isn't because he is Jewish. Shylock has a daughter, Jewish like himself, also wise, fair, and true. Anyway, her lover thinks so. To most in Shakespeare's nation until the other day, Jewishness, a concept dressed up in character, denies this possibility. But concepts and Shakespeare are like oil and water, and abstractions aren't part of his purview. A purview it is, provisional, not once and for all. This is the plus side of his skeptical view of perception.

In his tale of fathers and daughters, parallels show up everywhere, provoking speculation. Two fathers curb their daughters, a tyranny in nature, but in one case this works out for the best. Two daughters give away their rings, one precious, the other paltry. However, "what's aught but as 'tis valued?" Things are "seasoned," Shakespeare thinks (agreeable to taste), depending on the season that brings them to birth. Who wants a rose in winter? Some things taste best when mixed or seasoned with other things, justice, for example, mercy too. Shylock, simon pure, asks for one and Bassanio the other. So which is better? It all depends, and Dr. Portia, a Daniel come to judgment, disappoints them both.

"Nothing is good without respect," says Shakespeare's heroine, where "respect" means context, definitive for good and evil. The conventional reading, wanting things cut and dried, dispenses with context. It thinks "black is the badge of Hell," and so forth. Whatever the playwright thinks, his play is parochial, annulling the chance for shortcuts like this one. Taking leave of the typecasters, Shakespeare sticks to particular cases, and bringing on a Jewish villain brings on a Jewish heroine too. It isn't likely that he did this for tolerance' sake, a modern idea outside his ken. But he had an estimating eye.

Shakespeare's Jewish father and daughter, superficially the same, part company when he puts them through their paces. These two differ more, onlookers say, than red wine and Rhenish. Shylock's daughter Jessica is only this in blood, not in manners. Blood, distinguishing the "gentle" from the base-blooded man, tells of apparent truth, like clothing or color. Convention, in a hurry, pins its faith to this truth, and its cursory reading is vivid in the story of Jewish Dr. Lopez. What else should he be but a monster? Manners make the man, though, and lead that doesn't glister pays more than it promises. This is what old Belmont, setting up his lottery, hoped to teach them.

2

The Revolution of the Times

UNSUSPECTED IN THE AUTHOR of *The Merchant of Venice,* Shakespeare had an eye to social standing. In 1596 he achieved the rank of gentleman, more than mouth honor to an ambitious man. This year, however, he lost the son and heir without whom the honor would have seemed empty. Hamnet, dead of unknown causes at eleven and a half, took with him the chance to carry on the family name.

Honor's a lying trophy debauched on every tomb, Shakespeare's character assures us, but he himself pursued it, his stay against oblivion. A servant of Queen Elizabeth, later King James's groom, he wore livery and bought land and houses, flagging his status. Entailing this property, he meant to bind the future, and like his self-conscious heroes hoped posterity wouldn't forget him. Tell the tale of me, says his Richard II.

The pathos of Shakespeare's dynastic ambitions takes intenser color from the death of his son. His father's younger brother Henry died the same year but he was "sapless age," forfeit in the course of nature, Hamnet the "gentler scion." Shakespeare's daughters remained. Getting married, however, they became Hall or Quiney, not good enough. Though Judith, Hamnet's twin, produced male children, she outlived them. Shakespeare's brothers had no children except one, a byblow, dead of the plague. His wife Anne, living apart, and in the time's view an old woman at forty, bore him no second son. Like the phoenix in his poem he was one of a kind and his line petered out not long after he died.

Some biographers have him posting back to Stratford in the late summer of 1596 to kneel at his son's deathbed or stand beside the grave. No one records his presence, however, and he never mentions Hamnet by name. Some think he mourned his loss in the person of little Prince Arthur, who makes a pathetic end in *King John*. But this history play most likely antedates Hamnet's death. The greater life's impact on Shakespeare, the less the plays announce it, and rarely do things personal contaminate his art. But though he concealed them, befitting the artist, they constitute his principal truth.

Not acting out experience, the plays reflect its cost, e.g., in *Much Ado About Nothing* where a bereaved father, railing out of control, intimates the playwright's involvement. Hamnet's life is part of this generalized expense. His early death, insupportable fact no one could rationalize, might have served for melodrama and Shakespeare left it alone. When the funeral took place in Stratford, August 11, 1596, he was at work on history plays. Chronicles of the big wars, they develop a parallel story, the relation between fathers and sons, York and Aumerle, Northumberland and Hotspur, Henry IV and Prince Hal. This story, not his but an "abstract" of the divided kingdom, brims with felt emotion. Already in his first histories, archetypal figures suggest it. One, a new Aeneas, exits with his father, dead "Anchises," on his back. In the last *Henry VI* play, stage directions, Expressionist in their bold relief, introduce "a son that has killed his father . . . a father that has killed his son." The *Henry IV* plays pit son against father, and errant Hal, disappointing a parent's hopes, is to Henry as Absalom to King David. Shakespeare found his plot in Holinshed, fortified by memories of the Book of Samuel. Deeper down lay experience, matter for art to work on.

Named for Sadler the baker, Shakespeare's boyhood acquaintance, Hamnet is also Hamlet, interchangeable names. Four years after his son died, Shakespeare in *Hamlet* had to face him. The old tale, on the boards or soon to be when he arrived in London, isn't autobiography, and Shakespeare doesn't wear his heart on his sleeve. Transforming the given, though, he made his own play. In this impersonal labor, Hamnet figures as a reagent. Where the playwright is successful the reagent dissolves, all gone into art.

Bereft of the child that mattered, Shakespeare looked for satisfaction in his title to gentility. A coat of arms confirmed this, and both the playwright and his father John were privileged to display it. Medieval knights in armor wore the coat of arms when they went into battle, complemented by a crest on their helmets. Heraldic tokens, the crest and coat distinguished one man enclosed in armor from another. In the sixteenth century, on the way to modern times, the distinction didn't seem worth making but would-be gentry had a theory of the leisure class, the less useful, the more honorific.

John Shakespeare, coveting honor, petitioned for a coat of arms late in the 1560s, after his election as bailiff. He meant it to create him new, "a gentleman born" like the Clown in *The Winter's Tale.* Shakespeare, laughing at the Clown's pretensions, took them to heart, understanding that the laugh was partly on him. Gentleman's status didn't come cheap but John Shakespeare got money's worth and his handsome badge compels attention. The Heralds' College in London sketched it for him in pen-and-ink, their "pattern" or "trick" showing a silver falcon grasping a spear and shaking its wings. This was the crest or cognizance, punning on the name Shakespeare. The falcon stands on a silver wreath atop a gold shield. A "bend sable" or black band runs diagonally across the coat or shield from the top right corner, the wearer's right hand. Luminous on the black diagonal, the gold spear is tipped with silver.

Coming down in the world, John Shakespeare didn't pursue his application. In 1596 his son, established in Bishopsgate, revived it. He applied in his father's name, the oldest male of the line and as the world measured things the best credentialed. Garter King-of-Arms, approving, noted that John Shakespeare was bailiff, magistrate, J.P., married to an heiress, and officer of the Queen. This last counted most. Presiding over the Court of Record, a Crown court, Shakespeare's father had the right to call himself a royal servant.

The Shakespeare coat of arms needed its motto. This the herald supplied, first bungling the job. Above the shield and crest he wrote in French, the language of heraldry: *Non, sanz droict.* "No, without right." That had a frosty sound. Then, omitting punctuation, the herald tried again. This time he made a proper motto: "Not without right." The affair of the superfluous comma looks prophetic. In 1602, critics of the Garter King accused him of elevating base persons to the gentry. Of twenty-three cases alleged as improper, William Shakespeare's comes fourth on the list. He is simply and sufficiently "Shakespeare the Player." The family patent of gentility survived its challenge, though. Henceforward, said the Heralds' College, Shakespeares might bear the device awarded them "upon their shields, targets, escutcheons, coats of arms, pennons," etc.

Ben Jonson, Shakespeare's self-appointed conscience, renewed the challenge in two plays. Sneering at Shakespeare and the Heralds' "trick" or sketch, he said how rascally players forgot they were in the statute that still classed them with rogues and vagabonds. "They are blazoned there, there they are tricked, they and their pedigrees! They need no other heralds." Shakespeare's motto begot a cruel joke, and Jonson brought on stage a newly gentrified clown who has his crest, a boar's head, his motto too: "Not without mustard." Playgoers, amused, thought of Falstaff, gourmandizing at the tavern on Cheapside. Shakespeare swallowed his pique and pursued his claim to status.

A gentleman lived without manual labor, bearing "the port, charge, and countenance" of a man of substance. His wife, dressing well, was supposed to keep servants. Noblesse oblige defined them both. Money, a soilure, didn't stick to their fingers. Aristocratic propaganda, this reproved men of trade, also "upstarts" who lived by their wits. Some dissented from it, keeping their opinion to themselves. In the next century, Cromwell and his Ironsides spoke for these dissenters. The story of the Civil War, when rebels and royalists marched up and down in Warwickshire, postdates Shakespeare's time, but the quarrel between the parvenu and settled authority engaged him from the beginning. In his Lancastrian plays, he looks into the seeds of time. "Intestine" war, outs against ins, is the matter of these plays. Shakespeare the parvenu, "not propped by ancestry" but "force of his own merit," belongs with the outs.

But his deep skepticism spoiled the chance for a partisan's role. Though Coriolanus, his patrician hero, is a fool, his tribunes, who hurl the little houses on the great, are scoundrels. Who's in, who's out, a pressing question to many, left him unmoved. Protagonists in the theater of history got his attention but history itself seemed to him a game of "hoodman blind." (Steering clear of the present, he kept his reflections to the remoter past, from Alexander the Great to Henry V.) Contestants in the game put their trust in princes, the prince on the throne or some better surrogate they wanted to install there. In *Henry IV*, Part Two, a skeptical clergyman pronounces on their politics, saying what it got them.

> A habitation giddy and unsure
> Hath he that buildeth on the vulgar heart.

Getting things done absorbed him and he gives a great saying to old Henry IV, worn out in service:

> Are these things then necessities?
> Then let us meet them like necessities.

In the last resort, however, the stakes, in life and art, were personal. Private counted more than public, even in the public sphere. Falstaff, in the thick of it at Shrewsbury, has a bottle in his holster, not the pistol Hal is looking for. "What!" says the hero, "is it a time to jest and dally now?" But "every time / Serves for the matter that is then born in't." Characteristically, Shakespeare's men of affairs, full of bustle and poetry, dispute this—not a time to play with "mammets" (female breasts) or tilt with lips. He grants them panache but they deject him. A cold eye surveys their marchings and countermarchings, up the hill and down again like the grand old Duke of York's. Had he lived longer, he would have said that Cavaliers and Roundheads wore different costumes.

WINNING HIS SPURS with chronicle-history plays, he went back to this genre in the mid–1590s. Four plays in sequence remember the House of Lancaster, and some think other histories of the time, grouped together as the Shakespeare Apocrypha, are his. All feature the clang of swords on targets. His earlier histories, the Henry VI plays and their sequel, *Richard III,* open when the heavens, mourning Henry V, are hung with black. "In medias res" didn't suit the taste of panoramic Shakespeare, though, and a new tetralogy supplies the beginning of his bloody tale. *Richard II,* work of 1595, leads off, followed in a year or two by both parts of *Henry IV. Henry V,* saluting the Earl of Essex, was completed before the Earl returned from the Irish wars, September 1599. Shakespeare's four plays tell of a time when England's star lived greatly but that is only part of the story.

Everyone supposed that Essex would come home with rebellion broached on his sword. The record hardly promised this but the history play, something like the silver screen, cared less for truth than poetry. This explains its spectacular vogue. For roughly two decades after the Armada (1588), one play in five celebrated England's history. Shakespeare, digging up the past, was no antiquarian but catering to popular taste.

For the history behind the history books, he closed up his Holinshed and consulted "the quick forge and working house of thought." His version of history, played out on the world's stage, feeds "contention" in an act that never ends. Rumor introduced it and a Chorus, interpreting the action, said what the puppets were doing. Famous for fighting, they aren't otherwise remarkable, "warlike Blunt," brave Archibald "ever valiant," two bellicose Mowbrays, like father, like son. In the second Henry IV play, Shakespeare allowed himself a pair of Bardolphs, one in either camp. Perhaps he meant a comment, effacing distinction, or perhaps invention failed. Some of his lesser fry have names like cue cards: thievish Nym (= taking), Pistol, Mistress Quickly, Doll Tearsheet, Shallow and Slender. Too slight a peg for judgment to hang on, these morality types are complemented by Falstaff, so much himself that judgment stammers beside him. "Banish plump Jack, and banish all the world." The hero, faithful to history and its imperatives, undertakes to do this, cause for dismay.

History to Shakespeare's predecessors came down to "The Famous Victories of. . . ." In his Lancastrian plays, he felt for sequence, so wrought an unforgettable change. Readers who want a yardstick to measure his achievement have one in *Edward III,* an anonymous history of the earlier nineties. This baggy chronicle is often given to Shakespeare, and Tennyson was certain he wrote the first two acts, domestic back-and-forth between the kingly seducer and a virtuous matron. Rhetoric like Shakespeare's distinguishes the play, and Shakespeare in the sonnets is quoted directly: "Lilies that fester smell far worse than weeds." But *Edward III's* middle-class fervors, ingenuous and taking, suggest a sensibility less complicated than his, some eminent Victorian's in the womb of time:

> Away, loose silks of wavering vanity! . . .
> Give me an armor of eternal steel!
> I go to conquer kings; and shall I not then
> Subdue myself?

In this superior but staple version of the English history play, the issue isn't ever in doubt. Famous Edward the Black Prince, bayed by the dogs of France, stands like "a bear fast chained unto a stake," but though the dogs are many England's hero cuffs them soundly. Patriotic Shakespeare has similar passages. In his histories, however, doubt is of the essence. Three times in *Henry V* he puts us up on a mountain, the same one King Edward stood on, watching his embattled son. The King and his forces don't come down to help but "stand laughing by," half an army being adequate to confront the full power of France. The speaker who remembers this scene is partial, though, so perhaps not meant to be trusted. Henry's account of virile English and effeminate French is like that, begetting the same reservation.

Onstage history mustered a cast of thousands from beggar maid to king. Sometimes they crowd on stage together and we need a "stickler" to distinguish high from low. Shakespeare's characters often speak to this need, among them Sir Thomas More in the history play he lends his name to. "Seriatim" drama like *Edward III,* this old-fashioned play has the unity of what comes next. Two o'clock comes after one o'clock, an elementary pattern innocent of cause and effect.

A play by different hands, *The Book of Sir Thomas More* is memorable for one, "Hand D," supposed to be Shakespeare's. "Book," a technical term, refers to the manuscript, annotated by the company's bookkeeper and sent for approval to the Master of the Revels. "Allowed" for acting, it became the prompt copy. *Sir Thomas More,* falling foul of the censor, never got this far. Surviving in manuscript but not printed or acted in Shakespeare's lifetime, it dramatizes the adventures of an English folk hero. In Act II, scene iv, Hand D's contribution, the hero, then London's sheriff, faces down the mob. He does this on Evil May Day, 1517, when London's prentices, angered by rising prices, set out to kill and plunder the "strangers" in their midst. Self-interest went with xenophobia and removing these alien merchants couldn't help but advantage "the poor handicrafts of the city." That is what they tell themselves.

Evil May Day had a rerun in 1593, suggesting to some a date for the play. But the mob, noisome, comic, and dangerous, was always on the boil. Emerging from shops and tenements to part a fray or swell a tumult, prentices called for "Clubs!" or "Stones!" or fell to it with their teeth, like Shakespeare's bloody-pated servingmen in his first history play. Essex, leading his ragtag army against the Queen in 1601, hoped London's mob would rise with him. At the Revels Office, Tilney, eyeing such contingencies, wrote atop the first page of the inflammatory More book: "Leave out the insurrection wholly." More's chroniclers might begin, he said, with a report of the sheriff's good service in quelling "a mutiny against the Lombards." There weren't many Lombards in London.

Five men collaborated in the first version of *Sir Thomas More.* Anthony Munday, a prolific hack known to one contemporary as "our best plotter," headed this syndicate. Meeting or anticipating the censor's objections, the collaborators rewrote heavily, then called in Shakespeare to put the best face on their matter. This reconstruction of how the play was made depends partly on Shakespeare's autograph, surviving in six versions. Paleographers, comparing them with Hand D, give the mob scene to Shakespeare—a tenuous assignment, one of them conceded, like identifying "a face in the dark by the dim light of a lucifer match."

But style supports this assignment and locates "Shakespeare's" scene in the context of his Henry IV plays or a little later. Looking back to Jack Cade, it looks forward to *Julius Caesar, Troilus and Cressida,* and *Coriolanus*. More, reproving the rebels, has his "organic" metaphors, not like the Decalogue but appealing to experience:

> Whiles they are o'er the bank of their obedience,
> Thus will they bear down all things.
>
> by this pattern [anarchy]
> Not one of you should live an agèd man.
> For other ruffians . . .
> Would shark on you, and men, like ravenous fishes,
> Would feed on one another.

Concluding his catechism, the hero tells them what to do: "Give up yourselves to form."

Of all Shakespeare's words, form is the urgent one. Comely in itself, it takes power from its opposite, deliquescence, when life leaks away. "Innovation," More thinks, tears the bond that holds things together. This is suicidal and Shakespeare, invoking natural and social sanctions, arraigns it. The ocean, "overpeering" its banks (like Laertes in *Hamlet*), floods the mainland, at the same time dispersing itself. Men preying on others—e.g., the villains in *King Lear*—prey on themselves "like monsters of the deep." Not prescriptive but pragmatic, these analogies mean to persuade us. On one man's "charters and his customary rights" depend the rights of others. Take this man's rights from Time, says York in *Richard II,* and tomorrow doesn't follow today. Ranging from late to early, Shakespeare's contexts express point of view, the same view we meet in the More Book. His histories, tales of "damned commotion," fill it out circumstantially.

Everything he wrote derived from tradition, not the same as calling him a traditional writer. His patriotic genre took its materials, assumed to be true, from national chronicles like Holinshed's and Hall's. It put them to many uses, but like the Ten Commandments they boil down to two, glorifying England and instructing her ruler and people. Some playwrights invoke the past to buttress a theory like the divine right of kings. Or history plays (wearing kid gloves) criticize contemporary statecraft. One, ferocious comedy plus history, ends with an epilogue that admonishes the Queen; another, history plus tragedy, refers her to things past, wanting to insure a peaceful succession. This was the tradition Shakespeare inherited. Standard accounts, merging him with his inheritance, have him promoting a providential plan.

Drawing for his pattern on morality plays, he pieced it out with old stories of the falls of illustrious men, mainly princes. Up and down they go, these famous men of times past. Readers will find their stories, suitably moralized, in *A Mirror for Magistrates* (1559 and after), versified biography and one of Shakespeare's quarries. Incessant qualification marks his histories, however. Sometimes it seems to him that the evil men do lives after them, and even his happy endings have the feel of an ellipsis. Rebellion, like the Hydra, keeps renewing itself. In his culminating story, Agincourt, a famous victory, is behind, and England and France are going to breed a new scion between them. This is Henry VI who will go to Constantinople and take the Turk by the beard. But Shakespeare already had that story in his scrip, depressing reading.

Though his materials were given, they showed him a different grain. Meeting expectation, his epilogue in *Henry IV,* Part Two remembers the Queen. Shakespeare doesn't instruct her, however, but not because the Queen is wise. Instruction seems wasted on the likes of us, and the dancer who speaks his epilogue kneels down to pray. In *Richard II,* the story of a feckless king whose botched succession ushers in civil war, he is often said to be holding up the mirror. Caveat Regina. Essex and his friends read this history as a tract for the times. But Shakespeare's play is aloof from problems that admit of solutions, and his moral must exasperate hopeful men who think correction lies in our will.

> But whate'er I be,
> Nor I nor any man that but man is
> With nothing shall be pleased till he be eased
> With being nothing.

Sponsors of Shakespeare the Tudor apologist will want to ponder these lines.

Richard II, strong for divine right, says that all the water in the sea won't wash it off, persuasive rhetoric but events don't support him. Henry V has a second string to his bow. Picking a quarrel with France, he pleads "Salic law," pretty flimsy. Homespun philosophers worry about this, "a black matter for the King" if the quarrel he gets them into isn't just. But just or unjust, to disobey him "were against all proportion of subjection," i.e., theirs not to reason why. Not every subject was so tractable and some in Shakespeare's England made the tenure of kings and magistrates depend on their fitness to govern. But history plays have hard words for rebellious men who meddle in princes' matters. Shakespeare's aged Gaunt wants them to know that "God's is the quarrel." Against His minister, pious men will never lift an angry arm.

Spokesmen for the Tudors, promoting "degree," meant to admonish refractory subjects. Some eloquent speeches in Shakespeare partake of this intention, at the same time transcend it. But the rush of words, an imperious flood, has carried everything before it, and most assimilate Shakespeare to the World Picture he limned in the plays. Disconcertingly, though, his chief spokesmen for "the specialty of rule" are the "dog-fox" Ulysses, disingenuous Canterbury who has his ax to grind, bumbling Menenius in *Coriolanus,* Rosencrantz, both fool and villain, in *Hamlet.*

Canterbury on the honeybees makes a cunning rhetorician, perhaps a shade studied. Marshalling the same syntactic constructions, he means to run over us, subduing objection. But his iterated words and phrases: "The singing masons . . . The civil citizens . . . The poor mechanic porters . . . As many . . . As many," seem in their deliberateness to call in question the point they contend for. A formal oration, his ends with a sequitur, "therefore to France." This falls a little flat, unworthy of the long parade that forms up before it. These exemplary honeybees, doing as they're told, commended themselves to a politic Speaker of the House of Commons, addressing Queen and Parliament in 1593.

Shakespeare himself addressed the Queen by name in *Henry VIII,* patriotic piffle written long after her death. While she lived, he left the oily talk to others. She was vain as a peacock and the others weren't behindhand in catering to this. Diana, Oriana, Gloriana, they called her, also Sweet Bessy, ruler of the waves, the nurse of religion, joy of the zodiac, and empress of flowers. This rose had no thorns. Some, extolling her wisdom, identified Shakespeare's Queen with Pallas Athena. King James, the other sovereign he knew at first hand, was extolled for wisdom too. A drunken helmsman, running the ship of state on the rocks, he presided over a court that showed like a riotous inn. We hear about it in *King Lear,* safely prehistoric. Bacon, Shakespeare's great opposite, turned the King's vices to virtues, and Spenser hailed the Queen as chaste Belphoebe. Unlike these contemporaries, Shakespeare is silent on "Eliza and our James." In his history plays, however, he accommodated both. Neither would have been flattered had they read him through and through.

"Touchstone" speeches like Canterbury's have their obvious likeness to the Shakespearean part of *Sir Thomas More.* More's voice, authentic Shakespeare, isn't raised in defense of privilege, however, and his impartial strictures cut two ways. "Ravenous," his word, is apt for the commons, also, as analogy governs, for their betters. Shakespeare's histories, not counselling submission but discrimination, enlist the author on the side of life against death. In his first history play, he likens civil dissension to "a viperous worm" gnawing the bowels of the commonwealth. Analogies like this often occur to him, their opposites too, speaking for health. Ideal government, "though high and low and lower," keeps one "consent" or harmony, grateful to his ear. Compared to discord, harmony wins every time. But Shakespeare's reasons aren't prescriptive, his motives aren't partisan, and this considering witness isn't pro-king but pro-order. His allegiance goes to a polity where all "distinctly ranges." Distinction failing, "heaps and piles of ruin" succeed.

More than most, he felt the solid earth moving under his feet, and the specter of chaos, less political than total, haunts his plays. The consent he honors is artificial (a good word), not natural. Natural music is the ragged noise of time. Deep down, Shakespeare's histories are all sound and fury, "Alarum, Retreat, Excursions, Exeunt." Challenged by chaos, he imposed form on his recalcitrant fictions, understanding that this was partly imposition.

VEXATIONS AND SORROWS, crowding in on Shakespeare in 1596, tried the public man too. The summer his son died, he and his company faced a new rival, sponsored by the Earl of Pembroke and housed in an up-to-date theater, Francis Langley's. Destroyed by plague three years before but rising from the ashes, Pembroke's Men were led by theater-wise professionals like Gabriel Spencer. Young Ben Jonson belonged to the company, and later killed this Spencer in a duel.

Challenging the Henslowe-Burbage establishment, Langley enlisted

Pembroke's Men for his new playhouse. He built in Paris Garden west of the Rose on Bankside, and in the summer of 1596 Johannes de Witt went to see what he had made. "Of all the theaters," said this Dutch traveler, "the largest and the most magnificent is that one of which the sign is a swan." Perhaps Shakespeare's fellows, hunting a new location, played the Swan in the fall—"lately afore used to have plays in it," reads a contemporary record. Or perhaps Pembroke's Men, first noticed there in early 1597, were already on the ground well before this. For Shakespeare, harried by competitors while his company's lease ran out on the Theater in Shoreditch, it wasn't the best of times.

But Langley, notoriously a man of "greedy desire and dishonest disposition," overreached himself. Within a year his speculation failed, and Pembroke's Men, promoting a "seditious" play, fell victim to royal displeasure. In Shakespeare's age, actors and playwrights balanced on a narrow footing over dangerous waters. "If he fall in, good night! Or sink or swim."

Ben Jonson, a tyro in theater, dramatizes the peril they all stood in. In 1597 he and Tom Nashe, unlucky partners, collaborated on a political play, *The Isle of Dogs.* It had a mise-en-scène, downriver from the City, Londoners could actually point to. Unsettling to Privy Council, this blurred the line between fact and fiction. The play was called in, lost to the future except for its name, Jonson went to prison, and Nashe fled just ahead of the law. Shakespeare, watching from the sidelines, kept to history plays, things past. Once he set his scene in present-day England, making sure, however, that no one's withers were wrung. His lone contemporary play, *The Merry Wives of Windsor,* is full of topical allusion but bland.

Within weeks of the hullabaloo raised by *The Isle of Dogs,* Privy Council came down hard on the stage. Its anger, focused on the Swan, took in both Theater and Curtain, and meaning to close them all it had the support of London's Corporation. This was pro forma. Almost every year, the Lord Mayor and Aldermen, firing off letters, told the Crown that plays were evil. In 1594 Burghley's help was invoked to "stay" them. Next year Privy Council got the same request, reiterated in July 1597. Petitioning for the "final suppressing of . . . plays in or about" London, Mayor Billingsley urged that J.P.s for Middlesex and Surrey be empowered to see to this. "About" was important, all the public theaters lying outside Guildhall's jurisdiction.

The Crown consulted its own pleasure, not the London Corporation's, but for once the two coincided. Noting great disorders and a "confluence of bad people" in the common playhouses, Privy Council ordered an end to plays within three miles of the City. It put teeth in its order, instructing landlords to "pluck down" their theaters and requiring local magistrates to report on delinquents who didn't "speedily perform" as charged. One magistrate, William Gardiner, welcomed the requirement. A bitter enemy of Langley's, this Surrey J.P. had jurisdiction over Paris Garden and Southwark. Pursuing his enemy in and out of the courts, Gardiner spread his net for Langley's friends and acquaintance. Shakespeare, a lodger on Bankside or plying his trade there, got tangled in the net.

But the right hand didn't know or care to know what the left hand was doing. Venting their anger, the Lords in Council gave it limits and forbade playing only "until Allhallowtide next." For Langley, the ban on summer playing proved permanent. Reapplying for a license, he didn't get one, and when the theaters reopened five of his actors, quitting the Swan, joined the Admiral's Men at the Rose. The Crown's inhibition worked a hardship on Shakespeare too. Having no alternative, he went into the country, coming back with the others on All Saints' Day, November 1. Coming or going, they all lived on sufferance.

Sometimes this had a bright side, but like a summer's day, not to be trusted. In winter 1598, the remnant of Pembroke's Men, having lost their Bankside playhouse, began to act again in the City. Hearing of this, Privy Council had the Revels Office suppress "the aforesaid third company," licensing only Shakespeare's and the Admiral's Men. As the new century opened, these two companies were privileged once more, less a mark of the Crown's favor than its failure of nerve. Indifferent to genius, it wanted to restrict the "immoderate use" of the stage. The restriction was a boon for Shakespeare but one he couldn't count on, and his company's monopoly, ratified today, might be canceled tomorrow.

Later the boys' companies broke the monopoly. Waning popularity, not a royal injunction, sent the Chamberlain's Men on tour, some say as far as Aberdeen. "How chances it they travel?" Hamlet inquires. "Their residence, both in reputation and profit, was better both ways." But the wheel kept turning and later still the boy actors, not minding their manners, went the way of Pembroke's Men.

Ill-starred for Shakespeare, the summer of 1596 saw a fresh outbreak of plague. On July 22, Privy Council closed the theaters. The same day the Lord Chamberlain Hunsdon died, and Shakespeare and his company lost their patron. What the changing of the guard might mean to the players, they could only guess at. But they knew about plague and fall ushered in that time they dreaded most, a "tedious dead vacation" threatening work and means.

William Brooke, Lord Cobham, succeeded Hunsdon in the Chamberlain's office. He descended from the fat knight who diverted Prince Hal—Sir John Oldcastle, as Shakespeare called him first. This early name survives in a phrase from *Henry IV*, Part One, "my old lord of the castle," i.e., a roisterer. Cobham or his son Henry objecting to the name, Shakespeare changed it to Falstaff. Oldcastle, not the same man, died a martyr, he said. But the ghost of the roisterer wasn't easily laid and rival playwrights capitalized on Shakespeare's discomfit. Their version of Oldcastle, a "virtuous peer," differed, they noted smugly, from his "aged counsellor to youthful sin."

Deprived of a friend in power, the players found themselves "piteously persecuted" by the London Corporation. "In their old Lord's time they thought their state settled." Now, wrote Tom Nashe, it was "so uncertain they cannot build upon it." Then Fortune's mood varied again. Cobham died, having been Chamberlain for only seven months. His successor, old Hunsdon's son, George Carey, was St. George, the players thought, come to the rescue. All the dragons were still at large, though.

Marching step by step with Shakespeare's rising popularity, hatred of his theater, implacable, not spastic like Privy Council's, threatened to destroy it. (Some of his fellows lived to see this happen.) The theaters survived the edict of 1597 but the persecution continued, sometimes checked by the Crown, never deflected for long. Scurrilous pamphleteers like Gosson and William Prynne attacked the stage, some glancing at its royal patron. Prynne, a famous scourge of players, lost his ears in the pillory. Later, authorities cut off the stumps of his ears and branded him on both cheeks with the letters S.L., Seditious Libeler. In the next decade he was vindicated, though, Parliament ordaining that "public stage plays shall cease and be forborne."

Preachers and their satellites attacked the stage on moral grounds but were zealous for "pecunia" too. "The Venus of our time and state," Jonson called it. In their bill of particulars they cited "the charges that are laid out upon one stage play" or the "misspence of much precious time." Merchants chimed in with this, one ranking poets and playwrights with "shuttlecocks, tennis balls, apes, monkeys, baboons, parrots [and] puppets." The writer, a Jacobean businessman "conversant in weighty and profitable affairs," made his money in coal and saltpeter. The anti-theater scribblers are often called Puritans, synonymous with spoilsports. They weren't morose, however, but wanted to build the kingdom of God on earth. Shakespeare, provisional in his psychology, halfway to pessimistic, was their natural antagonist.

Not that he resembled the lilies of the field. His art, partly for art's sake, was meant for profit too, and like the new men who deplored him he had a gold thumb. Alone among contemporaries, he combined the roles of actor, playwright, and shareholder in his company. This brought him a percentage of the day's proceeds. Making money needed money and what he paid for his share is suggested by Alleyn's purchase of a share in the Admiral's Men. Pegged at £37.10 in 1589, it increased in value to £50 by 1602, to £70 a decade later, large sums. In time Shakespeare moved up to "housekeeper," part owner of the theater he played in. Wearing these different hats made him rich.

He got his money as he could, soaring or stooping. As actor he shared the revenue from the sale of beer, tobacco, fruit, and nuts. His company's "ordinary" poet, he enjoyed an "allowance" or was paid for his plays at the going rate of £6 or better. In James's reign, this payment tripled. By then Shakespeare had ceased acting, and his work as playwright and possibly director served as his return for the profits he realized as sharer. When he wrote a new play, however, his company gave him a "benefit," the whole takings of the house for the second or third performance. Some believe the housekeeper found these benefits beneath him, others that he took the money and smiled. This sounds Shakespearean.

From performances at Court, in the law schools, and noblemen's houses, he drew additional income. He invested his money, in Stratford and London, laying out more than £1,000. Also he lent money at usurious rates, and from interest on this, plus his rents and leases, gathered annually another £20 to £30. Husbanding these earnings, he left cash bequests totalling £350. Altogether, said a vicar of Stratford in the seventeenth century, "he spent at the rate of a thousand a year." That embellishes the saga of the local-boy-made-good but succeed he did and his biographers, scrutinizing the figures, put his yearly earnings between £250 and a little under £400. In 1598 his contemporary Thomas Dekker made £40 on plays, impressive but not up to Shakespeare. What with his "statutes, his recognizances, his fines, his double vouchers, his recoveries," he looks on one side like his lawyer in *Hamlet*. He saw the likeness and exploited it in plays, just as Henry James saw a piece of himself in Gilbert Osmond, the bloodless esthete who loves objets d'art.

GIVEN WHAT HE WAS, it isn't surprising that he looked at his history plays from different perspectives. "Natural perspectives," he calls them,

which rightly gazed upon
Show nothing but confusion, eyed awry
Distinguish form.

We hear about these tricky images in *Richard II,* and in *Henry V* they come up again. Shakespeare, confounding us, makes us see better. But he has his queer side, like those old typologists who turned the world and its history into a house of mirrors. To his uncanny eye everything looks like everything else, and the form his parallels distinguish seems coexistent with his catalog of persons, places, and things. Setting picture against picture or the word itself against the word, he leaves it to his auditors to say what he means. Sometimes you feel that meaning is exhausted in simple replication. This knack of seeing resemblances where no one saw them before marks the highest intelligence but verges on madness, "near allied," some say, to great wit.

Standing outside himself in *Henry V,* Shakespeare comments on his weird facility. Welsh Fluellen is his lookalike, a self-critical version. "There is figures"—parallels—"in all things," says this comprehensive man. Like and unlike Shakespeare's Plutarch making parallel lives, he illustrates by comparing Alexander the Great to Harry of Monmouth. Each was raised beside a river "and there is salmons in both." Downplaying distinction, he prefers a thesaurus of values.

Where modern ratios equate like with like, Shakespeare's instruct us that bad Falstaff is to Shallow (in *Henry IV,* Part Two), as Prince John to the rebels. But the rebels merit sympathy as they honor their word. Crookedness all round cancels sympathy, though, and Falstaff, "sealing" with his gull, is like the rebel prelate, "sealing" the lawless book of rebellion. Shallow himself, bearing out a knave against an honest man, mirrors the venal men at the top. Decorous, perhaps, for Shakespeare's play without heroes, this collapsing of distinction carries on in his heroic play, *Henry V.* Nym and Pistol have a quarrel, like the puerile quarrel of Fluellen and Macmorris over "the disciplines of war." Shakespeare isn't finished with his parallels, however, and the dispute between these fussy soldiers resembles King Henry's with the common soldier Williams. Perhaps it resembles Henry's quarrel with France.

Fluellen's pedantic discourse on the "ceremonies" needed for military science anticipates the King's great apostrophe to Ceremony. Oddly, each is accommodated in the same scene. Not separating out, oil and water make an emulsion. "Unto the breach!" the King bids them at Harfleur, rhetoric that tells on the pulses. In the next scene, however, his "choice-drawn cavaliers" are driven at sword's point "up to the breach." These juxtapositions might diminish the King and his gorgeous words but seem not to.

Other parallels come to mind but let us take them on faith and get on to a summary comment: in Shakespeare's emulsions nothing precipitates out. Judgment in the history plays isn't much pronounced, never ex cathedra, and good and bad "find no partition." If we have an index of value, Pistol, a moral nullity, supplies it. Others get hanged but he lives. Particulars are rendered with surpassing fidelity and this is much, perhaps as much as Shakespeare is ever willing to venture. But readers who catechize him will find that he turns a deaf ear. Is Bolingbroke a hypocrite? "God knows, my son. . . ." What really happened at Clement's Inn in the old days?

Modern readers, dejected by heroics, often decide that Shakespeare meant to undercut them. His kings have noble speeches but fight for an eggshell, and the discordant multitude, a "blunt monster," ratifies or annuls their achievement. Beneath the stirring rhetoric is "the law of nature." It says that the little fish is bait for the big one. Not all the rhetoric is stirring, some of it approximating Alleyn's fustian at the Rose. Sometimes patriotism resolves to bloodsucking, and Shakespeare's Christian king, let out of his cage, proves "deaf to the widows' tears, the orphans' cries." The rank-and-file, he avers, are brothers of his. But these common soldiers have a shrewd suspicion that when their throats are cut he may be ransomed and they never the wiser. Meanwhile the stay-at-homes, "civil citizens," coin money. "Look you," cynical Falstaff advises them, "that our armies join not in a hot day."

But Shakespeare isn't cynical, only circumambient, and his cool assessing doesn't preclude applause. Trumpets sound in his battle pieces and whoever doesn't thrill to this is dead, as they say, to all finer feeling. Outside the theater ignorant armies clashed by night, but his histories, reflecting a sure sense of theater, confess a grand moral design. Adjusting the historical record (Hal and Hotspur, mighty opposites, must be of an age), he cinches and compresses it (no room for that Emperor Sigismund who patched a truce between England and France). But his four-part chronicle is more notable for what it includes. In his tribute to England he finds a place for vulgar hijinks, pairing the ruler with a lord of misrule. This pairing is good for laughs and he liked to leave them laughing.

Getting down from his high horse in *Richard II,* too sober by half, he alternated sober with comic. Others showed him the way. "Bouncing Bess with the jolly buttocks" diverted the crowd in one of his source plays, and "A Lamentable Tragedy" of the 1560s is "mixed full of pleasant mirth." But where his predecessors stuff their Christmas stockings with something for everyone, his mix of jest and earnest honors truth to nature. He thought that order, not a cordon sanitaire but a living integument, needed its opposite. Like a wen on beauty's cheek, this saving imperfection completed what it marred. *Cos amoris,* they called it, "whetstone of love."

Disorder is the cohesive element for his comprehensive structure that fetters chaos and includes it. Harmony means contention, stasis is when things fall apart. Falstaff, a great disorder, dominates two plays, dying offstage in a third. Worcester the bad counselor and infatuated Hotspur are among his alter egos, and sometimes King Henry sounds like him. Mocking the time, the anti-hero has a context, low taverns and "leaping houses" or brothels. Against this disreputable but glamorous presence, the hero seems insipid and Shakespeare's morality verges on disaster. However, "two stars keep not their motion in one sphere." As *Henry IV,* Part Two concludes, Shakespeare's rising and falling curves intersect and "crescive" Hal meets Falstaff, bating and dwindling. At this nodal point, the reprobate is put away and the hero comes into his own. In the coda, they all sing "Te Deum."

This gives Shakespeare's scheme, masterly for architectonics. He doesn't undercut his scheme (modern writers, specializing in ironies, might do this), but he bends or refracts it as light is refracted when it enters the water. In his happy ending, much is gained but something is lost. Politics presenting its bill, family ties bow to reasons of state and "nice" or scrupulous customs curtsy to kings. York repudiates his son Aumerle and Henry V his second parent. This parent's role is Falstaff's too.

Also Shakespeare's ending blurs the moral paradigm, his formal commitment. Though the blood of King Richard cries for requital, the cycle that began with the murder at Pomfret doesn't end with requital but triumph. Partly the triumph is artistic, Shakespeare's Henriad making a coherence. Down the road, however, coherence breaks and the work is all to do again. That isn't because crime needs its punishment, rather because life is like that.

Happiness for the kingdom argued a sufficient ruler. But art has its own reasons and Shakespeare's Richard II, drastically incompetent, engages us more than the competent man who succeeds him. Falling like Phaeton he gets just deserts, but as he falls he glistens. This increment, modifying Shakespeare's given, makes a difference.

> I live with bread like you, feel want,
> Taste grief, need friends.

Made less than his name, Shakespeare's hero becomes his grief, a version of Everyman but idiosyncratic, so turning moral pronouncements aside.

"Oh, for breath to utter what is like thee!" Falstaff's baffled cry gives Shakespeare's intention, not polemical, artistic. Specificity, unexampled in the theater before or since, is his means to the end. It seemed to him important that holland (fine linen) brought eight shillings an ell. The word becoming incarnate, the parts that compose his plays are more than the whole and more than his ground plan requires. Generosity glamorizes his villains-by-convention, Hotspur, for instance, a portent of mischief to the well-ordered state. This rebel, though harebrained, jealous of honor, a woman in his shifting moods, is also the play's best poet. Estimating the stain, Shakespeare doesn't scant the beauty, and the blinkered man who leads his powers to death is at the same time the light by whom the chivalry see their way to brave deeds.

Sanctified by tradition, Henry V descended to Shakespeare as the mirror of Christian kings. His ceremonies apart, though, he appears "but a man" and tastes the same fears and desires as we do. Heard of first, he is getting a "favor" or token from a whore in the stews. Perhaps he never wins us more than in this parody of chivalrous behavior. Assuming the crown, he says how his father has gone "wild" into the grave, taking his son's wildness with him. That isn't all to the good and Shakespeare's hero wanes as he waxes. The public man, turning into his accouterments, is less substantial than the man who remembers small beer.

Tradition allowed his sowing of wild oats, a young man's partly amiable failing. But on Shakespeare's reading his younger time is only "plodding," no fun. Passion, soiling the rakehell, might acquit him.

What he does isn't passionate but cold-blooded, however, this rakehell "being in his right wits and his good judgments." Subjects who like a tidy commonwealth approve his change-for-the-better but see it as progressing "under the veil of wildness." Imitating the sun, he resembles the equivocal friend of the sonnets, and his "Euphuistic" discourse, "by how much / By so much," speaks of the stylist or calculating man. "Sunlike majesty" is most admired, politic King Henry tells him, "when it shines seldom in admiring eyes." But Hal knows all about this and Machiavelli has nothing to teach him. Though Shakespeare's story as he received it looks like a bildungsroman, it isn't his hero who learns things.

Falstaff is the hero's indispensable foil, by intention "sullen ground" to his brightness. As the story wears on, he runs to the bad, "a sow that hath overwhelmed all her litter but one." But the coarseness that declares him shows to advantage against others' squeamishness, e.g., the princely brothers Lancaster and Hal. One of Shakespeare's patented analogy-speeches puts the brothers before us. Likening the commonwealth to "this little kingdom, man," Falstaff looks forward to Canterbury on the honeybees. The comparative terms are similar, the end something else, though, praise for "good sherris sack." Falstaff thinks we get the point, not when we are sober but drunk. Jeopardizing the fable of the reformed prodigal, this makes brio the measure of value. The "grand jurors," fleeced in the robbery at Gadshill, play a part in this adjusting of value. Respectable men, "they hate us youth," so aren't felt as victimized but punished.

Part of tradition's legacy, Falstaff begins as the medieval Vice or the braggartly soldier, coming down from Roman plays. But Shakespeare's tun of vices lives on another plane, never visited yet by his antecedents. His lies, gross and palpable, are like the man who recites them. Scholars say they evoke the "Miles Gloriosus." "Gross" isn't vulgar but substantial, however, and these lies make a rival creation. The great scene in the Henry plays (1 *Henry IV*, 2.4), handed back and forth between the hero and anti-hero, tells of thieving, lying, cowardice, dereliction of duty. But Shakespeare's execution beggars report and under his hand this drossy matter turns golden.

Refining the method sketched in the Henry VI plays, he unfurls his plot in complementary scenes, associating things that don't look like each other or bidding us discriminate "true things" from their "mockeries," counterfeit copies. Disorder, challenging order, enters its fractious claim, and comedy, stalking history, makes rude gestures behind its back. But the gestures, rude or otherwise, are very compelling. Deferring to character, incident too, Shakespeare darkens his teaching play, not a mirror for magistrates but a "speculum mundi" (mirror of the world), reflecting life as it really consists.

History is when Hotspur, full of alacrity, will give battle "tonight." The winding up of a battle, better still a good feast, fits a dull fighter, though. This is comic Falstaff, quitting the stage as the King of Honor enters. Hotspur, ill-advised, pays the price for his alacrity and cowardly Falstaff survives. Inferring conclusions, Shakespeare's exegetes point out that discretion is the better part of valor. But apothegms, though always pleasing, make too tight a fit for truth, and Hotspur's rashness, like Shakespeare's poetry, doesn't count the cost.

Near the end of *Richard II,* two hotheads, wanting to kill each other, resume the fight in the tilting yard with which this play begins. The king, who seeks to compose a quarrel, fails where the usurper succeeds. Shakespeare's two scenes, like contrasting pictures, instruct us in the difference between man and man. Also they emphasize sameness. Never mind who sits the throne, his truculent heroes act like themselves and what's past is distressingly prologue. Movement there is but not onward and upward, rather from place to place. This is like a royal "progress," the only meaning of the word before that hopeful Bacon gave us our modern sense.

Tales of guilt and expiation, Shakespeare's histories are both moral and causal. To write the play of retributive justice needs assurance, however, that of the man who knows where truth is hid, "though it were hid indeed / Within the center." But perception in last things seemed to Shakespeare a casualty of "our dull workings"—hardly a play that doesn't catch us up with an observation like this one. He did his best for his cause-and-effect stories of crime and punishment and they made him famous. Under the surface, though, another pattern, deeply intelligent but owing nothing to intellectual or moral constructions, detects the unknowing man. Toward the end of his career this secondary pattern organized *Henry VIII.*

The graph of his tetralogy shows two lines, one volitional, meaning responsible, the other entropic, reflecting the normal tendency of things to fall apart. This two-in-one pattern makes the plays ambiguous, so more nearly true. In *Henry IV,* Part Two, the second line takes priority. Comedy gains on history or rather differences dissolve, and for the new amalgam the common term is decay. Immoral behavior participates in this and Shakespeare's Chief Justice thinks wasteful Falstaff ought to pull himself together.

As *Henry IV*, Part One begins, Bolingbroke presents the responsible man, culpable because free to choose. "So shaken as we are, so wan with care." He is saying that history is our lengthened shadow, step by step that there's no rest for the wicked. This is the perception by which posterity recognizes its Shakespeare. Univocal, it helps the playwright and his auditors see into the mysteries of things. Drama knows no more efficient an organizing principle and Shakespeare, harking back to churchly preachments and old homilists, made it the basis for his contentions between good and evil.

But unlike the historian on the lookout for God's providence, he sensed in history the working of flux. It had its sequences too, merely linear, though, like the turning of the wheel or the march of waves against the shore, and inevitably the end was dissolution. Sooner or later the great man falls but not because he transgresses. Composing his paean to Essex in *Henry V*, Shakespeare knew this.

In future time, his soldier-moralists tell each other, blood of English, rebels against King Richard, will "manure" the ground. That is certainly true and dependent on their wickedness. But this upshot depends on their mortality too, and is at the same time an earnest of new life to come. Shakespeare's didactic gardener, strong for cause and effect, relates the King's "fall of leaf" to his remissness. A bad husbandman, he didn't trim or dress the land. All those "dangling apricocks," etc. His successor, taking over the garden, "our commonwealth," finds other sprays (favored courtiers) growing inside the pale. Like violets, they please this successor, strewing the lap of his new-come spring, Shakespeare says. Both violets and courtiers are obligated to death, however, and good or bad husbandry won't change this.

Richard II's tragedy is often understood as a crime-and-punishment fable and has this side, strongly marked:

> Then all too late comes counsel to be heard
> Where will doth mutiny with wit's regard.

But the mutiny isn't much—platitudes mumbled by toothless gums announce it—and Time wastes the King in the nature of things. It could hardly repair him. Life's the fool of time, for good and bad alike, and having taken survey of all the world, must have a stop.

Some of Shakespeare's principals, like many of his readers, dispute the cyclic up-and-down, wanting to arrest it. One—it might be Essex—sees new life peering "through the hollow eyes of death." This emergent life is political, he thinks, personated by the usurper. But it isn't Bolingbroke's "new world" the play is pointing us toward, and the image of the skull suggests a different progress, from death to life and back again. As King Henry's life approaches its term, this image recurs, telling how his mind's labor has so thinned the wall around it that "life looks through and will break out." Within the skull of the king, the beggar too, death keeps his court, allowing a little scene. Then the word is "farewell" to either.

Bolingbroke, an apprentice or "journeyman to grief," is our principal surrogate in the Henry plays and his story makes a real Bildungsroman. Instruction ends when he walks the way of nature. Hopeful at first, he means to put a spoke in nature's wheel. "Awhile to work, and after holiday." But the corn is never threshed and the holiday they look to is only a respite. At the end of *Richard II,* Exton, banished by the King, goes into exile, like Mowbray as the play begins. This earlier exile travels to the Holy Land, the same voyage his adversary intends. So what has happened in that great gap of time between Acts I and V and what does Bolingbroke's victory add up to?

Subject to Time, the active-passive man is borne along the stream until it empties in the main of waters. His son's progress, superficially different, is like this. Describing it, he has in mind his reformation, an act of will.

> The tide of blood in me
> Hath proudly flowed in vanity till now.
> Now doth it turn and ebb back to the sea.

But whether vain or self-controlling, he can't order the ebb and flow.

Involuntariness, no good for theater, vitiates Shakespeare's Henry VI plays, and later he met his playwright's obligation to dream a form on the void. Paradoxically, though, the supervening of art carries with it a loss of conviction. *Richard III,* moralizing what happens, seems less credible than his first essays in history. In the greater plays that followed, Shakespeare, rectifying old-fashioned chronicles like the More Book and *Edward III,* includes their linear view in his story.

On this concessive view, death in the beginning draws the tap and lets it run. The pox pinches our youth, the gout galls our age, and though desire still plagues us it outlives performance. Like the King and the Pretender, both grown old, "the body of our kingdom" is lethargied too, foul and rank with disease. Shakespeare's imagery of mortal sickness surfaces first in *Richard II.* Sin, a pustulous boil, will break into corruption, deposed King Richard thinks. Merging moral law in nature's, this prophecy is verified in the next reign. King Henry, recollecting it, understands that his mistreadings are punished. A collateral truth says, however, that "we are all diseased," partly from surfeit, a moral failing, partly as we owe God a death.

Episodic, not inevitably cohering, *Henry IV,* Part Two looks to some like an afterthought exploiting Falstaff's success. But where Shakespeare's contemporaries, having no better idea, thread their multicolored beads on a string, he has a vision and his episodes succeed each other the way the sun climbs the sky, then sinks from its meridian. His structure that recalls the natural round is set to stunning music:

> I have known thee these twenty-nine years come peascod time.

> Thou art a summer bird
> Which ever in thc haunch of winter sings
> The lifting-up of day.

> We have heard the chimes at midnight.

Enigmatic Bolingbroke is privileged by this music. Old and soon to die, he meditates in his own voice on "the revolution of the times." Chicanery falls from him, royalty too, and this common man enters, Shakespeare's stage direction says, "in his nightgown." Is it guilt that afflicts him or a "whoreson tingling" in the blood? The question goes unanswered.

Revolution is revolving. Like Fortune's Wheel moving from apogee to perigee, it describes our up and down, saying how chances mock us and change, the only constant, fills "the cup of alteration." Not political or social and not much indebted to the war of wit and will, this is the revolution that beats in Shakespeare's mind. In any case, it was like that the day he wrote his speech for King Henry.

THOUGH THE HISTORY plays confirmed him as his time's greatest playwright, he needed a visible token. Having left Stratford in search of fame and fortune, he returned a dozen years later to buy the second-best house in town. This was New Place, built the century before by Hugh Clopton, Stratford's most distinguished son. Shakespeare's five-gabled house faced the Gild Chapel where priests in their orisons once remembered the soul of Sir Hugh. A mansion fit for a king, New Place was the Great House and later housed a king's consort, Henrietta Maria. In time of Civil War, this soldier queen held her court for three days in Shakespeare's house, the guest of his daughter Susanna.

Sir Hugh's descendants preferring Clopton Manor, two miles from Stratford, New Place went down hill, falling by King Edward's time "in great ruin and decay." Shakespeare built it up again, "modelled . . . to his own mind." Architecture rarely gets a hearing in his plays but this science engaged him in 1598, and *Henry IV,* Part Two has a prosy-earnest passage that airs his newfound interest:

> When we mean to build,
> We first survey the plot, then draw the model,
> And when we see the figure of the house,
> Then must we rate the cost of the erection,
> Which if we find outweighs ability,
> What do we then but draw anew the model
> In fewer offices.

"Offices" are rooms and Shakespeare wanted a lot of them. Soon after he moved in, Stratford's Corporation paid him for a load of stone left over from his remodeling. This went to repair Clopton Bridge, his starting-out point for the first journey to London.

In the seventeenth century when Shakespeare's line became extinct, another Clopton got the house back. Rebuilt sometime before 1702, it passed to the Rev. Francis Gastrell. This unsentimental clergyman, disliking the tourists who knocked on his door, also nourished a grievance against Stratford's Corporation. Spiting them all, he demolished New Place for good.

Shakespeare's house is gone, but two sketches exist, suggesting what it looked like. Rising three stories to a height of twenty-eight feet, it had a frontage on Chapel Street of more than sixty feet, ten feet longer on Chapel Lane. Neighbors in Stratford deferred to the landlord, wondering in their letters what he would do with his money. Partly he spent it fending off the English winter. Ten fireplaces warmed his house, each subject to a hearth tax. Evidently Shakespeare could afford it. The first brick house in Stratford, his was faced with ornamental timbers, brickwork filling the space between them. "Bricknogging," they called this, rare in a time when most reserved brick for chimneys. Plain glass windows, their panes set in lead, cut the facade, and a bay window on the eastern side looked over the garden, three-quarters of an acre checkered with trees and flowering plants. Shakespeare's vines were the glory of the garden, remembered for years by old Mrs. Temple who lived across the road where the Falcon Inn stands today.

Tradition pictures Shakespeare pruning his vines or meditating in the orchard, "circummured" with brick. In the years of his retirement he planted a mulberry tree in the garden, the first such in Stratford, but the Rev. Gastrell cut it down. Acquired by an enterprising woodcarver of Stratford, "Shakespeare's mulberry," multiplying like the loaves and fishes, supplied the tourist trade with goblets, fancy boxes, and inkstands.

Set well back from the road, New Place had an entrance porch looking toward the Gild Chapel. Between house and chapel, a brook or "mere" flowed down to the Avon. Visitors in Shakespeare's time entered from Chapel Lane and an early biographer imagines two of them, Ben Jonson and Michael Drayton, calling on their friend in his bucolic retreat. Passing through the gate house into a small green court, they have the house on their left hand, on their right a barn stocked with malt for brewing beer. All three, tradition says, liked their glass.

Storied in its own time, New Place had a sensational past. The year before Shakespeare's birth, the reigning Clopton, hard up for cash, sold the house to his agent William Bott. The craftiest merchant in the country, Bott was "void of all honesty and fidelity or fear of God." Once an alderman in Stratford, he suffered expulsion for defaming the council and yielded his place to Shakespeare's father. In 1563, having made a match between his daughter Isabella and a well-to-do but credulous landlord, John Harper, he arranged for Harper's lands to come to himself should Isabella die childless. Then he poisoned his daughter with ratsbane.

Had Bott got his deserts, said an unfriendly witness, he "had been hanged long ago." But the law, careless of distinctions, would have taken Clopton's and Harper's lands as well as his, and the murderer got off scot free. In 1567 he sold New Place to William Underhill, clerk of the Warwick assizes. Underhill the second inherited two years later. Shakespeare bought New Place from this William, May 4, 1597, paying £60 for the house with its two barns and two gardens. Though the deed records this figure, it was only nominal, a landlord's thoughtful expedient. Aware that the Crown was entitled to one-quarter of the property's yearly value, buyer and seller kept the purchase price to themselves.

Even for Shakespeare, connoisseur of violence, life in the country held surprises. Within two months, Underhill the second died of poisoning too, murdered by his older son Fulke. Brushing aside Shakespeare's deed of conveyance, the law took the forfeit of his estate, but a second son, Hercules, secured its regranting. Coming of age in 1602, he confirmed the sale of New Place, Shakespeare paying a small sum to clear the title.

For the rest of his life he commuted between city and country, bequeathing New Place in his will to Susanna and her husband. The Halls were still living there in 1631 when a local baronet sent for cuttings from Shakespeare's vines. Six years after this, Hall having died—in debt, a creditor protested—bailiffs entered Shakespeare's house. Ransacking the study, they seized "diverse books, boxes," etc. Posterity would like to know what was in those books and boxes, and publishing scoundrels have been on their track ever since.

In 1670 the Halls' only child Elizabeth, Shakespeare's granddaughter, died, leaving New Place to her husband. On his death four years later, the study, once Shakespeare's, still housed books and papers. Carted off to Clopton Manor when New Place was demolished in 1759, they came to the notice of William Henry Ireland. But this forger of Shakespeare manuscripts got there too late. Quizzing the gentleman-farmer who occupied the manor, he was appalled to hear this Williams say: "By God, I wish you had arrived a little sooner! why, it isn't a fortnight since I destroyed several baskets-full of letters and papers, in order to clear a small chamber for some young partridges which I wish to bring up alive: and as to Shakespeare, why there were many bundles with his name wrote upon them." Pitched on the hearth—this very one, the partridge-keeper said—Shakespeare's bundles made a roaring bonfire.

DEFENDING HIS HOLDINGS, Shakespeare litigated like his father before him. In the fall of 1597, he sued to recover Mary Arden's lost Wilmcote estate. Years before, improvident John Shakespeare had mortgaged this property to Mary's brother-in-law, Edmund Lambert. Still in possession when he died, Shakespeare's rich uncle left the estate to his son and heir, John. Shakespeare tried to get it back but failed, and his suit in Chancery, dragging on for years, prompted bitter reflections on the law's delay.

Different from Hamlet, he wanted more of the same. Early in the new century, he sued John Clayton to recover £7, then, back in Stratford, filed against Philip Rogers. This local apothecary, in his debt for some bushels of malt, owed him besides for a loan of two shillings.

Four years later, Shakespeare brought John Addenbrooke and his surety Thomas Horneby before the Court of Record, seeking £6 and the costs of recovery. When Addenbrooke decamped, Horneby had to pay. A master blacksmith, he ran the family forge near the Birthplace on Henley Street. Some think he and Shakespeare played together as boys.

Once at least the tables were turned on the litigating man. In November 1596, charged with breach of the peace, he was summoned with three others to appear in Westminster Hall. Two of his codefendants, Anne Lee and Dorothy Soer, are only names on the record, teasing posterity's interest. The third was Francis Langley, usurer, extortioner, and owner of the Swan. The whirligig of time turns up odd conjunctions in Shakespeare's biography and often his life seems to imitate the plays, a cruder version having no point but itself. Some of Shakespeare's scholars, wanting the life to look like the plays, construct a scenario around his day in court.

Allegations of fraud or violence came before the Queen's Bench, convening in the great hall where Shakespeare's Richard II gave up the crown. Elizabethans, "swearing the peace," told the court they were threatened with bodily harm. The peace-breaker who threatened them had to produce "surety" against an act of violence. In 1580 the Queen's Bench summoned John Shakespeare, moneylender of Stratford, and in 1596 his son William. Craving surety of the peace, William Wayte, the petitioner, said he feared death at Shakespeare's hands. Mindful of the epithets "gentle" and "sweet," many deprecate the suggestion; others imagine Shakespeare, newly created gentleman, wearing a sword at his side. Not splenitive or rash, this inoffensive playwright had in him something dangerous.

Wayte the plaintiff, a "loose person of no reckoning or value," survived Shakespeare's menaces and lived to die in the plague of 1603. He looks like a catspaw, the creature of his stepfather, that same William Gardiner who for three years had been trading insults with Langley. Moneylender, cheat, and sorcerer (a son-in-law said), Gardiner died in 1597. The same year, imaginative readers think, Shakespeare potted this bad man in *The Merry Wives of Windsor.*

His single through-and-through farce, the *Merry Wives* recycles characters from the history plays, notably Falstaff and his hangers-on. One is Justice Shallow, foolishly proud of the heraldic luces (fresh water fish) he wears on his coat. Like Sir Thomas Lucy, Shakespeare's supposed antagonist in his deer-poaching days, Gardiner wore luces, suggesting the man beneath Shallow's coat armor. Unlike Sir

Thomas, he really did have his deer park, substantially there for Falstaff to plunder. Wayte, his no-account stepson, pairs nicely with Slender, Shallow's simpleminded cousin, and Parson Evans, Welshman and pedant, with Shakespeare's old grammar school master, Thomas Jenkins. Though of London, not Wales, he had a Welsh surname.

The more exact the correspondence, the less Shakespearean, however. Tugging life into shape, he was crafty about this and his sorrows and vexations take a back seat to art. He left the satirical mode to Ben Jonson and didn't air his grievances, except in the law courts. Also he was prudent, a devout witness to the time's revolution. Chastened by the misadventures of Oldcastle-Falstaff, the last thing he needed was another roman à clef.

His *Merry Wives of Windsor,* an occasional play but hitching on easily to different times and places, defines without transcending its kind. Toward the end it pays attention to the Knights of the Garter. This Order of St. George, named for England's patron saint, helped the parvenu Tudors dress up their claim to the throne. Once every year on the eve of the saint's day, newly installed members sat down to a solemn feast in the royal palace at Windsor. Saluting the occasion, Shakespeare sends a troupe of fairies to scour the stalls and knightly crests in the chapel there, and a Garter Feast at Windsor looks like a good bet for the premiere of his play.

But other settings are plausible too. On April 23, 1597, Whitehall Palace housed the Garter Feast. George Carey, Lord Hunsdon, took his place among the new members, giving Shakespeare a chance to compliment his company's patron. Nobody doubts that compliments were called for, and the *Merry Wives* bears the stigma of a command performance. St. George's Day in 1597 saw Shakespeare turn thirty-three, but if this is when he wrote his play he wasn't pleasing himself on his birthday.

The *Merry Wives,* first published in 1602, looks backward, hinting at a Shakespeare with too much on his table. Perhaps, serving the time, not inviting the Muse, he cobbled up an earlier play. German visitors to England, noticed briefly in Act IV, were good for a laugh when they came on the scene in 1592, beside the point ten years later. Early days in Stratford live in Shakespeare's memory and his characters remember whipping the top, playing truant, or coursing the hare with greyhounds. At school a pedant to end them all lights a fire under young "William." This scene is harrowing and school is the best of his play.

Jokes on Shallow's function—he is keeper of the rolls in the county of Gloucester—evoke Shakespeare the tax evader, appearing on the Pipe Roll in 1596. This year, having won gentleman's status, he wrote himself "Armigero," bearer of arms. The resemblance to pompous Shallow didn't escape him and he didn't need Jonson to point it up for him.

But the *Merry Wives* has another face, turned to the future. Perhaps it tells of Shakespeare's attempt to cash in on the vogue of "humor" characters, stick figures. Jonson, putting his too-close-for-comfort *Isle of Dogs* behind him, began the vogue in a play of 1598. Corporal Nym, Falstaff's disaffected crony and a man of few words, seems to exploit it. Hanged for a cutpurse in *Henry V,* he returns from the dead, indulging his taciturn "humor." Shakespeare's Slender, a type of the foolish gentleman, is "humorous" too, like Hamlet's Osric, a chough or water fly, and Sir Andrew Aguecheek, at sea in Illyria. The run of type characters suggests an up-to-the-minute Shakespeare, checking to see what might please.

His watered-down version of Falstaff goes along with this. Having dismissed plump Jack to Abraham's bosom, Shakespeare brought him back again but tarnished and diminished, "the decay of lust and late-walking through the realm." This was unfeeling, conscienceless too, but his auditors, not cloyed with fat meat and missing the imposture, got as good as they deserved.

If an early tradition has the facts straight, Shakespeare's chief auditor was the Queen herself. Tickled with Falstaff in the two parts of *Henry IV,* she commanded her favorite playwright to bring him on "for one play more, and to show him in love." Likely, he did this in 1599–1600. Aggravating his trouble, the Queen instructed him to finish the job in fourteen days. A tall order, he thought, but he set to, and *The Merry Wives of Windsor* shows him on his merely professional side, competent, lively, and cold.

Mostly written in prose, it has some verse but no poetry, and some good comic scenes but they want decorum. Indifferent to plot and character, Shakespeare gets his laughs as he can. Graver business in his last act needing someone to take care of it, he foists this job on Mistress Quickly, not a grave bone in her body. Though his happy ending turns on disguise, the clothing is only clothing, no intimation here that "all hoods make not monks." Discharging his commission, Shakespeare doesn't exceed it. The reverberations that fill the silences in the greater comedies are missing in this one, and for once what goes on is all up front.

But *The Merry Wives of Windsor* ranks among Shakespeare's box-office successes. Being himself, he liked the plaudits. His play suggests that he felt the degradation, though, and his pseudo-Falstaff, reflecting it, says how "wit may be made a Jack-a-Lent when 'tis upon ill employment." In Lent, people who wanted to cheer themselves up threw stones at this easy target, entertainment for a dull season. Opportunist Shakespeare made it pass, however, and afterward, "as tradition tells us," the Queen announced herself pleased with the representation.

3

Sailing to Illyria

IN THE LAST YEARS of the old Queen's reign, Shakespeare's schoolfellow Richard Quiney made four visits to London. From his lodgings at the Bell Inn, still standing in Carter Lane near St. Paul's, he wrote Shakespeare a letter, the only one in existence. Bailiff Quiney had a mission, getting relief from the taxes and subsidies "wherewith our town is like to be charged." His Stratford neighbors and Shakespeare's, beset by runaway inflation, ruinous fires, and a long spell of wet weather, lived in "fear and doubt." Quiney's brother-in-law Abraham Sturley reports this, adding in a letter of 1598 that the town's great bell was broken, also the pavement of Clopton Bridge. William Wyatt was mending the pavement.

In London Quiney's suit went badly, crowded into the background by wars and alarms, and he complained in letters home of his "long travail" at Court. His correspondent, a former bailiff who knew about the law's delay, shouldn't be hopeful of things getting done. On October 25, 1598, he addressed his "loving good friend and countryman Mr. William Shakespeare." Quiney needed money, £30 to defray "all the debts I owe in London," and Shakespeare, supplying it, might friend him much. Offering security, he promised that "if we bargain further, you shall be the paymaster yourself." Shakespeare's willingness to help him went without saying, he told Sturley in a letter written the same day. But his brother-in-law, replying, ends with a dash of cold water. As to Shakespeare procuring them money, that, he said, "I will like of as I shall hear when, and where, and how."

Perhaps having second thoughts, Quiney never posted his letter to Shakespeare. When he went back to Stratford, he carried it with him, and it remains in the Corporation's archives. Explaining this, some imagine the two Stratford men meeting in London's streets. Shakespeare, they say, reacting with sympathy to his friend's tale of trouble, handed over the money or made arrangements to get it. This scenario, honoring Shakespeare's openhandedness, seems indebted less to life than the stage.

Money bought more in his day than ours, five to eight times more, said E. K. Chambers, the greatest modern Shakespearean. Chambers was far out when he wrote in 1923—even a decade earlier, another historian put the multiple at about double his figure. In the 1590s, when wages were set by statute, unskilled laborers earned from 5d to 6d a day, between £6 10s and £7 16s per year. This assumes constant employment, highly doubtful. James Burbage, a skilled joiner, lived on £15. One third of this, painfully little but enough to keep a man from starving, represented the bare minimum annual wage. Scrutinizing the figures, economic historians in our time reckon the proper multiple not at five to eight but more like five to eight hundred. Quiney wanted a lot of money, more than Shakespeare carried in his pocket. The creditor who was asked to furnish this sum looks like a man of means, with connections so far unguessed at. Commanding money on such a scale, he wasn't likely to cast it on the waters. The more affluent, the less openhanded, an unhappy fact of life often noticed in the plays. Sometimes you feel that Shakespeare, invoking an artist's privilege, sought to better everyday life in the plays, perhaps to make a better Shakespeare. If you needed money from his Merchant of Venice, all you had to do was ask. Bassanio does this, pleading "great debts" run up in the city. "My purse," Antonio tells him, lies "all unlocked to your occasions." The sea captain in *Twelfth Night,* another Antonio, is like that. Reserving nothing for himself, he gives what he has to his friend.

In *As You Like It,* a friend presses money on a friend-in-need, and tradition says that Shakespeare played the part of the generous man. This seems plausible. Dejected by the prudential virtues—nothing worse, he said in sonnets, than husbanding "nature's riches"—Shakespeare kindles in imagination when his prodigals come before us. Life and art weren't always the same, though. At home in Stratford, reports were circulating that "our countryman, Mr. Shakespeare, is willing to disburse some money," but this was for the purchase of land.

AMONG THE LORDS who convened to hear Quiney's petition, the imposing one was Essex, England's Earl Marshall. An enthusiastic councilor, he stood for aggressive war with Spain. In Shakespeare's England, inhabited by only four million people, fewer than live in modern London alone, the long-drawn-out struggle touched them all. Across the Channel in 1596, a Spanish army besieged Calais, recently an English enclave. On April 14, the noise of the cannonading sounded all day in London. Poets and playwrights like Ralegh, Lodge, and Donne knew the war at first hand, and Jonson, true to form, killed his man in single combat between the armies. Shakespeare, less vivid than these others, gathered what he knew from report.

But the war engaged him on his personal side. When hotheaded Essex clamored to relieve Calais, his protégé Southampton, once Shakespeare's patron, swelled this impatient chorus. The Queen declining to support them, her unruly favorites advanced their pride "against that power that bred it." This observation of Shakespeare's, surprising in its theatrical context, suggests that he couldn't help raising his eyes. Many think he lived vicariously in Essex and Southampton, "wild as young bulls," his phrase for the chivalry in *Henry IV*, Part One. This idea has symmetry, their flash to his quiet. But his eye, unlike theirs, was never less than steady, and folly by whatever name looked like itself to him.

In June the two earls took the fight to Spain. "Entramos!" cried Essex, flinging his hat to the waters as the expeditionary force sailed into the harbor of Cadiz. Next year, dreaming of the Spanish treasure fleet, he embarked for the Azores. Southampton went with him. But these gallants made a mess of things, the Spanish ships evaded pursuit, and the Islands Voyage ended in disaster. Donne, recalling it, wrote how "all our beauty and our trim decays, / Like courts removing, or like ended plays." In the wake of the fighting, London swarmed with returning veterans. A pair of them, reminiscent of Essex and Southampton, play an unheroic part in Shakespeare's comedy of 1598, *Much Ado About Nothing*.

Don Pedro is the general—amusing, Shakespeare thought, to make him a Spanish grandee—seconded by handsome Claudio. This soldier is full of dash, thick-sighted and governed by spleen. "He hath borne himself beyond the promise of his age," report says of him, "doing in the figure of a lamb the feats of a lion." But Shakespeare's character Antonio, a name he used in three plays when he wanted to speak in his own voice, finds the heroes out—

> Scambling, outfacing, fashion-monging boys
> That lie, and cog, and flout, deprave and slander.

Like antics or buffoons, they speak big words "and this is all." Much of the poetry, equated for once with fustian, goes to them.

The public war offstage serving Shakespeare for a lead-in, he shifted quickly to private business, a "merry war" or sexual encounter between a shrewish heroine and unromantic hero. Real-life characters who laugh at each other and can laugh at themselves, his Beatrice and Benedick "never meet but there's a skirmish of wit between them." Their back-and-forth, in prose but not prosaic, fulfills the promise of *Love's Labor's Lost,* memorable for "russet yeas and honest kersey noes" in the superheated world of Navarre. Taking leave of the little man and woman on the wedding cake, Shakespeare's adult lovers send up romantic courtship, meanwhile redefining it. Anyway, they do this until their heretic's faith melts in "blood" or sexual passion.

Unlike the pink and white heroine of ladies' magazines, Beatrice has a sound mind in a good-looking body and "to be merry best becomes her." An obstinate heretic in despite of beauty, Benedick must be won before he capitulates. This makes the ultimate capitulating important. "A notable argument," amused Don Pedro calls it, not given to "noting" or discerning himself. Theatergoers in the 1590s had a surfeit of cant, and Beatrice and Benedick met the taste of the time. Only let their names appear in the playbill, said one spectator years later, and "cockpit, galleries, boxes, all are full."

But Shakespeare's realistic play doesn't hold the stage alone. Retrieved from an Italian novella, a two-penny romance pops and fizzes beside it. Complications begin when Claudio "notes" or eyes the little daughter of his host, Leonato. But this noting turns into stigmatizing, and having won the lady he spurns her at the altar. Shakespeare's yen for verbal latencies won't let him stop at that, and in the last resort, noting means setting to music. We have to blame the music, his surrogate thinks, if pretty Hero, the ingénue, isn't wooed.

Harmony reigns in Shakespeare's happy ending and his last word, a stage direction, is "dance." But the persons of the play, at odds with their disposer, do their best to thwart him. A moustache-twirling villain, "out of measure" sad or morose, is their means to this end. No Iago, he disdains to hide his cloven foot but the others aren't quick on the uptake. They have eyes in their head, no good for seeing, though, and all nod in unison when a "good sharp fellow" or "white-bearded fellow" brings them false tidings. Clothes don't make the man, one of them says. However, the plot controverts this and fashion, "a deformed thief," is decisive for judgment. Early in the action, a masked ball diverts the revelers, and another is getting started as the play winds down. These entertainments sow confusion, mined for laughs. But the masque, a good "correlative" for this comedy, isn't really decisive. Even the hero, keener than most, has to ask "which is Beatrice?" Myopic in the grain, Shakespeare's characters make their own mischief.

Like other comedies of his, *Much Ado* seems theatrical, less like life than slick-paper romance. Many take comic Shakespeare for a mountebank of genius, and it isn't hard to see why. A barefaced expositor is reading a letter when the curtain rises, and eavesdropping, the stuff of melodrama, moves the plot along. Maladroit-seeming business, it has its decorum, though, saying how people learn things. Bad luck for some, what they learn is mostly partial. Guiltless Hero, traduced, is "but the sign and semblance" of her virtue, accusers say. The Prince, who ought to know better, thinks her "charged with nothing / But what was true, and very full of proof." ("Proof" and sundry cognates come up often.) Leonato, learning the truth, wants to confront the villain, "that, when I note another man like him, / I may avoid him." But Shakespeare's audience understands that the same "misprision" (mistaking) will trip him up again. In *Much Ado*, understanding is reserved to the audience. Though "noting" and "nothing," pronounced alike, mean different things, Shakespeare's characters tend to confuse them.

His Messina, like Navarre or Athens in earlier plays, divides into classes, at the top the governor, prince of Aragon, etc., on the lower rungs Dogberry, a constable, and his fellows of the watch. But this state is topsy-turvy, like the Beatitudes where the last are first, and the last, not their betters, bring the truth to light. That isn't because they are paying attention. On the contrary, they take no "note" of things. Shakespeare's upper-class persons are very arch with these inferiors, figures of fun like the rude mechanicals or the bumbling

"Worthies" in *Love's Labor's Lost.* Surprisingly, however, the least deserving man is the one who reads and writes. Dogberry has a good similitude: "as tedious as a king." But if wisdom is discovered in the mouths of babes, that is only as Shakespeare puts it there, and for highborn and lowborn the common term is imposition. Mustering the cast, Shakespeare's foolish presenter calls them "our whole dissembly."

Most in Messina reduce to their "bent" or "humor." One of them is saturnine, being born under Saturn, another, "Borachio," likely drinks too much. Don John, Shakespeare's heavy, is what he is, a plain-dealing villain, and seeking to alter this won't change him. Like a tailor's dummy, these characters are stuffed, but Beatrice, who says so, adds that the stuffing is mortal. Character isn't fate in *Much Ado About Nothing,* or, amending this, you can say that character, being slight or "humorous," is fate.

Both Adam and Hercules have bit parts in the play. However, the famous strong man belies his reputation. Turning a spit in the kitchen, he does what a woman tells him. Adam does that too, and Shakespeare's little people share this want of autonomy. All are Adam's kindred, i.e., "wayward marl" or earth, obdurate but easily kneaded. Leaving us impaired or frail, our first parent "transgressed." Shakespeare's heroine remembers this archetypal fall, and his soldier-heroes, reenacting it, bring comedy close to tragedy. But though of Messina they have the luck of the Irish, and backed by a greater power, "suffer salvation." Luckily for Benedick, "God saw him when he was hid in the garden."

In *Much Ado,* the all-seeing eye is personated by Friar Francis, another recurrent type left over from merry England before the new learning came up. This old religious man makes the difference for our happiness. At the end of the play he retires from Messina to an anchorite's cell, but reemerges to save the day in *As You Like It.* Gifted evidently with charismatic power, Shakespeare's friar-plus-aruspex arrives at truth by "noting of the lady." (Others, when they try to copy him, do this to their cost.) He has a gnomic turn, saying, e.g., how "greater birth" connects to "travail." Hero is his debtor but must lose her life to find it. "Die to live," he tells her, and honoring this injunction she sets the others clear. In the last act, graves "utter" or yield their dead.

Desert plays no part in this. Claudio, who gets a second chance, is sure to fumble it unless they hold his feet to the fire. Undeceived at the end, he still worships images and sees his betrothed in the same "semblance" that took his eye in the beginning. Extenuating his folly, he lays it to "mistaking." A miserable plea, heard again in the tragedies, later still in the romances, it might excite disgust but inclines the playwright to pity. "What men daily do," his ingenuous hero says, "not knowing what they do!" Shakespeare, tolerant or skeptical, catches the echo, though: "Father, forgive them, for they know not what they do," and his romantic entertainment ends with the remission of sins.

The sham context of the romantic play demands that we salute the tough-minded couple who dispute it. But Shakespeare has a surprise in store, and a greater context, natural prompting, assures that necessity will make them both forsworn. Head and shoulders above the rest, in last things they resemble the base foil that sets them off. Insufficient Claudio doesn't surprise us, not promising more than he pays. But Shakespeare's witty heroine belongs in his company, the plot locating her there, and this is much harder to swallow. An "approved wanton," the myopic man calls his mistress. Like merging with unlike, Beatrice echoes this in the play's most powerful scene. Claudio, "approved" a villain, deserves to die, she thinks. Not collected enough for villainy, he impeaches her conclusion, and the echo, hanging in air, associates the heroine and the hero manqué.

Benedick, lapsed in love, is part of their fraternity. Taking "infection," he can't be faulted, and the greatest note of what ails him, his melancholy, settles on him like a cloud. Gulled by friends, he figures in a pantomime, ending, like Claudio's, when they hear the dinner bell. Distinction blurs between the pasteboard man and the man of proof. Neither is his own man when the blood is up, and the smallest twine suffices to lead them.

"I will be flesh and blood," says bemused Leonato, meaning determined or moved. Complementary scenes in the garden (Adam and Eve used to live there) underline this equation. Benedick enters first, dancing to a tune played by others who mean to "fit" or entrap him. A kid fox, the others call him, elsewhere the fowl they stalk or the fish for whom the hook has been baited. "This fish will bite." Next comes the lady's turn. "Limed" in the same arbor, she is the lapwing who runs on her own snaring, another fish eager for the treacherous bait, a haggard or wild hawk who has to be tamed. Defined by this bestiary, Beatrice and Benedick aren't what we took them for. But the lowering of their stature is felt as judicious, declaring their humanity too.

Though Adam for his sins was driven from the garden, his fall turned out for the best. *Much Ado* records the consequence of this fortunate fall. It says that blood will have the victory when blood and wisdom combat, a distressing conclusion that might beget tears. But Shakespeare's play rejoices in it, converting sounds of woe to gladness. In his Act II song, as often a thematic highpoint, the "crotchets" that enfeeble us, perverse or whimsical things, are also notes in a musical score. This harmonious music sounds when the hero is gulled or "converted." Balthasar, a hanger-on about Court, supplies the music. Shakespeare's lookalike, he doesn't care to be pretentious, and says there's not a note of his worth the noting.

Harmony is when our bad parts jostle with our good ones, making a politic state. Benedick being a man, we may guess what he is. "Put down" by this hero, Beatrice will prove the mother of fools. "Dotage" describes them, too bad if your bias is hopeful. However, "the world must be peopled."

A cynical-seeming denouement, more patented Shakespeare, sees to it that a living daughter replaces the dead one. Shakespeare's conclusion is more than cynical-concessive, though, and the happy ending turns partly on bending the knee. (Mostly in his comedy this humble posture is enforced.) In Claudio's case, that means taking a wife without seeing what she looks like. Having learned nothing, he jibs at this, but the others know his talent for getting things wrong. At their bidding, the lady comes before him masked, like Alcestis to her husband, another hero with clay feet, or Rebecca to Isaac in the Old Testament story. Across the spectrum of character in *Much Ado About Nothing,* "there's one meaning well suited," and that is how Benedick must take his wife too. These older storytellers, Shakespeare, Euripides, and the author of Genesis, aren't about to let us choose for ourselves.

Announcing the end, an equivocal aubade or dawn song tells how "the wolves have preyed." Morning, gaining on night, is dappled with gray, and some are about to get married. Darkening this festive scene comes news of the villain, under guard but he still has his teeth. Like black-suited Mercade, the messenger of death in *Love's Labor's Lost,* he qualifies the happy ending. But Shakespeare's characters, though aware of his presence, won't think of him until tomorrow.

CLOWNISH DOGBERRY, fitted out with bits and pieces of Shakespeare's personal life, first appears in the minutes of Stratford's Court Leet. John Shakespeare, constable in 1559, presents him. Affronted by the butcher Griffin's "opprobrious" words—"Away! You are an ass," this naughty varlet is saying—he wants them set down in the record. A good joke, reminiscent Shakespeare thought, but Will Kempe ran it into the ground. Kempe, the Chamberlain's comic, took Dogberry's part in early performances of *Much Ado About Nothing.* Bellowing his lines like the town crier, he gave Shakespeare fits. "I am somewhat hard of study," another playwright heard him say, "but if they will invent any extemporal merriment I'll put out the small smack of wit I ha' left." Meanwhile the play had to shift for itself.

Hamlet-Shakespeare, complaining about this, bids the players speak their lines, nothing extra. But Kempe, notorious for "gagging," made a dull pupil. Known for jigs and "scurvy" faces, he could lap up drink from the ground and lay his leg across his staff "a pissing while," like Launce's dog in *The Two Gentlemen of Verona.* Barren spectators loved this. Their lungs, Hamlet said, were "tickle o' the sere," ready to laugh at anything.

Understudy to the ghost of Dick Tarlton, Kempe succeeded this early comic in popular favor. Later Robert Armin, taking over the jester's role for the Chamberlain's Men, tutored the age in a different kind of comedy. He created Shakespeare's wise fools. These three men among them, their careers spanning roughly three decades, illuminate Shakespeare's, beginning in the 1580s with knockabout clowns and running through the tragic fool in *King Lear.* Kempe in the eighties, a servant to the Danish king, played the castle at Elsinore and had a tale to tell, worth hearing. He has no part in *Hamlet,* though, withershins to his old-fashioned art.

One of the original sharers in Shakespeare's company, the bit player wanted the stage to himself. Quitting the company in 1599, he danced the morris from London to Norwich, hanging his buskins or boots in the guild hall. Perhaps he regretted this nine days' wonder. "I have . . . danced myself out of the world," he said, i.e., the Globe. Four years later, an entry in the registers of St. Savior's church, Southwark, records the burial of "Kempe a man." Out of breath with dancing, he took his parting dance with Death.

Most of the twelve sharers who joined Shakespeare's company when Kempe did stayed with it throughout their careers. One, George Bryan, a survivor from the troupe that played in Denmark, left the stage about 1596, and later John Duke and Kit Beeston moved over to Worcester's Men. When death claimed others, additional places opened up, but the number of sharers remained fixed at twelve. Shakespeare's First Folio, 1623, lists the principal actors in his plays, twenty-six of them, scholarship adding a few more to the list. All are male, and not until the Restoration when Mrs. Hughes played Desdemona and Mrs. Rutter Emilia, did women appear on the public stage.

Holding stock in the company, Shakespeare's fellows were "patented members," after the royal patent that licensed their joint enterprise. Though a business enterprise, it rested on mutual trust and affection. Members christened their children after one another, and dying, remembered the rest in their wills, "loving and kind fellows." Augustine Phillips, one of the fellows, left Shakespeare a thirty shilling gold piece.

Most plays needed more than a dozen performers, and hired men met the need. They worked for a weekly wage, paid by the sharers. This second group included minor actors, also prompters, stage managers, wardrobe keepers, and musicians. Like the others, the musicians took a part when called on. Jack Wilson had a good voice and did the singer Balthasar in *Much Ado*. Phillips, skillful in music, pleased the crowd with his "gig of the slippers," a short song-and-dance piece following the play. He owned a bass viol, cittern, bandore (guitar), and lute, leaving these instruments to his apprentices.

For most in Shakespeare's theater, music, an "intermezzo," diverted the crowd, not pointing the moral. On this side too, he shows his difference. In *As You Like It* and *Twelfth Night* his songs are nodal points, controlling for form and intimating the content. "Blow, blow, thou winter wind," sings a courtier in *As You Like It*, shrewd music for comedy. Later other singers, responding, make an antiphon: "therefore take the present time." If you put these songs together, you have Shakespeare's play.

Singers were often boys, as many as six in this third group. Playing female parts before their voices cracked, some lodged with the married sharers. One apprentice, Nicholas Tooley, rising to sharer, wrote with affection of Mrs. Cuthbert Burbage and her "motherly care." The model apprentice married his master's daughter or widow, whichever became available first. John Heminges, "old stuttering Heminges" as they remembered him, perhaps got his start as apprentice to William Knell. This eminent performer, dead in 1587, left a widow, Rebecca, nine months later Heminges' wife. Marriage, sometimes romantic, was more often convenient, and women with a portion weren't left alone for long.

Apprentices, enrolled in a "mystery," learned the actor's trade from their seniors. Nathaniel Field, among the stars of Shakespeare's company, beginning his career as a boy at Blackfriars sat as "scholar" to Ben Jonson. "It was the happiness of the actors of those times," said a Restoration annalist, "to have such poets . . . to instruct them." Shakespeare, living alone and moving from place to place, entertained no apprentice and kept his trade secrets to himself.

Turning out plays for a repertory company, he had to give each of them something to do. Good and bad went with this. *Romeo and Juliet,* not lacking in bawdy humor, doesn't need a clown but Kempe needed employment. Shakespeare grudged the need and Peter, the comic servant, is an unleavened lump in the play. Composers of opera in the next age, facing a similar problem, suggest how professionals make a virtue of necessity. Mozart, having skimped on the tenor's part in *Don Giovanni,* heard about this from his irate Don Ottavio, a self-important tenor who wanted his share of the limelight. Going back to the drawing board, he wrote a new aria to satisfy the tenor. This was "Il mio tesoro." Shakespeare, like Mozart, worked out of a context, and obligation to the fellowship sometimes quickened his art. Armin's Touchstone does more than dance a jig or tell a bawdy tale. This comic, a whetstone of wit, is our teacher.

Shakespeare's readers will want to follow him as he moves from the stage to the study. Some of his best things depend on the demands of his theater, the happy effect telling of its cause. Nothing said that Sir Andrew Aguecheek in *Twelfth Night* had to be thin. John Sincler was thin, though, and Shakespeare turned this to account. Joining the company as a hired man and becoming a sharer, Sincler "looked like" Aguecheek, probably Slender too. A short boy and a tall boy being at Shakespeare's disposal, he made his ladies short and tall, pairing Hero and Beatrice, Celia and Rosalind, others. But this matter-of-fact, though consequential, doesn't explain the plays. Reflecting the stage, they begin in the study, and their ultimate cause, mysterious, lies in Shakespeare's will.

Some, turning the relation around, think that his colleagues developed a "line," specializing in stock roles like the pert soubrette or lady's maid, the old pantaloon, low or high comic, etc. But this misses the point of a repertory theater, and Shakespeare's fellows wore a hundred faces. (Kempe, not understanding that, was left to go his own way.) William Sly's portrait shows a fat face, little malignant eyes, a frozen sneer on his lips. But the makeup man didn't care what he looked like, and cast lists of the time assign comic parts to this early member of the Chamberlain's Men.

Even with the supers, the group Shakespeare worked with was

often smaller than the list of dramatis personae. On the average, only sixteen players took part in his plays, a problem and "doubling" addressed it. Sincler in one play assumed five different roles. If he had an affinity for dim-witted thin men, he kept it to himself. Opposites attracted in Shakespeare's theater, part of his legacy. A popular play from the earlier years of Elizabeth's reign has the whore, a comic figure, doubling as a youth who sees his father skinned alive. This argued versatility, and Shakespeare the playwright enjoined it. His "tragedy of the first emperor Julius," a traveler remembered, was "excellently performed by some fifteen persons," though there are forty speaking parts in the play. Partly a convenience, the doubling of opposites comments on the inclusiveness of Shakespeare's psychology, medieval in its feeling for the *discordia concors*. He thought the well-assorted pairing associated like and unlike. During his lifetime, however, neoclassical critics, paying allegiance to simpler notions of truth, impressed on playwrights a fatal feeling for the proprieties. Flute, the bellows-mender, is Shakespeare's version of these critics. "Let me not play a woman," says this single-minded man, "I have a beard coming."

Puritans liked to say that the theater bred loose morals, a canard with its scruple of truth. Sly, though unmarried, begot a baseborn son "on the body of Margaret Chambers," and Richard Burbage, Shakespeare too, were sometimes "overlusty at legs." A contemporary diarist, John Manningham, tells how Burbage's playing of Richard III melted the heart of a citizen's wife. "Grown so far in liking . . . she appointed him to come that night unto her," using King Richard's name as his passport. Shakespeare, listening in, got there first, however, and "was entertained and at his game ere Burbage came. Then message being brought that Richard the Third was at the door, Shakespeare caused return to be made that William the Conqueror was before Richard the Third."

Mostly, Shakespeare and fellows, middle-class and "upwardly mobile," kept the romantic part to the stage. Five of them, like Shakespeare, aspired successfully to a coat-of-arms. Many sired large families. Burbage, living all his life on Holywell Street in his father's parish, St. Leonard's, had seven children, Richard Cowley, his neighbor in Shoreditch, had four. Thomas Pope, another of the troupe that went to Denmark with Kempe, remained a bachelor but stood as foster parent to adopted children. Henry Condell and Elizabeth had nine of their own, John Heminges and Rebecca fourteen.

These two fellows, bracketed in life, lie together in death in the parish of St. Mary Aldermanbury. Peripatetic Shakespeare lived near them for a time, on Silver Street in the next parish. Fire destroyed the old church they served as wardens but on its former site, red with tulips in springtime, an unpretentious monument remembers the editors of Shakespeare's First Folio. "They alone collected his dramatic writings regardless of pecuniary loss and without the hope of any profit gave them to the world."

This inscription, though just, is a little beguiling. The men of Shakespeare's company, living in a world of make believe, had an instinct for the verities, money and land. Heminges, handling the company's financial affairs, ran a grocery business too, no life more quotidian. Augustine Phillips, living quietly in Southwark with his wife and five children, had a head for money, saving enough of it to buy a country house at Mortlake, upriver on the Thames. Cowley, who played the simple-minded Verges in *Much Ado About Nothing*, owned property in London and an estate in the Cotswolds. "Pope the Clown" acquired three houses in Southwark. Burbage, he of the raffish anecdote, spent most of his life providing a legacy for his wife and children. When he died at forty-six, three years after Shakespeare, he left them "better than £300 land."

His early death seemed calamitous, "a visible eclipse." One eulogist said that "young Hamlet, old Hieronimo, / Kind Lear, the grievèd Moor," once living in him, "have now forever died." The creator of these tragic heroes baffles expectation, though, and the portrait at Dulwich, dominated by the bushy eyebrows, phlegmatic eyes, and pointed beard, suggests a well-to-do tradesman. With this masterful man, our modern neurasthenic Hamlet has little in common. Burbage enters history as a lad of seventeen, defendant in a lawsuit. Protecting his father's property, the Theater, against would-be sharers who wanted part of the profits, he beat them off with a broomstick, meanwhile playing scornfully "with this deponent's nose."

His life in the theater, like Shakespeare's, tells more of sweat than glamor, always the press of business and never enough time to get through it. Plays, physically taxing, were played at breakneck speed, and John Barrymore, reciting his lines at a snail's pace, wasn't wanted. Three hours sufficed for a play 3,000 lines long. This is the length of *Romeo and Juliet. Hamlet,* Shakespeare's longest play and hardly ever played uncut, is less than 1,000 lines longer. They could do it if they wanted to. Rehearsals in the forenoon preceded the play. When the Court or a noble patron summoned the players, the afternoon's performance was followed by another at night. *Pericles,* played "after supper" at King James's Court, went on until two in the morning. Actors who slept in, so missed the morning's rehearsal, were fined.

The next day's play was apt to be a new one. One theater historian, highlighting two weeks in an ordinary season at the Rose on Bankside, counts eleven performances of ten different plays. Putting on these plays in rapid succession, the actors promoted them too. Pied pipers charged with getting out the crowd, they paraded the streets, a drum beating before them. Sober citizens said how "they shame not in time of divine service to come and dance about the church." Some actors winced at this, like Shakespeare in his sonnets. If they were extroverts, that was lucky.

Shakespeare the playwright worked for years as an actor, no stranger to dust and soil. Feeling the thrill of mastery, he warmed to the work and they had all they could do to drive him from the stage to the study. Sometimes, though, he suffered from dry mouth, a "dull" or "imperfect" actor, "put besides his part." In the "wings" his colleagues dressed him down for this, "even to a full disgrace." Speaking his lines in yesterday's play, he had to keep them separate from the different lines he spoke today and tomorrow. To help him, the bookkeeper prepared a "plot," summarizing the action and pairing the actors' names with the characters they played and the episodes they played in. Written in double columns on foolscap, it was mounted on a sheet of pasteboard, cut with a square hole to fit a peg on the wall. Actors in the tiring-house, shuttling from *Hieronimo* to Jonson's *Sejanus,* kept the plot in view. Like a religious calendar, it appointed their movable feasts.

The plot got the actor onstage at the right time, the "part" told him what to say when he got there. Chopped up from a scribal copy of the author's manuscript, then pasted together, it made a continuous strip. One of Alleyn's survives, the title part in Robert Greene's *Orlando Furioso* (1591). Unrolling this roll, 6 inches wide and 17 feet long, the actor studied his lines, committing them to memory. Over a three-year period in the nineties, a leading actor like Alleyn memorized more than seventy roles.

Someone had to marshal and integrate the onstage traffic, and this was the director's function. Likely Shakespeare the dramatist directed his plays. "Even the most eminent actors," said a German visitor to his London, "have to allow themselves to be taught their places by the dramatists." Some dramatist-directors, lords of their creation, stationed themselves in the tiring-house, making "vile and bad faces at every line." Jonson represents them prompting the actors in a loud voice, stamping at the bookholder, cursing the tire-man, and railing the music out of tune. Himself a director, he meant to suggest his difference from these imperious men.

But Jonson's portrait gives his own likeness. Wanting things shipshape down to the last detail, he anticipates the modern artist. Dekker brings him on stage as high-and-mighty Horace, frightening the players out of their parts. This regisseur isn't Shakespeare, and it seems doubtful that he made an efficient director. Tradition has him directing the actors in *Hamlet,* the play suggesting that they set his teeth on edge. But unlike his officious Bottom, he didn't legislate by fiat. "What you will," he told them, throwing up his hands.

Onstage and in his study he was like that, blowing hot until inspiration waned or energy failed him. Then he grew bored or restive. Jonson, who understood that he never revised, wished more than once that he might have. "He flowed with facility," words meant in reproach. "We have scarce received from him a blot in his papers," said Heminges and Condell, introducing the Folio. This is overstatement approving a friend, and if Hand D in *Sir Thomas More* is his, it suggests that once, anyway, he blotted a line. As a rule, however, first thoughts needed no second thoughts, and this craftsman-in-a-hurry left well enough alone.

Blurbs announcing his quartos, "newly corrected, augmented, and amended," seem to argue to the contrary. But this was the publisher, puffing his wares. Playgoers, easily sated, objected when the "umbrae" of old plays walked the stage, and hacks in Henslowe's stable were paid to refurbish them. Dekker was one, "a dresser of plays about the town here." Shakespeare, even he, was put to this tinkering, internal evidence suggesting it for twenty-five of his plays. By and large this means abridging, though, or sprucing up the play with spectacular business, like Hecate's in *Macbeth* or the apparition of Hymen, the marriage god, in *As You Like It.* That isn't what Jonson meant by striking a second heat on the Muses' anvil. The year Shakespeare died, Jonson made his bid for immortality, revising his collected "Works" for publication. Shakespeare, leaving publication to others, gave them no addenda to work with.

This description of him appeals to the plays, full of loose ends and unresolved decisions. In *Love's Labor's Lost,* the play's great speech exists in two versions, standing side by side. Shakespeare wasn't helpful when the bookkeeper asked him about this. "Ghosts" crowd his margins, characters we hear of who never speak a line. Innogen, wife to Leonato, comes on stage twice in *Much Ado About Nothing,* but though her daughter is slandered, dies, and is brought to life again, she has nothing to say. Shakespeare meant to break her silence but finishing the play, found that he hadn't, and lacked the will or interest to go over the ground again.

Older scholars, "disintegrating" his canon (i.e., distributing the plays among different hands), cast him as an old-clothes man. Revising or patching other men's plays, he left a trail of solecisms behind him. Some recent scholars, holding fast to the reviser, come at him from a different perspective. Disbelieving in that Shakespeare who never blotted a line, they suppose that he blotted a thousand. For their scrupulous playwright, the model text is *King Lear,* first appearing in a quarto of 1608, again in the Folio fifteen years later. This second time round, the play adds a few new passages but drops about 300 lines. Most editors, conflating Shakespeare's two texts, date his play in 1605–6. Modern dividers of the kingdom think he revised his first version in tranquillity, creating a second play in 1609–10. But he wasn't James or Yeats, who could never let it go, and Shakespeare the revisionist looks like an aberration. Having written, he twitched his mantle and moved on.

None of the imperfections turned up by modern readers show in performance, and that was enough to appease him. At a deeper level he remained unappeasable, committed to nuance, no one more fiercely, in the interest of his comprehensive truth. Forward-looking thinkers in his century, boiling down the truth, sought to come to the spirit or heart of the matter. Impatient of nuance, they spoke satirically of "the choiceness of the phrase and the round and clean composition of the sentence" (Bacon in *The Advancement of Learning*). When you hear them do this, you know that the drama's great days are near an end.

Words and how they reticulate were Shakespeare's special province, even his obsession, and sometimes, pursuing them, he is like a belated traveler who finds no end in wandering mazes lost. Dr. Johnson, seeing this side of him, deplored it. But his language, vexed or sibylline, is always "to the matter," and has the density and texture of the greatest non-dramatic poems. In the theater this is hardly supportable, and much of what he has to "tell" us goes unnoticed. Lamb, a favorite butt of modern critics, was right about him. To get his quiddity, you have to read him in your closet.

Contemporaries, if they knew this, never said so. They ranked Shakespeare higher than anyone else, but their adulating is partial and their Shakespeare the merest shadow of himself. For the first time in 1598, title pages of the plays begin to carry his name, an earnest of value, and a year later, in *The Passionate Pilgrim,* he gets credit for all the poems in this poetical miscellany, though only a quarter are his. But the title is a telltale, "passionate" being amorous, shading to puerile. This pilgrim, not canvassing truth, is only pursuing a lady.

Thinking about Shakespeare in 1599, a young writer of epigrams praises his characters for their "sugared tongues." He is "sweet Mr. Shakespeare," heard of often in a trio of "Parnassus" plays produced by Cambridge students in 1597–1601. Francis Meres, the Lincolnshire clergyman who liked going to plays, mentions Shakespeare nine times in his "comparative discourse" of English and other poets (1598). Comparing him to Sophocles and Seneca, he sees the resemblance also to Doctor Legge of Cambridge, Doctor Edes of Oxford, and Master Edward Ferres. Scholars, coughing in ink, point out that this Ferres was George.

Meres's Shakespeare is "honey-tongued" or "mellifluous," but though he enriched the language his labor was superficial. Like Sidney, who wanted poets to pot their medicine in a syrup of cherries, Shakespeare "invested" his with "rare ornaments and resplendent habiliments." Already in the last years of the sixteenth century, they were saying that language is the dress or "habiliments" of thought.

MERES, calling to witness twelve of Shakespeare's plays, hadn't yet seen *As You Like It.* This work of 1599 invites comparison with the source Shakespeare drew on, Lodge's *Rosalind* (1590). Escapist fiction, written en route to the Canary Islands "when every line was wet with surge," *Rosalind* found a large public. Before writing *As You Like It,* Shakespeare inspected a later edition, seeing how it might and might not serve his turn. Critics of his play, not so different from Meres, tend to read both play and novel as chips off the same block, however. "Lighthearted comedy," they call it, "appealing to readers at all stages and in all lighter moods."

Turning away from the workaday world, Shakespeare set his scene in the Forest of Arden, né Arcadia, the Golden World all of us yearn for. Invented by old Greek poets with an assist from Renaissance Italians, this pastoral place offers a refuge to people wearied of the human condition. Poems hang on trees, some of them palm trees, and the fairy-tale ruler resembles "the old Robin Hood of England." You don't need books in the forest and don't have to go to church, there being books in brooks, sermons in stones, "and good in everything." Back in society, men and women learn corruption. In the country, "exempt from public haunt," things go better. That is the Arcadian tradition and many take it for true.

How Shakespeare took it distinguishes his play. Though the Court, our first venue, is corrupt and then some, quitting it we go from "the smoke to the smother," no difference. Shakespeare's young ladies are innocent of this, going, they think, to liberty, not banishment. But a winter wind blows through Shakespeare's forest, the bitter sky freezes, and even in Arcadia Death has dominion. Time, ticking inexorably, is his accomplice. Travelers in this uncouth desert faint with hunger. No one goes to church there, not a good thing. Beneath the melancholy foliage, wild animals lurk, and it wouldn't be Paradise without the serpent. "When I was at home," says one of Shakespeare's emigrés, "I was in a better place."

Dealing in absolutes, the Arcadian tradition says that God made the country, man made the town, disgraced with his tyrannies. But the country knows oppression too, personated by an absentee landlord. (This closefisted man isn't heard from in *Rosalind.*) If the Golden Age is what you're looking for, Lodge's nice old shepherd tells them, choose the life of shepherds. But Shakespeare won't let us choose, and his town vs. country setoff is fleshed out "in respect of" particular things. The shepherd's life is solitary, meriting praise, also lonely, deserving censure. Life in the country pleases but grows tedious, not being in court. This life is frugal, so far so good, "but as there is no more plenty in it, it goes much against my stomach." These tests or "touchstones" Shakespeare's clown applies, canceling each other, discover that absolutes aren't for us.

As Shakespeare's pastoral ends, all except his two malcontents leave the enclosed garden and rejoin "the full stream of the world." Romantic storytellers prefer a different resolution, and having got the hero through our vale of tears, dismiss him to happiness in "a nook merely monastic." But Shakespeare's good duke observes that men are "compact of jars," that is, made up of discords. If they grow "musical," harmonious through-and-through, discord in the spheres is sure to follow. Jaques, a gloomy philosopher, is the man in question, but plot and old cosmologies suggest that this concord/discord equation isn't peculiar to him. On Shakespeare's old-fashioned view, the music of the spheres depends on their colliding. In Elysium, however, all things are at peace and this music, growing dissonant, grates on the ears.

The most romantic-seeming of Shakespeare's major comedies, *As You Like It* picks up where *Much Ado,* famous for down-to-earth lovers, leaves off. Malice you can't explain describes his villainous elder brother and his usurping duke. Like Don John the Bastard, each of them hates but doesn't know why. Jaques has his points in common with Shakespeare's churlish Bastard too, likening civility to the encounter of a pair of baboons. "Monsieur Melancholy," he cultivates "extremity" in his behavior. But that is true of Shakespeare's hero Orlando, "Signior Love." These men are "humorous."

Shakespeare's reading of character owes little to the vogue of humors, though, and lands us in an unknown country where the roots of behavior go down into darkness. His unnatural Oliver has a natural brother, never schooled but knowing things, also practiced in virtue. "Why are you virtuous?" they ask this learned bumpkin, getting no answer. Vicious Duke Frederick is the mirror-image of virtuous Duke Senior, and has a generous daughter who gives where he takes. However, this daughter Celia is as spastic as he is, and the loving that overcomes her is like the onset of his hating. "Treason is not inherited," Rosalind says, recalling the Jewish daughter in *The Merchant of Venice.* So where does it come from? Shakespeare, looking into character, finds that genetic explanations don't explain, and already he has seen through behavioral science. The world of *King Lear,* where "twain" (daughters or first parents) dower nature with a general curse and a third redeems her, isn't more mysterious.

Press the playwright for answers and he is willing to hazard that good wombs have borne bad sons. Or he refers you to "complexion," a portmanteau word, meaning not only skin color but nature. Like his "affection" or natural bent, this word begs the question. Shakespeare isn't satisfied, his characters aren't either, and often their rumination involves them in a "humorous sadness."

Befitting men and women who find life full of briers, sadness qualifies his play. Orlando's is announced in the opening lines, and Rosalind's (like Portia's, greeting Antonio's) resumes it as the next scene begins. At court or in the country, the world's a stage where each plays his part, by turns a sad one. Irrational conduct is the norm, astonishing. "Is't possible?" they ask each other. Freedom belies itself and physiology governs. Lovers love "at first sight," oppressed by their "fantasy," a power they can't control and don't understand. Some butt heads like rams in their rut, and an erudite pun resembles others to goats, running into strange "capers." Like snails, all bring their destiny with them, i.e., horns. The crest is ancient, however, and sensible men aren't ashamed to wear it. Rosalind the heroine, one of Shakespeare's best, doesn't differ from the others, "country copulatives." This exile from society finds new skies but the same heart.

Lamenting the "condition of their estate," fettered, whatever else, Shakespeare's characters contrast it with a "s'ei piace, ei lice" world. "If it pleases, it's lawful." This "prelapsarian" world lives on in folk tales and in legends of a medieval Land of Cockaigne ruled by Charles the Great, part hero, part bully. (Two of the emperor's paladins, Oliver and Orlando, come down to Shakespeare as fast friends, but in his play, a modern comedy, they measure swords until a new dispensation "atones" them.) Further back in time is the lost Saturnian Age, glamorized by wistful poets out of love with the status quo.

A bawdy joke in the first act evokes this pristine time. "Come," says Charles the wrestler, "where is this young gallant that is so desirous to lie with his mother earth?" In the Golden Age before the clock started running, Uranus acts out this desire, siring new offspring on the body of his mother. But Gaea the Earth Mother gives Time an iron sickle. With this he castrates his father, and history begins. Sadness comes in with it.

Just here, the curtain goes up on *As You Like It.* An expository scene, bald even for impatient Shakespeare, lets us know how things are with his hero. "As I remember it, Adam, it was upon this fashion bequeathed me by will but poor a thousand crowns." The legacy or testament conferred on this speaker isn't much and he has to search his memory for details. However, an injunction supports it, reported by an old man called Adam. At first we aren't aware who did the conferring or laid down the law. This talky talk has to do with some antecedent time, "the beginning that is dead and buried."

Orlando, coming on stage "in medias res," has two brothers who help define him, sons of Rowland de Bois, i.e., of boys, also the wood. This wood is Shakespeare's Arden but remembers Ardennes Forest, familiar from medieval romance. Behind these real-life places is Eden, a near-homonym putting it before us. "Breaking of ribs" occupies them in Shakespeare's Eden, calling to mind old creation stories. In his play, this violent business is "sport for ladies." Three unnamed brothers furnish the sport but each takes a mortal fall, his ribs broken. "Yonder they lie," a depressing tableau. Bad news for Charles the bully, Shakespeare's hero resolves to try a fall too. "My trial," he calls it. Tutored, not least by Shakespeare, in dramatic competitions between good and evil, we think we know what this means. But a different kind of testing, not moral or transitive, brings the play to its climax. Time is the justice who examines such offenders as we are. Wisdom suggests that we "let Time try."

From Lodge and other romancers Shakespeare gathered his story, only bare bones like the "plot" that hung on the tiring-house wall. The Bible, endlessly his primer, elucidates this plot, however, also giving him his point of departure. Trusting to his audience to know where he is coming from, he provides his own account of creation and what happened next. Unluckily for Shakespeare, his chief thesaurus of meanings is no longer everybody's possession.

Where the biblical story emphasizes culpability, he has to plead ignorance, so leaves all that alone. "Something" happens between the acting of a dreadful thing and our inclination to it. But not having answers precludes a rush to judgment, and Shakespeare's tolerance is partly a consequence of his unknowing. His Duke Senior, though banished like our first parent, isn't a traitor, not that Shakespeare knows, and falling, doesn't get just deserts. How should he stand "in such a poverty of grace"? Debilitating for all of them, this poverty needs a good uncle, "obscurèd in the circle of this forest," to repair it. Meanwhile, Shakespeare's characters do what they can.

Silvius, a rustic lover unlucky in his suit, illustrates. Lacking grace, he hangs fire, gleaning "the broken ears after the man / That the main harvest reaps." But Shakespeare wants us to catch the echo of the Book of Ruth, a sad tale with a happy ending. The heroine, gleaning the ears of corn after the man who owns it, hopes to find grace in his sight. Letting things happen, she lights on that part of the field belonging to Boaz. In his eyes Ruth finds grace, and Silvius gets more than he bids for.

The joker in the pack and a puzzle to modern readers, grace, an absolute despot, complicates the relation between cause and effect. Good "Pelagians" in Shakespeare's time, emancipated men and women, restrict the governance of things to Nature and Fortune. A neat division, still familiar in our time, spells out their territorial rights. Nature governs in last things, Fortune, a lesser deity, only in material chances. Shakespeare's Celia mixes up Nature's office and Fortune's, however. "When Nature hath made a fair creature, may she not by Fortune fall into the fire?" If we are unlucky, i.e., devoid of grace, this fire, more than physical, consumes us.

Shakespeare's skepticism, full-blown in *As You Like It,* is implicit, not forensic, though, and what he means to communicate isn't couched entirely in words. Partly, meaning depends on complementarities, a familiar strategy of his. Sir Rowland and his three boys, lucky in the event, pair off with the old man and his three sons, done in by Charles the wrestler. Adam and Orlando make another pairing, one old, the other young. Convention wants the difference to mean things, but these two are more like than unlike. Underscoring their fraternity, one hoists the other, a "venerable burden," on his back. Shakespeare's "old" and "new" dukes activate St. Paul's injunction to put off the old man, put on the new. The distinction between them doesn't prove out, however, and at the "new" court the only news is the old news. Perhaps this bears on our dichotomy of town and country, social and rustic, regenerate and unregenerate man.

Wicked Oliver is a dead ringer for unregenerate man, lost and asleep in Arden beneath some druidical oak. (This scene recalls Shakespeare's dream play and the lovers who sleep and are changed.) We get a good look at the Cain-like older brother who pursues his brother's life, a "wretched, ragged man, o'ergrown with hair." Apparently he presents our worser part, the old Adam, a great bugaboo to convention. When our thinking part takes over, we will want to whip him out. Anyway, that is what convention supposes. Or the hairy man remembers Esau, the elder son of Isaac but condemned to serve the younger. Selling his birthright for a mess of pottage, this ignoble savage gets what he deserves.

But Shakespeare, finding his paradigm in Scripture, looks at it quizzically and it changes under his hand. Old Testament ethics, tit for tat, won't do for him, and though Orlando in reason should stay on the sidelines, he intervenes when hungry predators menace the villain. (One is a gilded serpent.) Nature impels him, "stronger than his just occasion." This welling up of nature—it isn't confined to the hero—resolves the crisis in the Garden. Oliver, waking from "miserable slumber," estates his father's house on his younger brother. This is a new testament, revising the old, and the man who confers it is Shakespeare's version of the Prodigal Son.

In St. Luke's gospel the prodigal wastes his substance, in Shakespeare's he gives it away. Unlike simple Esau, he knows what he's doing. Orlando, giving his "poor allottery" to the waters, is this kind of prodigal, Adam too, the selfless steward who prunes a rotten tree. Celia called Aliena, alienating her right, is the prodigal daughter. Plot, as always, warrants conclusions, and this giving that doesn't consult our advantage seems a way to thrive. It has its occasion, "kindness," another of Shakespeare's portmanteau words, meaning compassion but humanbeingness too. Following its dictates, we come from darkness into light, and as this journey ends, sorrow and grief are "extermined." Militant St. Paul, who wants us to put on the whole armor of God, isn't much honored in Shakespeare's happy ending.

Toward the close of the play another flood, like Noah's, is approaching, and Jaques sees strange couples coming to the ark. "Beasts," he calls them, true to his misanthropy, but they save the world when all is lost. That isn't as they triumph over their nature. In this community of unregenerate men and women, giddiness, being common, washes offenses clean. Shakespeare, up to his old tricks, takes this one step further, and in *As You Like It* our gyves or fetters convert to graces. The happy ending, affirming this, echoes *Much Ado About Nothing*. "Man is a giddy thing." But that is all to the good and we aren't to call the giddiness in question.

The juxtaposing of old and new—testament, law, or dispensation—is much to the front in Shakespeare's ending. "New" Duke Frederick, turned from what he was by "an old religious man," bequeaths his crown to Duke Senior. Also this good duke's cohorts, fellow travelers in the wilderness, get back their forfeited lands. Their reward is proportioned to their "measure" or rank, and partly they deserve it, a quid pro quo for virtue, patience, and endurance. Partly, however, happiness falls on them, like an acorn dropped from Jove's oak. Recalling the fateful tree in the Garden, this tree bears also, but the fruit that hangs on its boughs falls unbidden.

The end of *As You Like It,* making losses good, resumes and redresses the niggardly bequest we hear about in the beginning. Music salutes this change for the better, and Shakespeare's presenter bids the brides and bridegrooms fall to their measures (dancing) "with measure heaped in joy." This ample measure is their portion but means temperance too, and as they fall into their revelry, they rise.

The fortunate fall is contingent but not on girding up their loins. Leaving this to the villains, intentional men, Shakespeare's characters go in for concessiveness. Backing off, they think, is how you "take up" or settle a quarrel. "Much virtue in If." This doesn't dishonor them and they can't relinquish what they don't pretend to have.

These vagabonds in the forest challenge the rest of us, who mean to pull ourselves up by our bootstraps. Bernard Shaw, eyeing Shakespeare's play distastefully, has them conniving at falsehood, "pleasant and cheap." A woman's text ratifies their wanderings, though: "the wiser, the waywarder." Shakespeare's women are like that, deferring to Fortune, "the bountiful blind woman." Maybe these modifying words make a pair, defining each other. But we aren't to know how cause relates to effect, too thorny a problem for our natural wits.

JAQUES, reciting his Seven Ages of Man speech, is embroidering a line from one of Shakespeare's schoolbooks, "all the world's a stage." Another version of this commonplace says that the whole world acts history. *Totus mundus agit histrionem,* this was the motto that hung before the Globe, Shakespeare's theater on Bankside. Above the Latin tag on the signboard, Hercules the strong man bore the greater globe on his shoulders. In *Hamlet,* they speak of this.

Already "in the occupation of William Shakespeare and others" by spring, 1599, the Globe opened its doors that summer, at latest in the fall. In September a Swiss traveler saw *Julius Caesar* there, "very pleasantly performed." Old maps, the Delaram view and Wenceslaus Hollar's, show the Globe as a polygon, and excavations in our time confirm what it looked like. A contract for Henslowe's Fortune theater, built a year later, spells out the details. This playhouse was square, 80 feet by 80, otherwise a replica of Shakespeare's. Staircases, some on the outside for gallery patrons, also the great stage and all other "conveyances," were modeled on "the said house called the Globe." Henslowe grudged its glamor but knew a good thing when he saw it.

Rising in three tiers, the Globe surrounded the platform stage, thrusting forward to "the middle of the yard." Thatch crowned the galleries, plaster covered the facade, and the timber frame remembered the old Theater in Shoreditch. Building the Theater in 1576, James Burbage leased the ground it stood on. He owned the timber, benches, and equipment, however, and a clause in the contract allowed him to recover this. In April 1597, the ground lease ran out. Playing a cat-and-mouse game with Shakespeare's fellows, the landlord, Giles Allen, raised their rent and cut short their tenure. After five years, he proposed to evict them. While negotiations dragged on, a verbal agreement kept the lease in force. At any time, however, Allen could revoke it. The Chamberlain's Men lived from day to day, aware of this Damocles' sword.

Adding to Burbage's woes, the City Corporation was winning its campaign to banish players from the innyards. More than incidental, this threatened his company with the loss of the Cross Keys Inn where the Chamberlain's Men played in winter. Looking for an alternative, he found one in the ruined monastery, Blackfriars, above the Thames. At a cost of £600 he acquired and renovated the old frater or dining hall, turning this into a playhouse. But his upper-class neighbors blocked him from moving in, and early in 1597 he died. The Chamberlain's Men, quitting the Theater for the nearby Curtain, still hoped to come to terms with the landlord. When Allen upped his terms, they agreed morosely. This did no good, however, and he upped them again. In secret, he was planning to demolish the Theater and convert its wood and timber "to some better use."

But Burbage's sons Cuthbert and Richard, availing themselves of the old recovery clause, got there first. On the night of December 28, 1598, they led a party of twelve workmen to Shoreditch and destroyed what their father had made. Tough widow Burbage "did see the doing thereof and liked well of it." Away in the country for Christmas, Allen got the news and raged like a Herod of Jewry. In a lawsuit which came to nothing, he pictured his enemies "pulling, breaking, and throwing down the said Theater in very outrageous, violent, and riotous sort." This done, they ferried the dismantled timbers across the Thames, a herculean labor and perhaps it gave them their motto. Over in Southwark, Peter Street, the master carpenter, directed his work force, putting Humpty Dumpty together again. Thirty weeks later, the Chamberlain's Men had their new playhouse. Though the world had lain sick almost five thousand years, it was now wonderfully altered, wrote Thomas Dekker. What a workman was he "that could cast the *Globe* of it into a new mold."

Francis Langley, creating his own theater on Bankside four years earlier, built in Paris Garden close to the landing stairs but a long way from the bridge-foot. His patrons had to come by boat, a mistake Shakespeare's fellows didn't repeat. They located their playhouse close to London Bridge in the shadow of the old cathedral, St. Mary Overy (over the river), now St. Savior's. Patrons who took the water road landed nearby at Horseshoe Alley Stairs. Others, the most of them, crossed by the bridge. Passing the last gateway surmounted with its poles and heads, they proceeded a short distance along the High Street, then turned right through the alleyways south of the cathedral and the Bishop of Winchester's palace. Two hundred yards in from the river, they came to the Globe.

It stood on Maiden Lane, Park Street today, in Shakespeare's day "a long straggling place" paralleling the river with ditches or sewers on either side. Much of this area, sliced into garden plots, had only recently been drained and householders, like Venetians, entered their houses over little bridges. This was how Shakespeare's audience entered the Globe. Ben Jonson described it: "flanked with a ditch and forced out of a marsh." When fire leveled the Globe fourteen years later, a more sumptuous playhouse went up on the original foundation, piles driven deep into the swampy soil. This second Globe was torn down in 1644 and replaced by a sprawl of tenements. Later still, Barclay's brewery occupied the site. Henry Thrale, Dr. Johnson's friend, owned the brewery two hundred years ago.

From the turret atop the manor house of Paris Garden, a cicerone in Shakespeare's time looked down on three famous amphitheaters. Shakespeare's he called "the continent of the world." Half the year when the weather was good, "a world of beauties and of brave spirits" resorted there. Adjacent was "a building of excellent Hope"—after 1613 the name of the Bear Garden—"for players, wild beasts, and gladiators." Further west and just below Paris Garden Stairs, "a dying swan hangs her head and sings her own dirge." This was Langley's ill-starred theater, "now fallen to decay."

Beside the Hope stood Henslowe's Rose. He owned the bear pit too, a theater of cruelty. Shakespeare's contemporaries knew it as Paris Garden, the same name they used for the old manor lands on the west. Some bears, famous like professional athletes, had their familiar nicknames, Harry Hunks or George Stone. Mastiffs "of stupendous size" launched themselves at the bears, the Dutch traveler De Witt reported, "furnishing thereby a most delightful spectacle to men." Applause, often tumultuous, greeted the spectacle. Put out by the tumult in the yard of the King's palace, an angry porter in *Henry VIII* asks them if they took the court for Paris Garden.

Trouble with the law finished off Langley's Swan, competition with Shakespeare's fellows did the same for the Rose. Already twelve years old, this dowager looked faded compared to the Globe. Shunning the comparison, Henslowe and his son-in-law Alleyn sought a new location north of the Thames. Finsbury Liberty gave them their site, close to the open fields of St. Giles-without-Cripplegate. A half-mile east in James Burbage's old stamping grounds, the Curtain evoked earlier days. Peter Street, the Globe carpenter, supervised the construction of Henslowe's new theater. Opened in the fall of 1600, this successor to the Rose flew the flag of Dame Fortune. Imitating the Globe in its physical layout, it still honored Henslowe's old-fashioned priorities, i.e., he ruled the roost and his actors did as told.

At the Globe things were different. For the first time in the annals of the stage, actors, not businessmen—in the case of Shakespeare's fellows, actors who doubled as businessmen—owned the theater they played in. Seven of them participated in this new syndicate, Shakespeare, Kempe, Phillips, Heminges, Pope, and the sons of James Burbage. They were the "housekeepers," landlords to the Chamberlain's Men, and they split ten shares among them. A formal agreement, excluding outsiders, kept these shares in the syndicate's hands. Richard and Cuthbert Burbage, first among equals, each held two and a half shares, their five fellows holding one apiece. Half the income from the galleries belonged to the housekeepers, the company getting the other half, plus the takings at the doors. Shakespeare owned one-fifth of a "moiety," ten percent of the whole. When Kempe left the company, his share increased to one-eighth, dropping to one-twelfth when Sly and Condell bought in. Later he augmented this income. His company gaining the right to play at Blackfriars, he became a housekeeper in the private theater too.

On February 21, 1599, the members of the syndicate entered into their agreement, binding for thirty-one years. By then Shakespeare had moved to Southwark, of London's twenty-six wards the only one south of the Thames. Like a linchpin securing the arms of a cross, the bridge-foot gave the ward its center. Fanning out for half a mile east and west of the bridge, houses overlooked the river. A populated corridor extended south to Newington Butts, a mile away. Otherwise, woods, fields, and gardens covered this low and marshy terrain, crisscrossed by streamlets and bright with wild flowers. But life in idyllic Southwark had its price. Carried by underground streams, the leakage of cesspools and graveyards seeped into the wells, breeding fevers and agues.

Shakespeare lived in Clink Liberty, under the jurisdiction of the Bishop of Winchester. Privileged ground, it abutted Paris Garden, not the bear pit, the ancient liberty once belonging to the monks of Bermondsey. Together, these two enclaves constituted the Bankside. A long and narrow thoroughfare bordering the river between London Bridge and modern Blackfriars', the Bankside was for dubious fun. In 1601, Sir Walter Ralegh toured it with the French ambassador, after touring the monuments in Westminster Abbey. Bankside pleased more than the Abbey.

Clink Liberty, two hundred yards wide, ran half a mile from Clink Prison on the east to the liberty of Paris Garden. Behind the houses along the foreshore were the bear and bull arenas, west of them the Queen's pike-ponds. Malone puts Shakespeare in Southwark "near the Bear Garden" as early as 1596. Perhaps, evading the Subsidy Tax, he crossed the river this year, or having business on Bankside, he commuted. An easy walk from Bishopsgate led down Gracious Street across Eastcheap and over the Thames. What fire spared, German bombs flattened, and much of this district, old London, is gone. But St. Magnus the Martyr still stands at the bridge-head, "inexplicable splendor of Ionian white and gold." Miles Coverdale was rector there the year Shakespeare was born. He translated the Bible, wanting to afford the Word "not only to his own countrymen but to the nations that sit in darkness, and to every creature wheresoever the English language might be spoken." The Fire of London destroyed Coverdale's church but Wren, making art from chaos, rebuilt it.

Separated from London by water, Southwark for a long time kept itself separate in law. Criminals fleeing the city found refuge on the Surrey side. King Edward, in the generation before Shakespeare's, brought it under London's control, but it remained a byword for unruly living. Around Winchester House, the town residence of the bishops, whores plied their trade. Winking, the bishop took the rent of the brothels. In Shakespeare's first history play, he is the one who gives the whores indulgence to sin. Under Bloody Mary Tudor, this permissive churchman held his ecclesiastical court in Southwark, sifting dissent. Toward Reformers he was pitiless and many went to the stake.

Actors and playwrights found the Bankside, like old Shoreditch, congenial. Phillips, Pope, and Kempe were neighbors of Shakespeare's, also Henslowe and Alleyn and those famous bachelor-roommates, Beaumont and Fletcher, located by Aubrey in lodgings not far from the Globe. An aspiring actor, Shakespeare's younger brother Edmund lived in Southwark too, and is buried in its cathedral. Token-books of the cathedral (listing those who received communion) record the names of sixteen of the principal actors in Shakespeare's plays. Not less responsible than lawyers, bankers, and tradesmen, actors were different and lived outside the pale. On stage they summoned the glories of our blood and state, but behind the make-up was a lack of illusion.

Southwark's taverns were famous, among them the Anchor, the Falcon on the Stews, and the Cardinal's Cap. There, Taylor the Water Poet pleaded with the actors not to quit the Bankside when fire burned the Globe. (This poet and wherryman feared the loss of custom.) Tradition, as ever indulging its Shakespeare, says he liked the ale at the Anchor. At Southwark's largest inn, the White Hart, Jack Cade's ragged army left its hero in the lurch. In Shakespeare's play he calls the fickle multitude a feather "lightly blown to and fro."

Like Shakespeare, the law distrusted the multitude, and four prisons in Southwark dealt with its vagaries. Passing into the vernacular, one notorious prison, the Clink on Maiden Lane, became a common name for a lock-up. Proverbial lore said that "London juries hang half and save half." Those who were saved went to the King's Bench, the White Lion, and the Marshalsea, known to its victims as the Epitome of Hell. The Clink was for ruffians who "brabble, fray, or break the peace" on the bank or in the brothels, the White Lion for dissenters who put their conscience above the law. To the Marshalsea went men and women who offended too close to the Court. "I'll find / A Marshalsea," Shakespeare's chamberlain tells them, that "shall hold ye [in] play these two months."

Debtors' prisons, a clutch of them, little more than private houses, accommodated delinquents down on their luck. Called "counters" or compters, they stank to heaven. Falstaff walked uneasily by the gate of the Counter, as hateful to him "as the reek of a limekiln." Lean in purse but not otherwise, he presented quixotic Shakespeare, the fat man who wants to get out. Shakespeare, saluting him, kept him under lock and key. "Wouldn't be debauched," Aubrey noted. Thrifty and self-occupied, he had his careful man's precepts, letting others speak them. "Borrowing dulls the edge of husbandry," etc. This glorious poet talked like our grandmothers.

Acquiring interest in the Globe, he meant it to raise his fortunes. Obligations went with his prerogative. As a member of the syndicate, he laid out money for the ground lease and helped defray the cost of construction. Estimates, much lowered by the rescued building materials, range up to £600. Shakespeare's contribution came to one-eighth or £75 if, as seems likely, Kempe had already departed.

Connections, real or fortuitous, enliven his role in the building of the playhouse. His landlord, Nicholas Brend, had a brother-in-law, Sir John Stanhope, Queen Elizabeth's Treasurer of the Chamber. This officer of the royal household paid the players for performances at Court. Negotiating with Brend, Shakespeare and his fellows employed two trustees, both neighbors of Heminges in St. Mary Aldermanbury. One, the goldsmith Thomas Savage, arrived in London from the little town in Lancashire where "William Shakeshafte," player, once served Sir Thomas Hesketh. Some identify this Shakeshafte with Stratford's Shakespeare, thinly disguised and taking a roundabout path to fame and fortune. A speculator in the New World, William Leveson, merchant, was the second trustee. He played a part in the Virginia colony, of moment to Shakespeare's patron Southampton.

These peripheral characters might illuminate Shakespeare's story except that he soaks up the light. His story has its penumbra and sometimes, resembling the art, whets our curiosity but fails to appease it. In *Twelfth Night,* the disinterested sea captain who befriends the heroine is last heard of "in durance, at Malvolio's suit." This links the time-server and the man of fair behavior and suggests another play in the shadows "outside." But Shakespeare, intimating the connection doesn't elucidate, and his comedy ends with a hiatus.

THE GREAT SOUTHERN ROAD, beginning at London Bridge, ran to Dover and the sea. Travelers bound for the Continent took this road, and clumsy four-wheeled coaches, some gay with plumes and feathers, lumbered from the galleried inns on Bankside. Best known was the Tabard, immortalized by Chaucer's pilgrims on their way to Canterbury and "the holy blissful martyr." Shakespeare, though an "inland man" (one nurtured in cities), had his eye on far horizons, and the tang of salt water freshens his plays. When the Dutchman Willem Barents explored the Arctic ocean, he read up on this, and he followed the Shirley brothers on their travels to Persia. These adventures surface in his play of 1600, *Twelfth Night* or "What You Will." Hakluyt's "new map with the augmentation of the Indies" gave him an image for Malvolio, the wrinkles around his eyes radiating outward like rhumb-lines.

But Shakespeare's travelers, unlike Hakluyt's, have no definite end. "Go travel for a while," an attendant lord bids one of them, leaving the itinerary open. The offhanded titles Shakespeare chose for his middle comedies reflect this serendipitous progress. His young male lead in *Twelfth Night,* plucked from the sea but resolved to push on further, says his intended voyage is "mere extravagancy." An old-fashioned word, it doesn't mean costly but wandering without any purpose.

Putting his aimless to-and-fro on stage, comic Shakespeare verged on farce, real and pretended. (Jonson's strictures diverted him and he liked pretending that the plays were only fooling.) Witnessing a performance of *Twelfth Night* in February 1602, Manningham, the barrister who told a tale of Shakespeare, the man about town, remarked the kinship to Plautus, an Italian play called *Inganni,* and Shakespeare's *Comedy of Errors*. *Inganni* is tricks. Identical twins, not conspicuous in everyday life, appear in these plays, also in Shakespeare's immediate source. Adding to the unlikelihood, Shakespeare has a boy play a woman disguised as a man, codpiece, sword, and the rest of it. Cross-dressing revolted Church Fathers and Puritans, not him.

But Shakespeare's own twins rise before him in *Twelfth Night,* adding a new dimension to slapstick. "One face, one voice, one habit," twins aggravate the problem of identity. Shakespeare looked at this for the first time in *The Comedy of Errors,* strangely affecting.

> I to the world am like a drop of water
> That in the ocean seeks another drop,
> Who, falling there to find his fellow forth,
> Unseen, inquisitive, confounds himself.

The search for the fellow—other half of the apple "cleft in two," a mythy-minded character calls it—continued to occupy Shakespeare. In *Twelfth Night* he looked at it again. Seeking but not finding or not thanks to themselves, the persons of the play take hands only as nature draws "to her bias," sexual and involuntary. Plautus and the others, not looking this deep, are more cheerful.

Manningham liked *Twelfth Night* on its vaudeville side, but Dr. Johnson said the action "exhibits no just picture of life." The plot backs this up (one reason plot summaries won't do for Shakespeare). Dressed as the page Cesario, Viola falls in love with Illyria's duke, but sentimental Orsino pursues another woman, Olivia, in love with the page. Oddly, these women have names like anagrams, and the country they live in sounds like the world over yonder. "What should I do" in Illyria/Elysium? "I am not what I am," the heroine announces. But Olivia doesn't take the hint, and only the arrival of Viola's male twin saves her from a fate too gross for reporting. Thought to be drowned, this Sebastian escapes by miracle, like Arion on the dolphin's back. It runs in the family and his sister has that kind of luck too. Blighting Shakespeare's fairy tale, Malvolio, an ill-wisher, wants to put a damper on things in Illyria. (This dyspeptic steward doesn't like cakes and ale.) Two sots, Sir Toby and Sir Andrew, spoil his game, however, a dropped letter facilitating the business. Excepting Feste the Clown, all wear motley in their brain.

Farce depends for its modest charms partly on buffering but Shakespeare, averse by temperament to the proscenium, associates two fools or asses on stage with a third across the footlights. "The picture of 'we three,'" Feste calls this. Another image for *Twelfth Night* is the "natural perspective," first encountered in the history plays. This optical illusion, skewing reality, holds a concave mirror up to nature. Looked at with eye asquint, though, the thing "that is and is not" exhibits a just picture of life.

Some think Shakespeare wrote his play to entertain the Court on the twelfth night after Christmas, January 6. In 1601, revels on this occasion honored Virginio Orsino, Duke of Bracciano, a distinguished guest of the Queen. Perhaps this splendid youth gave Shakespeare's duke his name, and the occasion gave him his title. (Real-life Orsino, if he saw the play, wondered whether compliments were intended.) Pepys complained about the title, "not related at all." The feast of Twelfth Night celebrates an Epiphany, though, and this defines Shakespeare's comedy, meant to open our eyes.

Shakespeare's plays are all one play, variations on a theme, and *Much Ado* and *As You Like It* sketch the theme of *Twelfth Night.* But it isn't laid out in declarative statement, living rather in grace notes and asides. Antonio, they say, was captain of a "bawbling" (insignificant) vessel, "for shallow draught and bulk unprizeable." The big ships he grappled with found this hard to believe. That is better than a dissertation on Appearance and Reality, also truer, being provincial. But Shakespeare, though he recirculates old currencies, inspects them with a different eye from one play to another. In *Twelfth Night,* the considering eye is thoughtful.

Like the brothers Antipholus in *The Comedy of Errors,* Shakespeare's characters jerk to and fro, held by strings on the puppet master's fingers. In farce the playwright is the puppeteer, but in this play the manipulating power is nature's. Liver, brain, and heart are three sovereign thrones, one the seat of passion, another of judgment, the third controlling for the affections. Or the "houses" men are born in govern their behavior, e.g., Sir Toby, born under Taurus and predisposed to revels. This sign of the zodiac rules sides and heart, or was it legs and thighs. One way or another, fate and the stars above us dictate what we do. Olivia thinks this. Ending Act I she invokes their greater power, Sebastian doing the same as Act II begins. Malvolio, thanking his stars, chimes in later.

Fortune and "golden Time" making a coherence, *Twelfth Night* ends without the perdition of souls. But the end is a "happy wreck" and Shakespeare's principals come dripping to shore. Though they swear by reason and judgment, "grand-jurymen since before Noah was a sailor," ignorance confounds them, no darkness more puzzling. Around the corner the custard pie is being hefted, and an open manhole yawns at their feet.

A tale of vagrant lovers, *Twelfth Night* needs its still point, and perhaps the heroine supplies it. She bears a mind even envy calls fair. But the comeliness that sets her off is given, like the disordering that baffles the others. Not responsible enough to come before the bar of judgment, Shakespeare's characters in *Twelfth Night,* the fat one included, look thin. Unself-conscious Malvolio is likened to a trout, turkey cock, woodcock, etc., comic analogs for Shakespeare's gulls. But where Beatrice and Benedick, subdued to their nature, take vitality from it, Malvolio is only diminished. Atrophied in his senses, he is the victim all love to impose on, and sexual entendres go right by him. "These be her C's, her U's, and her T's." Witchcraft possesses Captain Antonio. Fleeing Belmont, he lands in Illyria but doesn't throw off his chains. He can't get rid of them, Sir Andrew can't either. Naturally fatuous, this lackwit isn't singular, having "no more wit than a Christian or an ordinary man." Thick-sighted Orsino thinks the cowl makes the monk. His exit line confirms this and Viola, he tells her, dressed "in other habits," will be his mistress and his fancy's queen. Shakespeare's comedies often end that way, to the accompaniment of the *Lohengrin* music. In *Twelfth Night,* though, the music is qualified, and Orsino, announcing the happy ending, makes us wince for what's to come.

Little things—interstitial, this being Shakespeare—put his characters before us. How does a brother know his sister? "My father," says Viola, "had a mole upon his brow." This looks back to Euripides, forward to Oscar Wilde, except that Shakespeare, unlike Oscar, isn't fooling. When Olivia seals her letters, she uses an "impressure," the image of chaste Lucrece. Stamped in wax, it gives her likeness. But the likeness has another side, telling of our native "frailty." Good-looking deceivers exploit it. They find it easy "in women's waxen hearts to set their forms!"

This sounds grave but gaiety goes with it, and *Twelfth Night* makes a composition, "truly blent." The play's great speech is Viola's, beginning: "Make me a willow cabin at your gate." Haunting in its melancholy but brimming with life, it raises this increment to the pitch of art, and the elegance, not denying the sadness, transforms it. Though the willow is the emblem of unrequited love, Shakespeare's delicate hyperbole won't let us pull a long face, and even before the mournful echoes have died comes the return to laughter.

Two songs hold the play, the famous one commending laughter. The other, stuffed with funerary trappings, summons us to death, and *Twelfth Night* turns away from this. Death isn't excluded from the comic round, however, and Shakespeare's songs need and complement each other. Olivia's beauty, all that red and white we dote on, is proper to her, she says archly, not like cosmetics. But it won't outlast wind and weather.

Viola, appearing for the first time in the play, thinks of her "estate" or condition, still unrealized. As the play concludes, the Clown, alone on a darkening stage, tells of this estate again. Shakespeare's words give the color of darkness, also closing the ellipsis with which his play begins. But the Clown's refrain mingles serious and whimsical, and singing, he hopes to please us.

Though resisting definition except in terms of itself, *Twelfth Night* has its burden, tricky to enunciate. Shakespeare isn't bidding us eat, drink, and be merry, and his drunkard, speaking for the epicures, is a drowned man. But Shakespeare pins his hope to what we do when most ourselves. Ambiguous counsels present this. Wheedling a second tip, the Clown wants the Duke to put his grace in his pocket. That is "bad counsel" but Orsino, letting flesh and blood obey it, takes out another coin. Only the niggardly man will call this generosity wicked.

Viola has a sister who never told her love, letting concealment feed on her damask cheek. Olivia's story as-it-might-be is a comic version of hers. Mourning a brother, this recluse, like a cloistered nun, renounces life and the light of heaven. But as she dies to life, life is dying all around her. Viola, bereaved also, is on the side of life, bestowing what isn't hers to reserve. In the end, Olivia is vindicated but not as she prevails, only as she succumbs, obedient to flesh and blood.

Showing us a crooked likeness of ourselves, *Twelfth Night* is a play without heroes. An analogy, one of Shakespeare's most telling, says we are like old clothes, mended by the "botcher" or tailor. "Anything that's mended is but patched: virtue that transgresses is but patched with sin, and sin that amends is but patched with virtue." This grants our proneness to error but disallows both total depravity and the chance for being reborn. Sebastian personates our middling condition, like standing water between good and bad. "A spirit I am," he tells them, but "grossly clad" in flesh and blood. This shape or dimension, imparted to him from the womb, is the index of our potential. Shakespeare in *Twelfth Night* doesn't give it high marks. Disguise is always his resort in comedy (more pulling their leg), and he gets a lot of mileage from it in this one. But he isn't harking back to his *Two Gentlemen,* and behind the mask a "pregnant enemy" connives at our disgrace. Invisible for once (no villains in the piece), the enemy lives within us, a "taint of vice" in the blood. Acquainted with its virulence, Shakespeare wonders how things will turn out.

It seems his denouement is up for grabs, or another five-act play is predicable of this one, the way *Figaro* follows from *The Barber of*

Seville, first the ardent suitor, then the faithless spouse. When wit and youth come to harvest in Cesario the page, his wife, Olivia thinks, "is like to reap a proper man." But Orsino opposes her hopeful construction, guessing what the youth will be when time has "sowed a grizzle" of gray hairs on his face. (Unexpectedly the philosopher, Orsino knows what he is talking about.) *Twelfth Night,* coming to terms with this rueful psychology, suggests a vade mecum for conduct. Suggesting is all it does, Shakespeare's "precepts" dropping casually from him.

Strong in the conviction that what we sow we reap, most read conduct in moral terms, but Shakespeare, eyeing our circumscribed estate, puts the accent on reaping and sowing. If we are lucky, occasion, growing "mellow," begets the wished-for thing. Better not summon it, though, "before 'tis ripe." There's a time for all things, and Shakespeare's heroine waits on its enlarging. In the end, process is verified and the "whirligig" of time brings in rewards and punishments. But this childish toy or top, drastically impersonal, is like the wheel of Fortune or the world on its axis, spinning between light and dark.

Setting out for Illyria's court, Viola knows already that her "intent" or purpose is subject to chance. Shakespeare, thinking about this, finds a plot for the matter of *Twelfth Night,* and the form of his intent is the voyage by sea. Inconstant men should put to sea, "that their business might be every thing and their intent every where." This abdicating of settled purpose "makes a good voyage of nothing."

A new nativity coinciding with the ending, Shakespeare's twins are "delivered to the world." But that is only "perchance." "Comfort you with chance," others tell the heroine, and she does this. *Twelfth Night* isn't a volte-face play (lost today, saved tomorrow) and the hero and heroine, emerging from their watery tomb, still look like themselves. The taint of vice that enfeebles them, unlike their beauty, is "in grain," and baptism or comic fiat won't ever wash them clean.

But against this endemic taint Shakespeare poses another, cited often. A whiff of mortality, it describes life and love when they molder. Shakespeare's protagonists do well to wear themselves, immersed in the blind waves and surges. Sometimes the tempest quickens and salt waves prove fresh in love. Morbid Olivia seasons or pickles a dead brother's love, hoping to keep it fresh. But her tears, devoted to the dead, are "eye-offending brine." "Present" love that won't endure is proper to the lady. She isn't going anywhere, and this is Elysium, the only one she will know.

Abiding the end, Shakespeare's characters hang on their driving boat, vexed or buoyed by accident and the flood of fortune. Looking for help, they don't find it. Reason is no lodestar but fetters itself, deferring to will. The riddle of things, too hard a knot for their wit to untie, eludes comprehension, and in the approved case they "wrangle" with their reason, going with the bias of nature. Darkened in reason, these characters attest the fall. It isn't wholly a fortunate fall, and this is the best they can do.

4

Fools of Nature

PIRATES ARE OUT THERE in *Twelfth Night* and the *Phoenix* is their spoil, en route to Illyria when Captain Antonio boards her. This salt-water thief, as they call him, is no ordinary pirate but gives where he takes. He takes the play's young hero from the breach of the sea, opposing to mortality his "sanctity of love." Later on the playwright hands back his prize, "tight and yare and bravely rigged," but that is matter for another play, *The Tempest.* Giving Orsino's vessel a name, the myth of the phoenix occupied Shakespeare as the new century succeeded the old. This fabulous bird, consumed on its funeral pyre but rising from the ashes, dies to live. Shakespeare expounded the mystery in gnomic verses of 1601, *The Phoenix and Turtle.*

His poem has a plot, farfetched even for him who cared little for realistic stories. Evidently an allegory, it remembers the death of a pair of constant lovers, the legendary phoenix and chaste turtle dove. Noisier than others, the phoenix takes center stage. Shakespeare says it has the "loudest lay." Being dead, it shouldn't sing but summons mourners to its funeral, oddly like a moot court or parliament of fowls. Participants include the kingly eagle, a kind of regisseur, and the swan that sings when dying, on their heels an upstart crow. Not everyone is welcome, and against some others, fiendish, feverish, and shrieking, the door is barred. "Treble-dated," the Shakespeare crow stands out from the rest. It lives a long time, one hundred years, some say four hundred. Not much to look at, crows are "carrion crows," feeding on dead things. Shakespeare's, though it triumphs over death, doesn't couple sexually but creates its "sable gender" through the mouth. "With the breath thou giv'st and tak'st" is how the poet puts it. Playing many parts in one person, Shakespeare merges with his presiding eagle and the priest that turns into a swan. He is the herald too, expert in valedictions. "O I could tell you," he is saying, "but let it be."

Flocking as to a theater, his auditors bear witness to a "tragic scene," rites of the Phoenix and Turtle, "stars of love." Up there on stage the lovers are distanced, and the audience, though engaged, is insulated too. Everybody dies, passing through nature to eternity, but this matter-of-fact, transformed to ritual, isn't the same as the shambles on the bestial floor. Confounding reason, Phoenix and Turtle obliterate number, their "simple" or separate elements being nicely mixed in them. In nature, you don't often see this, and most stories, rumorous with discord, peter out inconclusively, describing a broken arc.

Bringing up the rear, Reason takes the role of Chorus. Though a skeptical witness, it has to allow that Shakespeare's pair makes an integer, "two distincts, division none." (Division is dividing, as when you cut things in half, but means discord too.) In *Twelfth Night,* cast from the same matrix, this perfect integer is fractured. Incredulous like Reason, Captain Antonio asks how brother and sister have made division of themselves. "An apple, cleft in two, is not more twin." Legislating happiness, the comedies knit up this division. The sonnets go the other way and the Fair Youth, teaching his lover how "to make one twain," divides the concordant thing. But Shakespeare's line has its secondary sense. Look again and you find it saying that the Youth puts the pieces together, making a coherence from discord. If it didn't happen like that, it might have, and this is how art betters nature.

Departing from convention, Shakespeare ends his poem with a dying fall, no "flames in the forehead of the morning sky." A mesmeric rhythm, controlling for sense, removes the argument to another plane where discursive thought is helpless. Shakespeare's short lines and stanzas, plus the injunctive mode, add up to a pronouncement, not bullying, however, composed like an epitaph, one of Jonson's. In the last tercets, the rhymes, growing clamorous, mount to incantation.

Truth may seem, but cannot be;
Beauty brag, but 'tis not she:
Truth and Beauty buried be.

But Shakespeare's "defunctive music" isn't funereal. Sincerity and ingenuity go together and *The Phoenix and Turtle* accommodates wordplay. (One trouble with Laertes, grieving for Ophelia, is that his grief is artless.) Against the drag of the monosyllables that anchor the lines, words are insubordinate and forsake their customary order. Belying meaning, they assert it, or meaning is assimilated in magic. What can this poet mean, that "love hath reason, reason none"? Anyway, reason can't answer. Though sadness is the burden, Shakespeare's lament for the dead stretches the senses. Readers out to do him justice will want to read his poem aloud.

Every reader must feel that the poem is *con amore,* but Shakespeare wrote it to order, one item among several in a loosely unified collection, half festschrift, half vanity press. This was *Love's Martyr* (1601), meant to compliment Sir John Salisbury and Ursula his wife, a daughter of the fourth Earl of Derby. In 1587 these two had the chance to take the measure of young William "Shakeshafte," Sir Thomas Hesketh's player, when Hesketh's company stopped off at the Earl's country seat. Down in Lancashire that Christmas season, the Salisburys took part in the revels, perhaps seeing young Shakespeare plain. Many years later, Sir John's son wrote verses commending the First Folio. More "air" about the story, Richard Field, late of Stratford, printed *Love's Martyr,* the same Field who, years before, had printed Shakespeare's narrative poems.

One of Queen Elizabeth's Welsh cousins, Salisbury was a Cecil man, on the outs with Essex. At home in Lleweni, North Wales, he feuded with local partisans of the reigning favorite. Coming up to London to study the law, this sketch for Shakespeare's blustery Fluellen received his knighthood from the Queen in 1601. Maybe *Love's Martyr,* accreting over the years like stalactites, was published to salute the occasion. But Shakespeare's verses, though they honor an occasion, are less involved with life than death. Death environs his poem, that of Essex in February, later this year John Shakespeare's.

The emotion that suffuses *The Phoenix and Turtle,* flowing into these crevices, doesn't issue from them, though, and Shakespeare the elegist is evoking past things and heralding things to come. Fevered emotion from the same source produced his hothouse sonnets that tangle Poet and Fair Youth ("thou being mine, mine is thy good report"), also three plays that have betrayal for their theme, *Julius Caesar, Hamlet,* and *Troilus and Cressida.*

Robert Chester, Sir John's chaplain, leads off *Love's Martyr* with a long allegorical poem, "shadowing the truth of love in the constant fate of the phoenix and turtle." Chester has a subtitle, "Rosalin's Complaint," where Rosalin = Nature and "complaint," a catchall, intimates big questions like the decay of beauty. Having created the phoenix, a paragon of female beauty, Nature names and describes her parts. Some of the naming suggests a male presence—like Jove, like Apollo, etc.—and generally in Chester's verses sex differences blur. His "blazon" is standard for poetry of the time but convention doesn't save it. As a bonus, the poem describes England's chief cities, the nine female Worthies, the life of King Arthur, and includes rhymed catalogs of trees, precious stones, beasts and worms. Medieval encyclopedia-poetry, it seems remote from Shakespeare, not the encyclopedic bias, the naivete.

Dedicating the book to his patron, Chester eulogizes the Salisburys' wedding, ancient history in 1601. The donné is his, binding on his collaborators. Drastically absurd, it tells how the nuptial pair combusted to produce a new phoenix. Some cast the Salisburys' eldest child for the role, but this Jane was fourteen when *Love's Martyr* saw print. Though the pious chaplain intended to please, the wedding he wrote about looks like a martyrdom, Phoenix and Turtle brought to the stake. That is how Shakespeare took it.

Other poets, John Marston and George Chapman, contributed verses, and Jonson added an "Epode," worth the price of admission. (Scorning Chester's pyrotechnics, he says he brings his own true fire.) This muscular poem argues with a caddish observer just offstage. Never mind what the fellow thinks, Jonson's lovers don't restrain themselves because "lust's means are spent." Shakespeare goes on like this too. It wasn't "infirmity" that foiled his Phoenix and Turtle (a spent Squire of Lleweni?), "it was married chastity." Sir John and Lady Ursula produced a large brood between them, eleven children before they were done, but Shakespeare set the facts aside and accepting his commission gave more and less than was wanted.

Childless though not sterile, his Phoenix and Turtle are one of a kind and one and the same. This defies logic. "Either was the other's mine," and you need a keener eye than Reason's to tell them apart. Gender, like Property (meum vs. tuum), gets short shrift in the poem, and the turtle dove, sacred to Venus, ought to be female but isn't. Though these birds are dead, an insistent present (Shakespeare fudging his tenses) keeps them before us. Cleopatra, dreaming of Mark Antony, more vivid in death than life, is a comparable case. In the real world, devouring Time burns the phoenix in her blood, nothing left over, but in Shakespeare's poem, a "nest of spicery," death breeds, begetting images. Odd, that "what parts, can so remain."

Ovid (at second hand) gave Shakespeare the story of the Arabian bird. A small Latinist, he read in Golding's translation how it renews itself, defeating mortality. In this account of things dying and things newborn, Shakespeare found a clue to the labyrinth and didn't let it go. Golding's phoenix lives "by the juice of frankincense and gum of amomie," and Othello, about to die, recalls this. His tears drop as fast as the Arabian trees drop their medicinal gum. Antony, dying, is the Arabian bird, Timon and Imogen share the likeness, and Shakespeare's villains in *The Tempest* tell of the phoenix throne and the bird reigning there "at this hour."

But Shakespeare isn't converting sad to happy, and though his Ariadne's thread makes sense of the maze, not all come back alive. The salt flood claims Timon's bones (not his epitaph, however). Othello's death and Antony's are once and for all and Imogen's is only pretending. *The Tempest* ends in harmony, but prayers or banning charms are needed to sustain it, and failing them the ending is despair. As Shakespeare's poem concludes, his dove and phoenix reduce to clinker, leaving no posterity behind.

To the urn come all the others, not "concordant one" but fragments of a unity, broken for good. They don't come to renew themselves, piecing out their truth with beauty, still less to beg a pattern "from above." Shakespeare, unlike Donne in his "Canonization," doesn't appeal from our temporal place, and his last word, "sigh a prayer," is concessive. But *The Phoenix and Turtle* quickens with change, though not from death to life. Annexing experience, Shakespeare converts it to art, and where there was chaos the poem makes a figure. His rite of "transubstantiation," a secular model, invigorates the tragedies, beginning with *Julius Caesar,* and in this non-dramatic poem Shakespeare is working out his poetics. The tragedies are less pure than the poem, though. Clarifying experience, they acknowledge it too, so leave an overplus of value. Death is the common term but his heroes and heroines, evading a symbolic role, show the cinders of their spirit through the ashes of their chance.

THIS HAPPENS in *Julius Caesar,* an exemplary tale implying connections between crime and punishment. Things occurring "on account of" other things, Brutus takes his life or rather his evil deed turns his own sword against him. But an apparent gratuity comments on this, and Shakespeare's mouthpiece informs us that the hero-villain will be found "like himself." Mysterious information, it doesn't crown the whole but enlarges and perhaps oversets it. In the last scenes, a nimbus of affect surrounds Shakespeare's play, dark with excessive bright.

The play-in-outline hardly predicts this. Turning into Caesar, the hater of Caesarism becomes his new role, a fate worse than death. This miserable change holds for all the tragedies but another pattern, defying logic, cuts across the formulaic one, and the mortified man throws off his grave clothes. Though defeated, he has more glory than the victors, at least he says so. Bruised by "the dint of pity," Shakespeare's auditors take his part, and even the winners felicitate this loser. An unlikely comeback, begetting wonder and applause, it transforms the Q.E.D. ending.

Everything you know about Shakespeare says that he found the naked paradigm unlovely. He wasn't Jonson, an inspired cartoonist, or a maker of moralities like the author of *Everyman*. Paradigmatic-wise (a modern manner-of-speaking pioneered by him), he had two plays to choose from. One, a paean to freedom, casts Caesar in the heavy's role and Brutus and the other regicides as heroes. Coming down from the Middle Ages, a different reading puts Brutus in the lowest circle of Hell. (This type of Judas Iscariot kisses Caesar before he kills him.) So Shakespeare had his options, either adequate for tragedy, the "steely bones." True to his bias, he chose neither.

Readers and directors, choosing for him, often sponsor a patriotic play. But his republican heroes cut an unheroic figure. Mean envy gets them going and they want the uncommon man to "fly an ordinary pitch." Virtue can't escape the teeth of this envy. Dragging it down, they tell each other that ambition's debt is paid. Cassius, a type of political man, had rather not live than be "in awe of such a thing as I myself": a) another human being, b) common like this speaker. But the conspirators, "petty men," are also the "choice and master spirits" of the age.

One of convention's Nine Worthies, Caesar lives up to his billing, and sometimes when he speaks the stage is hushed.

> Of all the wonders that I yet have heard,
> It seems to me most strange that men should fear,
> Seeing that death, a necessary end,
> Will come when it will come.

Sometimes the oratory is only orotund, however. No Colossus but a sawdust Caesar, Shakespeare's strong man is a physical weakling, deaf in one ear and prone to the falling sickness. When the fever is on him he shakes like a girl, but has his don't-tread-on-me side and puts unfriendly critics to silence. Giving his name to *Julius Caesar,* the "eponymous" hero disappears halfway through it. But his spirit stalks the play, "mighty yet."

Jonson, scoring off Shakespeare, complained that he often "fell into those things which could not escape laughter, as when he said in the person of Caesar, one speaking to him: 'Caesar, thou dost me wrong.' He replied: 'Caesar never did wrong but with just cause.'" Ridiculous, Jonson called this, and a deferential Shakespeare ironed out the crooked logic. It gives Caesar to the life, though, sinister, unself-conscious, partly comic, and superb. Mixing negative and positive, standard practice with Shakespeare but aggravated in *Julius Caesar,* his "theory" of character leaves us at a stand. This confusion that looks like life reproves the conspirators. Appealing from it, they have their shibboleths, uncontaminated by the particular case. "Let's all cry 'Peace, freedom, and liberty!'" Brutus says.

Other heroes of Shakespeare's are poets plus soldiers, but this one, even in soldier's dress, is a wordsmith, all head and no body. Language as he manipulates it conceals the quick and membrane of things. You see this in his great oration (3.2), a tissue of words. Murder is the subject, evidently intractable, but the masterful rhetoric, taking order with experience, denies it. This triumph is artistic and Shakespeare's Brutus, another artist manqué, is a version of himself as he might be.

A forensic competition and notably formal, Shakespeare's play spills over with mindless and ferocious energy. His emblem for this is the stinking mob, clapping and hissing "as they use to do the players in the theater." Molders of opinion, unleashing the mob, seek to keep it at art's length—the tribunes, for instance, in the opening scene. Against a comic ruffian who challenges the play's intellectual veneer, they oppose their textbook rhetoric.

And do you now put on your best attire?
And do you now cull out a holiday?
And do you now strew flowers in his way. . . .

The smokescreen of words Brutus throws around Caesar's murder comes out of this textbook. But the physical world, brushing niceties aside, revenges itself on the artful dodger, and the mob is Brutus walking.

Not a "classical" tragedy where the Nuntius, reporting violence, spares us from seeing it, *Julius Caesar* is drenched in blood. Brutus hides bad deeds with good words but Shakespeare won't have this. His conspirators besmear their swords, waving these "red weapons" for everyone to see. Their "purpled hands" reek and smoke, their handclasps are bloody, fingers ends too, and they bathe in blood up to the elbows. Caesar, no sacrifice, is hacked like a carcass. This is butcher's work, matter for the tabloids. Shakespeare's grisly scenario needs its complement, however, "or else were this a savage spectacle."

It is and it isn't. E.g., purple hands, not only gory, are regal, and the victim, thrown to the hounds, makes a dish fit for the gods. The sensational death, like that of Phoenix and Turtle, is called a lofty scene, both ironic and just. Men not born yet will reenact it, taking comfort from a ritual observance. All the tragedies have this ritualized aspect, tangential to the story line. But the air they live in isn't perspicuous, like the air of heaven. Blood drizzles in the night sky—so say the Roman watchmen—and it always falls back on men.

A thesaurus of apt quotations, *Julius Caesar* lends itself to declaiming, and self-made men often tell us that the fault isn't in our stars but ourselves. Apart from the murder and the battle that winds things up, though, not much happens in Shakespeare's play. Structure, showing off the rhetoric, skimps on its other function, and action eddies vividly but doesn't throw forward. A sense of déjà vu, teasing the audience, suggests that this tale is twice told. Carnage is the most of it, importing little except itself, and in the future "another Caesar." One script fits all and Caesar, cuing his successors, backs up cronies who let money stick to their fingers, calls for a bowl of wine, spurns a begging petition, meditates on last things, turns into the third person pronoun. All this others do later, one reason the play is called *Julius Caesar.* Baring his breast to the knife, Cassius has Caesar's precedent. Octavius, "bayed about" with foes, looks back to Caesar too, brought to bay in the Forum. This is cyclical history where the present repeats the past and divination isn't needed to guess the shape of things to come.

Epiphanies there are, though mainly in language. Words and phrases reverberate, and on this side *Julius Caesar* looks ahead to *Macbeth*. Antony, who wants his own way, has seen "more days" than Octavius, Cassius, "older in practice" than Brutus, makes out the same case, and a cynical poet, intruding on their conference, has "seen more years" than either. Spared by the conspirators, Antony is "pricked" in the roll of their friends. The wheel turning, however, the survivor pricks out others, some of them friends but he kills them. Right from the start, they are talking of Pompey. This failed hero's name is a tocsin. Where should the conspirators meet if not at Pompey's Theater? Caesar, taking over as foremost man in the world, dies in this theater. Cassius at Philippi is Pompey at Pharsalia. Neither wanted to give battle but overruled by others, both go to their deaths.

As the curtain rises, supporters of Pompey's are catechizing the mob. This tag-rag people, blocks and stones, not men, doted on the great man until his wheel ran down hill. Antony, a flatterer, recalls this scornful language in his famous panegyric, only his people are men, not wood or stones. Whatever they are, it isn't hard to move them, and motion to no purpose is the play's chief constant. As the curtain falls a sequel play is being readied, and a new Caesar, parting or dividing "the glories" of the victory, resumes the carving up of the will. No play of Shakespeare's is colder.

This dismal replicating is his verdict on politics. A keen student of man in society, Shakespeare ranks high among political writers, but public men chilled his blood. So much is clear from *Henry V* where the hero, no sooner crowned, turns into Hotspur. Antedating *Julius Caesar* by only a few months, Shakespeare's English history shows him thinking "forward" from England to Rome. But past and present merge when London's Mayor and Aldermen, trailed by the mob, quit the city to greet the conquering hero. Already Shakespeare sees the likeness

> to the Senators of the antique Rome,
> With the plebeians swarming at their heels.

Essex, still in Ireland when Shakespeare wrote his Act V Prologue, belongs in this company. "In good time," the mob and their betters will fetch him in too. Many imagine Shakespeare sympathizing in secret with the aspiring man, soon to cross his own Rubicon. However, the stakes, merely public, were too low.

"High noises," appropriate to life at the top, go with Shakespeare's power struggle but are heard as dissonance, "a bustling rumor like a fray." This is politics, in case you didn't know it. Remote from politics, the essential play lives in homely detail. Caesar enters in his nightgown, Calpurnia can't bear children, an inoffensive poet takes a walk in the Capitol, Cassius has a birthday, Volumnius, an old schoolmate, instructs Brutus in the office of a friend. Against this personal fabric, Shakespeare locates his impersonal hero, the man who looks through flesh and blood.

Turning pages in North's translation of Plutarch (1579), he found what he wanted in Plutarch's life of Brutus, and this story, not Caesar's, organizes the play. Anybody's Caesar stands for the great man whose success is contingent on his lack of dimension. Brutus fails, disabled by "his own too much." Negotiating the hazards of the untrod state needs a less complicated hero. But the state is a version of the First National Bank and the hero has a chance to gain his soul or lose it. Less interesting, Shakespeare thought, to succeed with Caesar than to fail with Brutus.

That Brutus is the noblest Roman, nobody doubts. But he has his moral pockets picked. His eye doesn't see itself except "by reflection, by some other things." Phoenix and Turtle are like that, and flaming in each other's sight find out who they are. In the poem this suggestibility counts as a virtue, not in the play. Brutus, though ignorant of himself unless instructed, isn't fooled and like an alchemist turns drossy things golden. Aware that the "quarrel" won't bear looking into, he reads a lesson in stagecraft to the others, "Roman actors." Honor and Brutus, to hear him tell it, are twins, and playing on this word "honor" is how the conspirators snare him. But in a blood-boltered context abstractions disgust. Antony, urging the word derisively, understands this.

More ambitious than Caesar, Brutus yearns to escape our mundane condition, so tears the filaments that bind man to man. Reproving this quixotic enterprise, portents and prodigies—a lion in the streets, exhalations in the heavens—set the hero in a palpable context he can't get free of. Lapping the world's shores, a tide in men's affairs more potent than any steersman determines the course of things. Considering men, aware that we aren't self made, bid us wait on "the providence of some high powers / That govern us below." Brutus does this, supplying one of the play's familiar quotations, but the words go in one ear and out the other.

Though Cassius has a private grievance, reflected in his politics,

Brutus, rising into the stratosphere, invokes the "general wrong." But the violent act at the play's center is personal, not general, and meets us like a blow. All "fell down" with Caesar, Antony says, a vivid-prosaic phrase, no muffled Latinity about it. "Tyrannicide," a big word, lies outside Shakespeare's ken, and "private griefs," festering in his conspirators, prompt them to murder. Like every interesting motive, theirs is personal, therefore obscure. Provincial Shakespeare wonders what else it should be.

Late in the play, a gloomy Brutus, instructed like Macbeth, wishes "things done undone." In Brutus, however, different from Macbeth, the effect precedes the cause. At night he can't sleep, but this isn't a punishment, only a given, and throughout the play he labors to attain his final hour. On his own word, the passions that vex him are "only proper" to himself. "Some sick offense" within his mind, Portia calls this. Rest comes to the bondman when he kills himself, the only means to cancel his captivity. This phrase of Casca's, "overheard" in Act I, predicts the ending and describes it. Hoping to forestall the ending, Brutus undertakes his own purging. "Like an exorcist" he murders Caesar, "a piece of work that will make sick men whole."

Touching the life of the time at all points, Shakespeare feels and intimates times to come. In *Julius Caesar* he does the Age of Revolutions. Brutus, powerfully realized, attracts to himself every ideologue, and all find their justification in his eloquent speeches, suitably apothegmatic. This devotee of abstractions means to come at the spirit, leaving its carnal envelope unbroken. Pity drives out pity in the benevolent man, who has to be cruel to be kind. Nothing "personal" envenoms the cruelty, however, and Shakespeare has him say so. This is the unkindest cut of all.

Shakespeare's best-known valediction covers a multitude of sins. Sometimes you feel, however, that the resonant words are like insculpted sayings on gravestones. Both Antony and Brutus are good at obsequies but doubtful reporters. Is it really true that Brutus connived at murder "in a general honest thought / And common good to all"? What does Antony mean, that the elements were "nicely mixed" in him? Maybe he means that Brutus is one of a kind. Lulled by the Shakespeare music, playgoers don't invariably notice that the man who thinks it worthier to leap in himself is the same man who gives his verdict against self-slaughter. Though all are sorry for the husband whose wife has "swallowed fire," he comes across as pretty frigid when a messenger breaks the news, and though he says he found no man who wasn't true to him, the men of the "faction," using his "countenance," belie this. Blackening the hero and acquitting him too, Shakespeare has it both ways, and it isn't easy to say where piety leaves off and pietism begins.

Partly you can blame the poetry, glorifying whatever it touches. Partly, however, this comes from rendering the indigenous man whose like we won't see again. He makes trouble for *Julius Caesar* or you can say that he warrants its qualified success. Though Shakespeare's conclusion enforces a moral point, Brutus, appealing to "necessity," not a moral imperative, distorts it. Going into battle, he craves foreknowledge, then changes his mind. Sufficient that the day will end, "and then the end is known." Hamlet before the duel is like that. "If it be not now, yet it will come." Shakespeare's Roman hero sketches the tragedy of the aggressively intelligent man who wills a shape on the world only to discover that what we propose and what happens aren't always the same. Set against these laconic observations, moral strictures seem an afterthought. Not especially illustrative, only compelling, the play we remember has no point but itself and finishes when "time is come round."

TOWARD THE END of *Julius Caesar,* Cato, Portia's brother and the scion of a famous house, bounds on stage wanting something to do. "A foe to tyrants and my country's friend," the young regicide calls himself, but the words are hardly out when they kill him. In this cameo appearance, Shakespeare accommodates Robert Devereux, Earl of Essex. The second earl of the name and two years Shakespeare's junior, Essex was thirty-five when he staged his coup d'état. This was on a Sunday morning in winter 1601, and no event in Shakespeare's lifetime stirred England like the downfall of the very valiant rebel.

Soldier, scholar, courtier, and poet, he wanted to run the state himself. The Cecils, Burghley and his clever hunchback son Robert, stood in his way and he schemed to remove them. Luckily for England, he failed. Only Ralegh, his great adversary, rivaled him in pleasing, and he might have spread his cloak for Elizabeth to walk on. This soldier wrote sonnets and excelled at masques. Daniel, Chapman, and Jonson sang his praises. Spenser called him "great England's glory and the world's wide wonder."

Like a nova or vagrant star, Essex flashed across England's sky in the late eighties and nineties. His rise coincides with Sidney's eclipse, dead at the battle of Zutphen. Sidney, the age's paragon, left a gap in nature and Essex had to fill it. This was his misfortune. Dubbed knight banneret at twenty—i.e., honored for deeds done on the field of battle—he won his first fame at Zutphen and later took Frances, Sidney's widow, for wife. His sister Penelope, immortalized in sonnets, was the heroine of *Astrophel and Stella.* Essex House sheltered them both, the woman Sidney loved and the one he married.

Sidney was the real thing and Essex part counterfeit, befitting an age running down. In the long, attractive face the keen eyes, his best feature, riveted attention. The mouth suggested weakness, though, sensuality too. Loving his wife, he made an unfaithful husband. When he walked he stooped, as if to deprecate his height, and sometimes his air seemed abstracted. Bouts of melancholy went with this. The "Elizabethan malady," that was Hamlet's disease. Much given to reading and a book collector on the grand scale, Essex played a part in the founding of the Bodleian Library, his best memorial. Some think the scholar's bent went with Puritan leanings, and Puritans like Henry Cuffe were at home in Essex House. Once Greek Orator at Oxford and secretary to the Earl, Cuffe died with his master for ideology's sake. But Essex was no Puritan, only disaffected, and not thinking too much, thought too little.

In his early twenties, defying the Queen who meant to keep him in leading strings, he sailed on the Portugal Voyage. This attempt to set up an anti-Spanish pretender ended badly, like most of his ventures. But failing or succeeding, he coveted glory and generally found it. Shakespeare's child heroes remind you of him. Thrusting his pike into one of the gates of Lisbon, he wanted to know "if any Spaniard mewed therein durst adventure forth in favor of his mistress to break a lance." In *Troilus and Cressida* Shakespeare remembered this chivalrous challenge. His version seems absurd, though, and his Greek hero a pedant:

> And may that soldier a mere recreant prove
> That means not, hath not, or is not in love!

Men of action gravitated to Essex and he banked on their support to lift him as high as the throne. In periodic phrases worthy of Brutus, he said he loved them "for mine own sake . . . for their virtues' sake . . . for my country's sake. . . . If we may have peace, they have purchased it; if we must have war, they must manage it." Some, "wrecked on the Essex coast," went down with their hero. One, Sir Charles Danvers, died "rather like a bridegroom than a prisoner appointed for death." Shakespeare's Antony has an exit line that seems to recall this. "I will be a bridegroom in my death," he tells supporters but bungles the job.

Like his stepfather Leicester, once the royal favorite until he grew old and fat, Essex performed an elaborate mating dance at Court. Wooing Elizabeth, twice his age, he employed the idiom of sexual love. He said he was less subject to her power than her beauty, and kissing in spirit the fair royal hands thought of them "as a man should think of so fair flesh." The two windows of her chamber were the poles of his sphere. While it pleased her he remained there, fixed and immovable. He added, "When your Majesty thinks that Heaven too good for me, I will not fall like a star, but be consumed like a vapor by that same sun that drew me up to such a height." To England's Astraea no flattery seemed too fulsome, and refining on this luscious talk wearied her idolater. In private, he spoke caustically of the old woman whose behavior was "as crooked as her carcass!" At Court the walls had ears, and these outbursts got back to the Queen.

Presuming on his bonny looks, he forgot that the royal mistress was a daughter of Henry VIII. He knew how to pacify the Irish, he told her, and pushed his own man as commander-in-chief. This candidate not pleasing, he turned his back on the Queen like a petulant schoolboy. Boxing his ears, she swore at him coarsely. A two months' rupture followed, then they patched things up. In the end, he got the job himself, poetic justice.

When he went off to Ireland in March 1599, London's mob thronged the streets for more than four miles. Stow heard the people crying, God bless your Lordship! God preserve your honor! "Some followed him until the evening, only to behold him." Enemies, noting how he relished the applause, likened him to Shakespeare's Bolingbroke, plucking off his bonnet to an oyster-wench. The month before his departure, a young lawyer, John Hayward, told Bolingbroke's story in a history of *The Life and Reign of King Henry IV.* This biography reached its climax with Henry's deposing of Richard II. Imprudently, Hayward addressed it to Essex, "great in present judgment," more pointedly still "in the expectation of future time." The Queen and her Privy Council pricked up their ears at this and Hayward went to the Tower. But his past-as-prologue story, affording "lively patterns . . . for affairs of state," became an Elizabethan best-seller. Essex took it for proof of popular esteem. He meant to "barricade" himself in the love of the people, a contemporary said. But the "vulgar heart," endlessly Shakespeare's subject in his histories, proved an unsure habitation.

Richmond Palace on the Thames. Shakespeare's company, the Lord Chamberlain's Men, performed at Richmond for Queen Elizabeth shortly before she died there in 1603. Folger Library.

Some of Shakespeare's fellow actors. (a) Richard Burbage, principal star of Shakespeare's company from its earliest days. Delighting a grateful public, Burbage played "young Hamlet, old Hieronimo, kind Lear, the grievèd Moor." Painting, probably by Burbage himself, in Dulwich Gallery. (b) John Lowin in 1640. Old tradition says that Shakespeare, returning from Stratford, tutored this colleague in the part of King Henry VIII. Painting in Ashmolean Museum, Oxford. (c) Nathaniel Field. Beginning as a boy actor who learned his craft from Ben Jonson, Field graduated to leading roles with the King's Men. Painting in Dulwich Gallery. (d) Edward Alleyn. Leader of the Admiral's Men and creator of Marlowe's colossal heroes, he vied with Burbage for first place among tragic actors. The theater made him wealthy and in his retirement he founded Dulwich College, where this portrait is preserved. (e) William Sly. Cast lists of the time assign comic parts to this original member of the Chamberlain's Men. Painting in Dulwich Gallery.

Some of Shakespeare's fellow playwrights. (a) Sir Francis Beaumont. Until quitting the theater to marry a wealthy heiress, he collaborated famously with Fletcher in tragicomedy, an equivocal art where you could have your cake and eat it. Painting, 1615, in possession of Lord Sackville, Knole, Kent. Photograph by Courtauld Institute. (b) John Fletcher. Twice at least he and Shakespeare worked together on plays, and when Shakespeare retired Fletcher succeeded him as the King's Men's "ordinary poet." Painting, c. 1620, by permission of the Earl of Clarendon. Photograph by Plymouth City Museum and Art Gallery, Devon. (c) Ben Jonson. Shakespeare's self-appointed conscience and next to Shakespeare the time's greatest playwright, he had harsh things to say about his friend's work but wrote a glowing tribute in his memory. Painting by Abraham Blyenberch, the Guildhall Library of the City of London. (d) George Chapman. Famous for tragedy, comedy too, also a notable poet, he published a splendid translation of Homer. But his yen for big words got Shakespeare's bile flowing, and *Troilus and Cressida* records this. British Museum.

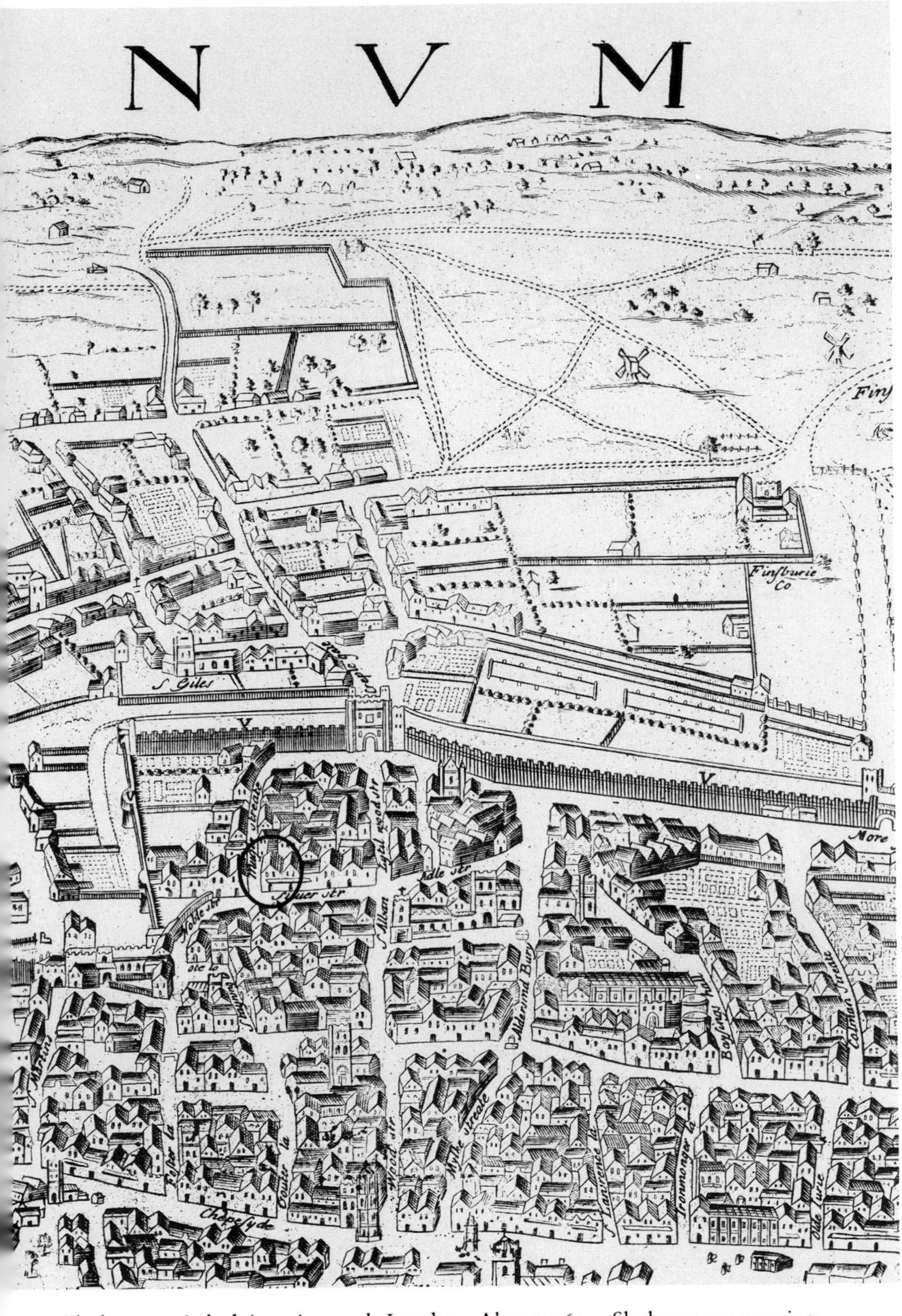

Shakespeare's lodgings in north London. About 1602, Shakespeare, moving to Cripplegate ward, took lodgings with a Franch "tire-maker" or hat-maker, Christopher Mountjoy. The house on the corner of Silver and Muggle streets, destroyed by German bombing in the Second World War, survives in Ralph Aggas's "Plan of London," c. 1570. Folger Library.

Robert Devereux, second Earl of Essex. Bad eminence to Shakespeare's patron Southampton, and Queen Elizabeth's favorite until he rose against the throne, Essex was the time's beau ideal. Beheaded in 1601, he lives a lurid afterlife in *Troilus and Cressida,* energizing this play's antiheroes. Painting after Marcus Gheeraerts the Younger, National Portrait Gallery, London.

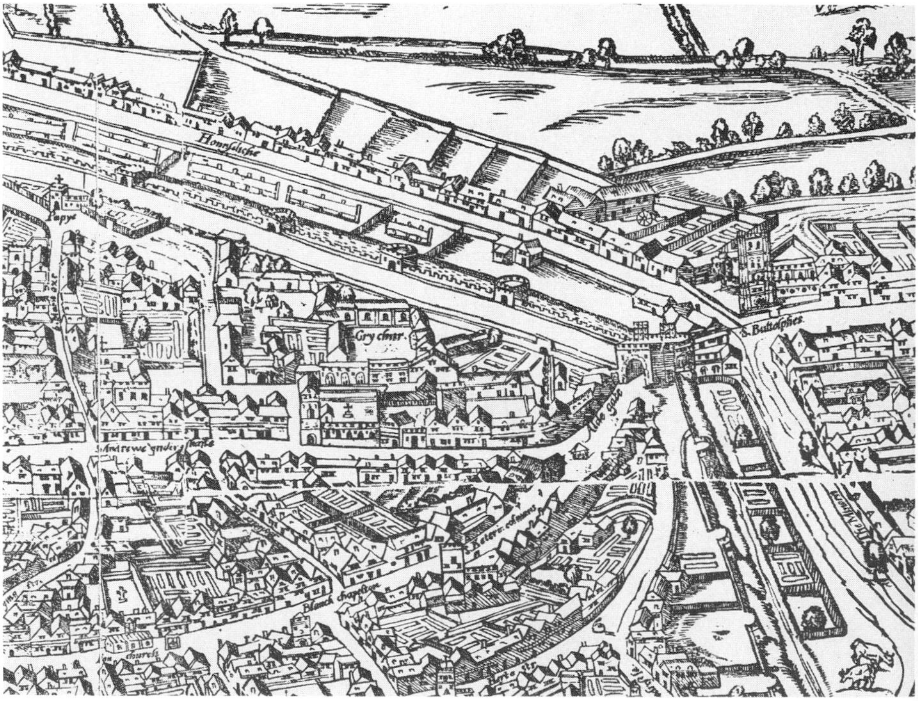

London Wall and Moat. Early in his career, Shakespeare lived in disreputable Shoreditch, outside London's Wall, moving in the mid-1590s to Bishopsgate, inside the Wall's northern perimeter. A ditch or moat, running with the Wall, stank to heaven, polluted by Londoners with "unsavory things." Ralph Aggas, "Plan of London," c. 1570. Folger Library.

Somerset House. Shakespeare, as Groom of the Royal Chamber, lived in this palace on the Thames, August 9–17, 1604, charged to "wait and attend" on the Spanish Ambassador. Folger Library.

King James. Invited down from Scotland, and needing no inducement, this first Stuart king in England succeeded Elizabeth in 1603. He brought the country to the verge of civil war but patronized Shakespeare's company, rebaptized as the King's Men. National Gallery of Scotland.

Father Henry Garnet on the scaffold. This Jesuit priest, remembered in *Macbeth,* died by hanging, May 3, 1606, a casualty of the Gunpowder Plot. Engraving from Matthew Tanner, *Societas Jesu,* Prague, 1675.

Middle Temple Hall. John Manningham, diarist, noted how "at our feast" in this London law school, February 1602, "we had a play called *Twelfth Night* or *What You Will,* much like *The Comedy of Errors.*" Gentlemen-lawyers liked their plays classical, not romantic, and perhaps Shakespeare's palled. However, he wrote in *Twelfth Night,* "we'll strive to please you." Picture Post Library.

The Globe. This open-air theater on Bankside gave Shakespeare a stage for some of his greatest plays. Built in 1599, the original Globe burned to the ground during a performance of *Henry VIII,* June 29, 1613. Reproduced from Visscher's "View of London," 1616. Folger Library.

Blackfriars and the Gatehouse. In 1608 Shakespeare and other members of the King's Men acquired the old Blackfriars monastery, using it as their winter theater. Five years later, Shakespeare bought the Gatehouse, once part of the ruined priory and notorious as a hideaway for papists. Ralph Aggas, "Plan of London," c. 1570. Folger Library.

(a) Henry Carey, first Lord Hunsdon. The nephew of Queen Elizabeth's mother Anne Boleyn, and England's Lord Chamberlain, he gave his title and patronage to Shakespeare's acting company. British Museum. (b) George Carey, second Lord Hunsdon. Old Hunsdon, dying in 1596, left the Chamberlain's office (after a brief interval) to his son George, shown in a miniature attributed to Nicholas Hilliard. Both men made a difference for Shakespeare's fortunes, their influence at Court protecting him and his fellows from the rising tide of Puritan hostility.

New Place. Shakespeare, doing well in theater, bought this Stratford mansion in 1597. The second-best house in town, it looked across the road to the Gild Chapel and Grammar School. An eighteenth-century owner destroyed Shakespeare's house but sketches survive, giving its likeness. Folger Library.

Southwark High Street and the cathedral of St. Mary Overy's as they appeared in 1543. St. Mary's Dock divides the cathedral from Winchester House. In 1599 Shakespeare lived nearby in Clink Liberty, under the jurisdiction of the Bishop of Winchester. From Canon William Thompson, *Southwark Cathedral,* 1910.

Shakespeare's coat of arms. In 1596 newly affluent Shakespeare applied for a coat of arms, signaling his gentleman's status, and the Heralds' College in London prepared this sketch for him. On the crest atop the shield, a falcon grasps a spear, punning on Shakespeare's name. Folger Library.

Jousting at "Barriers." In Shakespeare's time, couriers, denoted by an emblem or "impresa," fought in mock-medieval tournaments like this one. In 1613 Shakespeare and Richard Burbage prepared an impresa for the Earl of Rutland, a participant in the tournament that honored the King's Accession Day. Shakespeare in *Pericles* suggests what this device must have looked like. After a drawing by William Smith, c. 1597.

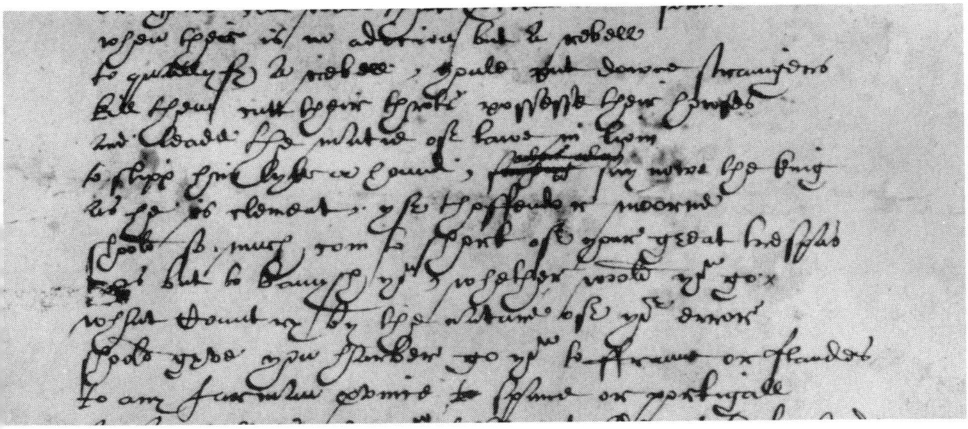

Hand D in *Sir Thomas More,* supposedly Shakespeare's autograph. Five men collaborated in this history play of the 1590s, then called in Shakespeare to refurbish their work. Paleographers say that the handwriting in this part of the manuscript is Shakespeare's, and parallels in style and thought to other plays of his support the assignment. British Museum.

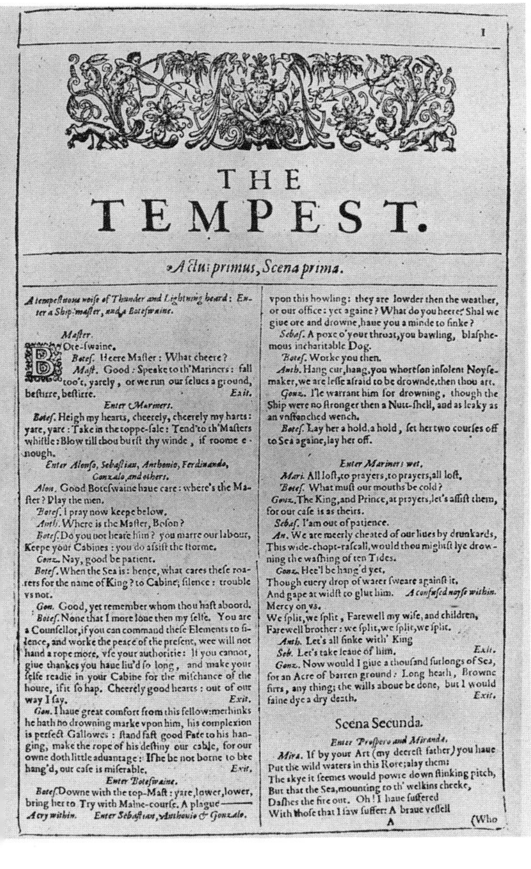

1

THE
TEMPEST.

Actus primus, Scena prima.

A tempestuous noise of Thunder and Lightning heard: Enter a Ship-master, and a Boteswaine.

Master.
Bote-swaine.
Botes. Heere Master: What cheere?
Mast. Good: Speake to th'Mariners: fall too't, yarely, or we run our selues a ground, bestirre, bestirre. *Exit.*
Enter Mariners.
Botes. Heigh my hearts, cheerely, cheerely my harts: yare, yare: Take in the toppe-sale: Tend to th'Masters whistle: Blow till thou burst thy winde, if roome enough.
Enter Alonso, Sebastian, Anthonio, Ferdinando, Gonzalo, and others.
Alon. Good Boteswaine haue care: where's the Master? Play the men.
Botes. I pray now keepe below.
Anth. Where is the Master, Boson?
Botes. Do you not heare him? you marre our labour, Keepe your Cabines: you do assist the storme.
Gonz. Nay, good be patient.
Botes. When the Sea is: hence, what cares these roarers for the name of King? to Cabine; silence: trouble vs not.
Gon. Good, yet remember whom thou hast aboord.
Botes. None that I more loue then my selfe. You are a Counsellor, if you can command these Elements to silence, and worke the peace of the present, wee will not hand a rope more, vse your authoritie: If you cannot, giue thankes you haue liu'd so long, and make your selfe readie in your Cabine for the mischance of the houre, if it so hap. Cheerely good hearts: out of our way I say. *Exit.*
Gon. I haue great comfort from this fellow: methinks he hath no drowning marke vpon him, his complexion is perfect Gallowes: stand fast good Fate to his hanging, make the rope of his destiny our cable, for our owne doth little aduantage: If he be not borne to bee hang'd, our case is miserable. *Exit.*
Enter Boteswaine.
Botes. Downe with the top-Mast: yare, lower, lower, bring her to Try with Maine-course. A plague——
A cry within. *Enter Sebastian, Anthonio & Gonzalo.*
vpon this howling: they are lowder then the weather, or our office: yet againe? What do you heere? Shal we giue ore and drowne, haue you a minde to sinke?
Sebas. A poxe o'your throat, you bawling, blasphemous incharitable Dog.
Botes. Worke you then.
Anth. Hang cur, hang, you whoreson insolent Noysemaker, we are lesse afraid to be drownde, then thou art.
Gonz. I'le warrant him for drowning, though the Ship were no stronger then a Nutt-shell, and as leaky as an vnstanched wench.
Botes. Lay her a hold, a hold, set her two courses off to Sea againe, lay her off.
Enter Mariners wet.
Mari. All lost, to prayers, to prayers, all lost.
Botes. What must our mouths be cold?
Gonz. The King, and Prince, at prayers, let's assist them, for our case is as theirs.
Sebas. I'am out of patience.
An. We are meerly cheated of our liues by drunkards, This wide-chopt-rascall, would thou mightst lye drowning the washing of ten Tides.
Gonz. Hee'l be hang'd yet,
Though euery drop of water sweare against it,
And gape at widst to glut him. *A confused noyse within.*
Mercy on vs.
We split, we split, Farewell my wife, and children,
Farewell brother: we split, we split, we split.
Anth. Let's all sinke with' King
Seb. Let's take leaue of him. *Exit.*
Gonz. Now would I giue a thousand furlongs of Sea, for an Acre of barren ground: Long heath, Browne firrs, any thing; the wills aboue be done, but I would faine dye a dry death. *Exit.*

Scena Secunda.

Enter Prospero and Miranda.
Mira. If by your Art (my deerest father) you haue
Put the wild waters in this Rore; alay them:
The skye it seemes would powre down stinking pitch,
But that the Sea, mounting to th' welkins cheeke,
Dashes the fire out. Oh! I haue suffered
With those that I saw suffer: A braue vessell
A (Who

The Tempest, First Folio, 1623. Among the last of Shakespeare's plays, this romance appears first in the great collection of Shakespeare's work, prepared by his fellow actors Heminges and Condell and published seven years after his death. British Museum.

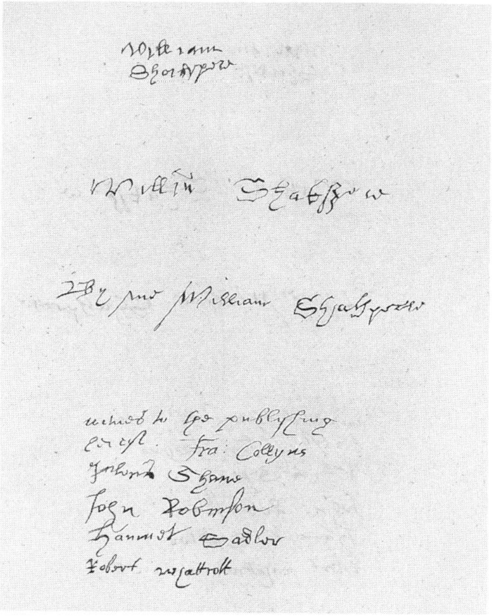

Top: Shakespeare's signatures. Preparing his will in 1616, Shakespeare signed it three times. Five witnesses, headed up by his lawyer, signed with him. Spelling in his day remained permissive and he spelled his name indifferently "Shakspere" or "Shakspeare." Folger Library.

Bottom: Welcombe Hills. In 1605 Shakespeare the rentier made his most ambitious investment, purchasing "tithe lands" in Stratford and its environs, including the village of Welcombe. "The West View of Welcombe Hills," 1777. Folger Library.

Shakespeare's epitaph. A few feet from Shakespeare's grave in Holy Trinity church stood Stratford's charnel-house where the bones of the dead, dug up from their graves, went to make room for newcomers. Shakespeare provided against this fate in a doggerel epitaph, cursing the man who moved his bones. Photograph by Edwin Smith.

Droeshout engraving of Shakespeare in the First Folio, 1623. Still a boy when Shakespeare died, Droeshout the engraver must have worked from a model, perhaps a painting by Shakespeare's fellow-actor Burbage. Though his version of Shakespeare has disheartened many, friends and family raised no objection. Folger Library.

Janssen bust of Shakespeare, side view. This work of a London stone cutter whose shop stood near the Globe overlooks Shakespeare's grave in the chancel of Holy Trinity church. Tradition says that the artist worked from a life mask or death mask. Folger Library.

A splendid army, 16,000 men, sailed with the new governor-general. Harum-scarum campaigning cost him his advantage, though, and in generalship, Tyrone, the Great O'Neill, beat him hollow. "Rough rugheaded kerns," guerrilla fighters, harried his English soldiers, and the bogs and mists of Ireland did the rest. In hysterical letters to the Queen, he called for fresh resources, got them and threw them away. When Elizabeth instructed him to march against Ulster, he disobeyed orders and agreed to an ignominious truce. Then, deserting the army, he ran for home.

Back in London on September 28, 1599, he tracked down the Queen at her palace of Nonsuch in Surrey. She wasn't made up yet when, without warning, he entered her bedchamber. This sealed his fate. Confined at York House, then banished from Court, he stood before Privy Council in June 1600, enduring the censure of men he despised. After all he wasn't Bolingbroke, more like degraded King Richard. Conciliating her favorite, Elizabeth had given him the grant of the tax on sweet wines, a government monopoly. In October this lapsed, beggaring a proud man. As he had prophesied, she sucked him up like a vapor.

Achilles in his tent, he sulked at Essex House. This mansion on the Strand, once Leicester's, overlooked the river just outside the City wall. Religious zealots and bravos with a chip on their shoulder haunted its precincts, infecting the Earl with harebrained schemes for his redemption. Mountjoy, his sister's lover, and Southampton, Shakespeare's patron, encouraged him to "root out" the Queen's advisers. Southampton, calling them "caterpillars" like the minions of Richard II, said they "laid plots to bereave us of our lives." A duodecimo version of Essex, he threw his life away or tried to, but Mountjoy lived to fight another day. Like the man in Shakespeare's plays who picks up the pieces, he returned to Ireland after the rising and succeeded where Essex had failed. In *Henry V,* Shakespeare's French herald, still there when the dust has settled, bears this survivor's name.

"I am Richard the Second, know ye not that?" Queen Elizabeth said. Promoting the resemblance, malcontents at Essex House engineered a performance of Shakespeare's play, February 7, 1601. The day before, a Friday, Sir Gelly Merrick and others crossed the river to visit the Globe. Augustine Phillips spoke for the Chamberlain's Men. *Richard II* being "so old and so long out of use," he feared no one would come to see it. But Merrick, determined "to have the play of the deposing and killing," dangled a large bribe before Shakespeare's fellows, forty shillings above their "ordinary" takings. "So earnest he was to satisfy his eyes with the sight of that tragedy which he thought soon after his lord should bring from the stage to the state."

Sir Francis Bacon said this in a declaration of the "Practises and Treasons" of Essex, noting with satisfaction how God had turned the treasons "upon their own heads." A hanger-on at Essex House, he served the Earl as literary and political adviser. Rejecting the advice, too sensible for his mercurial temperament, Essex urged the Queen to prefer this struggling barrister. That was his style and he spoke for friends like a Jack o' the clock when policy might have dictated silence. Later, at the trial, Bacon discovered much villainy in Essex.

On February 7, Privy Council, aware that the pustulous boil was near breaking, called the Earl to account. Begging off, he pleaded sickness. That night, his supporters slept at Essex House, a state-within-the-state. In the morning, a Sunday, officers of the Council hammered at his gates. Chief Justice Popham, a bit player in Shakespeare's story, read the riot act but the Earl cut him short. Seizing the councilors as hostages, he locked them in the famous library, then began his mad dash to oblivion. "For the Queen!" he cried. "The crown of England is sold to the Spaniard! A plot is laid for my life!" Perhaps he believed this.

Accompanied by Southampton and other "knights and gentlemen of great blood," he led a little army of two hundred men, poor perdus armed with swords "and some few with French pistols." The Queen, his ultimate prize, lay at Westminster, secure behind the barricades erected at Charing Cross. Heading the other way, he galloped up Ludgate Hill, hoping to raise the City. At Paul's Cross the Lord Mayor and Aldermen, attending a sermon, gaped in astonishment. Some in the crowd cheered feebly, not sure how the wind was blowing. Behind the rebels, however, came the Queen's herald, proclaiming Essex a traitor. Along Cheapside the streets emptied, men closed their shutters, and supporters fell away from the mockery king of snow. By afternoon, it was over.

At the trial in Westminster Hall, Bacon spoke tellingly for the prosecution, "not an office for a friend." Condemned to die with Essex, Southampton got off thanks to Robert Cecil, one of the caterpillars. Sir Gelly Merrick of the forty shilling bribe was hanged at Tyburn, however, and on February 25 Essex died on Tower Hill. Ralegh, he said, had plotted to kill him, but at the execution his great enemy wept. The night before Essex went to the block, Elizabeth attended a play, performed at her bidding by the Chamberlain's Men. This was her revenge on Shakespeare and his fellows.

Friendly biographers acquit them of blame. But treason was in the air that fateful day on Bankside, and playing to a cheering house packed with the Earl's supporters, they knew what they were doing. No doubt some sympathized with the rebels. Some, not all. Falstaff speaks for Shakespeare on Essex: "Rebellion lay in his way and he found it." Before the story was written, Shakespeare had it by heart. The history plays record his verdict and in *Julius Caesar* he judges the conspirators, not omitting Bacon and his reasons-of-state. Judging doesn't preclude emotion, but pity didn't blind him and what he wept for, he condemned without reprieve.

THE ESSEX CONSPIRACY begot no play by Shakespeare. He looked skeptically at the principals, suitably mythologized, in *Troilus and Cressida*, but absorbed in the stage set they swell a progress, little more. Dissenters, pointing to *Hamlet*, his tragedy of 1601, imagine an embittered playwright remembering the hero's fall. Shakespeare's Dark Period, a run of tragedies and "problem" plays, is often supposed to follow. He had dark periods but punctuated with light, also a long memory. If you could trace to their source all the threads in his carpet, you could reconstruct the life of the times. Perhaps the lawless or landless "resolutes" who march with Fortinbras for honor's sake first got his attention at Essex House. Characteristically, however, Shakespeare's eye is for minutiae, not the big wars but little business on the periphery.

Glancing at the sign of Hercules that hung before the Globe, his hero in *Hamlet* thinks of the rivalry between the boys' and adult companies, yesterday's favorites, and offers sound advice to ham actors. None of this seems to bear on the story, but wait. The taste of the age and the breaking down of class distinctions "this three years" prompt John Bullish reflections. Further back in time is the drowning of Katherine Hamlet, spinster of Tiddington. At the inquest in Stratford, they had to decide if she took her own life or was this death "*se offendendo*."

John Shakespeare's death in 1601 passed without comment but his minor adventures enliven the play. In 1599, wanting a higher gloss on his gentleman's status, he sought approval from the Heralds' College to combine the Shakespeare coat of arms with that of his wife's family, the Ardens. Though no grant of impalement answered this request, *Hamlet* seems to take notice—all that to-do about honor. Self-important Laertes wants his duel ratified by "masters of known honor," like that earlier duel, "well ratified by law and heraldry," between old Hamlet and Fortinbras. The infatuation with honor comes up again in *All's Well That Ends Well,* another fathers-and-sons play. Shakespeare's quarrel with his father extended beyond the grave.

The death in Stratford increased his holdings, satisfying to a man who set store by material things. As the eldest son, he got the Henley Street houses, renting one to his sister Joan Hart and her husband the hatter, the other to Lewis Hiccox of Welcombe. Renamed the Maidenhead by Hiccox, the eastern house became an inn. Shakespeare was writing *Hamlet* while absorbed in this business, petty but hardly beneath him. Like his lawyer in the Graveyard Scene, he sought assurance in parchment. But acquisitive Shakespeare is the same man who could be bounded in a nutshell, except that he has bad dreams.

In January 1601, less than a month before Essex raised his standard, Shakespeare's Stratford neighbors got in trouble with the law. Falling foul of Sir Edward Greville, lord of Stratford manor and a voracious land whale, they found themselves on Bankside, under arrest and bound for the Marshalsea prison. All eyes were on Essex across the river, and other than Shakespeare no one noticed. Men like Stratford's lord, enclosing public lands, threatened small farmers with ruin. Their plight interested Shakespeare, not the humanitarian but the connoisseur of situations, and a few years later he wrote about it in *Coriolanus*.

As the new year began, the manor lord enclosed the Bankcroft, common pasture beside the Avon where in John Shakespeare's bailiwick local citizens took archery practice. Promptly, Stratford rebelled, led by Shakespeare's schoolfellow Richard Quiney, John Sadler, twice the town's bailiff, and Henry Walker, mercer in the High Street. (In time to come, Walker fathered Shakespeare's godson William, and Sadler's son John, looking beyond the seas like Shakespeare's Southampton, made a fortune in Virginia.) On January 21, Quiney and the others broke down the man-made pale. Armed with spades and mattocks, they rooted up Sir Edward's new hedges and drove in horses, cattle, and swine, for good measure carting off six loads of willows. These "enormities" cost the landlord £40.

Committed to the Marshalsea, the rioters got out on bail, then carried their grievance to Sir Edward Coke, the Queen's Attorney General. Thomas Greene of the Middle Temple advised them. This sometime tenant at New Place called Shakespeare "cousin" and named his children Anne and William. He and Quiney waited on Coke "three days together" but "could not have him at leisure by the reason of these troubles," i.e., the Essex rising. Meanwhile, the rape of England's common lands continued.

Background, not foreground, this is part of the soil *Hamlet* springs from. Denmark, the play's locale, is ripe for insurrection, and outside the palace the "distracted multitude" has taken the law into its hands. (In England where madness reigns, things are worse.) Already in the first act we hear that the state is rotten. Corruption, an "imposthume" or abscess, undermines it. Other ways of seeing Denmark include a pocky corpse or mildewed ear. Compelling Shakespeare's attention, the disjointed time inspires loathing. Action stops while he indulges this, and things are well along before we meet Prince Hamlet in the play that bears his name.

Not an isolated ego whose notorious problems stem from private unease, Hamlet has a graver problem, how to negotiate the fallen world he lives in. Time servers, skilled at getting on, run the state, one the supple chamberlain, another the courtier whose trough stands beside the King's table. Their knees have "pregnant hinges" and their "wisdoms" endorse the King's parody of statecraft. A vice to know them, Hamlet says, but they own much land and fertile. Shakespeare knows them, the exacerbated tone telling of his revulsion. "'A did comply, sir, with his dug before 'a sucked it."

But a more virulent strain envenoms Shakespeare's critique, and his indictment of society comprehends the playwright. "In's time a great buyer of land," Shakespeare is this and many odious things besides. In the Closet Scene he takes Hamlet's role, then shifts to Gertrude's, playing both accused and accuser. Black and dyed in the grain, the offenses that spot his soul are more lurid than imagination can shape them. Like self-accusing Richard II, he turns his eyes upon himself, limning his own portrait. "What should such fellows as I do, crawling between earth and heaven?"

Raging almost out of control, *Hamlet* continues the story, first sketched in *Julius Caesar,* of the tormented hero obsessed by hatred of the drossy age and its best chronicler. A major obsession, it overflows its "list" or boundary, contaminating whatever it touches. Some "leprous distillment" infiltrates the play, and poison all round manages the ending. The court turns into the world, an unweeded garden noisome with decay, while servile retainers, false friends, and too pliant ladies stand for the whole of creation. Man in the aggregate is knavish. Historical time disintegrating in *Hamlet,* a continuous present runs together the Trojan War, Golgotha, and Doomsday. No waking from this nightmare except by endless sleep.

More penetrating than others, Shakespeare's fascinated hero sees the puppets dallying and sees the skull beneath the skin. This moralist in Sodom has a horror of sexuality. Though bedroom doors are closed he looks through them, estimating the sweaty lovers "honeying . . . / Over the nasty sty." Replete with visions like this, *Hamlet* is variations on an old theme, "de contemptu mundi." But Shakespeare, penning his hate-filled letter to the time, is purged of hatred, including self-hatred, and the ending is quiet, "all passion spent."

Perhaps the generalized hatred exceeds the facts as he gives them. Rosencrantz and Guildenstern, surrogates for the rest of us, suppose this. Looking for the source of Hamlet's distemper, they can't find it, but being themselves how should they? Closer to Shakespeare than any other of his protagonists, Hamlet has depths, not easily sounded. The King, a middle-of-the-roader ("weighing delight and dole"), thinks his grief excessive. It shows a heart "unfortified." Truth clamors for a hearing but even-tempered Horatio is "fortified" against it and you have to assail his ears to get at him. The Gravedigger, devoid of feeling, sings at his work, "custom" making the job supportable. Custom hardens Gertrude's heart, "proof and bulwark" against feeling. And so on. The hero in his sable suits of woe stands apart. Self-conscious in a "pursy" (bloated) time, he looks eccentric, possibly mad. But that is a comparative judgment.

Writing for the theater, Shakespeare needed a scenario to focus and escape from his rage. He found it in the Revenge Play. Descending from Roman Seneca, more recently from Thomas Kyd, likely the author of an earlier *Hamlet,* the time-honored story has all the clarity of simpleminded things. "Hamlet, revenge!" its initial datum, is absolute, the Ghost's word is sterling, and the hero doesn't have to think twice. He has a problem, only technical, though, how to get past the King's Switzers. An antic disposition, put on to lull suspicion, takes care of this. No one less complicated than convention's Hamlet. And no hero more ferocious. Bristling with male aggression ("splenitive and rash"), he belongs in the lockup but the culture eggs him on, only Shakespeare withholding applause. The right sort of revenger drinks hot blood and likes the witching time of night when graveyards yawn and the croaking raven bellows for revenge. Mouthed by Shakespeare's hero, this is fustian and sends up the conventional play.

Smiting the guilty, Hamlet is prompted to his executioner's work by Heaven. Shakespeare's Hamlet adds, however: "and Hell." With this addition, the old-fashioned play begins to destruct. The stagy hero is still with us but he isn't the Prince. One-dimensional Pyrrhus, heating up the air in the Player's speech, presents him. Another son requiting another father's death, this gore-encrusted man is Hamlet as they liked him, mincing an old man's limbs with his sword, "malicious sport." Alert to his "cue," no hanging back for him, he drowns the stage with tears and makes horrid speeches. Laertes is like that. Incensed at his vulgar passionating, the hero mocks him in language appropriate to farce. "Woo't drink up eisel? Eat a crocodile?"

Farce (mounting to something more) is when Hamlet swears the Watch to silence while the Ghost makes obbligato noises beneath the stage. This hysterical interlude draws for its black humor on the presence of the King that was, dead but still on the rampage. An "extravagant and erring spirit," he raises eyebrows or ought to. At sunrise he skulks off like a guilty thing, and in the Christmas season doesn't stir abroad at all. Killing and that hallowed time don't go together, and murder, even "in the best," works out to rash and bloody. That is what the Ghost says, but Hamlet to this point doesn't hear him.

Marching into the play, Hamlet Senior has a warlike form and a reputation to suit. When he parleys he gets angry. Some in his neighborhood regret this. "Smote the sledded Polacks. . . . Did slay this Fortinbras." Shakespeare's hero is born the day old Hamlet kills his man, a nice conjunction of virile past and less strenuous present. Hamlet stands for the present and many think it effeminate. No doubt Shakespeare intended a contrast. Sharpening the contrast, other figures from the distant past loom on the play's edges. Two are military men, Caesar and Alexander, both of them good at grasping the nettle. Hercules, another Worthy, comes up four times. This type of the active man strangles a lion with his bare hands. Hamlet isn't like him.

Bad luck, says the hero, that the job of putting things right goes to him. Perhaps he fits the Ghost's contemptuous portrait, duller than the weed that grows beside the river of forgetfulness. Laertes, a barbarian, takes on the job, however, and is apt at calling offenses in question. Claudius has this alacrity. "To the quick of the ulcer" is a phrase of his. Wanting them to get on with it, he hopes to cure the "hectic" that rages in his blood. Desperate diseases are only relieved "by desperate appliance." This sounds like good medicine but lumps action and sickness together.

Veering between his will and the matter in hand, pre-Act V Hamlet lacks poise. The Ghost wants him to kill without tainting his mind, but this injunction isn't one he can follow. A good Coleridgean, Shakespeare's Prince tries hard to accept the proposition that "action is the chief end of existence." In a self-reproving soliloquy, he says his resolution is "sicklied" over with the pallor of thought. So thought equals sickness and "conscience" makes cowards? Maybe like the multitude, sweeping aside old sanctions, the considering hero ought to close his eyes and leap.

Examples "gross as earth" exhort him, and partly that is the trouble. His rival Fortinbras, another military man, doesn't think too much but "makes mouths at the invisible event." (Only picture it.) He fights for an eggshell but never mind:

> Rightly to be great
> Is not to stir without great argument,
> But greatly to find quarrel in a straw
> When honor's at the stake.

Tidying up the syntax, Shakespeare's editors suggest that his sense needs a "not not" construction. But the sense isn't confused, only equivocal, asking us to stir when there's not much to stir about, also to sit still, consulting the occasion. Interesting questions have this Yes and No look and answers worth the name reflect it.

Innocent of ambiguity, the persons of the play, Hamlet excepted, hold fast to a single truth. "Revenge should have no bounds," etc. Always? sometimes? But they don't raise the question. Theirs isn't a truth you need to "unfold," and they can bring it to light "though it were hid indeed / Within the center." The play, all hints and interstices, challenges assurance, however, and takes a doubtful view of perception. Our wills and fates run contrary, and though "our thoughts are ours," their ends quicken with a life of their own. Hamlet's activity, real and purposed, comments on these observations. He shoots his arrow over the house and it finds a target, but not the one he aimed at.

In the precincts of Elsinore, night merges with day and weekdays aren't divided from Sundays. "Yonder cloud," Hamlet thinks, looks like a camel, or possibly a weasel or whale. A gentleman of Normandy, reporters say, has witchcraft in horsemanship. Lookers-on can't tell this rider from his horse. The blurring of distinction is efficient in other ways, suggesting that perfect equipoise when doubts aren't resolved but persist in a lifelike tension. Death comes when the tension breaks and things precipitate out.

An image for *Hamlet* is the mixed-up duel that ends it. "In scuffling they change rapiers." Shakespeare's tragedy depends on mischance and maybe it serves decorum but Horatio, our preceptor, tells us more than he knows. The Prince, who says nothing, might tell us but runs out of time. The Ghost promises to tell us. However, he reneges. He "could a tale unfold" but not to ears of flesh and blood. The last scene, muffled drums and a catafalque, leaves Shakespeare's protagonists, his auditors too, in the dark.

Checked or driven by flesh and blood, all are "fools of nature," Hamlet's phrase. Perception failing, freedom is abridged, a casualty of our natural condition. But this description, borne out by plot, isn't felt as diminishing. Exploring one man's fate, Shakespeare is its celebrant, and much of this play's excitement comes from our sense of limitations pushed as far as possibility allows. Hamlet, fettered in last things, is the most nearly free of tragic heroes. In the event, time and chance have their way with him, but dying, he runs out the tether.

The natural condition, a radical impairment, goes by different names, "the stamp of nature" or "vicious mole of nature," elsewhere "our old stock." Do what we can, we "relish" or taste of it. A rueful psychology, Hamlet's is descriptive, not prescriptive. Christian doctrine is where it comes from, though Shakespeare nowhere mentions original sin.

Many take comfort from this reading of how things are with us, laying our trouble to some "particular fault." Tragedy ensues (they hear Hamlet saying) when we enlarge in ourselves "the stamp of one defect." This defect or "tragic flaw" is (choose one) ambition, pride, jealousy, lust, anger, etc. A one-to-one correspondence relating effect to cause, it rationalizes the misfortunes of Shakespeare's tragic heroes. But the tragic flaw, an ancient misunderstanding, isn't much involved with volition. Not special but generic, it tells of "contagious blastments" waiting to strike us or the "canker" in the grain that galls or kills. Against this endemic flaw, "pales and forts" are no good.

Shakespeare isn't the Buddha, looking passively at the world and its business, and the hero's supposed insufficiency doesn't argue quietism or paralysis of will. On the contrary, it argues "readiness," different from that anxious screwing up of resolution we feel in the man who says: "and now I'll do't." Generosity urging its claims, he wipes the slate clean, forgetting "to pay ourselves what to ourselves is debt." The Player King, who has cause to remember bad debts and revenge them, enjoins that kind of forgetting. Not only generous, this is wise, and Hamlet, tarred with the same brush as others, declines in common prudence to use them after their deserts.

In heaven but not on earth, Claudius tells us, "the action lies / In his true nature." Taking the point, the hero asks for "relative" grounds to proceed on. Also, needing all the help he can get, he asks help of conscience, this word meaning itself plus introspection. The natural world, where organic process rules, offers pointers or seems to. Our meditated purpose, says the Player King, is like unripened fruit. When the fruit is green it sticks on the tree but falls without shaking when mellow. Shakespeare is himself as he complicates responses, and perhaps this little homily casts too clear a light.

Claudius and Hamlet, though they fight to the death, resemble one another, each bearing a "heavy burden." Best not to call it guilt, a question-begging word; better to call it awareness. Claudius, "like a man to double business bound," sets Hamlet before us, the would-be avenger at war between will and will not. In the last resort, however, this familiar dichotomy is too slight to carry the play. Less specific and more poignant, the double business engaging the hero and villain, also the playwright who participates in both, isn't open to codifying, resolution either. Most plays are classifiable, and single-minded Polonius enumerates the different kinds. In *Hamlet,* however, "individable," "unlimited," demarcations collapse and antithetical things make a pairing. For the hero, asked to entertain them without losing his mind or will to action, this is hard.

Being in the world but not of it, he loves where he hates, lives and wants to die, thrills to the consciousness of angelic or godlike power while acknowledging a "limèd soul," tangled in its muddy vesture of decay. Wild surmises shake him but he knows them beyond his reach. Hamlet, who means to sweep to his revenge, will do this, he announces, "with wings as swift as meditation or the thoughts of love." But what does meditation mean if it doesn't mean delay? So the hero's purpose, even as he avows it, is baffled.

Not fully fledged in the beginning, Hamlet arrives tardily at the hero's role. As the last act impends, his thoughts, bloody or "nothing worth," still declare the purposive man who has his hands on all the ropes. But enlightenment in the form of a mysterious sea change dispels the dark thoughts that beset him. Spared by "thieves of mercy" and set "naked" on the kingdom—implicative phrases both—in the end he puts off his unease.

Failing to play the man is often said to be his vice. But it takes a man at full stretch to live equably with his bifold truth. Learning to do this, Hamlet becomes himself, of all Shakespeare's heroes the one who touches us most. The play's final speech—ironically, it goes to the strong-armed man—salutes his transformation. Bear Hamlet to his rest "like a soldier," Fortinbras bids his captains, and they do this.

A WAR of the Theaters marched step by step with the writing of *Hamlet,* reaching its climax in 1601. Guildenstern describes it, "much throwing about of brains." Ben Jonson began it or was glad to take the offer of a quarrel. Shakespeare ended it when he gave Ben a "purge."

The Poets' War, "that terrible Poetomachia," pitted Jonson, a seriocomic Hamlet, against the age. For three years, he complained, "they" provoked him with their petulant styles. Determined to see "if shame could win upon 'em," he lashed out at contemporaries, Marston, Dekker, others, also whipping up a "contention of the two houses," i.e., public and private theaters. The Globe, a public theater, got the worst of this. Berattled by "goosequills" (satiric pens like Jonson's), the Chamberlain's Men lost ground to the boys' companies, newly popular at the century's end. Do they carry it away? Hamlet asks, and is answered: "Ay, that they do, my lord—Hercules and his load too." No tempest in a teapot to Shakespeare, the Theater War meant money out of pocket.

As to money, "We have need on't," Jonson makes one of Shakespeare's fellows say, "for this winter has made us all poorer than so many starved snakes; nobody comes at us." Unless things looked up, they would have to tour the country, stalking on "boards and barrel heads to an old cracked trumpet." That is how Hamlet finds them, driven from town "by the means of the late innovation." Shakespeare's play, a first version, spells out what this means. Abandoning the Globe, "the principal public audience" (Hamlet's schoolfellow says) "are turned to private plays / And to the humors of children."

Troubles bore down on the Chamberlain's Men not as single spies but in battalions. "Allowed" by Privy Council, another company, the Earl of Worcester's, rose up to challenge them. First housed at the Boar's Head in Whitechapel outside Aldgate, it moved within six months to Henslowe's newly vacant Rose theater on Bankside, too close for comfort. Kempe, returned from one more morris dance, this one over the Alps to Rome, starred for Worcester's Men, and Thomas Heywood, the "prose Shakespeare," joined them as their principal writer. Toward the end of Elizabeth's reign, four companies, each with its own playhouse, were competing with Shakespeare's for favor.

Like the adults, the children had their ordinary poets, John Marston and George Chapman writing for Paul's Boys, Jonson for the Children of the Chapel at Blackfriars. Second only to Shakespeare among playwrights of his time, Jonson spoke loudly and carried a big stick. In 1598 he duelled with Gabriel Spencer, leader in Alleyn's absence of the Admiral's Men. Henslowe wrote Spencer's epitaph: "slain in Hogsdon Fields by the hands of Benjamin Jonson, bricklayer." The bricklayer's trade was how Jonson began and enemies didn't let him forget it. Tried and condemned, he might have swung, but got off, pleading Benefit of Clergy. This meant conning a scrap of Latin, the "neck verse." He lost his property, however, and had his thumb branded with the felon's mark, T for Tyburn prison. Spencer the actor was his second victim and people quarreled with Ben at their peril.

A newcomer to the stage in the mid–1590s, he owed his first success to Shakespeare. Offered the manuscript of *Every Man in His Humor* (1598), the Chamberlain's Men "turned it carelessly and superciliously over, were just upon returning it," said Nicholas Rowe, "when Shakespeare luckily cast his eye upon it." This judicious critic recommended "Mr. Jonson and his writings to the public. After this they were professed friends."

Being friends with Jonson needed tact and a sense of humor. Valiant like a lion, he was churlish as a bear and slow as an elephant, and though he had a hundred eyes saw nothing when he looked at himself. These are words for Shakespeare's Ajax who resembles him except for the mountain belly, still to come. In middle age he made a grand tour, like that other Johnson, walking from London to Edinburgh to visit the poet Drummond of Hawthornden. His host sized him up thoughtfully: "a great lover and praiser of himself; a contemner and scorner of others; given rather to lose a friend than a jest; jealous of every word and action of those about him, especially after drink, which is one of the elements in which he liveth; a dissembler of ill parts which reign in him; a bragger . . . passionately kind and angry; careless either to gain or keep; vindictive, but if well answered, at himself . . . oppressed with fantasy, which has ever mastered his reason, a general disease in many poets."

Fantasy, not reason, made Jonson a great poet, one of the half dozen in English. Scholars, stressing his bookish classicism, haven't served him well. Partly this is the revenge of Bardolaters on the judgmental man who loved Shakespeare too but "this side idolatry." Bishop Fuller in the next age delivered both to posterity, "a Spanish great galleon and an English man of war." Jonson, galleon-like, "was built far higher in learning, solid but slow." Shakespeare, "lesser in bulk but lighter in sailing, could turn with all tides, tack about and take advantage of all winds by the quickness of his wit and invention." Jonson's triumphs depend on emotion, however, Shakespeare's on myopic study and the close pursuit of words. The aptly entitled "Ode to Himself" gives the essence of Ben:

And since our dainty age
Cannot endure reproof,
Make not thyself a page
To that strumpet the stage,
But sing high and aloof,
Safe from the wolf's black jaw, and the dull ass's hoof.

Like Yeats three centuries later, Jonson combined in himself the time's scapegoat and its best censor. He is the romantic, Shakespeare the intellectual. Whatever Jonson got from Camden his teacher, he had in his psyche small Latin and less Greek.

Befitting a novice playwright, still in his twenties when he took on the age, he liked verbal fireworks and thought fancy words better than plain ones. One of his affectations, "element" for "sky," gets the back of Shakespeare's hand in *Twelfth Night*. But Jonson, patient of himself, had no patience with others. Marston in particular made his hackles rise. Converting private pique to everybody's business, his great talent as a poet, he lampooned this rival in *Every Man Out of His Humor* (1599). An all-purpose attack on other men's vices, it zeroed in on the man who loved big words. "The ingenuity of the time and the soul's synderisis . . . doth demonstrate to us the vegetable circumference and the ventosity of the tropics." You could read all about it in Marston.

Jonson was beside himself when the worm turned. Though vain of his scholarship, he didn't like hearing that he smelled "all lamp oil" with study. An invitation to a duel going unanswered, he hunted down his enemy, "beat him and took his pistol from him," afterward "wrote his *Poetaster* on him." This comical satire, written the same year as *Hamlet,* shifts the scene from London to classical Rome. Thinly disguised as magisterial Horace, Jonson is his own hero, "poet and priest to the Muses." Crispinus-Marston is the villain. Given an emetic, he vomits up his gallimaufry of words.

Ben made more enemies than he needed. One was Marston's friend Dekker, "play dresser and plagiary." Shakespeare and his fellows felt the lash too—men of "the common stages, so they call them," says Rosencrantz. This was what Jonson called them. Warming to the work, he sneered at their part in the Essex rebellion. "Forty, forty shillings," says a character in *Poetaster,* bribed to attack the play's hero. This evoked the ill-timed revival of *Richard II*. Privy Council didn't like the political innuendo, and later took satisfaction in sending Jonson back to jail.

The Chamberlain's Men devised a crueller revenge. Enlisting Dekker's facile pen, they brought Jonson on stage, untrussing the humorous poet. Crowned with stinging nettles, he became a laughing stock in theaters on both sides of the Thames. "Not famous enough yet for killing a player," the "foul-fisted mortar-treader" aspires to satire and eats men alive. His "mastic" jaws work slowly, though. "Horace Junior," Dekker called him, already the pedant of subsequent times, "a candle by him burning, books lying confusedly."

Some think Shakespeare had a hand in Jonson's untrussing, and a Cambridge student play gives him credit for ending the stage war. In the second part of *The Return from Parnassus* (1601), "Kempe" and "Burbage" are talking about it. "That Ben Jonson," says Kempe, "is a pestilent fellow! He brought up Horace, giving the poets a pill; but our fellow Shakespeare hath given him a purge that made him bewray his credit," i.e., befoul himself. Later Jonson looked back, more in sorrow than anger. He wasn't moved by "what they have done against me," only sorry for some "better natures" among them, enticed by the others "to run in that vile line."

AN ARMED PROLOGUE lords it over the audience as *Poetaster* begins, high-and-mighty Jonson throwing down the gage to "base detractors and illiterate apes." Naturally, the armor was defensive. A year later, Shakespeare picked up the gage in *Troilus and Cressida.* His play, tilting at Ben's, has an armed prologue too, but not brought on "in confidence / Of author's pen or actor's voice." Shakespeare's suits his story, the Trojan War.

Surprisingly, he found the story comic. No play wittier than this one, said a commender of the first edition (1609). Full of "the palm comical," it stood comparison with the best comedies of Terence and Plautus. Theatergoers didn't agree and *Troilus and Cressida,* a fleering, scoffing kind of play, was never "staled by the stage," anyway the public stage, or "clapperclawed" by the vulgar. In our time where old verities aren't true, only old, Shakespeare's bitter comedy has come into its own.

On his bilious side he has more bile than most, and Thersites, a "stool" or privy for a witch, functions as Chorus. Dogging the heroes, he gives their character and says what they are up to. Some die, but tragedy gets its quietus from this scabrous reporter. Incandescent with hatred, his vision of humanity down in the depths might drag us down too, and when the hatred is felt as merely pettish this happens. But ugliness, sufficiently clarified, has its luminosity, like putrescent wood.

Fresh in Shakespeare's mind from *Hamlet,* the "Matter of Troy" had always absorbed him. Already in his early work you find him brooding on Sinon's treachery, a pendant to the rape of Lucrece. Treachery is his theme in *Troilus and Cressida,* prompted partly by thoughts of the Essex rebellion. Chapman, a rival playwright and poet, saw to it that he made the connection. His translation of Homer's *Iliad* (1598 and after) identifies Essex with "most true Achilles," the all-virtuous hero, not the man who sulked in his tent. Shakespeare accepts the identification, but his Achilles, like Essex, is only a valiant ignorance. Raging in commotion, he batters down himself.

A poet who mingled much smoke with his fire, Chapman got Shakespeare's bile flowing. Packing his play with outlandish words, he mocked the "proud full sail" of Chapman's verse. Hector, Latinate on the "dexter" side, Teutonic on the "sinister," catechizes boastful Achilles: "Think'st thou to catch my life so pleasantly / As to prenominate in nice conjecture / Where thou wilt hit me dead?" No one ever talked like that and Shakespeare knew it. Agamemnon's battle piece, a mouthful, tells how fierce Polydamas has beaten down Menon and how bastard Margarelon, holding Doreus prisoner, "stands colossus-wise, waving his beam / Upon the pashèd corses of the kings." Epistrophus and Cedius are dead, also Polyxenes and possibly Amphimachus and Thoas. Shakespeare left the actors to make of this what they could.

Medieval chroniclers imagined the Trojan War as a sort of knightly jousting, fair play, not fool's play. Inspecting these sources, Shakespeare used them as a backboard to hit off. Though never in Ireland with Essex, he knows what went on there, and the cormorant, a gluttonous bird of prey, is his image for the war. Helen, whose rape begins it, ought to be fair, painted daily with blood. Shakespeare's Chorus sees a war for a "placket," the slit in a petticoat, with anatomical suggestions. Popinjay heroes attitudinize colorfully, but common soldiers do most of the fighting and dying. Pandarus, a stay-at-home, calls them crows and daws after eagles.

Resuming the strategy of *Julius Caesar* where the noblest man of history becomes the hook-nosed fellow of Rome, *Troilus and Cressida* does a number on heroes. Nestor, the type of the sage councilor, turns into Polonius, an old mouse-eaten cheese, Ulysses is the dog fox, and Menelaus a louse infesting a leper. The Greek general Agamemnon, "six-or-seven-times-honored," loves prostitutes, to his credit, but hasn't as much brains as earwax. A high point of the play, the aborted combat between Hector and Thersites retouches Falstaff's fight with the Douglas but the lines are bolder, appropriate to farce. Thersites, not "of blood and honor," lives to tell the story. Hector, drunk with honor, is murdered and dragged over the field.

Here, Shakespeare meant to end with a sonorous couplet.

> But march away.
> Hector is dead, there is no more to say.

This needs peals of ordnance and the rites of war, flights of angels. But the "Shakespeherian Rag" seemed out of place for once and Shakespeare added an epilogue, telling of venereal disease.

An exercise in backing and filling, almost an anti-play, *Troilus and Cressida* votes against theatricality. Leading up to climactic scenes, Shakespeare undercuts them. Expectation locates the apex of his play in the duel between Hector and Achilles, "fell as death." Unlike the epic combat of Hal and Hotspur, however, this one never comes off. Troilus and Diomed are all for killing too, but can't get at each other. Not the stuff tragedy is made of, they hark back to Lysander and Demetrius, angry young lovers in *A Midsummer Night's Dream*. Ulysses speaks beautifully, not to the purpose, though. His counsels, one witness says, aren't proved worth a blackberry. This partial judgment might be suspect but plot backs it up and at the end things are worse than before. The famous "degree" speech, persuasive when you meet it in discussions of the age, is followed by bromides and gets nothing done. Swotting up Aristotle for their great debate in

Troy, Hector wins the argument but throws in his hand, no anticlimax more stunning.

To one ear, parts of *Troilus and Cressida* sound like early Shakespeare, reprocessed to serve an occasion, the Poets' War. Couplets, often banal, evoke the Player King and Queen. Meant to be heard as old-fashioned in *Hamlet,* in *Troilus and Cressida* this poetry that counts syllables isn't intentional, only itself. Giddy Troilus recalls the lust-besotted hero of *Willobie His Avisa.* A roman à clef that dates from 1594, it includes in its cast the "old player" W. S. Shakespeare's sluttish heroine, handed round among the Greeks, evokes the heroine of *Love's Labor's Lost.* Perhaps a vestige of the shadow play, *Love's Labor's Won,* is before us in Shakespeare's tale of love's pains earned.

But *Troilus and Cressida,* if designed as polemic, is too big for the job, like most of Shakespeare's occasional plays. Sometimes the sawdust heroes, getting beyond themselves, disconcert us with their truth, Agamemnon's, for instance—

> What's past and what's to come is strewed with husks
> And formless ruin of oblivion.

Sometimes the pompous diction, forgetting its target, turns jest to earnest:

> there is a credence in my heart,
> An esperance so obstinately strong
> That doth invert the attest of eyes and ears,
> As if those organs had deceptious functions,
> Created only to calumniate.

Making a "recordation" to his soul, Shakespeare's hero is saying "remember." But it isn't Troilus who stands before us, confessing his love's disgrace. Shakespeare is the speaker, his mind troubled "like a fountain stirred," and the graver context in which his new-old play is set is that of the sonnets, *The Phoenix and Turtle, Hamlet,* and *Twelfth Night.* "But oh, how vile an idol proves this god!"

Betrayal, not political but sexual, is the play's important business, and sexual anxiety the grease it runs on. The anguished poet of the sonnets speaks in the coarse disvaluing of Helen of Troy, kept with "a hell of pain and world of charge." "Things won are done, joy's soul lies in the doing." Cressida knows this. Any man may sing her, tormented Shakespeare says, "if he can take her cliff"—or clef or cleft! He is standing in the wings, all ears, when she tells them: "I will not go from Troy." This "daughter of the game," like the Dark Lady Rosaline, is like Juliet too, but a maculate Juliet, soiled in the working. Looking with a different eye at his tragedy of romantic love, Shakespeare mocks his achievement, and his new aubade or dawn-song replaces nightingales with ribald crows.

Eros, a perverted god, presides over the action (the war inside and outside being the same), and Shakespeare's ruttish heroes turn indifferently to women and men. Soldiers in his plays sometimes have trouble sorting out Mars and Eros, Hotspur, for instance, who longs to embrace his opposite with a soldier's arm, or York in the Henry VI plays, in love with an enemy's bearing. The rapt heart of Aufidius beats a tattoo when he looks at Coriolanus. *Troilus and Cressida* brings this ambiguous stuff to the front. Silky Patroclus, a male varlet or masculine whore, is Achilles' "brach" or bitch. But Achilles has a woman's longing to feed his eyes on Hector and sickens with this appetite until he can peruse him "limb by limb." In the air of Shakespeare's play, tainted with memories of Essex and Southampton, the whiff of decadence hangs heavy.

Like the Titans, old gods confined to the dark underground but always rebelling against the gods of light, emotion personal to Shakespeare seeks to control the play. *Hamlet* is still with him, *Othello* soon to come, and he is the cuckold, eaten up with passion, who sees his woman "bolster." Self lacerating makes great poetry, though.

> What hath she done, prince, that can soil our mothers?
>
> Nothing at all, unless that this were she.

The disappointed lover, Troilus—perhaps Shakespeare—banks on "rule in unity," supposing, i.e., that one can't be two. But the play disproves the rule. Bifold like the psychology it develops, it mingles different voices. Shakespeare's "comical satire" means to keep experience at the safe remove of laughter, but the buried life, recollected, contaminates the play. An impure medley of raucous laughter and pain, *Troilus and Cressida* is Shakespeare's version of the fortunate fall. Stumbling on its own reality, it invades us to the skin.

Time, a barrister or pilgrim, has a wallet at his back and into it go all our virtues, "alms for oblivion." Self-knowledge disappears in this all-eating receptacle or was never ours to lose. From the great *sic transit* speech, passed back and forth between Achilles and Ulysses, we learn that no man is lord and owner of himself, only knowing what he is "by reflection." Shakespeare is remembering his Phoenix and Turtle, realized in each other's sight. Unexampled for their constancy, his two "distincts" remain undivided. In *Troilus and Cressida,* however, a "bifold authority" distracts the lovers and the "inseparate" or indivisible thing falls apart. Abdicating its office, reason panders to will, or the will dotes, subservient to the poisonous thing it desires. This is why in the teeth of reason we have Hector's amazing turn for the worse. Self deceived and deceiving others, he seems much inferior to antiquity's famous hero, "enchanted" like his brother Troilus, almost a fool. But he isn't a figure of fun.

5

Treason in the Blood

On March 24, 1603, Queen Elizabeth died in the forty-fifth year of her reign. Before Shakespeare was born, the great Queen ruled England and was still there when he reached middle age. Most of her subjects knew no other ruler and most who did were sorry. She said her desire had been to reign for their good, her glory that she had reigned with their loves. English "never had, nor shall have, any that will love you better."

At seventy, Elizabeth still hunted, hawked, and went to plays. The Lord Chamberlain's Men played before her one more time the month before she died. But the execution of Essex, the unworthy favorite she cherished most, left her brooding on mortality, and in June 1602 she told the French ambassador that life had lost its savor. Ever stingy in matters of state but lavish in dress and liking to display herself, she owned two thousand gowns, some say three times that many. Toward the end, however, vanity palled and her wardrobe gathered dust. Listless with pain, she ate just enough to keep body and soul together, but though dying, she wouldn't lie down.

The Queen left no offspring. This troubled the realm—no tyranny worse than a ship without a rudder—and her councilors implored her to name an heir to the throne. She refused, perhaps believing herself immortal or perhaps not unwilling to anticipate a deluge "après moi." On her deathbed she gave in, whispering in Cecil's ear the name of "our cousin of Scotland." He was James VI, the first Stuart in England where he reigned as James I. Shakespeare in his *Henry VIII* tells how the "maiden Phoenix" begot him.

An era ended with Elizabeth's death and many poets memorialized it, not Shakespeare. "Bestow your time to write for England's Queen," an anonymous versifier urged him but got no response. Others among his acquaintance, angling for preferment in the upcoming reign, helped speed the transfer of power. Sir Robert Carey, the youngest son of Lord Hunsdon, first patron of Shakespeare's company, waited through the night outside the palace at Richmond. Getting the news of the Queen's death between two and three in the morning, he put spurs to his horse, then raced for the North and Holyrood Palace. Bonfires in the streets, lamenting the dead and saluting the living, saw him out of London. By nightfall of the third day, Carey was in Edinburgh, kneeling before a new king.

The man who received him didn't cut a kingly figure. James at thirty-seven shambled like an ungainly boy when he walked, his fingers fiddling with his codpiece. English ridiculed his big head, his rickety legs, goggle eyes, and slobbering tongue, too big for his mouth. Drinking, he seemed to eat his drink. He wore quilted clothes and hoped they were proof against an assassin's dagger. A coward, hence a despot, he might have said, "I am the state."

Taken unawares by manhood, the King lived with terrors, the legacy of childhood. His mother, Mary Queen of Scots, died at the axman's hands, a victim of the woman he succeeded. Murder stalked the famous and glamorous Queen, first Rizzio's, the secretary, killed in her sight while James was still in the womb, a year later that of the killer Darnley, her husband and James's father. Beleaguered by his nobility, most of them kilted ruffians, a lash-wielding tutor, and the bigots of the Kirk, he took refuge in books, stuffing his head with tracts on witchcraft, theology, and the divine right of kings. Profanity burned his ears, and at his instigation the Master of the Revels blue-penciled oaths by God's bodykins, His lid, liggens, lugges, lights, and sonties. Tobacco offended him too.

Not hypocritical, only frail, the King drew a line between precept and practice. Drowning his terrors, he turned the Court into a grog-shop. Even the ladies rolled about in their cups. An epicene, he drank mostly in the company of handsome young men. One, Philip Herbert, became Earl of Montgomery, a reward for favors rendered. "He pretended to no other qualifications," said Clarendon, the historian of the Great Rebellion, "than to understand horses and dogs very well." Later, Shakespeare's first editors dedicated the Folio to this vacuous nobleman and his elder brother William, Earl of Pembroke. Southampton, another favorite, got the grant of the tax on sweet wines, once conferred by Elizabeth on Essex.

Robert Carr, Earl of Somerset, adulterer and poisoner, was the fixed star in James's constellation. Vicious "Italians" in the tragedies of Webster and Tourneur give his likeness. As Groom of the Bedchamber, this pretty young Scot built an immense fortune, part of it plunder from the wreck of Ralegh's fortune. Out of favor with James, the old Elizabethan languished in the Tower, under sentence of death. In plays like *King Lear* and *Timon of Athens,* Shakespeare drew the picture of the Jacobean Court, less a gracious palace than a tavern or brothel.

James's Queen, Anne of Denmark, making the best of a homosexual husband, reared her three children, all ill-starred. Typhoid killed Prince Henry; Elizabeth, married to a German prince, lost her petty kingdom in the wars of religion; Charles, succeeding his father, died on the scaffold at Whitehall. The Queen, bony and plain to look at, had her own refuge, the theater, where wishes came true. Scandalizing her subjects, she appeared on stage in spectacular entertainments mounted by Jonson and Inigo Jones. Shakespeare in *The Tempest* created his own version, but his "insubstantial pageant" serves a greater whole. Blackness titillated Queen Anne and her contemporaries and once, daubed with makeup, she played a blackamoor herself. Her predecessor's wardrobe still hanging in the closet, she cut it up to furnish a masque.

James came down from Scotland like a wolf/sheep on the fold. In Newark-upon-Trent by April 21, he emptied out the local prison but hanged a cutpurse caught working the crowd. Conflicting signals, they typified the royal autocrat who posed as God's vicar. Like the new Leviathan or new God of the Calvinists, he moved in mysterious ways. Though the law penalized most felonies with death, it excepted petty larceny, the theft of goods under twelve pence in value. James, "newly in the seat," had a point to prove, however, and wanted the body public to know he could command. He wasn't crueller than Elizabeth, only less tactful, and both hanged eight hundred a year.

Like Shakespeare's duke of dark corners in *Measure for Measure,* the King didn't care to stage himself to the people. He wished England's Parliament would leave him alone but felt "obliged to put up with what I cannot get rid of." When he reached London, such multitudes thronged to meet him, "in high ways, fields, meadows, closes, and on trees . . . that they covered the beauty of the fields." This argued their love, smirking courtiers said. Not mollified, he answered: "I will pull down my breeches and they shall also see my arse."

Plague afflicted London in the spring of 1603, cutting short the royal progress. A portent of mischief, it seemed to comment on the end of Elizabeth's reign. Twenty years or so later, a more terrible visitation heralded the end of King James's. "Philosophical persons," scientists like Bacon, scoffed at these conjunctions. Making sense of portents and prodigies, they had their "modern," i.e. ordinary, reasons. Shakespeare, like his courtier Lafew in *All's Well That Ends Well,* differed from the "new philosophers." Monstrous evil engaged him and sometimes its opposite, good that is its own reward. But how these things should be eluded comprehension. Deferring to the event, he forbore to explain it and read what happens as "supernatural and causeless."

In the first year of the new reign, plague carried off more than 35,000 in London and environs, a sixth of the population. Those who could get away quit the city for the country, among them Ben Jonson, leaving wife and children behind. In Huntingdonshire with his old tutor Camden, he saw in a vision his eldest son, "child of my right hand," a bloody cross marking his forehead. Soon after came letters, telling of the boy's death. When the sickness abated, Jonson hurried back to town to welcome in the King. Handing a panegyric up to the throne, he said that James had been placed upon it by Heaven "to rule like Heaven." In last things, however, a sad equality governed, and kings, being men, had no more "their own" than others.

Fearing infection, James postponed his royal entry and accepted the crown in private, July 1603. In the new year, however, the mob had its traditional pageantry, a dramatic and symbolic occasion like Shakespeare's theater. The King was the cynosure, attracting to himself the loves, hopes, and fears of his subjects. "Afar off they spy him," riding a white mule, above his head a rich canopy, the "heavens." "The Tower serving that morning but for his withdrawing chamber," he stepped from it "into his City of London." Bound for Whitehall Palace, he came on through seven gates, like the doors at stage rear that opened on the platform stage. This costume drama moved slowly and it took the King half a day to reach Westminster from the Tower.

At Fenchurch, the site of the first gate, Jonson had the duty, deploying allegorical persons for the pageant. Beneath the feet of the British Monarchy sat Divine Wisdom, also the Genius of Man, presented by Edward Alleyn. Shakespeare and his fellow actors, Grooms of the Chamber, walked in the procession. Among the hangers-on who attended the King, they ranked above boys and pages, below sergeants and yeomen. From the Master of the Great Wardrobe, each received an allotment of red scarlet cloth. Four and a half yards of it made a doublet, hose, and cloak, the sleeve emblazoned with the royal arms. In the Wardrobe accounts recording this issue, Shakespeare's name comes first on the list. Some playwrights he knew wrote about the Coronation but he let it pass without comment.

For almost a year the theaters stayed dark and Shakespeare's company traveled, south to Bath and north to Coventry. Stratford wasn't far away and nothing says he didn't detour to buss wife and children. This scenario looks out of character, though, and the closer you get to him the less domestic he seems. Christmas revels saw him acting before the King at Hampton Court. Nearby, at Mortlake-on-Thames, lived his fellow actor Augustine Phillips. Late in November, the players, rehearsing at Mortlake, received a summons from Wilton, the palatial home of the Herberts, earls of Pembroke. James, keen on hunting and glad to be out of the plague-ridden city, had taken up residence there the month before. But his stay was off again, on again, and Salisbury, the county seat where things were livelier, lured him as the old year wound down. The invitation to the players, partly an expedient, was meant to provoke his return.

Wilton House, once a Benedictine abbey, came to the Herberts at the Dissolution of the Monasteries. Fire ravaged the house that Holbein built but later Inigo Jones rebuilt it. Grander than the work of either were the Cedars of Lebanon that still stand above the lawns. At Wilton Sidney wrote *Arcadia,* and his sister Mary, poet and patron of poets, married the second earl. "We have the man Shakespeare with us," she wrote to her son, telling him to make sure of the King. Lady Mary, a friend of Ralegh's, hoped to heal the breach between this friend and his sovereign, and though she failed, James's time wasn't wasted. Back in Wilton, December 2, 1603, he had his entertainment, *As You Like It,* with Shakespeare, tradition says, in the cast.

A reward of £103 compensated Shakespeare's fellows for their part in the Christmas revels. In February, when they played at Whitehall, the King added another £30, a "free gift" to make up for their losses in plague time. Generosity like this had no precedent in Queen Bess's reign, "good" but cheeseparing. Even before his arrival in London, James took the Chamberlain's Men under his wing. Newly baptized, they became the King's Men and wore the royal livery. Letters patent of May 17, 1603 licensed "these our servants" to play where they pleased "within our said realm and dominions." Mayors and aldermen thought this a bitter pill.

Pride of place among the servants went to Laurence Fletcher, "comedian to His Majesty." But this favorite from Scotland, not listed among the chief actors in Shakespeare's plays, looks like a sop to the King. Shakespeare's name comes next, acknowledging his leadership among the working professionals, after him Richard Burbage, Phillips, Heminges and Condell, William Sly, Armin the new clown, and Richard Cowley. The King's servants, James told them, were to exercise their art "as well for the recreation of our loving subjects as for our solace and pleasure." Solace him they did and he made an enthusiastic patron. Over a twelve-month period beginning November 1, 1604, he saw seven plays of Shakespeare's, old war horses like *The Comedy of Errors,* also new plays like *Othello* and *Measure for Measure*. Intrigued by *The Merchant of Venice,* he called for it twice. Father Gobbo in this play swears "by God's sonties" (saints) but when he played at Court in February 1605, kept a civil tongue in his head.

In the first decade of James's reign, the King's Men entertained him an average of thirteen times a year. This more than quadrupled Court performances under Elizabeth. Other companies enjoyed the royal favor too. Queen Anne lent her name to Worcester's Men; Alleyn's company, the Admiral's, became Prince Henry's Servants; and the boys at Blackfriars the Children of Her Majesty's Revels. No company came close to Shakespeare's, however.

Groom or flunky, he had his special duties, sometimes a cross to bear. In August 1604 he waited on the Spanish ambassador, the first such in England since Armada days. Don John de Velasco was the ambassador, Constable of Castille and Legion, Duke of Frias, Earl of Haro, Lord of Villapano and the Seven Infants of Lara, etc., etc. Lodged at Somerset House, he brought with him a small army of retainers. The splendid palace, second only to Whitehall, had room for all and then some. Once the residence of queens, in later days it preserved Shakespeare's will, under glass to discourage visitors from tearing off bits of the margin. Shakespeare and the other grooms made themselves helpful to the marquises, earls, barons, and knights. One scholar thinks they acted as tour guides.

On August 19, Spanish and English put their names to a peace treaty, then marched up the Strand to Whitehall. At Elizabeth's cavernous old Banqueting House, the King gave them a state dinner. Pembroke and Southampton, favorite claimants to the title of Shakespeare's Fair Youth, served as gentlemen-ushers. Lesser lights, the King's servants, brought in the dishes, bowing and scraping "four or five times." Dancing followed dinner, then the guests of the nation watched the King's bears fight with greyhounds. This, said an eyewitness, afforded great amusement to all.

WHILE DOING HIS DEVOIR in the summer of 1604, Shakespeare put the finishing touches to *Othello*. Though an exotic play, none more "romantic," it has its roots in early Jacobean London. At its deepest level, however, *Othello* tells of private anguish. Sometimes the beating heart breaks through the "continent" that holds it in this most painful of Shakespeare's tragedies.

First performed on Hallowmas Day, November 1, his military plus domestic tale led off the year's Christmas season. Whitehall's Banqueting House where he waited on the Spanish Constable furnished Shakespeare his stage. His public role has its complement in a public play, Venetian Doge and Senators standing in for Spanish grandees. Though the hero is burdened by "particular grief," official business needs attending to and "duties to the Senate" take a lot of his time. He isn't a mere sworder hired to fight the Turk but traces his lineage to men of royal "siege" or seat. Shakespeare's tragic heroes are like that, outsize "mirrors" in which we see a bigger version of ourselves.

But Othello, black like the "hollow Hell," is unique among the heroes, and it seems right to ask what Shakespeare thought he was doing. His black man, getting first place in the play, unsettles the hierarchies men lived by. Both glamor and scariness go with his "sooty" skin. An "extravagant and wheeling stranger," i.e., a traveler who knows about places beyond the civilized pale, he has seen the stuff of nightmare, cannibals and men with heads beneath their shoulders. Running through his life's story, vexed with chance and accident (but "hair-breadth scapes" set him clear), is how he sweeps away Desdemona. English, guessing at vast caves, empty deserts, and hills that touch the sky, shared her fascination. Jonson's *Masque of Blackness,* starring Anne of Denmark, capitalized on this.

Outside the theater, glamor shaded into scariness, and in 1600–1, ambassadors from Barbary found London not yet ready to accept them. "Strangely attired and behaviored," they killed their own meat, "sheep, lambs, poultry, and such like," converting their house in the city to a shambles. A portrait, still surviving, shows the leader in his flowing robes, turban, and carved scimitar. Above the black beard the eyes are full of menace. On a superficial view, these "barbarians" had nothing in common with Shakespeare. But like Joyce in *Ulysses,* drawn to Bloom the Jew, he saw in Othello's countrymen a distorted image of himself. For Shakespeare the outsider, different in his inmost place from everybody else, the black man seems an indicated hero.

Most in his time, instructed by old paintings and morality plays where the Devil is black, smelled a villain. *Plus ça change,* etc., and they didn't want their daughters covered with a Barbary horse. "Moors, Moorens, or Negroes" all looked the same to them. This "people of beastly living" had a wily side, however, remarked by Sir John Hawkins who "seldom or never found truth" in a Negro. (Hawkins was hunting slaves on the African coast and his victims did their best to elude him.) "Discontented at the great numbers of Negars and blackamoors which are crept into the realm," Queen Elizabeth planned to deport them. A popular proverb said you labored in vain if you tried to "wash an Ethiop" or wash a black Moor white. Shakespeare, writing *Othello,* meditated on the common wisdom, his taking-off point for the play.

Desdemona's love for the Moor has puzzled many, beginning with her parent, outraged Brabantio. "Monstrous," thought Coleridge, "to conceive this beautiful Venetian girl falling in love with a veritable Negro." But veritably Negro is what he is. Racial epithets, explicit and demeaning, sketch the man Shakespeare pictured, "the thick lips," "an old black ram," like the Devil himself. Even the hero wonders wistfully if blackness isn't ugly, at least in the eyes of his beautiful Venetian. Insisting on negritude, Shakespeare activates stereotypes, still recognizable, Othello as King Kong, Desdemona as Fay Wray in "the gross clasps of a lascivious Moor."

Shakespeare's immediate source, an Italian novella antedating the play by only a few decades, illuminates "everyman's" notions of color. Incidentally, it shows the playwright in his workshop, making a silk purse from a sow's ear. Venetian Cinthio's Othello-story, a vulgar and brutal tale of miscegenation, tallies with Shakespeare's earlier reading of blackness, vivid in plays like *Titus Andronicus* and *The Merchant of Venice.* Behind Othello stand Aaron the Moor and the Prince of Morocco, one a sexual athlete, the other hopelessly dim.

This has its minstrel-show side, potentially trivializing. See the black man roll his eyes and rack his brains. Two centuries later, that is what Pope saw, taking a hint from Iago:

> Not fierce Othello in so loud a strain
> Roared for the handkerchief that caused his pain.

Then comes the surprise, a great coup of theater but more than theatrical. Color in *Othello* functions as a straw man, and Shakespeare, who sets it up, wants it knocked over. This done, the dupe who might provoke laughter merges with the rest of us, "perplexed in the extreme." Convention, ever incurious, lives on the surface but Shakespeare, having learned things, insists on making "incision." Or rather Desdemona, his surrogate, does this. She sees Othello's "visage" in his mind.

But race, though not color, remains decisive for the play, and a racial opposition supplies its energizing power. Iago's malignity, not "motiveless," stems from sources you can point to, mean envy, egotism, greed, maybe lust, but shows at bottom as racial hatred, the little man's for his natural superior.

> He hath a daily beauty in his life
> That makes me ugly.

This sinister line, lifting the lid on a dismal soul and its secrets, tells of Cassio the lieutenant but takes in the general too. "Free and bounteous" in manner, no skulking in the shadows for him, he is the one who "must be found."

Style is the man and Othello's has the glory of far-winding horns.

> Keep up your bright swords, for the dew will rust them.

> Oh, now forever
> Farewell the tranquil mind! Farewell content!
> Farewell the plumèd troop and the big wars
> That makes ambition virtue!

Against the poet who can feel and sing like this, Shakespeare poses the commonplace man, incapable of singing and feeling. Menaced by amplitude, littleness calls it bombast, "horribly stuffed."

Shakespeare's positive includes its negative, and he accommodates the possibility his up-front play denies. The Moor, Cassio too, has a yen for big words. Each "paragons" fame, exceeding what others say of him, also making an extravagant reporter. Ambition in Othello, like a "just equinox" mingling light and shadow, doesn't always show as virtue, and sometimes the grand manner seems less grand than "exsufflicate" or windy. Approving the hero, Shakespeare looks at him shrewdly, not least when he resembles the playwright. Ardent beyond the common run in language and gesture, he pays a price for this, and *l'homme moyen sensuel* finds him an easy mark.

Self-criticism like all the plays, *Othello* introduces Shakespeare in his various guises. He is the poet who soars above an "ordinary pitch," also the icy regisseur. His villain comes close to capsizing the play and sometimes the villainy sheds a fiercer light than the virtue it darkens. Prodigious, whatever else, the fathomless evil Iago's artistry discloses wrings a tribute from his victims. "This is thy work." The work showing as imperfect, evil's instrument is blunted, but Shakespeare goes on undeflected. Like his baleful Don John in *Much Ado About Nothing,* another playwright manqué, he blocks out the stage, and his dramatic creations, "planted and placed and possessed," can't escape him. Others, wielding the world, had armies; he did it all with words. In Iago's chilling retort on the eminent man, raised up by birth or station, he put something of himself: "You are a senator."

Othello, no match for the villain, falls in his "practice," but Shakespeare won't call him not guilty. Compulsive like the Pontic Sea in faraway countries where the Ottoman rules, he surrenders to passion, judgment's enemy, abetting the "treason" that murmurs in his blood. This hero is culpable. Others in the play are like him, e.g., cynical Emilia, a willing tool in Iago's hands ("nothing but to please his fantasy"). Maybe Desdemona is like this, "obedient" to Othello's fantasy. Cassio, drunk on duty, is certainly like this. Roderigo turns the wrong side out and whose fault was that?

Readers who track Shakespeare from one play to another will recognize their old familiar, the moral poet of the Psychomachia. A fair fight between good and evil, this spirit war can go either way, and how the mighty opposites carry themselves makes the difference. So far, Shakespeare's crime and punishment play looks like the morality play it takes off from.

Bodies litter the stage as the curtain descends but survivors keep going—always, in Shakespeare's tragedies. Though darkness reigns in the *Othello*-world, light is the norm, and after the drunken brawl the dawn comes up on Cyprus. Nature abhorring dissonance, the dreadful bell that frightened them from their "propriety" is silenced. Defective psychology trips up the villain. Stunted himself, he measures others against his own littleness, Desdemona, for instance: "And knowing what I am, I know what she shall be." A different reading of psychology invigorates Emilia. Much falling, she has to speak, though it kills her. That is what it means to be human.

But the reasserting of norms and sanctions comes a little too late, not only for the dead, for those of us who must abide the ending. True, the ship of state rights itself and sails on. All the same, who cares that Cassio rules in Cyprus? Resuming *Julius Caesar* and its murder in the Forum, a pitiless Shakespeare makes us bear witness to the dragging down of the titan. In his secular version of the Beatitudes, first and last change places. Yea-saying won't do for *Othello*.

All men taste defeat but Shakespeare's tragedy tells a graver story, the fall of valor in the soul. "Once so good," the hero matches in his fall the height of his goodness, throwing in at last with the "general" (universal) enemy. This is the Ottoman, figuring the beast in man. Sexual torment, burning like the mines of sulphur, envenoms the story, and the buried life seems to fester just under the surface. Shakespeare's biographer, taking note of the fury that seethes in the words, must ask himself if the playwright threw a pearl away, richer than all his tribe. Shakespeare allows the customary "Addios" and a splendid gratuity summons the better past. "And say besides, that in Aleppo once." But Othello's valedictory is a clamor in a vault and the play's last tableau poisons sight.

The will vs. wit play, Shakespeare's model text, has its fearful symmetry, and desert, enacted, makes the ending endurable. Shakespeare's bleak recension spoils all that, however. Not "desert" but "wretched fortune" catches the heroine, "rash and most unfortunate" are words for the hero, and in the end the "dart of chance" brings him low. Imposed on by flimsy evidence—"modern seeming" is Shakespeare's phrase—he looks less guilty than dull or abused.

Another reading of man's estate, different from the homiletic one, is nagging at Shakespeare. It says that some are saved but others must not be, and whether Providence discriminates, nobody knows. Mystery envelops the play, blotted by tempests and a huge eclipse. Something prowls in darkness outside the walls, knocking to get in. Venice, not the shining city rising from the waters, is like a "grange" or lonely outpost in the jungle. Bulletins reaching the beleaguered place lack "composition," and reason, our tried-and-true resort, can't sift them.

Taken by surprise, Shakespeare's characters wake from sleep to find their city on fire. Though fear is epidemic, they can't tell you why they fear, and the questions they raise go unanswered: "What had he done to you? / I know not. / Is't possible?" In the night's dull watches, understanding seems palsied, and appeals to "proof," often ventured, echo like mocking laughter offstage. A sacrificer, no murderer, Othello strikes where he loves. Nature could hardly err like that without witchcraft, and you must invoke arcane power if you mean to make sense of the play.

Shakespeare does this, glancing at forbidden arts or the pull of the moon. (As the murder prepares, it comes too close to earth.) Unwitted by some planet, the hero runs lunatic. Trifles ensnare him, the famous handkerchief, for instance; however, as he tells them, "there's magic in the web of it." Corrupted by the "pestilence" Iago pours in his ear, the sufficient man falls in a trance. Readers will think of *Hamlet's* play-within-the-play, but *Othello* needs no poisoner making antic faces and the evil that destroys them is begotten on itself.

Making little of the "tragic flaw" (Othello is one not easily jealous), Shakespeare gives us instead a sense of frailty all round. "Treason of the blood," it doesn't preclude judgment, but where all are guilty, all are innocent too, and inevitably the scales tip toward pity. Moralizing is at least fatiguing: "the fruits of whoring," remissness, drunkenness, etc. Men being men, the best sometimes forget, and no one is so pure but some unclean thought keeps "leets and law days" in his heart.

Shakespeare's women characters comment on this. One is a courtesan but another is all innocence and the third, a maid-in-waiting, is no better than she should be. All speak for womankind. Recognizably themselves, at the same time they live along the same spectrum, so differ less in kind than degree. Some women, willing to do the deed in the dark, "abuse" their husbands, possibly Emilia among them. This self-righteous wife calls Bianca a strumpet. However, the "fallen" woman is as honest as those who "abuse" her. That is what she says, but Bianca's innocence carries guilt. Though Desdemona is guiltless, she has her Willow Song, a tale of loose loves. "If I court moe [more] women, you'll couch with moe men." Lodovico, "a proper man," hasn't escaped her notice. This hardly suggests that Iago is right about her. No supersubtle Venetian but not carved from alabaster, Desdemona is only human.

Near the end, Shakespeare's heroine prays for forgiveness, her prayer remembering Cassio's: "God forgive us our sins!" Neither is much of a sinner. Othello, who sins greatly, is guilty and not guilty, an equivocal condition underlined in the wretched heroes of Shakespeare's later plays. Acquitting him in part, it fails to save him, however. Bystanders, an ineffectual Chorus, want to moralize his tragedy but the best they can say is "I am sorry."

FOR SHAKESPEARE and his contemporaries, Venice meant fashionable women, some free-and-easy like Bianca in the play. Thomas Coryat, a roving reporter, told them about the women in his travel book called *Crudities*. Martyrs to fashion, they crowned themselves with towering headgear, nets of gold or silver dusted with precious stones. These "tires" took strange shapes—one, like a ship under sail, caught Falstaff's eye—and it needed dash and a high forehead to carry them off. London's tire-makers, promoting the taste of Venice, lived in Cripplegate, north of the river. Early in the new century, Shakespeare took lodgings with one of them, Christopher Mountjoy. In 1604 this artist-craftsman furnished Queen Anne with tires worth £59, a small fortune.

Mountjoy, a French Huguenot, fled to London in the wake of the St. Bartholomew's Massacre (1572). He ran his hair-dressing business out of the large house on the corner of Monkswell (Muggle) and Silver streets, inside the northwest angle of the Wall. Centuries after Shakespeare's time, German bombs destroyed the neighborhood, but an old map shows the house he lived in, twin-gabled with its penthouse "lid" extending over the shop-front. Lodgings on the second floor accommodated the Mountjoys, including daughter Mary, their apprentices, and "one Mr. Shakespeare." A legal document of 1612, looking back "ten years or thereabouts," says he "lay in the house."

Shakespeare moved to Cripplegate before or just after 1602, "thereabouts" allowing a year's latitude either way. Earlier work of his suggests that this wasn't a leap in the dark. His French Herald in *Henry V* (1599), recalling that Mountjoy who married Sidney's Penelope, recalls his humbler landlord too. A king's trumpeter, Humphrey Flood, is part of the shadow text. This latter-day herald, stepfather to an apprentice of Christopher Mountjoy's, carried messages between Paris and London. Shakespeare himself, though not traveling to Paris, had "*fausse* French enough to deceive de most sage *demoiselle* dat is *en France*." The lodging house in Cripplegate looks like his schoolhouse.

Some equip him with a language mistress, Mary Mountjoy. (He had bought a beginner's manual in Stationers' Row and she helped him turn the pages.) Cherchez-la-femme readers cast the tiremaker's daughter as Shakespeare's Dark Lady. But if he learned his schoolboy French in Silver Street, this was before he moved there, and Richard Field, an old acquaintance, was his means to the end.

Field, a distinguished printer, had his press around the corner at the sign of the Splayed Eagle on Wood Street. Early in the 1590s he gave Shakespeare's narrative poems to the world. Though of Stratford, he was no savage Boeotian, and texts in half a dozen languages, French included, appeared over his name. Thomas Vautrollier, another Huguenot refugee, helped get him started. Well-known in London's French Protestant community, Vautrollier printed fiery John Knox, lowering the temperature with King James's "Poetical Essays." When he died his press went to the widow, and Field, a model apprentice, took this Jacqueline for wife. Shakespeare, not yet installed in Cripplegate, likely got to know Mountjoy through her Huguenot connections.

The quarter he lived in mirrored the age, raffish and respectable, benighted, brutal, and caring. Stow walks us through the churches, more than were needed, but Shakespeare's neighbors didn't reason the need. One, St. Michael's in lower Wood Street, had a grisly trophy, the head of James IV of Scotland. A half century before Shakespeare was born, he died at Flodden Field with the flower of his chivalry. Romantic Scots were like that, good at throwing their life away, but English, already a nation of shopkeepers, meant to inherit the earth. Silversmiths, hardworking artisans, gave Shakespeare's street its name, and Jonson in a satiric comedy noticed the wigmakers: "All her teeth were made i' the Blackfriars, both her eyebrows i' the Strand, and her hair in Silver Street."

The halls of city companies, temples to profit, leaned over the narrow alleyways—Barber-Surgeons, striking fear in the hearts of the bravest, Curriers or leather workers, Hurrers or hatters, Bowyers who made archery bows. East of Bowyers' Hall, almshouses, twelve of them, sheltered the old and infirm. A compassionate benefactor saw to it that these poor folk, casualties of time, got seven pence weekly, also charcoal and faggots to keep off the cold. Monkswell Street, where the almshouses stood, remembered the well and the monks who lived beside it. But the age before Shakespeare's, looking with contempt on the mendicant life, drove out the monks, "lazy drones, unprofitable burdens."

In the parish church of St. Alban, grocers, masons, and haberdashers were the most of the congregation. Pope in his life of Shakespeare lays this author's failures to rubbing shoulders with the likes of them.

Some, rising in the world, became Lord Mayor. Sir John Cheke, a great scholar, had his monument in the church. His learning was intentional, like his fellow humanists' but unlike Shakespeare's, and he hoped to make the world a better place to live in. A jingle preserves his memory, Cheke who taught Cambridge and King Edward Greek.

St. Alban's faced Love Lane, "so called of wantons." Collared by policemen, they were whipped through the streets at the cart's tail. Worn-out whores went to the "sweating tub" but left a legacy, venereal disease. Young lechers in *Measure for Measure* joke about this, Lucio among them. Gone bald from disease, he points regretfully to his "French crown."

Behind the prostitute stood the wealthy burgher, plating sin with gold. Generally a Puritan, he raised his voice against whoring in the suburbs but left the brothels in the city alone. In these "houses of resort," part of his investment, whores like Kate Keepdown made their "metal" breed too. Usurers with a difference, they bred bastards. The law put down the merriest kind of usurer but the worser kind wore a furred gown. Faced with fox and lambskins, Shakespeare's Pompey said it was.

Riffraff like him kept an eye on the law, enforced by Sir John Popham, England's Chief Justice. He played "rex" among the whores and bawds, hounding "poor pretty wenches out of all pity and mercy." Shakespeare knew him at a distance. Prosecuting Essex at the trials in 1601, he appeared first as witness, then reappeared as judge. This took panache and even Popham's detractors allowed it. Though "mealed" or spotted with the faults he scourged in others, he liked wielding the lash. Donne, on the wrong side of the law in these days, said that only a guilty conscience stung worse. Shakespeare's wicked deputy Angelo reminds you of him, sanctimonious in public, something else when he shrugged off his robes. "What corruption in this life, that it will let this man live!" Readers and playgoers, agreeing with Isabella, look forward to the bad man's comeuppance. But Angelo cuts a figure—his evil "quits" him well, is how Shakespeare puts it—and in the happy ending the villain has a place with the others.

Nine constables kept the peace in Cripplegate ward and the local prison, called the Counter, awaited citizens who broke it. Pompey, rising in status from bawd to hangman's assistant, found this prison a faithful copy of the world outside the walls. Bullies and debtors, fops, gamblers, and drunkards looked out from the grating, all of them "for the Lord's sake," i.e., appealing to the charity of passersby in the street. Simon Forman, famous for astrology, spent much time in the Counter, dogged by his enemies, the "congregated College" of physicians. A sketch for Jonson's Alchemist, he could conjure and cast figures, cure the plague, piles, and pox. Some of Shakespeare's acquaintance, like the printers Field and Jaggard, were clients of his. Shakespeare's landlady, a client in need, went to see him on the sly. Madame Mountjoy had a roving eye and having got herself pregnant by one of the neighbors, wanted Dr. Forman to read her fate in the stars. Later he predicted the day of his death, a great triumph of the astrologer's art.

The open country, still lapping the borders of Shakespeare's city, began at St. Giles Cripplegate, within the postern of the Wall. In the Jews' Garden west of the church, Jews buried their dead, for centuries their only burying ground in England. Coming to London about the time Shakespeare did, Forman the magus lodged in these precincts where the Barbican stands today. Of old a watchtower that looked over the city, now a showcase for plays, it hides the bones of medieval Jewry. Ancestors of Shakespeare's patron, the Earl of Southampton, were laid to rest in St. Giles, also Foxe the martyrologist. In early days he served as tutor to the Lucys of Charlecote where once, tradition says, young Shakespeare went poaching. Joining Foxe in the chancel came Milton, in 1674.

Shakespeare's lodgings put him far from the Globe (though nothing in his London was all that far from anything else) but close to Finsbury Liberty, a pulpit for famous Ned Alleyn. This actor worked his magic at the Fortune Theater, half a mile to the north. If Shakespeare walked south, down Wood Street or Foster Lane, he came to the markets on Cheapside. Nearby in St. Paul's, "tall fellows" like his scandalmongering Lucio thronged the nave. Even the King couldn't tie the gall up in their slanderous tongues. Bookstalls in the church close made a dropping-in place for Shakespeare and the rest of London's literary life. Part of this life, the Mermaid Tavern on Bread Street hosted monthly meetings of "sirenical gentlemen," poets who sang like sirens. Legend, sprucing up Shakespeare's life, assigns him his place at the table.

Ben Jonson and his unfriendly collaborator Inigo Jones belonged to the "worshipful fraternity." Venerated by posterity, they look across the years like graybeards, and it comes as a surprise that both were only thirty in 1603. "Mad Jack" Donne came to the tavern on the appointed Fridays, joined by Beaumont and Fletcher, a pair of bohemians before the word was thought of, also the poet Hugh Holland. He wrote a sonnet for Shakespeare's First Folio, his one claim to fame. In letters from abroad, Coryat the traveler saluted them all but sent no greetings to Shakespeare, who lived only minutes away. Fifty years later, though, an anecdotal clergyman has heard of "wit-combats" between him and Jonson. This reminiscence puts Shakespeare before us, convivial as we would wish. But his fevers and ecstasies were all gone into the work, and among the worthies at the Mermaid he seems out of place, not a man to set the table on a roar.

Just east of Silver Street lived Heminges and Condell, in the parish of St. Mary Aldermanbury. As near anonymous as men can be, they defined the actor's trade. Both labored for the parish, one as churchwarden, the other as assistant or "sidesman." What these long-time associates had to say to Shakespeare, he to them, is a question. Perhaps their even tenor pleased him, calm after storms.

Domestic squabbles enlivened the years he spent in Cripplegate. In 1604 his host and hostess engineered a marriage of convenience between their daughter Mary and a former apprentice. He was Stephen Belott, French stepson of Humphrey Flood, the English herald. Having completed his six-years' apprenticeship, the bridegroom-to-be went "to travel into Spain," then came back to serve as Mountjoy's assistant. For this businesslike alliance, money was the linchpin. Shakespeare, with a head for same, acted as go-between. Neighbors spelled out his role in a protracted law suit, uncovered three hundred years later.

Though Madame Mountjoy "did give countenance unto" the lovers—through the screen of legalese you can see her smirking and ogling—young Belott hung fire. Not an ardent suitor, he wanted his dowry before he pledged troth. Shakespeare, deponents said, offered assurances, "the sum of £50 in money and certain household stuff." Belott in his testimony recalled a larger portion, £60 down, £200 more on the death of Mountjoy. In the event, £10 was what he got, plus assorted linens and household furniture on the order of Shakespeare's second-best bed. A bobbin box was part of the dowry, also two pairs of scissors, little ones, this son-in-law noted.

On November 19, 1604, he wed his master's daughter in St. Olave's church, Silver Street. For a year and a half the newly married couple lived and worked at home, gratifying the tire-maker who got them on the cheap, then, to his distress, set up as rivals. The death of Madame Mountjoy in October 1606 brought them back to Silver Street to keep house for the widower and help in the business. But this reunion soured quickly and in the spring of 1607 the restless couple moved again. Shakespeare stayed in touch, so said their new apprentice. However, he had to listen to a tale of woe, "divers children" now, "to the great increase of their charges." By 1607 he had had enough, and quitting his lodgings returned to the Bankside.

But he wasn't done with Silver Street, where old Mountjoy was drowning his sorrows. Powerless to stop this, his son-in-law watched the promised legacy melting away. On January 28, 1612, he brought suit for dower in London's Court of Requests. Belott vs. Mountjoy has its comic side. Witnesses swore by all that was holy but told conflicting stories, and on June 30 the court washed its hands of Frenchmen. Referring the case to the Huguenot church in Threadneedle Street, it appealed to the native shrewdness of the reverend overseers and elders. They gave their verdict for Belott but saw little difference between plaintiff and defendant, both "debauché." The judgment that went with the verdict had yet to be paid a year later.

Much depended on Shakespeare's testimony. Summoned from Stratford, he gave his deposition, May 11, 1612. He acknowledged his long acquaintance with both defendant and complainant and agreed that a marriage portion had been talked of. What this portion was, though, the witness "remembreth not." It appeared to him that defendant showed complainant great good will and affection. On the other hand, complainant was a very honest fellow. More than this he couldn't depose.

The year Shakespeare testified, he began a final history play, *Henry VIII*. Frenchmen show as foils for English in his patriotic hymn, and giving their likeness he went back in mind to Silver Street. French manners and dress ("fool and feather") irked his Englishman's reserve. Frenchmen curtsied, made moues ("fits o' the face"), and when it came to amours had no rivals. That didn't endear them either. Some English he knew learned from these lewd tutors tricks "to lay down ladies." Unbuttoned Shakespeare, his feet up on the fender, doesn't differ much from Tom, Dick, and Harry.

His recollection of life in Cripplegate, being heartfelt, is partial, though, and on his artistic side he tells a better story. In his so-called dark comedies, work of the time, corruption bubbles until it overruns the stew. Unexpectedly, this gave him pleasure. Absorbed in the work, he got out of himself or transcended himself. If he had "views," he checked them at the door of the playhouse.

VITALITY is the common term for Shakespeare's Cripplegate plays, *Measure for Measure* and *All's Well That Ends Well*. Scabrous and splendid, they celebrate the triumph of our erected flesh. Virtue is buffeted, manly strength melts in weakness, and though this has its deplorable side, you hear the note of self-congratulation. Tolerant maybe to a fault, Shakespeare likes acknowledging that we are all frail. His ribald clown Pompey speaks for both plays: "The valiant heart's not whipped out of his trade." The trade is a bawd's and the man who pursues it crams his maw with the wages of filthy vice. But his bum is enormous—even virtue takes notice—and this makes him in a beastly sense Pompey the Great. In Shakespeare's London, known also as "Vienna," "Florence," "Rossillion," the wicked throw their weight around. Virtue, altogether less substantial, can't do this, and its "steely bones" look bleak in the wind.

You can say of Shakespeare's twin comedies that a pair of shears went between them, i.e., they were cut from the same piece of cloth. For both, "a sinful fact" speeds the happy ending. This is "the bed trick" where one woman lies down in place of another. (Shakespeare is telling us that all cats look gray in the dark.) His ruttish heroes, easily imposed on, impose on others too. Heroic they aren't, and how we should reconcile our hearts to either has been a stumbling block for critics, beginning with Dr. Johnson. This critic, his eye on plot, thought one play would serve.

But Shakespeare, though always himself, never repeats himself. *Measure for Measure,* ostensibly a primer, unfolds the properties of government, but being indigenous, its truth is complex. Truth in *All's Well* isn't simple exactly; however, the "point" is more firmly established. Neither a first essay nor a twice-told tale, it presents the radical case. Saying which play came first is a labor for critics not less than scholars, and involves a comment on the nature of Shakespeare's art.

Measure for Measure, played before the King at Whitehall on St. Stephen's Night, December 26, 1604, likely dates from the summer before this. Evidence, both factual and critical, suggests to one reader that *All's Well* came a year later. Much occupied with current events, it steals covert glances at James's negotiations with the Spanish and Dutch, "front page" news in 1604. The King of France and Frenchmen represent the King of England and his subjects, and Florentines the Dutch insurgents. (English shouldn't favor either Spain or Holland, King James considered, and Shakespeare's French King is a neutralist too.) First Lord in the play, telling of a "peace concluded" between "Florence" and "Siena," has in mind the 1604 treaty between England and Spain. (Cooling his heels in Somerset House, Shakespeare kept an ear to the keyhole.) Within a year, says a letter to the English envoy at The Hague, the players were presenting "the whole course of this" on stage.

All's Well failed to score, however, and its vindicating has awaited modern times. No need to fault the public. It knows what it likes, prodigal Shakespeare who upends the horn of plenty. In *All's Well* he doesn't do this. His play stirs us powerfully but unlike its predecessor isn't thickened with matter-of-fact—no stewed prunes in a fruitdish of threepence—and though the moral law gets short shrift in both plays, only in the former do they bite it by the nose. Grossly physical imagery, not disgusting but cheerful, sets off *Measure for Measure.* Making love is "untrussing," elsewhere a game of tick-tack (inserting pegs in holes), filling a bottle with a "tun-dish" or funnel, groping for trouts in somebody else's river. Puritanical Angelo wrinkles his nose at this. People say that when he makes water, his urine is congealed ice.

Fishy in his origins, the villain is inhuman, but the others come from somewhere. We hear of Mariana's brother, gone down at sea, and young Claudio's "most noble father." A shadowy presence who never appears on stage, he helps render the sinful hero and qualifies his sinning. Not a Morality type, Claudio takes substance from the context he lives in. Angelo, merging people in their symbols, would like to deny this, as when he disposes of the hero's intended, merely a "fornicatress." But the play in its circumstantiality reproves him. This "dependency of thing on thing" is less conspicuous in *All's Well,* not so cluttered with messy life.

Like other "old" masters, Michelangelo in the age before him, for instance, Shakespeare grew more skeptical as he grew older, also less patient, another word for naturalistic. Fining down denotes the playwright of the late romances, already a-borning in his exemplary tale of Helena, St. Jaques' pilgrim. Showing defers to telling, vivid but declaring the mumbler of old proverbs. This role, attracting Shakespeare from earliest days, gets scope as the great wheel of his oeuvre comes full circle. Devoted to simple statement, he anticipates the synoptic theater of *Henry VIII* where First and Second Gentlemen report the joys and sorrows earlier Shakespeare would have put before us. Late Shakespeare is anxious to get on to other business. *All's Well,* reflecting this, looks like his second and more skeptical version of the way we live now, in Cripplegate and elsewhere. First Lord, cluck-clucking, moralizes this for him: "As we are ourselves, what things are we!"

A homiletic saying, it comprehends our mortality. As Shakespeare's comedy gets started, all enter in black. His comedy is leavened, not the same as calling it "dark," also marked by a certain brusqueness, appropriate to little people whose time and function are abridged. One woman being dead, why not take another? Birth looks forward to death, and the Countess, "delivering" her son, buries a second husband. Though Bertram's father lives a long time, sooner or later "haggish age" usurps his life. The heroine has a dead father too. Skilled in medical lore, he might have lived forever "if knowledge could be set up against mortality." But no contingency is more remote.

Against the mortal sickness that attacks the King, defenses go down. (In last things he's a beggar.) "Embowelled" of their doctrine, physicians at Court agree to let his disease run its course. His enfeebled condition that can't be redressed describes the rest of us, "as we are ourselves." Falling in our "flaws," gusts of passion or cracks in the fabric of our being, we blister reputation and only grace can reprieve us. Unluckily, though, "skill in grace" isn't part of our equipment. Lavatch, a clown, intimates this, bad news for Shakespeare's dramatis personae. But when hope is coldest the greatest Grace lends grace, and this is how the ending is happy.

Shakespeare's play isn't religious ritual or an "auto-da-fé" (act of faith), and grace needs its visible presenting. The fairy tale, mistaken by many for romantic hocus-pocus, supplies it. Helena, paging through her father's recipe book, finds a magic potion that can quicken a rock, breathe life into a stone. On her efficient side, however, she isn't like the girl next door raised to the *n*th power but a heavenly actor, and there is more to the ending than nature was ever conduct of.

Downplaying human agency, *All's Well* is less dramatic than *Measure for Measure,* also more severe on our pretensions. Captive to "blood," Shakespeare's characters remember their beginning in their ending. Though his King of France stands in for King James, in his own eyes a latter-day Solomon, the French King is no Solomon but "wrapped in dismal thinkings." (At Whitehall they didn't draw conclusions.) Trying on the role of god-from-the-machine, he fumbles it badly, and the power he confers on Helena starts a palace revolution. Later, learning nothing, he empowers Diana too, making sure that things won't end well. "All yet seems well," says this innocent, however, as all go off to a flourish of trumpets.

Even Helena is hoodwinked, "idolatrous fancy" prompting her

love for Bertram. This reprobate who can't see but wants to choose for himself is Shakespeare's root or radical hero, not tested or matured, only confirmed. (He has his antecedents, pale carbon copies, Proteus in the *Two Gentlemen* or that other Claudio in *Much Ado About Nothing*.) The ending subdues him to his fallen condition, but the scales never drop from his eyes. Shakespeare's Second Lord disputes this, saying how Bertram, stung by a letter we aren't privileged to see, changes "almost" into another man. Maybe Shakespeare intended us to credit this change. But he reserves it to the wings or the green room.

Measure for Measure has its deus ex machina but for getting things done, character is the critical agent. Emergent in the Duke, it shows as nobler than its just occasion in Shakespeare's gimlet-eyed Isabella. In the beginning the ducal hero sneaks away "privily," lending his deputy his terror. Like squeamish King James, he keeps the wind between his subjects and his nobility. (Truth to tell, they stank "in some sort.") Oddly, Shakespeare's villain resembles Duke and King and complains that the common people, barging into the great man's presence, stop the air.

But where fastidious Angelo is a villain dismissed to happiness and King James a fool in the grain, the Duke isn't static and his unfolding character keeps this kettle on the boil. Lessoned at the end, he forsakes his monastic nook and rejoins the full stream of the world. Also, driven by the flesh and the devil, he gets married. We didn't expect that of the standoffish man, not "much detected for women." Some think sexual slings and arrows force him to take cover, but he says he is proof against "the dribbling dart of love." "Dribbling" (like a weary penis) makes us laugh and blanch but doesn't do justice to Eros, and by-and-by love's shafts find their mark. The Duke, who boasts a "complete bosom," isn't himself until this happens.

Isabella, met in Act I, has entered a nunnery but wants a stricter restraint than her order imposes. Life in "Vienna," a cauldron of unholy loves, offends this custodian of the negative virtues, and taking refuge she means to escape it. By their similitudes you shall know them, however, e.g. death, like a bed that longing has been sick for. As Act V concludes, the heroine is preparing to strip herself to this bed and yield her body up to "shame." Anyway, the Duke hopes so and the ending is happy as she falls in with his wishes.

In *All's Well's* less forgiving world, metamorphoses are out (but not the volte-face change, defying explanation). A "fated sky" operates, modifying our slow designs when we ourselves are dull. Intolerably, though, it does the same when we are quick or forthcoming. "Philosophical persons," problem-solvers who look the Sphinx in the eye, beg to differ. Disbelieving in fatality, they write Self Reliance over their lintel. Helena, Shakespeare's heroine, is one of these persons. Down in the dust, she turns compliments aside, only a "babe," "the weakest minister," etc. In her closet, however, she sings a different tune. Her remedies lie in herself.

Not a villain, only pertinacious (but what pertinacity!), she puts you in mind of villains like Cassius, no "stars" in his psychology, or Iago who sees the business and banks on his will to transact it. Emancipated Edmund, a self-made man in *King Lear,* sounds like her too. In *All's Well,* dark clouds are building. Shakespeare gets above the battle, though, and inspecting self-assurance, finds it less wicked than comic. The same point of vantage buffers him in *Measure for Measure.*

Helena, partly his target, casts herself as love's martyr, plodding barefoot along the cold roads. The letter that draws her picture is written in heart's blood but means to wring tears from a penitent husband. (He'll miss her when she's gone.) This type of Patient Griselda is weak where men are strong. Real Helena has all the weakness of those acts of God underwriters wash their hands of. Her intentions being "fixed," she won't take No for an answer, and marks down her man like a predator appointing its prey. (Bertram quailed when he saw the look in her eye.) Parolles, the comic villain whose evils are "fixed" in him, has this integrity, aloof from praise or blame. Both are full of sap and you can't embarrass either. The immemorial bluestocking, not long on humor or self-consciousness, Helena anticipates Ibsen's New Woman. Shaw, sensing the resemblance, supposed that Shakespeare for once was on the right track.

Posterity prefers its Shakespeare democratic, and in *All's Well* he seems to oblige. Bertram, rejecting his lowborn wife, gets a lesson in priorities:

> Honors thrive
> When rather from our acts we them derive
> Than our foregoers.

Promoting a competition between virtuous acts and inherited virtue (i.e., noble blood), *All's Well* backs the former, personated by little Helen, a version of the country boy from Stratford. The blood in her veins is the same as the King's, and if you poured the two together, the eye couldn't tell them apart. So much for titles and the hierarchy they pretend to.

This genial egalitarianism is too easy, however, and Shakespeare, though deep down a leveler, has more and less than politics in mind. His meanings are multiple and blood, meaning an inherited title, also means our inherited flaw. "Treason of the blood" (harking back to *Othello*), it brings the king and the beggarmaid down to one level, not a plateau, ground level.

Unlike puffed-up Bertram, Shakespeare doesn't belittle them for what they don't have. All "fill a place," villainous Parolles no less than the King. Both say so and linguistic parallels insure that we make the connection. Parallels are everywhere in *All's Well That Ends Well,* like a children's cutout that shows the same on either side of the fold. As language echoes itself, incidents recur, asserting a community between villain and hero and villain and clown. King and Countess have things in common, so do Helena and Bertram. Parolles deceives Bertram, Helena following suit, while Bertram & Co. deceive Parolles. Shakespeare's characters come from opposite ends of the spectrum but one touch of nature makes them kin, Angelo's discovery in *Measure for Measure.* All are frail, not much discriminated either by birth or activity. In this democracy all are equal, i.e., insufficient. Equalizing our chances for getting things done, Shakespeare doesn't rate them highly.

The Ruritanian war in *All's Well,* bungled business where they charge their own soldiers, gives activity's likeness in the public sphere. Even Caesar, unrivaled for military virtue, couldn't cope with this disaster. Caesar = Helena (as greater things speak to less), and Helena as romantic heroine can't cope either. But Heaven delights to hear her prayers and she unravels the "goodly clew" or tangled skein the fates toss in her lap. We mustn't lay it all to Heaven, though, and partly she can thank herself, not her strength, her weakness. Both *Measure for Measure* and *All's Well* act out this surprising conclusion.

Adulterating her goodness, Shakespeare's heroine wins as she loses, the point of the bed trick. (The loss of men is the "getting" of children, and though women don't "lose" the way men do, the clown's bawdy paradox holds.) Morality finds this expedient offensive but nature or blood, aspiring to sovereignty in our little kingdom, overrules its counsels. This "treason of the blood," just what you would predicate of our fallen condition, has its decorum, however. Roses are known for thorns, and passion, resembling them, goes with us as we are human. Many rue its power but Shakespeare's Countess, worldly wise, calls it "the show and seal of nature's truth."

"Natural rebellion," overbearing reason's force, destroys the hero in *Othello,* but in *Measure for Measure* and *All's Well* passion's victory works out for the best. Even for readers familiar with Shakespeare, the man who sees all round, this apparent contradiction is hard to come to terms with. Consulting Italian Cinthio for Othello's story, he turned the page and found the ground plan of *Measure for Measure.* In both, the fire in our blood rages out of control, and that is true for *All's Well.* In his trio of plays that date from the same period and sort through the same materials, the same question governs. "Who can control his fate?"

But in the comedies it isn't heard as despairing. Capitulating to fate, Shakespeare's characters are equable about this. They put on "the destined livery," taking service with "the prince of the world." Out of pocket or out of grace, they don't have much option. One, a poor fellow, says he would live, while another must go the way the devil drives. But these observations, parceled out between the clowns, aren't simply concessive, as when we make the best of things. Much good comes from taking service with the devil and his livery fits those who wear it. Shakespeare's pharisee, seeing the light, thinks we ought to write "good angel" on the devil's horn.

The comedies, like a debate that never gets resolved, go back and forth, and the backsliding deputy, coming down to earth, is rebutted by the heroine, still "enskied and sainted." Posing weak-kneed Claudio, she has a question that expects its prompt disclaimer. "Wilt thou be made a man out of my vice?" Playgoers in our time, easygoing as to vice and indifferent to chastity, wonder what the problem is, but the context demands a negative answer. The last scenes of Shakespeare's play bid for a different answer, however. (Readers will note the different context.) All are "molded out of faults," Mariana tells us, even best men, and the best become better for being a little bad.

This mix of bad and better presents our "mingled yarn," embodied in Helena, her name recalling Helen of Troy. Both virgin and mistress, friend and enemy, wise counselor and traitress, she plays different parts in one person. Her maculate parts don't kowtow to her good ones, and "pilgrimage," with its overtones of expiation, is a misleading figure for *All's Well.* Expectant readers expect an agon but get a "composition," auspicious for good. The great speech in the play, turning drama into apothegm, tells of this: "Our virtues would be proud if our faults whipped them not, and our crimes would despair if they were not cherished by our virtues."

Moralists think Shakespeare must mean that our virtues whip our faults. But his "cherished" is intractable and has to raise eyebrows.

What! Are we not to whip out the old Adam? Accommodating Shakespeare won't let us do this, though. He thinks the relics of bad behavior are "incensing," like perfume.

Angelo's crude question, "which had you rather," justice or mercy, does nicely for the play as pièce bien faite. But a graver opposition pits Barnardine, our "gravel heart," against the Duke who must correct it. Toward the end of the play, when "the unfolding star" calls up the morning, these two salute each other. On his way to execution, Barnardine comes first, "desperately mortal," i.e. lapsed in mortal sin, at the same time incorrigibly human. How do they know he is coming? Pompey answers: "I hear his straw rustle," no line in Shakespeare scarier than this one.

But the Duke has a charm, efficient against the darkness. Laying down the law in Sodom, he undertakes to do this "by cold gradation [deliberate steps] and well-balanced form." His form is comprehensive, though, and takes in what it schools. This insures that our worser half will live to disgrace itself again.

"Scope," meaning latitude, is one of Shakespeare's words in *Measure for Measure*. Angelo, parsimonious as ever, asks for "the scope of justice" when the great ax, falling, bruises to death. Sentimentalists, all for latitude, would rather make the law a scarecrow. But the Duke is at fault in giving the people scope. Excessive for Claudio, its immoderate use turns into restraint. Meanwhile Shakespeare, canvassing his special cases, looks for ground to stand on. He knows what proper scope isn't, not the mercy that confuses liberty with license and not inhuman justice but the jar between. In this ambiguous place, mercy and justice season each other. This seasoning that cancels absolutes is another of his words.

All's Well takes its cue from *Measure for Measure* and the villain, though crushed, gets back up on his feet. But it isn't lenity that saves him. Simply the thing he is makes him live. Shakespeare's bad means to good ends, Parolles is the one who guarantees the happy ending. Lucio, the knave who verifies the Duke, has this role in *Measure for Measure*. Others in Vienna or Rossillion grudge these bad instruments, e.g. the Duke, our emblem of rectitude. Haunted by Lucio, he means to stop his wagging tongue. The scurrilous man is our old Adam, though, and at the end has yet to be silenced. This burr will stick.

6

The Wine of Life

JACOBEAN SHAKESPEARE is primarily the tragic playwright, executioner of Othello, King Lear, and Macbeth. Impersonal, a word for the playwright, describes the headsman too. Steeped in blood, he kept going until wearied with carnage, then turned to romance. Outside the theater his days went by routinely, occupied with money making, births, marriages, and deaths. Punctilious in business matters, on his personal side he lacks definition, and for this his readers, perhaps the playwright too, must appeal to the plays. In the summer of 1605 he became an uncle for the second time. Thomas Hart was his nephew, christened by Stratford's vicar on July 24. One of the three sons of Shakespeare's sister Joan, he lived for many years in the Birthplace, surviving into the Restoration. Shakespeare's will remembers two of his nephews but the name of this Thomas escaped him.

The year 1605 brought a visit from Katherine Rogers, up from the country to marry Robert Harvard, butcher of Southwark. Two years after the marriage, they had a son, John. Rejecting the past, this Puritan clergyman started life afresh in the New World, later giving his name to Harvard College. Thomas Rogers, Katherine's father, served Stratford as ale-taster, rising to bailiff. Elaborate wood carvings, offensive to Puritans and their cult of simplicity, adorned his house on the High Street. The bear and ragged staff remembered the earls of Warwick, whose family crest this was. Shakespeare in his histories, chronicles of the old days, not always good but worth preserving, is their annalist.

Weddings and christenings brought joy but sadness followed—predictably, on the "heel of pastime"—and these first years of the century deprived him of some he knew. An early acquaintance, Richard Quiney, died in 1602, killed in a brawl with retainers of Stratford's manor lord. Pope the Clown, like Shakespeare a charter member of the Chamberlain's Men, went two years later, then, in 1605, Augustine Phillips. The loss of this multitalented man—actor, dancer, and musician—left the company poorer. In his will, Shakespeare's name heads the list of legatees. But the master of valedictions wrote no memorial for Phillips or anyone else. Words were "mouth-honor," breath without substance, or he was like the expert fixer who can't fix things at home, so left his personal life unrecorded.

Plague, never quiet for long, sent his fellows on tour in the fall of 1605, again the next summer. They traveled west to the coast of Devon, north to Leicester, east to Dover and its cliffs. Halfway down the cliffs hung a man who gathered samphire, "dreadful trade." Edgar, reporting this in *King Lear,* sees nothing, however, and perhaps what Shakespeare wrote was all hearsay. More than once, he and the others played Oxford and Cambridge. Some picture faculty and students in these university towns rolling out the welcome mat, and the students may have done this. The faculty, preferring plays in Latin that kept to the unities, extended no welcome to Shakespeare.

Traveling or at home, he paid attention to his portfolio. Two days before Richard Quiney fell wounded in the fight with Greville's men, he bought land in Old Stratford, down the road from New Place. Most of it was farm land, 107 acres, pieced out with another 20 acres in pasture. William Combe, lawyer of Warwick, and his nephew John, a Welcombe money lender, sold this property to Shakespeare for £320. Tenant farmers, Thomas and Lewis Hiccox, occupied the land. Subsequently, Lewis Hiccox turns up as an innkeeper on Henley Street. Shakespeare a) sent him packing, b) boosted this former tenant into a better job. He himself was in London when the Combes made over their right, and his younger brother Gilbert took possession for him, setting his hand and seal to the conveyance.

He couldn't own too much in Stratford. Though London offered a fairer field for investment, he put his money in the place he grew up in. For most, this argues deep-rooted affection but another guess says that old memory rankled and the newly successful man had something to prove. Less than five months after the purchase of the Old Stratford "yardlands," he bought a garden cottage and its quarter-acre plot on the south side of Chapel Lane. The Gild Chapel, a house of memories, overlooked it, and opposite lay the gardens of New Place. He had been planting fruit trees, like the famous mulberry, and wanted the cottage for his gardener. Or he wanted it because it was there. This was "copyhold" land, held by Rowington manor, and he had to swear fealty to the dowager Countess of Warwick. Shakespeare's tenure was fee simple but old forms prescribed his oath of allegiance. "Ratifiers and props," as he called them in *Hamlet,* they set him in a context, linking past and present. The context was partly fictive but the more it receded, the more he insisted on it in plays.

The same day his nephew Thomas Hart was christened, he made his most ambitious investment, buying up "tithes" in Stratford and three neighboring hamlets. Shrewd Abraham Sturley had suggested years before that Shakespeare involve himself in a purchase like this one, saying how it "would advance him indeed." A medieval holdover like the oath to the manor lord, a tithe was a tenth, the fraction of each year's produce that supported the parish priest. New "presbyter" replaced old priest, but the practice of tithing—legalized extortion—continued. First the Crown took this tribute, later the village corporation. Money knew no creed.

Even before the Dissolution, the Church, farming out its right, helped line the pockets of local investors. In 1544, the Barker family got the right to the tithes of Stratford's College, this lease running for ninety-two years. Pocketing a rental fee, the Barkers sublet to others, forty-two in all when Shakespeare bought in. From Ralph Huband he acquired one-fifth of the whole, paying £440 for the right to collect half the tithes on "corn, grain, blade, and hay" in the villages of Old Stratford, Welcombe, and Bishopton. Also he enjoyed a one-half right to the "small" tithes (on wool, lamb, etc.) in the parish of Stratford. Farmers in Stratford and the outlying districts still worked their "pelting farms" in the medieval way, not yet cramped by enclosure. Pasturage remained common for sheep, horses, and kine, and farms were tilled in strips or allotments. This would change.

Shakespeare's investment, vindicating lawyer Sturley, returned 14 percent, a price to earnings ratio of 7 to 1. In money terms, it brought him £60 a year and rising. A common laborer's annual wage in the previous decade came to roughly £7. Well-to-do Shakespeare grew in prestige with the growth of his personal income. Already, as master of New Place, he had his special pew in Holy Trinity church. Buying the old religious tithes made him a lay rector, with the right to be buried within the rails of the chancel. In 1605, having restored the fallen fortunes of his father, he stood at or near the top in his home place.

ALSO IN 1605, Shakespeare wrote *King Lear.* As disjunctions go, none seems more absolute, first the prudent businessman, then the angler in the lake of darkness. Notorious for unsignaled switch-overs, many of his characters are like him. Or he is like them, jumping but not bridging the gap from here to there. This volte-face way of doing things shows in his first history play where Burgundy, a Frenchman, switches sides at a word. "Done like a Frenchman," says a scornful reporter. "Turn, and turn again." Shakespeare, quick-change artist, had this facility. He wasn't going over to the enemy, though, only paying his respects to friends and foes, public and private.

Absorbed in his business deals, was he vamping till ready? No reason to think so. Business was his pleasure, including theater business. Others in the older time share his sedulous but laconic concern for detail, and you glimpse him in the craftsmen who built the great cathedrals. *Ghiselbertus hoc fecit* ("I, Ghiselbertus, made this"), one of them said, letting it go at that. But Shakespeare wasn't a type, and no other artist gives his special quality. Here and there his plays elucidate—*King Lear,* for instance, where two energies oppose one another. "Ripeness is all," First Philosopher says, a passage that sets the heart beating faster. But it doesn't stand alone, and Second Philosopher has an answer, banal as everyday: "And that's true too." Telling of essential Shakespeare, this line of Gloucester's counts as much as the famous line it responds to.

Chaotic in matter but not form, *King Lear* makes an order, accounting for its basilisk-like fascination. Playgoers as toughminded as Johnson had to avert their eyes but terror is Shakespeare's element. At his Atridean feast, "pelican" daughters drink their father's blood or stick their boarish fangs in his body. An old man, tied to the stake, is like the blind bear in the arena. Lust for profit, a commonplace motive, made the bear-garden run but a vision drives the play. Across the dark stage, lighted fitfully by commotion in the heavens, madmen lead the blind. Humanity preys on itself and bestiality, like the Centaur's, describes the human condition. Shakespeare's prime truth is the snuffing out of virtue, and though an Act V reprieve looks potential—only "send in time," they say—this regisseur with a play to finish hurries on the business. At the end he gets the job done, cause for bleak satisfaction.

Shakespeare isn't reveling in bleakness exactly, but the executive impulse is paramount for men like him, and he likes managing his quarries of the slain. Also he likes wheeling on the persons of the play, pleasure incident to artistic composition. A good example is the Blinding Scene, introduced by back-and-forth between Gloucester and Cornwall:

> But I shall see
> The wingèd vengeance. . . .
>
> See't shalt thou never. Fellows, hold the chair.

Albany, an all's-right-with-the-world kind of man, is Shakespeare's special target. Meant to point the play's "moral," a too-smooth speech of his says that friends will taste reward, "and all foes / The cup of their deservings." But the line is metrically deficient and Albany's "O, see, see!" directing attention to the death of the king, must repair it. This is instruction.

Shakespeare's "counterpointing" speaks of design but his play is asymmetrical and he gets low marks in the moral calculus that fits the punishment to the crime. Later in the century, revisers put their hook into the nostrils of his Leviathan, wanting to make these things square. Cyril Tourneur, one of his contemporaries, said what that means for drama: "When the bad bleeds, then is the tragedy good." But Shakespeare, though not averse to bloodletting, doesn't discriminate between good and bad. His text is St. Paul's, the unknowing philosopher: "on whom it will, it will; / On whom it will not, so." It was never his business to justify God's ways to man.

Some of his characters are more sinned against than sinning, and often the best are the ones who find out the worst fortunes. Gloucester's "flawed" heart bursts, and in Kent, tough but sorely tried, the strings of life begin to crack. Shakespeare's heroine dies too, perhaps compromised by goodness. Cordelia's refusal to heave her heart into her mouth makes some uneasy, but her silence, not a fault, tells of virtue. Different in the grain from Goneril and Regan, Cordelia cannot speak "because" the heart of a fool is in his mouth but the mouth of the wise is in his heart. Later, going about her father's business, she dies. Fellow-feeling, washing her eyes with tears, begets the ending. A looker-on says how pity in Cordelia, resembling our worser part in the old spirit war, seeks, "rebel-like," to be king, a surprising way to put this. In the context of the Lear World, provident men and women will turn pity's counsels aside.

Panoramic where *Othello* is focused, *King Lear* shifts its scene from the palace to the open country, a field of battle, the British camp. But Shakespeare's to-and-fro seems aimless, and no eye watches over the sparrow. Both good and bad deny that, more than one of them assigning a supervisory role to the stars. Villainous Edmund creates a tutelary goddess, while others think the gods throw stones of sulphur at the wicked. Or they kill us because they like to, malignant purpose being better than nothing.

Shakespeare, unclear as to purpose, doesn't "anthropomorphize" the world of the play. "Visible" spirits were for masques, his stars look on impassively, and the gods don't come down on call. But *King Lear* infers connections, different from that Shakespeare whose personal life denies or conceals them. Bad things happen to the wicked when they turn the wrong side out. "A tailor made thee," the good servant tells his opposite number. This bad man's soul is in his clothes, not enough soul to stead him. Cornwall and the others, sweeping aside the forms of justice, unstop the vials of wrath. This works out to suicide, the life dissolving that wants the means to lead it. A common term, dessication, associates Shakespeare's villains. "Slivered and disbranched," they cut themselves off from the source of their being. So it happens that they wither or their hearts turn to stone. In the Trial Scene, macabre fooling with a point, one of them turns into a joint stool.

Transformations for the better enliven the play. Gloucester learns to see when he loses his eyes and ingenuous Edgar becomes the hero, adept in "the art of known and feeling sorrows." Lear, losing the world, gains his soul. In the beginning his love, others' too, is a commodity, measured in ponderable ways. The notorious Love Test follows from this misreading. "Which of you shall we say doth love us most?" Subsequently he discovers that plainness is more than eloquence, and meager lead buys more than silver and gold. St. Paul, Shakespeare's study from earliest days, is on his mind when the mad king comes to himself again. "In the heaviness of sleep / We put fresh garments on him." For the play as "Commedia," this putting off/putting on is decisive.

But the saving change Shakespeare's metaphor announces doesn't change the course of the plot. Climbing the mountain that leads up from our vale of sorrows, Lear is like Sisyphus, pushing his stone before him. (If you call the mountain Purgatorial, you have to have a Heaven in prospect.) The stone, a dead weight in the present, figures guilt, not particular but generic. Shakespeare's king hopes to discharge it and to hopeful readers his penitential suffering looks like the means to this end. "Protestant" Shakespeare is indifferent to works, however, and the stone rolls back to the beginning.

Breaking new ground in *King Lear,* Shakespeare presses further on the dark country already staked out in *Othello*. Though new and old are never quite the words for him, the accent marks are new. Still compelling his attention, sin's wages seem less exorbitant now than the wages of being human. We come wailing from the womb, spirits but "grossly clad," and the air we breathe smells of mortality. The tragic life reflects this carnal dimension.

An emblem for tragedy is Lear's "wheel of fire," descending from medieval accounts of the damned. Farther back is Greek Ixion, often noticed in the emblem books bound to his wheel. This type of unbitted lust meets and focuses much turbid emotion in Shakespeare. The emotion is sexual, another instance of biography infiltrating the art. Disordered sexuality, livid in half a dozen plays beginning with *Hamlet,* rages unchecked in this one. Haunting the maddened King, it arouses his wicked daughters, also the Bedlam. The beadle whips the whore he lusts to use "in that kind." Like the father, the bastard son finds the "forfended place." This playwright wants "civet" (perfume) to sweeten an inflamed imagination. Readers have a clue to Shakespeare's tragic period in his too-potent ravings, "his" because heard from the wings or the flies. What sets him going remains a mystery, though, vexing in our age of cocksure etiologies.

Keep your hand out of "plackets," slits in a petticoat, the chastened man advises them. They can't do this, however, "unless things be cut shorter." Copulation thrives and the polecat and ruttish horse go to it, none with more appetite than a simpering woman. Though her face "between her forks" promises snow, the gods inherit only to the girdle. Beneath is the sulphurous pit, "burning, scalding, stench, consumption."

This "dark and vicious place" costs Gloucester his eyes. The moral calculus equates the cost with the wages of sin, and the old sensualist, nudging his straightman, appears to go along. "Do you smell a fault?" etc. But the fault is more and less than Gloucester's youthful peccadilloes. Shakespeare, speaking through an anonymous Gentleman, calls it the "general curse" laid on nature.

Like a leitmotif, "nature" is heard from often. Sometimes "tender-hefted" or compassionate, it isn't this invariably, so what Shakespeare wants us to recognize is moot. Natural "bias" in the king gets our assent, not in Cornwall, however. Weighted or biased like a bowling ball, one of Shakespeare's metaphors, he runs all one way and you can't "rub" or deflect him. Edmund, a self-acknowledged captive to natural "law," is like that. In comedy, Shakespeare, cheerful or rueful, goes with nature's bias. Here the maker's role is uppermost, and he seeks to correct it.

Animals are natural, a lot of them in *King Lear* as everyone has noticed, most only eating machines like the cuckoo. Let it into your nest and you regret this. Animality in man or woman is unnatural, Lear thinks, and his shocked surprise meets filial ingratitude, perverse in the child, not in the sea monster. Schooled by experience, he changes his mind.

Man in the state of nature, a poor, bare animal only "forked" or two-legged, has a place in Shakespeare's bestiary and we cringe when we meet him. Though some think poverty is riches, Shakespeare, no St. Francis, isn't bidding us strip ourselves and his poor, naked wretches merit pity, not applause. Naked Lear, crowned with furrow-weeds and nettles, is more vividly present than Lear with his fifty followers, but that is an esthetic judgment. "What need one?" they ask him, a question to ponder. Another way to put this is to ask what "true need" consists in.

Questions punctuate the play, an essay in definition. "Who am I, sir?" "Now, good sir, what are you?" "What art thou?" This last addresses the man whose loyalty is a mystery, also the Bedlam, our primeval slime. "Hog in sloth, fox in stealth, wolf in greediness, dog in madness, lion in prey," the Bedlam incarnates natural man. Swimming up from night thoughts but still there in the morning, this apparition strikes terror.

The exorcist, a sleight-of-hand man, puts it to flight. But Shakespeare, resembling the God of the Creation, makes a better nature from the dust of the earth. Different from Michelangelo, who thought he was freeing the shape within the stone, he finds this shape amorphous, so blesses it with form. Pseudo-natural histories, telling how the bear cub is licked into shape by its mother, offer a version of his activity.

Lear on the heath, like a Puritan or "New Philosopher," is feeling for essential man, uncontaminated by context. "Lendings" is his word for the trappings of civilization, e.g., silk, hide, wool, and perfume. Simplifiers think they deform us or spruce us up, either way a falsification. "Unaccommodated man" throws off these lendings, reducing to the thing itself. True to his meagerness, he lacks interest for drama, though.

But in the best-case scenario, elected by Shakespeare, art amends nature and this lack is repaired. Gratuities or grace notes—pity, remorse, an emergent sense of "fitness"—supply what is wanting. Not laid on like veneering, they participate in what we are, the way the form participates in the content. Something happens in *King Lear,* a metamorphosis play like so many of Shakespeare's, and though it doesn't redeem our sorrows, it makes us capable of them.

The villain, sketching a "behaviorist" psychology, thinks men are like the time, responsive only to the itch of ego. Picking a quarrel with custom, as in "the plague of," he sneers at nice distinctions, dear to lawyers and some poets. This "Epicurean," not a hedonist as in our modern sense but man in a vacuum, is himself alone. Against him Shakespeare recites his litany of forms and sanctions, spells that bar the pit. Creating a context, they help to define us, so endow our helter-skelter with meaning.

But the meaning is coterminous with the play, hard on those who want things settled. This foils the playwright too, committed to bringing order from chaos but always at a new beginning. Though many imagine him handing down the Decalogue ("not for an age but for all time"), universal Shakespeare is largely the creation of our modern taste for conceptualizing. His matter-of-fact, uncommonly realized, suggests general statement, but his cases are special and he never ventures far from this man in his habit or the provincial place he starts out from. Intimating parallels to the major story, *King Lear* looks like a universe of horrors, "he childed as I fathered." Shakespeare's universe is particular, however, both its glory and its limitation, and his tragic hero isn't Everyman, only himself.

Figures of speech are this poet's stock-in-trade and employing them he means to say what his particulars add up to. But like an eyes-to-the-ground "nominalist" in the time before him, he looks with too much sympathy at the matter in hand, and when all is finished his "there" turns out to be "here." Bridging the gap between them, modern readers improve on his ad hoc psychology. This is the characteristic habit of the academy, benevolent and wanting to apply things.

A curious species of synecdoche (when a part is put for the whole) distinguishes his play. Interesting in its own right, maybe all-absorbing, the part comes near displacing what it stands for. Met in "fields near Dover," crazy Lear, blind Gloucester, and the beggarman who functions as Chorus compose a tableau beyond paraphrase or codification. Shakespeare's scene has its "heuristic" content, and his expositors, zeroing in on the king's bitter schooling, fillet it out. But the "side-piercing sight" must deject exposition and the hero's schooling pales beside his substantial presence, "every inch a king."

A high-sounding word for this, Aristotle's, is "megalopsychia," greatness of soul. With the play as moral paradigm, it has little to do. Questions of "how," "when," and "where" engage the playwright, less ambitious than the moralist who wants to know why. The effect transcends its cause when we front the cold wind that blows through the hawthorn or the thing that grumbles "there" in the straw.

Ideological Shakespeare, feminist, Marxist, or Freudian, is often introduced in our time, but -isms are what he isn't capable of, or rather he entertains them all. Shakespeare the Socialist comes to the podium when Lear and Gloucester hand over their "superflux" to the wretched. "So distribution should undo excess." Shakespeare's socialism is a cry of pain, however, and Lear's great apostrophe, addressed to "houseless poverty," only merits a hearing as it begins with the Fool.

Readers who like to classify lay bare Shakespeare's "poetics," recurring patterns in his work. But context, a great solvent of general truth, distorts them. Restraint urging its claims in Albany, he declines to let his hands obey his blood. Elsewhere, though, restraint goes out the window. The "hot-blooded" France is one of our heroes, and we understand from Kent that anger has its privilege. (Pleading it, he has to sit in the stocks.)

Like other plays of Shakespeare's, *King Lear* asks us to mind "true things" by their mockeries. Against the wicked daughters, Shakespeare poses Cordelia. His wicked duke pairs with a virtuous duke, and a selfless suitor with the mercenary man whose suit is exhausted in "respects of fortune." Though Edmund has no pity, his brother is "pregnant" to pity. And so on. Plucking comfort from these comparisons, commentators say how good, a refreshment, mitigates the aridity of evil. But on another view, all we have are setoffs. Shakespeare's Fool, who doesn't run away, is at least no knave. Oswald, a knave, doesn't do this either, though, and both earn a place in the story.

Bearing witness to "the mystery of things," Shakespeare lets others resolve it. But he isn't a neutral looker-on at the play and you hear his voice in his surrogates. Strongly cadenced, sometimes thrilling, this voice is raised for life. Better to live, though we have to endure the pain of death every hour. Gloucester at the bottom of the wheel invokes the blessing of Heaven, and Edgar, blown to the worst by the "insubstantial air," bids it welcome. "World, world, O world!" says the embattled man,

> But that thy strange mutations make us hate thee,
> Life would not yield to age.

Driven from Court, Kent says he goes to "freedom," i.e., the "to-and-fro-conflicting wind and rain." But Shakespeare intends no irony. Near the end he offers us a long and generous description of Dover Cliff, logically in excess of his play's requirements. This speech of Edgar's means to summon great heights. Putting before us "the crows and choughs that wing the midway air," the fishermen on the beach, the murmuring surge that chafes the pebbled shore, it says to the despairing man that the end he craves is near. But all that wealth of detail, crying out against death, tells of our lives' sweetness.

PLAYED BEFORE the Court at Whitehall, December 26, 1606, *King Lear* contributed to the holiday season, revels time. Sir John Harington, Court poet, ribald jokester, and not easily scandalized, said what the audience was like on these occasions, the ladies "sick and spewing," their male counterparts abandoned to riot and excess. Drunk or sober, they needed waking up, a job for a playwright. Extravaganzas tickling the viscera were in, and this is what they thought Shakespeare gave them. Readers will want to set him "on the top" like Prospero, looking down on the new three-ring circus.

Most who catered to the reigning taste for sensation live only for antiquarians but a few transcend their time. Cyril Tourneur is one, the same who said tragedy should confess poetic justice. He made a permanent mark with his *Revenger's Tragedy,* acted by the King's Men soon after they acted *King Lear.* On his official side, this gifted Son of Ben and slip of Marlowe's stock wants us to know that crime doesn't pay, but he discovers a rich lode in crime and other perversion. Mounting a full-scale assault on the senses, he spreads before the audience a gothic novel's worth of horrors. His hero, toting them up at the end of the play, gives the playwright's point of view, incidentally posterity's: "'Twas somewhat witty carried." For much Jacobean theater when it works, that seems a fair assessment.

Relishing his dark byways, Tourneur is the laureate of the Grand Guignol. His Paris Garden brutalities stale with repetition, and later work of his shows him preying on himself. Shakespeare's plays were another mine to plunder. Rifling them for good things, he liked especially the woman hater in *Hamlet. Hamlet's* misogyny is corrosive, however; in Tourneur a flattering unction. Never tell a woman a secret overnight: your doctor may find it in the urinal in the morning. Any kindred except a sister is men's meat in these days. That shocked them in 1607 but Jacobean playwrights kept upping the voltage and John Ford made this reservation obsolete.

When Shakespeare left the King's Men, he helped take up the slack. Meaning to keep the audience on the qui vive, Ford tries harder than Shakespeare and his plays show the strain. A model Jacobean, he can't think causally, so rings down the curtain by fiat. Everyone knows his *'Tis Pity She's a Whore,* old *Romeo and Juliet* spiced up for the time's jaded palate. In his tragedy of incest, he has a stage direction: "Enter Giovanni with a heart upon his dagger." A surprising scene, it stops the show—the hero says it darkens the midday sun—and that is the playwright's intention.

Older drama doesn't skimp on spectacular effects and the mysteries and moralities Shakespeare went to school to appealed as they could to our senses. Adam sleeps in the Garden and God, creating Eve, lifts "a rib colored red" from his side. Christ, nailed to the Cross, rises from the dead but this needs corroborating, and the Doubting Apostle traces the wounds with his finger. Mostly, however, onstage reality demanded an act of faith. Property lists, not inspiring conviction, suggest this, e.g., half a yard of Red Sea, two worms of conscience, a link or torch to set the world on fire. But older playwrights had something to say.

At James's Court, spectators, no longer "auditors," made ocular proof the touchstone of merit. Gloucester with his "bleeding rings" passes this test but adds an increment, putting Shakespeare at odds with the temper of his time. His play, though it tells on the senses, is less a tale of horrors than a crucible for meanings. But the "Jacobean Temper," nihilistic to his skeptical, dissolves meaning in rhetoric and gesture.

Chapman, for instance, in *Bussy D'Ambois:*

> Man is a torch borne in the wind: a dream
> But of a shadow.

Let it be said for this histrionic playwright that his heroes hold the torch aloft. Most are glamorous roughnecks braving the heavens, a gesture that mocks itself. Short on pia mater, they can't disperse "passion's fumes" with their weak labors, and in their arias you hear the death knell of the old Psychomachia. All have the gift of poetry, handed round impartially to the hero or villain. If you mean to tell them apart, you need a playbill.

Characters in Webster hope for sharper definition and some, for a luminous instant, break free. Trapped in the final toils, his great heroine is "Duchess of Malfi still!" But she pays for her enfranchisement. In Webster the way to freedom is through suffering, whether you endure it or inflict it. Accounts of Jacobean theater always put him and Tourneur together, but Webster, throttled and elliptical unlike his self-pleased colleague, grudges what he has to tell us. Echoing Shakespeare's words in two powerful plays, he said he wanted to be read by Shakespeare's light. He has no results, though, only events.

> We are merely the stars' tennis-balls, struck and bandied
> Which way please them.

This is like Gloucester on the gods who kill us for their sport. But Gloucester isn't speaking for the playwright.

Essentially a Pyrrhonist (know-nothing), Webster makes it hard on his doomed protagonists. Dying "in a mist," they don't know anything either. The snow preserves their footprints but the sun shining, melts both form and matter. Though his Duchess, marrying beneath her, dies her monstrous death, only Pharisees will call it contingent. She is going into a wilderness, life itself.

Websterian tragedy falls apart toward the end, and generally the ending takes place in a waxworks: "Gives her a dead man's hand. . . . Here a dance of eight madmen. . . . Enter executioners. . . . [They] strangle the children." Not "hoist with their own petar," beleaguered characters are done in by contrivance. This has its comic side, like a Road Runner cartoon in blank verse, someone said. But coincidence in Webster is less an expedient than a principle. A question torments him: "is it true thou art but a bare name, / And no essential thing?" Groping for an answer, he flays his characters in order to know them. Horror is a means of grace.

Having no yardstick except for the self, Jacobean playwrights don't know any more than Iago how one man should differ from another. To verify the new cipher hero, they dress him in real habiliments ("costume drama"), or set him in a real context. Though the tailor's dummy on stage lacks reality, bric-a-brac are real and so are gouts of blood. Jacobean theater, Shakespeare's apart, exploits both. Life perhaps is phantasmal but realism, the cinematic kind, lends a spurious solidity to the shadows on the other side of the footlights.

The Red Bull, a public playhouse, fleshed the shadows out. It promoted a world of papier-mâché, substantial to the eye but flimsy when you leaned against it. Webster—his *White Devil* premiered in this theater—looked in vain for an "understanding auditory" at the Bull. "Ignorant asses" sat in judgment there. Deaf to the good, they brayed for the new, poisoning with their breath even the most "sententious" play (i.e., Webster's). Decidedly a snob, he expected this from the hoi polloi.

Located in Clerkenwell, north and west of the city, the Red Bull opened in 1606. Nearby stood the Revels Office where James's state censor looked with a moody eye on playwrights who didn't say what they ought to. At the Bull they made his job easy. Dialog reduced to home truths or deferred to special effects, as when Heywood in one of his classical-legend spectaculars has Hercules enter "from a rock above tearing down trees." Historians of theater imagine Shakespeare getting in step, and across the river at the Globe, Dr. Forman the astrologer noted how Macbeth and Banquo rode about the stage on horseback. This intrusion of the real world is rare in Shakespeare, though, and runs counter to his art, an imitation of reality.

In medieval times, an ancient well beside the Bull provided a meeting place for London's parish clerks. Assembling there once a year, they played "some large history of Holy Scripture." Their entertainments meant to teach and delight, and though they had their eye on Heaven, represented the "brazen world," everyday life as they knew it. Jacobean theater, both public and private, abridges this two-in-one esthetic. Careless of instruction and indifferent to our middle earth, it prefers a golden world, stuffed with "forms such as never were in nature."

Persons of quality didn't go to the Bull, "so open and black," supercilious Webster called it. But their preference for the golden world was the same. It flowered in the masque, a courtly entertainment forever linked with Ben Jonson and Inigo Jones. They made an odd couple, Jones the camel who got his nose under the tent, Jonson sulking in the corners. In the masque, a disgruntled poet said, "the art and invention of the architect gives the greatest grace and is of the most importance; ours, the least part and of least note." Irate Ben didn't like this:

> Shows! Shows! Mighty shows!
> The eloquence of masques! What need of prose,
> Or verse, or sense, t'express immortal you?

Verse of high quality distinguishes his Court shows, but none add up to a play.

In the masque, the play, still there vestigially, functions as a picture frame. The appeal to the eye comes first (it "loves to look on something beautiful"). The ear takes second place, "charmed" but only by the musical accompaniment. Bringing up the rear, the players make "graceful discourse." Jones, faithful to his genius, knew what he wanted, though, "Hamlet without words." By-and-by, getting rid of the graceful discourse, he created the essential masque, "nothing else but pictures with light and motion."

The year Shakespeare wrote *King Lear,* the proscenium arch, an Italian import, came to England. Jonson's *Masque of Blackness* introduced it. Behind Queen Anne and the other ladies, separated from the audience by a front curtain, verisimilar settings authenticated the play. They showed streets, palaces, churches, and "various kinds of cornices," all in relief and looking "as if they were real." Inside the picture frame, the architect-designer manipulated scenes and machines. He knew how to make the sun rise in the heavens, move on its course, and set at the end with such skill that spectators "remained lost in wonder." Clouds at his command changed their shape and size and the sea grew tempestuous, darkening in color. Marine monsters broke the surface, spouting water while they swam.

Shakespeare's Dover Cliff, like the sea that beats against it, is a tissue of words, but Jones had a real cliff, standing four-square. Parting it in the middle with his "scena ductilis," he called up "an illustrious concave," filled with artificial light. Prospero, though skillful in magic, couldn't do this. But Shakespeare, denied the new technical resources, didn't want them. (Trecento painters didn't want perspective.) Toward the end of his career, fresh opportunities offered, sliding flats, "revolves," a drop curtain, etc., and still his stage remains dynamic, polyscenic if he says so, and mostly naked to the eye. Action on the great platform, not so different from the medieval *platea,* flows between fixed stations, unlocalized except by the word. All-creating, it appealed to the senses but courted intellect too, and for Shakespeare the play was still the thing.

HIS TRAGIC PERIOD coincided with a time of troubles, not the "mythical sorrows" of Shakespeare, public troubles. (In his plays he addressed and composed them.) Catholics and Puritans hoped for better days when King James came in, but finding their hopes dashed, turned violent. Puritan violence, culminating in Civil War, ruined "the great work of time." The young Catholics who engineered the Gunpowder Plot, November 1605, brought about their own ruin, bringing down many who were guiltless. Life imitates Shakespeare's art in this tale of crime and random punishment. In *Macbeth,* pleading not guilty is a "womanly defense," no good at all.

More than another tale of ill-weaved ambition, the Gunpowder Plot activated deep springs of emotion in Shakespeare, "a companion in tribulation though not in the cause." Characteristically, his response is muffled, recalling the speaking silence with which he greeted the fall of Essex. Others wrote up-to-the-minute plays like the anonymous *Gowry* (1604), telling of an attempt on the life of King James. Transforming life to art, he set his version of the plot in medieval Scotland, long before his Stuart King was ever heard of.

"Remember, remember the Fifth of November." That was the government talking. The important point, Cecil said, was "to demonstrate the iniquity of Catholics." The account put about by his agents underlines this but doesn't always bear looking into. Some, beginning in Shakespeare's time, called the plot a provocation, intended to lay the ghost of the old faith. Twentieth-century readers, brought up on show trials, won't find that out of the question. But though history may or may not repeat itself, historians always repeat each other, and the official version has held the field from that day to this. How Shakespeare received it comments on the man he was.

Robert Catesby, "dear Robin" to friends, led the plotters. Handsome in person, captivating in manners, in soldier's harness every inch the commander, he cast a spell like magic, said one who knew him. No ordinary malcontent but worthy to be a rebel, he meditated confusion's masterpiece, the destruction of England's government "at one fell swoop." The opening of James's second Parliament on the 5th of November gave him his occasion. King, Prince of Wales, all the nobility, the bishops, the Privy Councilors, and most of the principal gentry were to perish. On the ruins Catesby meant to erect a Catholic state, headed by a puppet ruler, the young Princess Elizabeth. Across the Channel, a volunteer army waited to support the popular rising he hoped for. Holy Communion, consecrated by a missionary priest, sealed the Gunpowder Plot. It almost succeeded and but for twelve hours' grace, the King and the rest would have died.

Hiring a building adjacent to Parliament, the plotters tunneled beneath it, intending to blow their victims at the moon. By March 1605 they had reached the halfway point when a vault beneath the House of Lords fell open for rent. This they stored with thirty-six barrels of gunpowder, one-and-a-half tons' worth, hidden under faggots and coal. Guy Fawkes, a Yorkshire squire who had fought for Spain in Flanders, volunteered to detonate the powder.

For the site of the rising, the plotters picked Warwickshire where Catholics were thick on the ground. They met at Clopton House outside Stratford, on the border of Shakespeare's tithe lands. Hugh Clopton, who built the bridge across the Avon, laid its foundations in the reign of Henry VII. Recusant Catholics worshipped in the attic, comforted by black-letter texts on the walls:

> Whether you rise early or go to bed late
> Remember Christ Jesus that died for your sake.

Joyce Clopton and her husband, Sir George Carew, owned the house but toward the end of September 1605 leased it as a hunting lodge to Catesby's pawn, Ambrose Rookwood. Gathering there on the Sunday after Michelmas (September 29), the hunters concerted final plans. Eclipses, "strangling" the moon and sun on October 2, advertised the displeasure of the heavens, "troubled with man's act," Shakespeare's character said. But portents mean what men want them to, and Catesby, sure of the heavens, pressed on.

Back in London, he and his confederates feted one another at taverns like the Mermaid and its rival the Mitre, on the other side of Bread Street. William Johnson, Shakespeare's friend, subsequently his trustee, was their host at the Mermaid. Early in October, a supper party at Catesby's lodgings in the Strand brought the inner circle together. Unsuspecting Ben Jonson, just at present a Roman Catholic but up to date on Court business, came as an invited guest. No doubt they hoped to ply him with Canary. Only days since he had got out of jail for his part in *Eastward Ho!* Poking fun at the King and his fire-new nobility, impolitic Ben had a Scots voice exclaim: "Ah ken the man weel, he's ane of ma thirty-pund knights." His topical jibe recalls a cryptic line of Shakespeare's, supposed by some to glace at James's bartering of knightly honors: "our new heraldry is hands, not hearts." Whatever this means, it doesn't mean mischief, though. Shakespeare knew what to do when the wind was rising.

Pity betrayed the Gunpowder Plot. All must be blown up, iron-willed Catesby said, were they "as dear unto me as mine own son," but Francis Tresham made an exception. In a letter to Lord Monteagle (October 26), he warned this brother-in-law to stay at home on the 5th of November. Regret proved the fruit of pity and Monteagle took the letter to Cecil. Though the First Secretary knew treason when he smelled it, only James knew where it lurked. Gifted with prophetic powers, he pointed straight to the cellar. "God put it into His Majesty's heart" to do this, said Attorney General Coke.

Cutting it fine, a search party mustered on November 4, headed by the Lord Chamberlain, formerly Shakespeare's lord. At midnight the searchers netted Guy Fawkes, "the owner of that hand which should have acted that monstrous tragedy." On the rack, he named names. But his confederates, forewarned, took horse for the Midlands and loyal allies, like Brutus and Cassius after the failure of another coup d'état. Crying rebellion "for God and the country," they didn't incite it. "We are for King James as well as for God and the country," said the villagers who heard them, striking their sticks on the ground. It sounds most Shakespearean, including the bleak denouement.

On Wednesday, November 6, Stratford's bailiff, arming his constables with calivers, light muskets, broke into Clopton House. By then the birds had flown, leaving behind a bag full of copes, vestments, crucifixes, and chalices. George Badger, woolen draper of Stratford and sometime neighbor of John Shakespeare's on Henley Street, had the custody of these "massing relics." A sheriff's posse ran the fugitives down at a Catholic "safe house" over the border in Staffordshire. Catesby, mortally wounded, took in his hands a picture of Mary, God's Mother, "and so, embracing and kissing the same, he died." Three others died with him, the survivors dying later on the scaffold. Justice in Shakespeare's England had a taste for ironies and Guy Fawkes met his end in Old Palace Yard, overlooking the Parliament he had meant to destroy.

To Shakespeare's contemporaries, the Gunpowder Plot looked like Essex's rising all over again. Most who conspired with Catesby were with him in 1601 when he rallied the Earl's soldiers to shouts of "Ça, ça! Tirez!" This romantic posturing in a bad cause stole men's hearts four years later. The same William Barlow who preached at Paul's Cross on the trial and sentencing of Essex ascended the same pulpit, November 10, 1605, to give the first public account of the plot. At the trial in Westminster, the same Justice Popham who harried Essex presided. England's sovereign, facetious in victory, wasn't just like his predecessor, though. Had treason succeeded, the King told his subjects, he would have died in good company. At least ages to come could never have said against him that he had died in an alehouse or stews.

EVER AN INTERESTED SPECTATOR at the scene of the crime, Shakespeare jotted down the facts (who could say how they might germinate?), but if he had sympathies, concealed them. Most think he recoiled in Protestant outrage at Gunpowder Treason, e.g., in *Macbeth* where "dire combustion" signals the death of a king. (Probably this is part of his macrocosm = microcosm shorthand.) Others, a Catholic minority, cast him as recusant Shakespeare, deploring England's breach with Rome. Inference tends to support them and their case needs a hearing. Shakespeare the secret Catholic, if that is what he was, must alter our sense of the plays.

Guilty by association, he descended on his mother's side from the Catholic Ardens, old Warwickshire gentry. Most of the plotters were distant relatives of hers and most came from the Shakespeare Country. One owned land in Snitterfield where Shakespeare's grandfather Richard once worked his little farm. At Coughton Court west of Stratford in the days that followed the debacle, the women waited for news of their men. Poor birds, they didn't fear the net or lime but it caught them.

Shakespeare's kin, the Catholic Throckmortons lived in the manor house, and Father Robert Southwell left his calling card there. Posterity remembers him as author of *The Burning Babe,* the poem Jonson would have given many of his own poems to have written. Executed for treason in 1595, he asserted his right to "equivocate," telling a lie when you had to. Catholic pamphleteers promoted this doctrine and First Clown in *Hamlet* is one of their scholars. An "absolute" knave, i.e., notably finicking, he tortures words for their latencies. We have to speak by the "card" or compass, Shakespeare's hero tells Horatio, "or equivocation will undo us." So far, perhaps, omniverous Shakespeare, feeding on current events.

But Southwell, dogging Shakespeare's footsteps, turns up again. Government spies note his sister's visits to Southampton House in London, where the Dowager Countess sheltered missionary priests. Genealogists, surprising us, connect him and Shakespeare's noble patron, unlikely cousins by marriage. For Shakespeare's biography, bizarre conjunctions seem the rule, and in 1616—Shakespeare by this time being safely dead—published work of Southwell's salutes "my worthy good cousin, Master W.S." In Shakespeare's England, they all seem related to each other.

If you trusted the Crown, Jesuit missionary priests were the plot's first instigators. With these cunning "casuists," men who wrested the truth, Shakespeare had much in common. What is his poetry but lying like truth, Macbeth's phrase for the fiend's equivocation. Supremely casuistical, he "set the word itself / Against the word." Father Henry Garnet, head of the English Jesuit mission, plays a part in *Macbeth,* and Father Edmund Campion in Shakespeare's early biography. This soldier-priest aimed to win benighted English to Heaven or die upon their pikes. Likely he ministered to Shakespeare's father at Lapworth, the family seat of the Catesbys, when Shakespeare was a boy. Whatever he was in life, John Shakespeare died a Catholic.

Simon Hunt, recusant Catholic and English confessor at St. Peter's, Rome, appears briefly in Shakespeare's story. Master at the King's School, Stratford, he chose exile in 1575 to study for the priesthood at Rheims. A great English Bible, work of militants like him, began appearing from that city a few years later. Shakespeare, no friend of schoolmasters, seems to remember this one with affection. In *The Taming of the Shrew,* his young hero Lucentio disguises himself as a "young scholar that hath long been studying at Rheims," famous or notorious for Jesuit priests. But "seems" is shaky ground to build on, and Lucentio is only pretending.

Hunt had an acolyte, Robert Dibdale. Shakespeare's schoolfellow, he quit Stratford when his master did, took holy orders, then came home to martyrdom in 1586. Exorcizing the devil from young Protestant girls (one way or another he was going to save them), this zealous seminarian made his presence known in England, so died on the gibbet. Rev. Samuel Harsnett, a Protestant propagandist, rehashed the details with attention to their lurid side (much groping in the girls' "park," etc.). In 1604 or thereabouts, Shakespeare, leafing through Harsnett's *Egregious Popish Impostures* (what didn't he read?), found the names of the devils who possess his Tom of Bedlam. Perhaps he was looking for young Dibdale in Harsnett. The story, pointed with invective, is there.

Late in the 1580s a missionary priest, not Shakespeare's friend but his lookalike, swung on the gallows in Finsbury Fields, facing the Theater and Curtain. Some have Shakespeare a witness to the hanging. Cottage gardens, marked off by ditches, bloomed on the site, once a priory of Black Nuns. In *The Comedy of Errors,* old Aegeon walks through country like this, on his way to hang in

> the melancholy vale,
> The place of death and sorry execution,
> Behind the ditches of the abbey here.

In Ephesus things go better than in Shoreditch, however, and in the nick of time Shakespeare's kindly Abbess takes a hand.

Skeletons rattled in the Shakespeare family's closet and in April 1606, a time of mass hysteria, Shakespeare's elder child opened the door. Though savage punishment threatened the "popishly affected," Susanna skipped Easter Communion. In the aftermath of the plot, James's government imposed this sacramental test on Catholics. Fines, rising to £60, penalized the stiff-necked, and most, unlike Susanna, fitted their necks to the yoke. There was "something of Shakespeare" in his daughter, people said easily, and perhaps they shared the same features. Later the vicar's court dismissed the case against Susanna, lucky for all concerned.

Many Shakespeare knew stayed loyal to the old church, too many to tell of, but one at least deserves mention. He was Thomas Reynolds, father of that William Reynolds remembered in Shakespeare's will. The Reynoldses lived on Chapel Street, home to Shakespeare too. Only a year before Gunpowder Treason, Thomas Reynolds gave shelter to a priest on the run. Fleeing from the Gild Hall—in green breeches, high shoes, and white stockings, sharp-eyed neighbors reported—the fugitive made a beeline for Chapel Street and safety. What happened to him afterward isn't reported but history, rehearsing other stories like this one, fills in the blanks. Though Catholic priests in James's reign armed themselves in conscience, raison d'état prevailed and judges hanged them routinely.

This was the fate of Father Garnet, "Pecorella" as they knew him in Rome, the little sheep who went to the slaughter. Flushed from his priest hole not far from Stratford, he died in Paul's Churchyard, May 3, 1606. Cecil appointed the place of execution, the very spot where the "late dread and dear Sovereign Elizabeth" had thanked God on her knees for the defeat of the Spanish Armada. En route from the Tower of London to hang, Garnet bade farewell to his "good friend," Tom the cook. "This day," he said, "I will save thee a labor to provide my dinner." In the Age of Shakespeare, they had such words at need.

But Garnet gave Shakespeare better than this, the Drunken Porter Scene in *Macbeth*. He is the "farmer" (an alias of his) who hanged himself in the expectation of plenty, also the equivocator who committed treason "for God's sake" but couldn't equivocate to Heaven. Cruel of the Porter to urge this against him but Garnet's own testimony fed him his cue. At the trial in London's Guild Hall where wretched Dr. Lopez had stood in the dock before him, he admitted to prior knowledge of the plot. However, he said, echoing Father Southwell, "reservations in some cases are lawful." So many threads in this carpet. Perhaps they make a figure, Shakespeare the papist who had his ax to grind?

Equivocation didn't trouble Dr. Johnson, no casuist but strong for common sense. "If, for instance, a murderer should ask you which way a man is gone, you may tell him what is not true." Shakespeare's characters take a different line, however. "What is a traitor?" young Macduff wants to know. "Why, one that swears and lies," his mother answers. "Everyone that does so is a traitor, and must be hanged."

But Shakespeare lets them all have their say. Much on the point for our sense of the man, he made capital of rebellious Catholics and Protestant loyalists, standing with neither. All were only sectaries to his lower-case catholic, and the house they worshipped in was too narrow to hold him. Unlike that other Jonson, anxious to clear his skirts, he didn't write poetry celebrating treason's failure, and he couldn't have said with Father Garnet that you had to be a Catholic if you meant to be saved. Imagining heroes, he wasn't one himself, and thought the cause, any cause, too good or too paltry to fight for. "Two truths" organize *Macbeth,* his Gunpowder play, not the unitary truth others owed allegiance to. "Prologues" to the theme, Shakespeare's hero calls them. Enriching it, however, they darken it too, and we see things as through "fog and filthy air."

SHAKESPEARE wrote his play at full gallop, probably in the first half of 1606. A "royal play," it compliments the King, who included Scottish Banquo in his family tree, and a reasonable guess says that a Court performance diverted this sovereign and his brother-in-law of Denmark, visiting in England that summer. James liked his plays short, else he fell asleep, and *Macbeth* is shorter than most. Tailoring is incidental, though, Shakespeare in last things pleasing himself.

None of his tragedies matches this one for intensity, partly a consequence of radical stripping-down. But *Macbeth* isn't thin, rather a narrow causeway descending into Hell or ascending to Heaven. Shakespeare's hero, a Prince of Darkness, is also the light bearer, "Lucifer," Prince of the East. The generosity that touches minor characters with life, a hallmark of Shakespeare's, isn't much lavished here and the hero-villain and his wife, burning the air around them, have the play pretty much to themselves. Shakespeare's imagination, roused by the arch-equivocator's story, allowed nothing to deflect it. He is his Macbeth, not the king-killer, the man who swears in both scales against either. In the end, his testimony is impeached and the world, imposed on for a long time, destroys him.

Equivocation is the play's burden, sounded in the opening lines. "Fair is foul, and foul is fair." Macbeth when we first meet him catches up this saying of the Weird Sisters. Women though bearded, they seem "corporal" but melt into air. Riddling poetry is their medium, "mnemonic" like nursery rhymes, not discursive like blank verse and not easy for reason to cope with. "Lesser" works out to "greater" in their extra-rational world, not so happy is happier. Mysterious intelligence, it can't be ill, can't be good.

A doubtful battle, both lost and won, figures the hero's story. Promising comfort, it brings discomfort in its train. Which is which is a problem, though, the auspices tricking us "in a double sense." (Later the hero, much deceived, says they keep the word of promise to our ear but break it to our hope.) Shakespeare's Captain, describing the mighty opposites, sees them clinging together like exhausted swimmers who choke each other's strength.

But these opposites aren't substantial, as when good son and bad son face off in *King Lear.* Forget Macduff and thin-blooded Malcolm: internal war is *Macbeth's* important business (Shakespeare going back to *Dr. Faustus*). Pitting "rebellious arm 'gainst arm," the hero batters down himself. Insurrection shakes his little kingdom, man. The heart quits its seat to knock at the ribs; the eye, fooled by the other senses, entertains visions, or it winks at the hand, abdicating its censor's office. Open to wicked suggestion, the ear does this too. Mutinous dreams unsettle Macbeth, and in the end his "pestered" senses, embarrassed by the company they keep, rise against him. Lady Macbeth's story is like this. "Perturbation" in her nature pulls her two ways and she dies a suicide, by "self and violent hands."

Confusion, much of it lexical, eddies outward as scene follows scene. Words run into each other, and "success" equates to "surcease" when the plot against the king nears its climax. The equivalence is only formal or "homonymic," though, and no conclusion seems possible for the fatal act that levers the play. Heavy with unlooked-for consequence, it ramifies forever, a world-without-end bargain the hero never meant to strike.

The future, dictated by fate, seems written as the play begins. Lady Macbeth says she feels it "in the instant" or present, but this is ghastly irony, Shakespeare's, not hers. Though words have their latencies, they don't "latch" the ear the first time we hear them and Shakespeare's characters must wait on the end to possess the full range of their meanings. Lamenting Duncan's murder, a mock-remorseful Macbeth predicts his own fate and the beggaring of all his achievement. "The wine of life is drawn," he tells them, speaking better than he knows.

Typical sequences go like this:

A. What's done is done. [i.e. over and done with]
B. What's done cannot be undone.

Memory is a fume, the heroine thinks, easily dispersed in the mind's alembic. At last, though, sorrows, "rooted" deeply there, consume her. Double-edged prophecies lull the hero. No need to fear until the earthbound tree "unfixes" its root. But already in the first act, horrid thoughts "unfix" his hair, a "proleptic" image, intimating things to come. In the last act, trees uproot themselves and give in their evidence against the unnatural man. "Known . . . to speak" in past times, they resume this uncanny power in *Macbeth*.

"Rooted," a countryman's word, suggests the natural round, Shakespeare's touchstone for behavior. Banquo is the "root" of kings, "scorched" or slashed but still potent. Instrumental to the denouement, the "mortified" man gets up from the dead. This happens for cause but isn't probable to thinking. Most times, "when the brains were out, the man would die."

Equivocal in person but also in his fate, Macbeth a) inculpates himself, b) has a grievance. No villain blacker (no hotter name in hell). Shakespeare, standing in for prosecutor Coke, wheels out his biggest guns, an impressive battery of moral and natural sanctions. Though the play enacts perversity, focus goes to use and wont. The villain lives in chaos but nice gradations reprove it. "You know your own degrees. . . . Stand not upon the order of your going." Hospitality and the breach of this complement each other. Lying in wait on the roads, a murderer with a turn for poetry tells how the belated traveler gains the timely inn. In the banquetting scene, feasting after killing, Shakespeare's hostess keeps her state, the host, mingling with society, drinks a "measure" with the others. "Measure" is good and heard from again in the benediction that blesses the ending.

Much in *Macbeth* about ceremony, health, good digestion, the general joy of the table. (Great nature's second course, sleep occupies the playwright too.) Much about babes, bloodied and otherwise. Macbeth, however, has no children. "How many children had Lady Macbeth?" readers used to ask, not a frivolous question.

"Kindly" relations fill out the play's background. Conjugal love, asserted by homely terms of affection ("dearest chuck"), goes hand in hand with murder. Nature's bond is canceled but procreation opposes it. The martlet, summer's guest, likes to build its bed in churches. Where this knowing creature breeds, the air must be delicate—if not yet, then sometime, when the sickly commonwealth is purged of disease.

"Reflector" characters, à la Henry James, illuminate the central character, saying what he is and isn't. One is a sailor, master of the *Tiger.* Tempests, loosed by the witches, shake his bark but can't sink it. Shakespeare's villain is free to choose but gives away his freedom, and in the great weighing and choosing scene (1.7) you see him do this. Good confronting evil, the next scene begins with Banquo who keeps his bosom "franchised" or free. Malcolm in the Testing Scene (4.3), cataloging his supposed iniquities, looks like Macbeth but takes a different direction. Also the play has two doctors and two kings. Pious Edward the Confessor, king plus medicine man, heals his country's maladies, Macbeth in the meantime throwing "physic" to the dogs. Edward has a gift of prophecy, heavenly, though.

All this, the prosecution's case, bears out Shakespeare's play on its moral or exemplary side. But the same materials sponsor another reading and Shakespeare, honoring his "two truths," does it justice. Perhaps this second reading distinguishes the play we most remember.

Though comparisons and contrasts tell against his villain, he sees how they raise as many questions as they answer. If Banquo but not Macbeth stands in God's hand, why is that? Both pass for men in the catalog that describes us, the way all dogs are dogs, mongrels, pure bloods, etc. Evidently how they differ depends on some "addition" Shakespeare doesn't put a name to. Bountiful nature confers this on one but not the other.

Some, "good and virtuous" like Macbeth in the beginning, go to the bad, submitting themselves to "an imperial charge" or injunction. Malcolm, our reporter, declines to venture reasons. Early Shakespeare has reasons, and in *Richard III* a sententious character wants us to accept that "avoided grace makes destiny." Good theology, it doesn't put us any farther along. Who avoids what is good for him? Tragic Shakespeare wonders about this.

Only once does he elect a villain for his hero. (In *Richard III* the hero-villain, larger than life, i.e., not lifelike, is mostly a vehicle for sinister fun.) Fascinated with evil and alert to its spoor, Shakespeare is asking where it comes from.

Old philosophers told him that the will never moves except under the shadow of good. Maybe "ambition," apparently good, spurs Macbeth to murder. Or maybe "great love" or "violent love," coincidentally a "spur," makes him run faster, outrunning the pauser, reason. The race going to the swift, reason doesn't help him much and its counsels aren't much involved with the ending. Shakespeare's tragedy ends well, anyway for some, but that is thanks to "the grace of Grace," a more concessive and less hopeful reading than *Richard III's*.

All those images from husbandry—Macbeth newly planted, full of growing at first but fallen at last into the sear and yellow—what do they do but argue natural process, an iron "rigol" or round he can't appeal from. Clothes, they say, make the man, and the hero learns about this too. Dressed in ill-fitting clothes, he isn't sure they become him. "With the aid of use," these borrowed garments cleave to his form, though. This is how the dyer's hand assumes the color of the dye.

Lengthening the odds, Shakespeare sets his scene in some *selva oscura* ("rooky wood"). Darkness enshrouds the action (the moon is down, heaven's candles are out). Under cover of this, a mysterious Third Murderer goes about his business. He isn't dispensable and Macbeth's officer isn't called "Seyton" for nothing.

Intoxication abets and foils Shakespeare's husband and wife. (The Porter says it sets them on and takes them off.) We hear of drugged "possets" and an "insane root" that imprisons the reason. Maybe this narcotic helps explain the inexplicable, Macbeth's stunning turn to the bad. "Metaphysical aid" sets the crown on his head and a "vaporous drop," distilled, engineers his confusion. Outrageous in tragedy, this recalls the magic potion that seals their eyes in Shakespeare's dream play.

Here are some foci for *Macbeth* on its anti-exemplary side.

> Who can be wise, amazed, temperate, and furious,
> Loyal and neutral, in a moment?

> Being unprepared,
> Our will became the servant to defect.
>
> we are traitors
> And do not know ourselves . . .
> But float upon a wild and violent sea.

This unknowing is tragic, diminishing too, and assimilates *Macbeth* to *Othello*.

A sufficient reading of *Macbeth* will summon the hero/villain who might have "wrought" or acted freely but wouldn't and/or couldn't. Contradictory ways of seeing him, they don't cancel out but face each other in a lively stasis. Shakespeare's tragedy isn't static, however, and the energy it brims with drives us on conclusions the story line doesn't point to. Judicial readers will conclude that Macbeth is guilty and not guilty, but Shakespeare is bidding for more. He wants our applause, different from our judgment, and in the last scenes he achieves it.

Macbeth who might end as the sport of prophecy, "perplexed in the extreme," isn't just the same as hoodwinked Othello, and his tragedy exhilarates where it might cast us down. Though dregs or "rancors" await him at the bottom of the cup, he drinks this poisoned chalice, so reduces to a "dwarfish thief," the role his enemies assign him. Their account of what happens isn't plenary, however, and Shakespeare's account doesn't register diminishing but growth.

As ironies are vindicated, the "usurper's cursèd head," brought on stage at the end, ought to evoke the fate of that earlier rebel whose head they fixed on their battlements. But Shakespeare's parallel, while emphasizing likeness, also asks discrimination. Who is "Macdonwald" that we should be mindful of him? Macbeth dies in harness, visibly there. Like Marlowe's Faustus, tempted to his damnation, he differs from Faustus, resisting the last temptation, repentance. The ending, memorable for the beating of dark vans, belongs to him, and playgoers, not moralizing, only bearing witness, salute this.

Rebirth (as per usual) gets our attention, but not only nature's or the kingdom's. Heeding St. Paul's injunction, the "mortified " man puts on the new man. (Properly, this is Banquo's part but Macbeth steals the show.) Or bathed in "reeking wounds," he recovers his youth like old Aeson, restored by the witch Medea. You could call these echoes grim parody but "affect," triumphant, not mocking, won't allow that. The blood Macbeth can't get rid of argues "guilt" but "gilds" him too, showing as a badge of honor, and this villain is also our hero. Dr. Johnson, eyeing Shakespeare suspiciously, wondered if he meant a "similitude," "guilt" suggesting "gilt." Yes, he did, releasing latent meanings that govern for our sense of the whole.

Refined by experience, Act V Macbeth is grander by far than the efficient swordsman of the opening scenes, and a mournful philosopher dominates the ending. All Shakespeare's tragedies have their special insignia, distinguishing one from the other. *Macbeth's* is gain-in-loss.

Crudely ambitious in the beginning, not, let us say, ambitious like Shakespeare, the hero reaches for his minor prize, "the sweet fruition of an earthly crown." This competition lacks interest. But Shakespeare knows how to retrieve it, and as his plot thickens, the stakes, motive too, are aggrandized. A rival creation, "the great doom's image," compels our notice in *Macbeth*. Scotland merges with Golgotha, "the place of the skull," and the hero, no petty thief but unexampled for sacrilege, breaks open the Lord's anointed temple. Ambitious beyond the common run, this version of the brightest angel means to encompass another fall of man.

Though plot (morality in motion) undoes him, saws and sayings approve this sequence and stick figures announce it, their slightness qualifying our response. The hero is precipitate but "modest wisdom" holds them back, seeing to it that they don't make the wrong choices. Impoverished on her imaginative side, Lady Macbeth doesn't measure up to her role of "fiend-like queen." (Partly this lack of stature acquits her.)

But someone in our play has the stature great villainy needs. Macbeth, self-conscious in evil, so "worthy to be a rebel," stands alone in a world where none of them sees beyond the sight-line. He pays for his access of being, and the breadth of his imagination is the measure of his pain, the possession of tragic heroes and poets.

Wading through every hopeful perversion, the hero—it might be Lucifer, Prince of the East—dies with the taste of dust and ashes in his mouth. Inevitably, perhaps, an image from the theater presents him. Life is a stage play and all are poor players, permitted their few hours' traffic. "Struts," the incomparable word, says what they do, kings and commoners, sectaries of whatever persuasion, rebels and loyalists. Macbeth is part of their company but unlike the others, he knows this.

7

Bravest at the Last

GOING BACK every year to his "native country," Shakespeare broke the journey at Oxford. Seventeenth-century reporters say he stopped off at a local wine house, the Tavern. Rising two stories and faced with twin gables, it overlooked the Cornmarket near the main road to Warwickshire and the north. In an upper room, once a bedroom, mural paintings of vines and flowers decorated the walls, and an inscription beside the fireplace admonished the traveler to "Fear God Above All Thing." Uncovered in 1927, the murals and inscription prompted headlines in the local paper, saying that Shakespeare once slept there.

Playing Oxford in 1603–4, he returned the year after, a red-letter year for town and gown alike. Oxford that summer scrubbed its image nervously, awaiting a state visit from the King. Addicts of tobacco put away their pipes and great clerks studied speeches, their "practiced accent" throttled with fear. By August 27 all was in readiness and James entered on horseback, followed by his family and a crowd of retainers. Isaac Wake, the University's public orator, extended official greetings. During the visit, he shadowed the royal eminence, recording his sayings and doings for the future. At Oxford, James said later, "one Wake made him sleep."

Entertainment, meant to edify, featured ten "disputations." Professor X, leading off, said, e.g., that money smelled sweet, never mind how you got it ("lucri bonus est odor ex re qualibet"). Denying his major, Professor Y called money the root of all evil. Four plays, under the direction of Dr. Gwinn, complemented the learned back-and-forth. Some, willing a connection between the theater and the university, think this Oxford don invited Shakespeare to help him. A classical tragedy headed the bill, followed by a comedy, allegorical, though. Both, like the disputations, were in Latin. Inigo Jones, on hand to see that things went smoothly, designed the sets in the Italian manner, and the Revels Office sent down properties and costumes. James found his entertainment wearisome, however, and "spoke many words of dislike." He never heard the allegory, nodding off when it began.

The Stuarts, kings in Scotland for a long time, prided themselves on their ancient lineage, and the welcoming committee took note. Materializing before the King at the city's north gate, three women from the "elder world," i.e., students of St. John's College, promised enduring fame to "Banquo's descendant." Propagandists invented this part of the lineage but it got respectful mention in Holinshed's *Chronicle,* Dr. Gwinn's source for his playlet of the Three Sibyls. Scholars and tourists looked on, the scholars "all on one side of the street, and the strangers of all sorts on the other." A latter-day scholar posts Shakespeare with the strangers, collecting ideas for *Macbeth.*

Next year he wrote his play and King James, much gratified, honored him "with an epistolary correspondence." The Duke of Buckingham, one of Shakespeare's Restoration "improvers," remembered it, and an early editor of the Poems told readers how "King James the First was pleased, with his own hand, to write an amicable letter to Mr. Shakespeare." Now lost, it "remained long in the hands of Sir William Davenant," the fourth child of John and Jane, Shakespeare's landlords at the Tavern. Christened William in St. Martin's church, March 3, 1606, this poet and playwright was Shakespeare's godson.

John Davenant, a grave, melancholy man, later Oxford's mayor, "was seldom or never seen to laugh." He loved and admired plays and playwrights, however, especially Shakespeare, who "frequented his house in his journeys between Warwickshire and London." Jane, his wife, "a very beautiful woman, of a good wit and conversation," gave him seven children. Robert, the eldest, remembered the hundred times Shakespeare kissed him as a boy, and William, after Shakespeare's death, wrote a youthful ode warning poets to keep away from the banks of the Avon. He said the flowers and trees had withered with grief and the river had nearly dried up with weeping.

Later, improving on this performance, he called himself Shakespeare's natural son. "It seemed to him" (said gossipy John Aubrey) "that he writ with the very spirit" Shakespeare did, and sometimes, drinking with intimate friends, owned up to a closer relation. In this way "his mother had a very light report, whereby she was called a whore." Nineteenth-century biography amended this to "a perfect Thaïs," the famous courtesan of antiquity.

The story of Shakespeare's Oxford affair, embellished with an anecdote from somebody's jest book, got better as time went on. In Pope's version, young Davenant, then seven or eight, "would fly from school" whenever his godfather Shakespeare came to town. "There's a good boy," says a local wag approvingly, "but have a care that you don't take God's name in vain."

Davenant, growing up, outstripped Shakespeare in honors. Knighted by King Charles I, he became Poet Laureate of England. Opera in England begins with him, and Shakespeare's popularity in the Restoration years is largely his doing. Some thought he looked like Shakespeare (the same "open countenance") but though his portrait survives, the resemblance isn't apparent, venereal disease having eaten away the nose.

In the post-Civil War time—"this refined age," a complacent diarist called it—"old plays" like Shakespeare's had begun "to disgust," but Davenant, a great mogul in the theater, made them "fit." He scored with *Macbeth,* "dressed in all its finery, as new clothes, new scenes, machines, as flyings for the witches, with all the singing and dancing in it." Collaborating with Shakespeare in ten of the plays, he emasculated all of them, his best claim for being Shakespeare's son.

OTHERS AFTER DAVENANT put their hook into Shakespeare, notoriously Thomas Shadwell. Dryden said this Restoration playwright "never deviates into sense" but his instinct for theater, though tuned to the least common denominator, is unerring. Revising *Timon of Athens,* he confessed that it showed "the inimitable hand of Shakespeare" but found it wanting in love interest. This Shadwell supplied, boasting that he had made Shakespeare's play into a play. Purcell supplied the music, worth a thousand words, and for more than half a century, Shadwell's *Timon* "wonderfully pleased" both Court and City.

Not so, the original. Pleasing few if any in its own time, it isn't much favored in ours. No performance is recorded in Shakespeare's theater and not until the mid-nineteenth century did his version see the stage. The parochial playwright who remembers small beer for once doesn't do that. He has his eye on the world over yonder, and not one allusion to any contemporary person or event has ever been verified in *Timon of Athens*. Most think it fell from Shakespeare's hand unfinished. Marred by inconsistencies in character and plot, *Timon* is very short (but so is *Macbeth*), mixes prose and verse haphazardly, and some of the verse is hardly that at all. In the consensus view, Shakespeare quit on the play, finding it intractable. But *Timon,* though rough and ready (perhaps like Michelangelo's roughened figures in the Laurentian Library), seems, at least to one reader, less unformed than unexpected. Just when we thought we knew him, this "English man of war" takes a new tack.

Riding the mighty wave that produced *Coriolanus* and *Antony and Cleopatra,* Shakespeare wrote *Timon* about 1607. He was in his forties, getting on but not flagging, and kept all three projects going, on the hob or on the boil. Impatient of his own success, he experimented with each, stumbling with two of them. You can almost see his eye moving critically from one to the other.

Plutarch's parallel lives of noble Greeks and Romans, the source for his two Roman tragedies, suggested Timon's story. Greek Alcibiades, the hero's friend and a rebel in Athens, pairs with Coriolanus in Plutarch's account, and in the life of Antony, Timon appears again. After the defeat at Actium (says North in his English translation), embittered Antony lived for a while in a "solitary house he had built by the sea." This he called Timoneon, remembering the hermit's cell where Timon entombs himself "upon the very hem" of the waters. Sometimes these heroes, when their great pine is barked, sound like one another. "To Lacedaemon did my lands extend," Timon says ruefully, poetry shining through the ashes of his chance. Drowned in his own bile, he doesn't expire like Antony, though. This makes a difference for posterity's verdict.

Shakespeare's plays, like his Sonnets, often group in pairs, and *Timon* and *Lear* have this relation. (Shakespeare wanted another look at his mightiest tragedy but from a different point of vantage.) Each has a hero who gives "unwisely, not ignobly," also a wise fool, hypothetically this, "not altogether a fool." Each hero loses his life to save it, and nothing brings him all things. The profligate man who won't hear until he feels might be Lear or Gloucester, and the play's greatest speech, summoning "confusion" against the city and the world, remembers the maddened King on the heath. Like Lear, Timon is much imposed on but the misery that scourges both of them "outlives incertain pomp." At the end a survivor patches up the gored state, decking his sword with the olive.

But all this is paraphrase. Scanning the plays, computer-wise, for their ideational content, it never notices the distinguishing thing. Shakespeare's continuities, not unifying *Lear* and *Timon,* highlight a new departure, and no plays differ more in the grain.

Older critics and scholars, assigning *Timon* a place in Shakespeare's mythical biography, said a great gloom was on his mind when he wrote it. Having labored through his Valley of the Shadow, he suffered a nervous collapse. "A wave broke, then an illness followed." The tragedies tell of triumph, however, and writing them he wasn't depressed but fulfilled. His "topics," often merest rags he pulled from the rag bag, mattered less to him than the way he stitched them together. For this master of means and ends, the absorbing question is always "how."

Where *King Lear* is centrifugal, "images of revolt and flying off," *Macbeth* changes direction, forcing great emotion through a narrow bore. (First the expansion, then the contraction.) *Richard III* is *Macbeth* from the outside, the face of the clock, appropriate to grim comedy. Later, resuscitating his hero-villain, Shakespeare studied the clock's inner workings. After *Macbeth,* the indicated play is *Coriolanus.* Impenetrable in armor, its soldier-hero moves like an engine, grunts like a battery of guns. *Antony and Cleopatra,* uniquely itself, grows out of but transcends all that goes before it and presages things to come.

Though *Timon* turns over familiar materials, it isn't an "after vibration" but appeals to a kind of theater Shakespeare doesn't often visit. A cyclical pattern, profoundly reactionary, organizes his story of the misanthrope who goes from everything to nothing. Like the up-and-down of Fortune's Wheel, this pattern is less indigenous, i.e. peculiar to the play, than all-purpose, right for the moralist. Shakespeare had points to make or views to enforce, and *Timon* casts them in relief, accommodating his preacher's impulse.

This modern morality, Shakespeare as by Brecht, gives the view from the watch tower. Particulars aren't much rendered and characters move behind scrim. Shakespeare locates his play in our "beneath world" (under the moon), but his hero and the others are only passing through and their halfway house doesn't detain them. Most are embodied types, Poet, Painter, Jeweler, and Merchant. "Certain Senators" cross the stage, an "Old Athenian" enters, then Lords not worth naming, three Strangers, etc. Railing Apemantus comes on "discontentedly, like himself," says a stage direction, i.e., a Cynic philosopher. Women, brazen ones in this play, though made up to suit, are only "a sweep of vanity." Shakespeare's Poet engages to bring before us "all kinds of natures," and "kinds" is what we get.

Tested one by one, Timon's fickle friends are rubbed on a golden touchstone, but their difference turns out to be sameness. Ingratitude is "the world's soul," common to all. The testing of pretension, a standard plot device of Shakespeare's, recalls earlier plays like *Measure for Measure:* "What figure of us think you he will bear?" For this question to signify, the playwright needs a master-of-his-fate kind of hero, and his truth needs a world to back it.

In *Timon,* however, "sentences" are free-standing, whether the hero's or somebody else's. For example, First Bandit: "there is no time so miserable but a man may be true." The play neither approves nor reproves this. It has some great lines and some powerful passages but pasted up as on a billboard. "Faults that are rich are fair," sententious Shakespeare allows, perhaps acquitting the hero, except that he isn't there when we need him. First Stranger wants us to "see the monstrousness of man" but Shakespeare doesn't oblige. Evil, intolerably before us in *King Lear,* is only posited. The tears that scald like molten lead are missing, and sometimes, when tears are called for, this play makes us laugh.

Shakespeare takes it much to heart, though. Anger, felt as personal, is a red spot in his cheeks, and the playwright isn't broken down but ready to take on all comers. Smarting at every pore, he skimps on dramatic business, preferring an illustrated sermon. His allegory of Fortune, a "moral painting" wheeled on from the wings, shows us didactic Shakespeare, catechizing the crowd. If the crowd won't listen, that isn't because it can't hear him. Much of *Timon's* verse is anti-discursive, gnomic couplets often running down to doggerel. This goes with the pronouncing style (fevered Shakespeare taking hold of our lapels) and suits the diminishing of his dramatis personae. Some are his butts, others his surrogates. Timon, a surrogate, has sex on the brain. E.g., this scandalous bit, raising eyebrows:

> Down with the nose,
> Down with it flat, take the bridge quite away.

Invoking plagues on them all, he means to defeat "the source of all erection." Playgoers, eyeing the rabid man, want to know what "erection" has to do with his distemper.

Lawyers, priests, and soldiers feel the lash of his tongue, also young folks and the lady of the house. (She's "o' th' brothel.") Mostly, this impartial hatred scourges the money lenders. In Shakespeare's world, superimposed on Timon's, "the learned pate / Ducks to the golden fool." Old dotards, men of the "usuring Senate," count their money lovingly, letting out coin on large interest. Well-to-do Shakespeare might have sat for their portrait. "Banish usury," his Alcibiades tells them. Unexpectedly a social critic, the bluff soldier speaks for Shakespeare. Marxist critics, alert to the money talk, promote his play as a tract for the times. More permissive than usual, he indulges their polemical reading. Biographical critics, not out to use the play, only to assess it, must wonder if what we have here is Shakespeare on Shakespeare.

Doctors, like lawyers, are always fair game, and Shakespeare seizes his chance to get at them. But his rancorous laughter exceeds its occasion, or rather there isn't one you can point to. "Trust not the physician," this ex-patient advises a trio of thieves, "he slays / Moe [more] than you rob." But not only doctors give theft a green light. In *Timon's* scoundrely universe, "each thing's a thief," not excluding sun, moon, sea, and earth. "Scientific" Shakespeare makes this good.

Handed back and forth between Misanthrope and Cynic, his Jeremiad verges on Billingsgate, tautened beyond the ordinary, though. Insults like this are worth having: "Thy father" (says First Fishwife) "put stuff / To some she-beggar and compounded thee." *Timon* goes on like that, *Hic* demolishing *Ille*. It goes on too long, one reason the play is short, but we admire the verbal legerdemain.

Whatever Shakespeare had in mind, he evokes this impersonal response, spoiling and retrieving the moral exemplum. A competition in railing, villainy too, *Timon* hopes for tragedy but stumbles on farce. This doesn't say it isn't serious, only that no one's withers are wrung. Shakespeare's targets, beneath contempt or transcending it, evade his slings and arrows. Honor is cudgeled from their limbs but like Ancient Pistol, practiced in survival, they do without it. The Devil, when he made them politic, defeated himself. Timon's servant, taking off his cap, salutes this all-too-human nature that can't be put down. In the end, he thinks, "the villainies of man will set him clear," i.e., excuse him.

"Multiplying bans" or curses, the hero has more and better lines than the villains, giving him his modicum of glamor. In Shakespeare's game for mortal stakes, all are subdued to their nature, however. This nature isn't deep, only volatile, or the springs of behavior run so deep that it seems idle to plumb them. Shakespeare after *Timon* leaves explanations alone. Some of his characters are willing to explain things but the plays don't support their "If . . . then" formulation.

Different moods assail the hero or he plays different roles, "a madman so long, now a fool." The roles don't connect and volition isn't in it, no doing more or less than becomes a man. Timon, a cartoon, never makes acquaintance with the middle of humanity, only its extremes. He doesn't grow, so can't be redeemed unless fiat redeems him, and if he changes, this is only as the weather does.

Shakespeare, resuming his beginnings in his endings, is harking back to the far-off world of his first histories where character is mysterious and action a bolt from the blue. The moralist looks out of place in this spasmodic world (but not the sage who mutters proverbs), and terms like "hero" and "villain" aren't felt as useful except as they help structure the play. Shakespeare's new-old psychology is stony ground for drama, the wit vs. will kind, and some find it enervating, possibly depressing. But it has its auspicious side and others may feel that the plays of his age, though often wild and whirling, come closer to things as they are.

DR. JOHN HALL, when he called on Shakespeare's daughter Susanna, left his pharmacopeia at home. "His antidotes are poison," he heard Timon-Shakespeare say. Some of Dr. Hall's fit this description, mixing precious stones, excreta, and animal innards, e.g., the powdered windpipe of a cock. He treated hemorrhoids (his own) by cutting open a live pigeon and applying it to his feet to "draw down the vapors." Vertigo, afflicting "one Hudson, a poor man," yielded to dried peacock dung infused in white wine. Success depended partly on the phases of the moon and treatment continued from new moon to full.

Tradition assigns Dr. Hall and his Susanna the half-timbered house in Old Town road—tourists know it as Hall's Croft—leading from the churchyard to the borough. Walled-in gardens about the house supplied nature's remedies, like rhubarb and senna. Macbeth, scorning "physic," had no use for these cathartics but they banished melancholy, and Dr. Hall could have told him. For more than thirty-five years he ministered to rich and poor, in and around Stratford. Most of the distinguished families in the neighborhood consulted Shakespeare's son-in-law. Michael Drayton, the poet, living two miles away at Clifford Chambers, was a patient of his, dosed with syrup of violets. This emetic "wrought very well both upwards and downwards." The doctor's casebook, crammed with a thousand recipes and published after his death, advertised his high repute "in the county where he lived and those adjacent."

Some of his recipes got him in trouble with the "congregated college" of physicians. For scurvy he prescribed his home-brewed scorbutic beer, boiled with plants like Lear's fumiter, rich in vitamin C. English, skimping on fruits and vegetables, lived through the winter on fish and salted beef, and this medicine worked wonders. Advanced for its time, it gave scandal, however, provoking hostile comment from "those most famous in the profession."

Dr. Hall was thirty-two to the bride's twenty-four when he married Susanna, June 5, 1607. Well-wishers, pointing to his scholarly and other credentials, propose him as a likely companion for Shakespeare, eleven years older. He held an M.A. from Cambridge, had traveled on the Continent, and kept his medical diary in Latin. Perhaps he spoke French. Also he bore arms, emblazoned on his tombstone: "sable three talbots' heads erased or." Familiar to heraldry, the talbot is a large white hound with long ears and great powers of scent. In his later years plain Mr. Hall might have been Sir John but when offered knighthood, declined it.

Elected against his will to a seat on Stratford's council, he didn't come to meetings or when he came irked the others with his "continual disturbances." He was a Puritan, Zeal of the Land Busy. As churchwarden of Holy Trinity, he reported parishioners for "loitering forth of church" while the sermon was in progress or sleeping in the belfry, especially with hat on. Men who put their hands in plackets got cited for "beastly behavior." "Laughing and rumbling" he couldn't abide. His epitaph says he was "most celebrated in the medical art," Susanna's that she was witty and wise. These two rubbed together for nearly three decades.

Propriety suggests that Shakespeare gave away the bride at the wedding. He and the King's Men were back in Oxford that September, close enough to accommodate an earlier visit to Stratford. No epithalamion saluted the occasion but a recent biographer involves him in another wedding this year, commemorated in poetry, perhaps devised by him. The poem itself, long known and up to now attracting little notice, does nothing for Shakespeare's reputation and the case for his authorship isn't proved. But attempts to glimpse him outside the limelight—doing piecework on commission, eulogizing an acquaintance, taking his ease at his inn—are always worth a hearing.

An "occasional" poet, he left the Muse to those who needed her, drawing his inspiration from the matter of everyday. Dynastic struggles, up front in the plays and more glamorous than the price of bullocks, obscure this. He had an eye for glamor but his histories reveal a "pots-and-pans" historian, absorbed by petty business, not least his own. The year Susanna married offered him an occasion. Discontent in the Midlands erupting this spring in small-scale civil war, he made it his taking-off point for another modern tragedy, disguised as ancient history. This was *Coriolanus,* among his most topical plays.

ACROSS THE BORDER in Northamptonshire on the last day of April, a knot of artisans and laborers rose against the Crown. Spilling over into Warwickshire, the Midlands Revolt freshened six-year old memories of Stratford's rising against the manor lord. Friends and neighbors of Shakespeare's led that earlier protest, giving him his personal fix.

Rebels in the Midlands were "Levellers" and "Diggers," code words in the next age for utopian socialists and communists. Leveling the estates of gentry and clergy "as they leveled banks and ditches," they aimed to "bury all which yet distinctly ranges." Coriolanus, a hell-for-leather man, no good at "bolting" or sifting, is like them. Revolts in the villages—hundreds before and after Shakespeare's time—appealed to God and Country. In 1569 Shakespeare's father, then bailiff, coped with one, the Northern Rebellion. Men who were willing to die for the faith, whether Catholic or Protestant, couldn't live by faith alone, though. Empty bellies bred rebellion, complicating the melodrama Shakespeare might have written, black hats against white hats.

Vox populi, mute in the days of Gunpowder Treason, spoke out in 1607. Shakespeare's people had a grievance, enclosures. Withdrawing land from tillage, this evil brought with it a shortage of grain and skyrocketing prices. Misery bore down harder in the Shakespeare Country than elsewhere, and "many carts laden with victual" and "good store of spades and shovels" kept the rebellion well supplied. England's worst disturbance in almost forty years, the Midlands Revolt corrects the picture of a placid English countryside, redolent of beer and good feeling.

Shakespeare's most prosaic tragedy asks to be read against the backdrop of a new economic faith, turning his world upside down.

Capitalism had an appetite, not sated yet. It laid the ax to England's woodlands, like the Forest of Arden, drained the fens, and threw up hedges around the wastes and common lands. Nimble Shakespeare prospered but many of his countrymen fell off the ladder. By 1596, "nothing but poor people" lived in Bletchingdon, near Oxford. Historians know the sequel as the Enslow Hill rising. In the year of Shakespeare's First Folio, enclosures took the last common land in this parish.

May 1607 saw three thousand rebels mustered in Warwickshire. The voice of officialdom, a village Menenius, told them to go home again but they stuck to their guns, i.e., bows and arrows. Ultras in Privy Council, types of Shakespeare's irascible hero, thought it "very strange to expostulate with such insolent, base, and rebellious people." They said officers of the Crown should have "set upon them," meeting force with force. In the upshot this happened, and on June 8 a bloody skirmish put down the rebellion. Ragged footsoldiers fought hard but broke before the charge of armed horsemen. Hanging and quartering followed.

Warwickshire's rebels, recalling Quiney et al., merge with "poor suitors" in *Coriolanus*. In Jacobean England, a model for Shakespeare's Rome, countryfolk felt the smart of ever-encroaching tyrants "which would grind our flesh upon the whetstone of poverty." Wary of the censorship, Shakespeare transposed town and country but his tale of insurrection comes hot from the press. He knew the protagonists, both "plebs" and "patricians," e.g., the Combes, Warwickshire landlords and prominent among his acquaintance. In rebellion's aftermath, William Combe, High Sheriff that year, opened a window on the time. Through it, we catch a glimpse of Shakespeare.

The people, Combe reported, wanted corn, i.e., wheat, rye, and oats, and maltsters wanted barley for brewing. But "the chief townsmen in every corporation," though well stored with both, refrained "to bring the same to market." One of them, the villain of a popular ballad, turns his widowed tenant's house into a barn, filling it "in harvest time / With good red wheat and corn." Waiting on a rise in prices, he keeps the harvest "safely from the poor." This landlord looks like Shakespeare, no oppressor of widows but first or second among Stratford's chief townsmen and not slow to exploit his advantage.

Soon after he purchased New Place, no later than February 1598, Stratford's commissioners looked into his barns. This community's livelihood depended on malting, and the corn crop gave its people their food. But a lean harvest in 1594, followed by three wet summers, thinned out the crop. Malt was scarce in 1598 and the "dearness of corn" exceeded that in "all other counties." Near-famine brought with it the threat of rioting among the poor. Rich folk, "their storehouses crammed with grain," made light of this, like Shakespeare's patricians in *Coriolanus*. "Yield us but the superfluity," his plebeians say, but the hero, not long on social conscience, doesn't listen. The corporation's survey, intended to detect hoarders, found ten quarters of malt, about eighty bushels, in Shakespeare's possession. Of his thirteen neighbors in Chapel Street ward only two had larger holdings, or you could say that two neighbors held more than he did.

However you read the statistics, they enjoin a look at *Coriolanus*. Adjusting Plutarch's history, it downplays other troubles in republican Rome while emphasizing one, the corn riots. England's caste system shackles the republic—patricians are English "gentry"—pointing up an anxious sense of class war. But Shakespeare isn't writing a democratic broadside. His commoners are fickle, also they stink—who doesn't remember "the mutable rank-scented many"—but more to the point, they challenge the status quo. Landlords trembled and this one wrote his play.

The mob, among his recurrent nightmares but mostly making offstage noises, takes center stage in *Coriolanus*. Carnivorous like Shakespeare's rebels in the *More* play, Rome's plebeians feed on one another or would unless their betters kept them in awe. They want to turn your channel, maybe his, into a ditch, or, unbuilding the city, lay everything flat. Getting rid of the "enemy of the people," all throw up their caps, crying "Hoo-oo!" In a moment, however, they call him home again, allowing the playwright his chance for heavy ironizing. Over in Corioli the people are Volscians, but what's in a name? Today they glorify the hero, the same who slew their children, tomorrow they tear him to pieces. If you depend on their favor, you swim with fins of lead. Coriolanus says so but the voice is Shakespeare's, speaking for "the graver bench," men like himself.

The eye that looks all round must look beyond self-interest, though, and Shakespeare allows his plebeians a case. His play's first act, mixing blame and something else, makes ten scenic "refractions." Armed with staves and clubs like London's prentices, mutinous citizens have to be blamed. But Shakespeare's are starving, and though they smell have strong arms, also a sense of humor. Fighting "pro patria" isn't to their liking and Coriolanus taunts them for this. In the mold of Essex and Southampton, he likes a good fight. The war with the Volscians, "audible" (noisy) and "full of vent," gives his mindless heroics an outlet.

The fable of the belly, more Act I business and one of Shakespeare's "touchstone" speeches, sings the praises of "degree." Shakespeare found it in Camden, Jonson's old teacher, equipped with a customary moral: "respect the common good of the whole public estate." Upper-class Menenius works the moral hard. He says that all suffer when the body's members, grudging the belly's privilege, rebel against it. But his rococco analogy serves a cunning man's turn—fobbing them off, shrewd plebeians say—and signaling this he makes the belly smile.

Comparisons between the greater world and man's little "kingdom," though much in vogue in Shakespeare's time, don't always beget conviction. The night is a buttocks? Elaborated to the point of fussiness, Shakespeare's verge on parody, perhaps by design. In the well-run body, laborers in a common cause store the food in cupboards or refine it in "shops" or factories, en route to the kitchen. An auditor with his checkboard supervises the work, discriminating flour and bran. According to Menenius, the good society is like that.

This following up of analogies is very Shakespearean, recalling Ulysses on the "string" untuned by discord or Falstaff whose fertile wine "manures" the blood. But all that nice equivalence—blood for rivers, tendons and veins for our "cranks and offices"—must sooner or later strike the ear as absurd. First Citizen thinks this happens sooner. Willfully pedantic, he populates the "microcosm" with engaging cartoons—the kingly head and trumpeter tongue, the arm our soldier, our steed the leg—sending up Menenius and his easy talk of "incorporate friends." In this citizen's little kingdom, the belly is a "sink" or sewer.

Things fall apart in *Coriolanus* and *disjecta membra* walk through the play. Severed from the body, the part becomes the whole. A "bosom"—it can't digest things—stands for the people, and First Citizen is rebellion's great toe. At the other end of the social scale, the hero reduces to his foot, elsewhere his knee. "Bussing" or kissing favorers, it bends at the "waist" like a beggar acknowledging alms. No knee more sufficient than this one.

The "metonymic" habit, abstracting in its tendency and congenial to late Shakespeare, comments on the way an older playwright reads the world. In *Coriolanus* this reading is oddly surrealistic. Menenius and his party will say that things are like that when men suffocate degree. But you can't moralize Shakespeare's part-for-the-whole constructions, black hats and white hats being the same. Parts don't connect to parts any more, that is all there is to it, and Shakespeare, surveying his disarticulate world, is sponsoring a vision of life.

Physiology (cribbed from his son-in-law) furnishes details but his focus on our bodily functions doesn't put an organism before us. In *Coriolanus* we see a machine. Stoking its fires, the hero, not dining like everybody else, stuffs his "pipes and channels" with wine and feeding. (Until then his blood is cold and he pouts, making faces at the morning.) Living outside our sphere, the prodigious man resembles a god or planet. Other ways of seeing him include the dragon, a rock or oak, a disembodied sword (the swordsman gone into his weapon). Emptying out the city (like the plebeians), he means to "be every man himself." With a hero like him, Shakespeare doesn't need a villain. The evil he does lives after him in Coriolanus Junior, killing butterflies for sport. Volscians on the rampage, like "boys pursuing butterflies," take their cue from this son.

Directors have a problem with *Coriolanus,* not good vs. bad but bran and chaff all round. Sympathizers on the left, deodorizing the mob, diminish the hero who doesn't need diminishing. Others do the other thing, creating an anti-republican tract. Meanwhile the playwright balances on his tickle point. But his above-the-battle posture makes it hard to warm up to his hero.

Commentators, beginning with friends in the play, do what they can for him. The man they speak of can't be "counterpoised," nobody weighing as much as he does. Bearing this out, however, they present "a thing of blood" that runs "reeking" over other men's lives. "Worthy man!" says Menenius, but it seems unlikely that Shakespeare wants us to concur.

Many of the play's readers, supposing that language must be the dress of thought, assimilate the hero to Shakespeare's swelling organ tone, a great builder-up of character. But felt emotion in *Coriolanus* is heard less as earned than delivered from the wings, e.g., when Volumnia soothes the savage breast (5.3), not a speech you would predicate of this leather-lunged virago. Like mother, like son, and the hero, though his rhetoric is generally repellent, can pull out the stops when he wants to. We never thought to hear him meditating on the world and its slippery turns. He is of Shakespeare, however, often the prisoner of his own blank verse, and the great lines, whether decorous or not, keep on coming.

Plutarch's hero has the gods on his side and a display of celestial fireworks ("sights and wonders in the air") goes with his banishment. But these portents and prodigies, much featured in other plays of Shakespeare's, are too grand for this one, and though an impressive theme organizes *Coriolanus*—Shakespeare bowing respectfully to old forms and customs—only the playwright entertains it. Both the hero and anti-hero, joining with the mob, overleap "rotten" custom. All stand as if a man were author of himself. This disgraceful unanimity denies the audience its point of rest.

Plutarch and his translator, offering reasons, repair Shakespeare's deficiency, and if you don't love their hero, at least you can figure him out. (Sparing the rod spoiled the child, or perhaps it was the early loss of his father.) Shakespeare's "dull actor" can't be "other than one thing" but has to play the man he is. Or too many reasons go to explain him, pride or defect of judgment or strength opposing strength. Maybe "sovereignty of nature," a phrase that begs the question, determines what he does. One way or another, the options close down. This is how forty-ish Shakespeare understands things.

Not liking the look of this, some in our time introduce a voluntaristic hero who gets rid of his Iron Duke persona. At their hands, more tender than the mob's, he dies a ritual death, purging and renewing his country. This sad but august ending is like a reprise of earlier tragedies, drums beating, pikes trailed for the dead. "Take him up," says the victor, suddenly remorseful. But Shakespeare is only clearing his curtainless stage. "Let's make the best of it," says Second Lord, giving tragedy its quietus.

Shakespeare's first editors led off the tragedies with *Coriolanus*. It seems out of place in their company, though, looking back to *Troilus and Cressida,* the play that precedes it in the Folio edition. Both, stuffed with parochial business Shakespeare's blueprint doesn't allow for, want to be something other. *Troilus and Cressida,* coming close to the bone, aspires to tragedy. *Coriolanus* wants to be comedy, the corrosive or comical-satire kind.

A risible eye assesses the hero. (He'd help a friend if he could but can't remember his name.) Before his last adventure, he had twenty-five wounds. "Now it's twenty-seven." Lovelier, his mother calls them, than the breasts of Hecuba when she suckled her son. (Shakespeare's simile lets us know that she's mad.) Barging into the play—Enter cursing, says the stage direction—he carries noise before him, leaving widows behind. "Who's yonder," incredulous spectators ask each other, "that does appear as he were flayed?" This is Coriolanus, absurdly like that ranting Pyrrhus in *Hamlet's* Player speech, "o'er-sized with coagulate gore."

Titans in the "cellarage" menace the house that Shakespeare built, giving his play its particular tension. Things left over from the personal life enter their claim, and the playwright, generous beyond the call of artistic duty, lends an ear. Shakespeare's quarrel with the given is lucky for him and us, though, and *Coriolanus* is most alive in its interstices. Though the setting is urban, old crab trees "here at home" need looking after, and Warwickshire and the English countryside insist on a hearing. This world outside the margins isn't recollected in tranquility, however.

Someone other than the hero hates his native country. Revolted by the "common file," Shakespeare seems more fastidious than usual. Plutarch's would-be consul shows his wounds to the people, not his. Men of the "right-hand file" smell better but otherwise the honors are even. "I banish you," says this disaffected surrogate, turning his back on them all.

Inadvertent asides trouble the play's surface, a Roman soldier instructing us in "the fittest time to corrupt a man's wife." Freudian critics, for whom there are no inadvertencies, notice the "muscular and psychological hardness" of a hero who can't help "penetrating everyone he meets." He has his special target, the Volscian general Aufidius. Were this villain on the hero's side, Coriolanus would revolt, making "only my wars with him." But the villain is an "odi et amo" man too, and twining his arms about his mighty opposite embraces both a rival and mistress. In dreams the two of them have been down together, fisting each other's throat. Waking from sleep, however, the frustrated man finds himself "half dead with nothing."

Imagined by Shakespeare from the merest hint in his source, a Strindbergian female dominates the play. (Her "boy of tears" has to regret this.) "Here comes his mother," say the tribunes, ducking for cover like schoolboys. German critics, eyes on Vienna, wonder if the hero's mother wasn't prompted by Shakespeare's. Maybe a real-life son confronts us in *Coriolanus,* paying tribute and/or getting his revenge.

Little more than a "gracious silence" in contemporary accounts, Mary Arden comes on strong in a recent biography, badgering her feckless husband. (He wasn't well-connected like his wife.) Shakespeare's play drops the husband, long gone as things get started, but he isn't missed. Her son's her husband or might be, Volumnia says. She takes more pleasure in thoughts of him fighting than "in the embracements of his bed."

At the play's apex these two have a reunion, like and unlike Lear's and Cordelia's. Historical Volscians, possibly embarrassed, averted their eyes at this Act V tableau, she kneeling, he kneeling, etc. "Clucking" the boy-hero to the wars and home again, Volumnia wins the battle but transforms the play to an Oedipal fantasy, "Coriolanus' Complaint."

BITTER COLD, bringing with it the hardest frost in Shakespeare's lifetime, gripped London the year he wrote his play. Before Christmas 1607, the Thames began to put on her "freeze-coat." Ice floes piled up against the piers of London Bridge and the river, hewn in rough blocks, turned into a gray marble pavement. Crossing from one bank to the other "as safe now as in her parlor," the citizen's wife gave example to multitudes, greater in number than in any street of the city. On the Twelfth Day after Christmas, London's archbishop, having business at Court, took this route to Westminster from his episcopal palace at Lambeth. Warming travelers like him, fires blazed on the river, and hawkers stood "ready with pans of coal to warm your fingers." *Coriolanus* recalls this. Plebeians back in Rome were no surer, says the hero, "than is the coal of fire upon the ice."

The Great Frost brought in carnival time and Londoners went bowling where there used to be water, shot at "pricks" with bows and arrows, wrestled, and played football. "Certain youths burned a gallon of wine upon the ice and made all the passengers partakers." Costermongers in makeshift booths peddled fruit and sundries, and barbers, a pair of them, hung out their signs. There was even a tavern on wheels.

The best of times for some, for others the winter of 1607–8 meant disaster. Barges laden with fuel moved over the ice, drawn by pulleys and engines, but demand outran supply and woodmongers and chandlers boosted their prices, laying the poor on the rack. "Rich men had never more money, and Covetousness had never less pity." God help the fish! said a whimsical reporter. "They use not to lie under such thick roofs."

This iron December, young Edmund Shakespeare died. The family's latest born, he was twenty-eight and like his brother a professional actor. "Edmund Shakespeare a player" reads the laconic entry in the register of St. Savior's church, Southwark, December 31, 1607. A few months before, his baseborn son Edward had preceded him in death. Plague, closing the theaters between July and November, probably killed both father and son. The son lies in St. Giles, Cripplegate, near the house on Silver Street where Shakespeare lived with the

Mountjoys. Moving back across the river in 1607, he buried his brother in Southwark.

The funeral took place on a Thursday, New Year's Eve, and "a forenoon knell of the great bell" tolled for Edmund's passing and the old year's. The fee for the bell came to 8 shillings, plus another 20 shillings for burial inside the church. Ringing the lesser bell cost only 12 pence, and 2 shillings bought a grave in the churchyard. Someone didn't grudge the extra charge. Afternoons were reserved to plays at the Globe, and this was why the bell tolled in the morning. About Shakespeare's brothers, Gilbert, Richard, and Edmund, little is known. Two bear the names of his greatest villains, an attendant lord recalling the third.

Players and watermen suffered most from the cold. The watermen, deprived of custom, wrapped up their smoky sails, but on the Bankside the show went on, though few came to see it. The King's Men had a resource, the Court, and it kept the wolf from the door. Between December 26, 1607 and Shrove Sunday in the new year, they put on thirteen plays at Whitehall, taking home £130. But the Court was for holidays, never enough of them, and comparisons were odious to their open-air playhouse, the Globe. Hoping to keep off the chill from their bones, Shakespeare's fellows handed round pans of coal, small solace, like a "spark in an old lecher's heart." Even in meaner days when they were Chamberlain's Men, they could count on the Cross Keys Inn for winter, no more.

Then the insolence of the boy actors, long-time rivals, gave them the winter playhouse they needed. This was Blackfriars, the covered theater on the north bank, southwest of St. Paul's and a hundred yards in from the Thames. Part of a "liberty" where the city's writ didn't run, it sheltered the Children of the Queen's Revels. As their fortunes rose and fell, they were called by different names but under whatever name they pretended to amateur status, a great point with English then and later. Respectable citizens, murmuring at professionals like the King's Men, left the Children alone. For boys and adult actors, strictly business was the rule, though. Blackfriars, a private theater, catered to a higher-toned audience than the Globe, meaning that it charged higher prices.

Ghosts, among them Shakespeare's familiars, walked this Thames-side quarter. On the west across Fleet Ditch, Bridewell, the house of correction, stank with the sweat of torment. Dissenting Catholics and some players and playwrights knew it from the inside. To the north on Carter Lane, the Bell beckoned to travelers up from the country.

From this tavern Richard Quiney, dead now for years, addressed his "loving good friend and countryman, Mr. William Shakespeare." Where Carter Lane and Blackfriars Lane come together, James Burbage built his theater in 1596, desecrating or reconsecrating what was once monastic ground. In the open space before the theater, Playhouse Yard, coachmen in Shakespeare's time turned their horses.

Within the precinct of the old Dominican priory, dissolved by Henry VIII, stood the church of St. Anne. Before Shakespeare came to London, the Master of the Revels used it as his office, a storehouse for tents, pavilions, and masks. The Clown in *Twelfth Night* swears by St. Anne and lives in a house "by the church." Later, Shakespeare purchased his own house in the neighborhood, on a street leading down to Puddle Wharf beside the Thames. When he crossed by wherry to the Bankside, Puddle Dock was his jumping-off point.

Blackfriars, recently fashionable, attracted upper-class residents like Sir George Carey, patron of the Chamberlain's Men. William Herbert, Earl of Pembroke, one of the "incomparable pair of brethren" to whom Shakespeare's fellows dedicated the First Folio, lived in Baynard's Castle, overlooking the river. Shakespeare's Good Duke Humphrey rebuilt this ancient pile and his Richard III (said John Stow) "practised for the crown" there. Nearby, on modern-day Queen Victoria Street, the College of Arms prepared a pedigree for newly affluent Shakespeare.

The middle class, always rising, flocked to Blackfriars in the wake of its betters. Glovers, recalling Shakespeare's father, and painters like Cornelius Janssen—he did the Lucys of Charlecote—set up their shops in alleyways around the theater. Before moving to Wood Street, Richard Field, Shakespeare's fellow Stratfordian, had his printing press in one of these shops. Neither Field nor the Lord Chamberlain wanted professional actors on the doorstep, and both signed a petition to keep them out. This foiled James Burbage's scheme to pair his theater in Shoreditch with a roofed-over playhouse for winter. Having glimpsed the Pisgah-sight, he died disappointed in 1597, never reaching the Promised Land.

Three years later the boy actors, led by Henry Evans, scrivener and shrewd businessman, leased Blackfriars from James's son Richard. Theater historians call this troupe highbrow but the term seems better suited to Shakespeare, looking down from his high forehead and appealing to the best in us. Snobbish, another word for provincial, describes the boy actors. Hamlet's "little eyases" (young hawks or nest-birds), they appealed less to intellect than class. When the new King came in, the Queen granted them her patronage. They fouled their nest, however, and the wonder is they survived for so long.

Jonson, Chapman, and Marston, troublemakers all, were three of their playwrights, and in 1605 got together to lampoon the royal Scot. This cost the boys the Queen's protection but they didn't retract their claws. Next year, a satire on the not-so-happy relation of Scots and English sent some of them to Bridewell. John Day was the author, potted centuries later by Eliot in "The Waste Land." In 1608, the boys drew blood again. Marston, snapping and snarling until he dwindled to a clergyman, brought on stage a drunken James and his favorites. (Long-suffering Queen Anne, a member of the audience, enjoyed the laugh against her husband.) Chapman, weighing in a few days later with an *au courant* tragedy, not at all like one of Shakespeare's, showed the Queen of France boxing the ears of the French King's mistress. For James enough was too much. Expelling the boys from their nest, he swore they "should never play more." Enter the King's Men and their "ordinary poet."

All this while, they were waiting in the wings, and their chance, when it came, found them ready. On August 8, 1608, Richard Burbage, joined by Shakespeare and five other sharers, bought back the unexpired lease to Blackfriars. "Housekeepers" or owners for the duration of the lease, the men of the syndicate each committed £5, 14s., and 4d. toward the yearly rental. Within days, death took one of them, William Sly, an original member of the Chamberlain's Men. This boosted Shakespeare's share to one-sixth. Though his stock in the Globe varied from 1/8th to 1/12th of the whole, at Blackfriars it never fell below 1/7th. He and his fellows did well by their investment, getting "more in one winter . . . by a thousand pounds than they were used to get on the Bankside." I.e., they nearly doubled their take.

Neighbors in Blackfriars thought they did too well and later asked the city to evict them. Mobs coming on foot and in four-wheeled hackneys clogged the streets, they said, flowing over into Ludgate. This went on "every day in winter from one or two of the clock till six at night." Playgoers then, like soccer fans in time to come, were a trouble to themselves and others, breaking down stalls and throwing goods from the shops. Irate householders couldn't get to their houses, "nor bring in their necessary provisions of beer, wood, coal, or hay." ("Hay" tells us that the country still survived in the city.) Descending to the common water stairs, they risked life and limb. Shakespeare and the King's Men, persona non grata from day one, walked a tightrope in Blackfriars.

The elder Burbage's fate might have made them think twice but they didn't consult it, even though their privileged enclave was about to come within the city's jurisdiction. This says something for their trust in the King and the ever-closer connection between the Crown and the stage. Ironically, the connection undid them, and when the Long Parliament shouldered the King aside, Blackfriars closed its doors, September 2, 1642. In the next decade, tenements replaced Shakespeare's theater.

A long siege of plague, the last such in his lifetime, kept the King's Men "on the hoof" for more than a year. Back in London for the winter season 1609–10, they moved into Blackfriars but didn't abandon the Globe, playing there from the last week of April to the first week of November. Performances, summer and winter, divided equally between the two houses, about 150 for each. Modern scholars, making much of Shakespeare's yearly change of venue, think it caused a shift in his art. This view of him, reflecting the optimistic materialism of the nineteenth century and later, says that you can explain the "product" in terms of its physical context. Modern "theory," Marxist (shading to new historicist), Freudian, and feminist, owes much to this old-fashioned reading.

A new kind of audience bought the product at Blackfriars. Groundlings weren't welcome and everybody sat. Playgoers, ascending by a winding staircase at the northern end of the building, took their seats in the galleries that rose on three sides or in the cockpit at stage level. The cheapest seat went for sixpence. It doesn't sound much but cost six times more than standing room at the Globe. In years to come fewer patrons laid out their money, and what this coterie wanted it got. By then, however, Shakespeare was dead.

Blackfriars when he and his fellows took over had fallen "far into decay," and likely the housekeepers assessed themselves for repairs. Maps of the time show their state-of-the-art playhouse, the long narrow building crowned by its gabled roof, just west of Baynard's Castle. Lead covered the roof, not about to go up in flames like the thatch-covered "heavens" at the Globe. Sea-coal fires and stone walls, three to five feet thick, kept off the weather, and six dormer windows let in the light. Performances no longer required this, however. Chandeliers hung from the ceiling, torches flared on the walls, and later, footlights—candles in sconces—illuminated the stage. The

King's Men, if they cared to, could put on their show at night. But Shakespeare's plays, like his Falstaff, have little to do with the time of the day, summoning both night and darkness in words.

Out of the Great Hall or Upper Frater of the priory, Burbage the joiner carved his auditorium, 46 feet across and 66 feet deep. First of all, this theater was small. On a good day, 700 spectators filled the auditorium, maybe a quarter of the audience that came to the Globe. Pressed for space, the King's Men did without the huge isthmus that jutted into the yard at their public theater on Bankside. The stage, less deep than wide, covered at a guess about 537 square feet. If you doubled the playing area, it still wouldn't approximate the platform stage of the Fortune or Swan. This drastic down-scaling might argue a reining in of the playwright's imaginary powers, no more panoramic drama on the "vasty fields of France." But readers will want to look at *Cymbeline,* a three-ring circus.

Running east and west at the southern end of the building, the stage butted on the side walls. Playgoers no longer surrounded it, left, right, and center. This forfeited the old cheek-by-jowl proximity, bane or blessing of the actors in earlier days, and you could say, reversing what is often said, that Shakespeare's private theater was less intimate than the Globe. But no plays tell more on our pulses than the plays he ended his career with. Which ones he wrote for the Globe and which for Blackfriars, nobody knows and he himself betrays no intention.

Standing 4½ feet above the paved floor, his stage, like the Globe's, had a trap in the middle, a place for the ghosts in *Cymbeline* to vanish into. From the cellarage below it came the sound of hautboys in *Antony and Cleopatra*. Music "above" sounded from a gallery over the stage, in the Globe from the tiring-house at stage rear, more a distinction than a difference. This dressing room, paralleling the stage, extended across the width of the hall. Three doors cut the facade, the middle one serving as a "discovery-space" where the actor stood framed for an instant. The facade in *Coriolanus,* wherever they played it, does duty scene by scene for Rome, Corioli, or the hero's house. In both theaters the same sketchy props helped create the scene, low stools, a few cushions, a simulated gold throne in Act V. In both, spectators pieced out these imperfections with their thoughts.

Built into the wall of the tiring-house, three boxes accommodated musicians, a Lord's room, and action as they needed it. Curtains, hiding the music room, allowed for a discovery-space above. Dead space between the ceiling and the outer roof of the hall housed a stationary winch and gear for flying effects. Through a trap in the ceiling, a suspension line descended to the stage, drawing actors up and down like buckets in a well. Shakespeare in his romances put this machinery to spectacular use.

Dr. Forman the astrologer witnessed two of his late spectaculars—probably at the Globe, though. Shakespeare, furnishing plays for both public and private theaters, saw to it that they played with equal ease in either. Opening Blackfriars late in 1609, he might have pleased them with bric-a-brac, some tale of a faithful shepherdess. The guess here, as good as any, is that he opened with *Antony and Cleopatra*. His most panoramic play, it ignores the theater's dimensions, crosscutting from Rome to Egypt and points in between. Making them credible was up to him.

BUT PLACE IS IMPORTANT for *Antony and Cleopatra* and Shakespeare's settings stand for different states of mind. Egypt means "Alexandrine," congenial to sybarites, also sinister, courtesy of the Soothsayer, always there in the shadows. Cleopatra's ladies-in-waiting speak for Egypt. One of them, Charmian, loves long life even better than "figs." She hopes to play her husband false but doesn't put it just like that, saying that she means to load his horns with garlands. This sexy talk is the business of the play's second scene, and no doubt you could call it immoral.

Caesar speaks for Rome. His powerful rhetoric acknowledges "strong necessities," and Antony the woman's man appears frivolous beside him. But Roman Caesar is a landlord, nobody's favorite, and hasn't much hair on his chin. Young in person but gray on the inside, the mirror image of Antony, he calls the Rome-Egypt setoff in question.

Giving Shakespeare a plot, such as it is, civil war divides his competitors, a pair of jaws that grind each other. Both ask the love of the "slippery people" but this common body doesn't love the deserving man until his deserts are passed. *Coriolanus* is still casting its baleful afterglow and Shakespeare, nosing the mob, overhears it too, rumbling in a theater where "quick comedians" act out a vulgar farce. Antony, brought on drunk, is the butt of their laughter, approving the common liar who speaks of him in Rome. His soldiers are killing Parthians, and a dutiful commander should be on the scene but this one isn't. (Possibly, like a subordinate of his, he prefers the loss of reputation to the gain that might darken him.) The thin-lipped morality that reports his doings needs a second look, however, its spokesman being both a liar and common.

Shakespeare's tragedy, not notably dramatic, resembles the swan's-down feather Antony tells of. Held by conflicting currents, it goes back and forth between extremes. No midway between them, a desponding character says, but this is where the hero lives, upon the swell at full tide. Caesar has a similar image, likening the people to a drifting iris that "lackeys" the water until it rots with motion. This single-minded man thinks the people ought to choose, coming down on one side or the other.

Too much history clogs Shakespeare's story line and everything happens twice. Twice Antony meditates one more gaudy night before a next day's battle. Twice Cleopatra and her navy turn tail. Two defeats at sea follow, and in two scenes the hero reviles her. Two deaths, both self-inflicted, bring down the curtain. Meanwhile time passes, but synoptic Shakespeare, like an old-fashioned moviemaker, flips the pages of his calendar so fast you can't see them. He wants to be on to other things.

None of his plays has so many scenes, 13 in Act III, 15 in Act IV. This busy proliferating is partly thanks to editors, but he himself shifts the camera's eye from Caesar's house in Rome to Antony's in Athens to Cleopatra's palace in Alexandria, etc. As to the history transacted in his many locales and his great gap of time, it doesn't seem of first importance. Perhaps the play's real center is remote from history "and all that."

Antony and Cleopatra occupied Shakespeare no later than spring, 1608. Most scholars, lining up the great tragedies in order of composition, put it next to last, before *Coriolanus.* Some put it earlier, citing other men's work, maybe or maybe not revised in the light of his. Reaching the summit in *Antony and Cleopatra,* he might have climbed down again, addressing himself to *Coriolanus,* even *Timon of Athens,* "essays" en route to something better. (Lawrence, having written *Sons and Lovers,* might have followed this masterpiece with *The White Peacock,* the novel he limbered up with.) But the artistic probabilities go the other way. To one reader it seems likely that Shakespeare finished the tragic cursus with *Antony and Cleopatra,* "bravest at the last." What more was there to say?

Running the course needed energy that has no parallel, and only a few years sufficed for his Matter-of-Britain plays, *Lear* and *Macbeth,* his Roman tragedies, and *Timon. Pericles,* the first of Shakespeare's romances, belongs in this period too. The work that engaged him in 1605–8 took its toll, however. After *Antony and Cleopatra* a wave did really break, and he never went back to tragedy again.

Sitting down to the fierce dispute between damnation and impassioned clay, he cast it in his familiar wit vs. will mode. Two of his principals give the play's terms. "Is Antony, or we, in fault for this?" Cleopatra's question gets a no-doubt-about-it response from Enobarbus: "Antony only, that would make his will / Lord of his reason." We know this much from word one, "Nay," heavy with censure. Unexpectedly, though, the Roman soldiers who look askance at the hero bear witness to an apparition that ties up judgment's tongue. Overflowing all measure, self indulgence in General Antony has its best analog in the fertile and life-giving Nile. The higher it swells, the more foison it promises.

All Shakespeare's tragedies enact a cause-and-effect pattern, all adjusting it too, their saving distinction. But none does this more desperately than *Antony and Cleopatra.* Opera is like it, the music, incomparably suave, stopping our ears against the strictures of morality. "Grates me," we say. A "fundamental sound" points the moral but an "overtone series," running with it, modifies what we hear. Meaning goes one way but diction and image, even as they assert it, quicken with new life. Fulvia, cast off by Antony, *broaches* mischief like wine from a barrel, and the Italy she pesters *shines* over with swords. Her idle spouse *breeds* danger or *hatches* ills, and what he loses he *kisses* away. The kissing revives him.

Blood ought to stain the scene but this play that tells of carnage brims with light and health. No comedy of Shakespeare's is more richly comic than *Antony and Cleopatra,* and some critics, uneasy about this, won't call it tragedy at all. Shakespeare's greatest poem discovers "high order" in its ambiguities, fusing different parts that shouldn't go together to compose a new heaven and earth. "Behold this man" is our rubric, both the defeated man and the one who comes smiling from the world's great snare uncaught.

Language and gesture never coalesced to more stunning effect but it carries a price tag, and Antony in defeat merges with besotted Ajax. A type of the anarch (= villain), he pulls down the temple or "wide arch" of the empire. In the procession of Shakespeare's despairing heroes, led off by Young Clifford in the first history plays, he brings up the rear. Lear, Macbeth, and Timon, all invoking the death of order, swell this tragic chorus. But Antony mitigates it, not in outline, in words. Harbingers of chaos call up the wild flood or want horrors to multiply "even till destruction sickens." Different from them, he wants Rome to "melt" in Tiber, a sensuous image that leaves paraphrase threadbare. Intellectualizers assimilate him to the others, life-denying men. But the ear, if consulted, won't allow that.

Preying on his reason, valor, something like Dutch courage, eats the sword he fights with. Friends, even his ancestor Hercules, fall away, instructed by this "diminution" in our captain's brain. His sorry change recalls *Macbeth* where the tyrant's supporters, taking the van against him, upbraid his turn for the worse. See how he "becomes" or takes his flaw, says the victor complacently, closing the book on "poor Antony."

But Caesar is saying also how Antony's flaw becomes him. No spectacle more riveting than greatness going off. Wine peeps through his scars, and though the midnight bell sounds for his last hour, he mocks it. Macbeth the dead butcher, his dark splendors notwithstanding, belongs in another universe of discourse.

Laying down the rules for this one, Antony's own "particular" aspires to control the play. He ends where he lives but friends renege, testifying more to their corruption than his. E.g., the fortunes of Enobarbus. Reason challenges the loyalty this second holds to his chief, but rejecting what it tells him he earns a place in the story. Later, going with reason, he dies convicted of "turpitude." So what shall be said of reason's counsels?

Good or bad, they don't get Antony's attention but the man who won't listen to them looks less willful than bemused. Isn't this hero "beguiled" by forbidden arts? Asides, glancing at magic, make us think so. Cleopatra, a "witch" or "charm," binds him up in "poisoned hours," and even his Hercules-connection isn't proof against her spell. On the contrary, his fate and the god's are one, and the play, summoning ancient stories, Omphale's and Dejanira's, enforces the parallel between them. Cleopatra, a cold morsel of Julius Caesar's, remembers the widowed queen who robs the god of his virility (wears "his sword Philippan"). Or she is Dejanira who gives him the poisoned shirt of Nessus the centaur. Antony, putting it on, tears himself in agony. But his death, like the god's, translates him to the heavens. At least this is what the heroine supposes. "The noble ruin of her magic," others call him, emphasis falling where you want it to.

Between the hero's culpability and his "wounded chance" lies a murky country, lit by half lights. Faults in Antony appear inherited, not what he chooses but "what he cannot change." This suggests his kinship to Coriolanus who has to be what he is, perhaps to comic characters like Lucio and Parolles. "'Tis pity of him," says Lepidus, but the "spots" or faults that darken his goodness are like the spots of heaven, "more fiery by night's blackness." Is Shakespeare drawing an equation between faults and stars? He seems to treat our moral sense cavalierly.

For the dotage that ensnares the hero, his word is "fetters," remembering the Samson and Delilah story where the seductress, a version of Shakespeare's heroine, binds her lover with fetters of brass. Break them he must, and the play shows him tossing and turning. In the end he fails to get free, so dies a suicide, Cleopatra too. But their deaths, a different kind of fettering that works out to freedom, "shackle" accidents and "bolt up" change.

Cleopatra says this, and our response to the ending vindicates and reproves her. In the roll of Shakespeare's heroines none is so equivocal, a "boggler" without a fixed point, "triple-turned whore," fragment (as in greasy scraps and orts), "salt" or lascivious. She makes defect perfection, though, and even the holy priests bless her when she's "riggish" or wanton. Dante puts Cleopatra in the second circle of Hell, and Spenser in a dungeon below his House of Pride. Others, caught like Antony in her strong toil of grace, enshrine her in accounts of good women. "Not a humble woman," said Horace, Shakespeare's teacher. He hadn't thought to venture praise. Shakespeare, upending praise from his horn of plenty, qualifies it, however, and his legend shows the other side too.

Women's hearts are waxen, according to Viola, the heroine in *Twelfth Night*. But Shakespeare's male lead has a mind like an opal, endlessly changing, and in *Antony and Cleopatra* a single image, the swan's down feather that moves with the tide, comprehends both the man and the woman. Elsewhere, though, Shakespeare insists on the difference between them. His heroines are feline, versions of himself. Convention to the contrary, this assures their priority, and in his world of theater the woman is the head of the man. That isn't as she plays at being a man, like Volumnia in *Coriolanus*.

Aloft on her burnished throne, Cleopatra, Venus-like, forces reason's devotee to adore her. But Shakespeare's theophany is a tissue of words, perhaps an imposition, and the life-giving goddess has the "aspic" in her lips. A "serpent of old Nile," she puts us in touch with archetypes or racial memories that go back to the beginning of time. Who is Cleopatra but the Serpent in the Garden, also Eve, the mother of us all? Antony, believing her, will never be saved. This piece of work is wonderful, though, and not to have seen it would have discredited his travels.

In Shakespeare's emulsion, contrarieties live together, none precipitating out. His encyclopedic art, already alien in these early years of the seventeenth century, remembers the older time when devil and lamb of God share the same cradle and Lux + fero stand for Lucifer and Christ. This is preposterous, perhaps like life itself, and moderns must shake their heads in wonder. "'Tis a strange serpent." Shaped like itself, so once and for all, it makes a clarity beyond explication.

Later in the century, two great poets, one English, one French, had a go at Shakespeare's story-in-outline. Dryden's version is univocal, commemorating a world well lost for love. In Racine's, another Egyptian queen, Berenice, takes the role of Cleopatra, the Roman Emperor Titus standing in for Shakespeare's hero. The poignant conflict of public and personal is still Shakespeare's, however, and organizing both plays is the same important question, which counts more, "the sides o' th' world" or "the sides of nature."

Dolabella, a skeptical guest at Cleopatra's feast of words, looks forward to Racine, pitting *l'empire* against *faiblesses d'amour.* A grand sensibility that earns what it decides for, Racine doesn't resolve this conflict easily and his last word is "*hélas.*" But the issue isn't ever in doubt.

Cleopatra looks forward to Dryden. He has his grandeur too and she is herself but each, tilting the balance, abridges Shakespeare's vision of "all that is won and lost." Against the "huge sphere" where it becomes us to play the man, his hero lets his "best love" draw to the point which best preserves it. But the conflict, like the hero, is "well-divided," even fearfully. "Taints" and "honors" balance and Shakespeare, poised, not irresolute, accommodates both. So he leaves us darkling or you could say enlightened, ambiguity being the hallmark of the full life and this dramatic poetry that presents it.

8

Unpathed Waters, Undreamed Shores

EARLY IN 1608 Shakespeare entered on his last phase with *Pericles, Prince of Tyre.* Forty-four this year, he had eight years left. Byron and Mozart died in their thirties, Shelley and Marlowe at twenty-nine, and Wordsworth, though living long, dwindled to "Wordswords." Shakespeare, luckier than some and more resourceful than others, got it all down, nothing left over. Toward the end he was putting out fresh shoots. Four romances and a coda record his final flowering, *Pericles* leading off.

But how much of the play is his? "Rugged and defective" (said Edmond Malone), perhaps it reflects some "reporter's" fallible memory. Verse that doesn't quite make it tells of a bad ear or an imperfect transcript, and bits of buffoonery raise eyebrows. The clownish father Simonides, bundling his daughter and the hero off to bed, isn't too indelicate for a playwright versed in country things but hasn't wit enough for Shakespeare. Heminges and Condell failed to include *Pericles* in their First Folio, no one knows why, and though uncommonly popular it had to wait half a century before editors allowed it in the canon. Even today, when its fortunes are on the rise again, many give it the back of their hand. But the play confounds its detractors. Go to a performance and see.

Scholarly opinion, picking its way through a minefield, says that Shakespeare 1) wrote all of it, 2) wrote only the last three acts, assigning most of the rest to somebody else, 3) revised the finished work of others. This biography supposes that *Pericles* is largely his. Some collaboration there was, betrayed by an oddly elliptical style. For instance, this from Act I where Pericles' ships "are like the Trojan horse / was stuffed within / With bloody veins." Clarity needs a pronoun but someone likes his utterance throttled. Conspicuous in the first acts, this tic of style persists to the end, suggesting that Shakespeare's collaborator kept his hand in. Doing this, though, he played second fiddle to Shakespeare.

Eighteenth-century editors reversed the relation, laying the work as a whole to "some friend whose interest the 'gentle Shakespeare' was industrious to promote." Improving the dialog, he augmented the "catastrophe," and was "most liberal of his aid" in Act V. But this picture of the master adding "a few flowery lines" affronts sensibility. From the stunning first scene straight to the end, the design of *Pericles,* a grand conception, is Shakespeare's.

The collaborator who dropped his pronouns looks like George Wilkins, a hack writer whose vice this was, also a "friend" whose dubious career and Shakespeare's intersected. (The author of *Measure for Measure* wasn't choosy about the company he kept.) Registers of St. Giles, Cripplegate say that in 1605 George Wilkins, "poet," lived in the parish, neighbor to Shakespeare and his landlord Mountjoy. Wilkins knew the Mountjoys and their litigious son-in-law, testifying in 1612 to an acquaintance going back seven years. When he gave his deposition in Belott vs. Mountjoy, he was living nearby in St. Sepulcher's parish. Mountjoy's daughter and her husband, quitting the house on Silver Street, set up on their own in this parish. George Wilkins gave them lodgings. Did an avuncular Shakespeare direct his young friends to this friend's house? Having brought them to the altar, it was the least he could do.

The minor playwright who tinkered plays for the King's Men kept an inn on the side, i.e., a brothel. At odds with the law, he sheltered whores accused of theft. Some he beat "outrageously" and Judith Walton, when he was through with her, had to be carried home in a chair. Haled before the Middlesex Sessions, he brought with him his respectable "guarantor," Henry Gosson, the publisher of Shakespeare's *Pericles*.

Exploiting his Shakespeare connection, Wilkins reworked the play he and the eminent friend had made together. In 1608 he turned it into a prose romance, something like the rushed-into-print "novel" that follows the popular movie. The play's "true history," he called it, "recently presented" by the King's Majesty's Players. Sprucing up his romance, he cribbed from another version of the Pericles story, in the public eye this year, thanks to a new edition. Next year came the play itself with its attribution on the title page to "William Shakespeare." Editors, accepting this badly printed quarto as the "skeleton" of his *Pericles,* flesh it out with Wilkins' novel, a quarry of lines and phrases, some of them blank verse lines, omitted in the published play. One recent commentator sees a broken vase, not a few pieces missing, the rest roughly patched and glued together. But whatever its defects, the vase is still of great price.

BACKWARD-LOOKING IN STYLE, *Pericles* is what it is deliberately. A Chorus, recalling *Henry V's,* gets each act under way but doesn't apologize or summon reality in language. This Chorus wants to distance us from the world outside the playhouse. The hero's daughter Marina, strewing flowers on her Nurse's grave, sees a "carpet," i.e. tapestry work, and *Pericles* is something like that. Scene follows scene, though not "on account of this," and structure is less modern than linear-medieval. Apprentice Shakespeare chose the same form for the loose-limbed history plays he began with. Resuming it at the end, he thought it more nearly expressive of life's content. The tossing sea, all swells and troughs, gives the pattern.

Hamlet begins in the middle of things ("Who's there?"), *Pericles* with the egg. This flattens out perspective. Progress there isn't, unless from one place to another, and moving we never move. Shakespeare's play is marvelous brooding, a meditation on the vagaries of things. The playwright we know best absorbs "ideas" in character and plot, but the pronouncing impulse, often in the service of social and political truth, is growing on him. E.g., the "fishers" who "tell the infirmities of men." Diction, sometimes archaic, is often sententious, more matter with less art.

Old enthusiasms revive when Shakespeare's heroine enters the play and her involvement in the brothel scenes (4.2 and 6) sets them apart from the rest of this bare-bones drama. Brutal and jocose, they recall the particularities of *Measure for Measure.* But Shakespeare's interest in the lower-case world is on the wane. Home truths hitch on indifferently to his different characters, and Cerimon the magus sounds like good King Simonides. Impersonal Shakespeare isn't speaking *in propria persona,* however, and the voice that serves for all of them suggests Holy Writ.

"Motes and shadows" people his stage. Not the same as Plato's shadows, they look to him like the thing itself. "She here," Antony's phrase for Cleopatra, says that no one else is like her, "lass unparalleled" and wanton nag. But characters in *Pericles* reduce to their type, "the mean knight," "a murderer," Two or Three Gentlemen. Marina, though herself, is assimilated to these others, a "new seafarer" whose destiny is already written. When she was born, the wind was north. The hero reminds us less of Lear on the Heath than Everyman, moving painfully across a universal stage. Want teaches him to know himself, a man oppressed with cold.

Contemptuous of personality, Shakespeare risks leaving us too little to take hold of. His cursoriness has its virtue, though, and the least showing of this poet's back above the element he lives in is felt as remarkable, giving the play its enormous power. Pericles has no time to pay his wife the rites of mourning

> but straight
> Must cast thee, scarcely coffined, in the ooze;
> Where, for a monument upon thy bones,
> And e'er-remaining lamps, the belching whale
> And humming water must o'erwhelm thy corpse,
> Lying with simple shells.

Nothing in Shakespeare betters this poignant farewell.

All the same, *Pericles* turns a new page. No hero more guiltless than Shakespeare's peregrine and none less able to fend for himself. Sending this wanderer on his voyage, Cleon, King of Tarsus, gives him up "to the masked Neptune and / The gentlest winds of heaven." But the winds blow as they list and a "visor" hides what's coming on. The play's resolution, coinciding with the "triumphs" of the inscrutable god, must wait until this visor is lifted. Gifted with the armor from the sea, the hero puts on the new man. But the gift is gracious, not earned, only conferred, so the elation appropriate to happy endings is tempered.

A far cry from Renaissance man, challenging the universe in these early years of the seventeenth century, Pericles must obey the powers above him. His medieval knees lack health until they bend. Wrathful or kindly the powers may be, but he himself is their plaything,

A man whom both the waters and the wind
In that vast tennis court hath made the ball
For them to play upon.

Escaping the land to perish at sea, he rides out the tempest, but not as he steers, as he submits.

Like plants and animals, Shakespeare's characters owe allegiance to nature, their parent and grave. "Infirmities" define them, sin playing no part in this. The pregnant wife Thaisa, shipped at sea on her "eaning time," is a ewe about to foal. Pericles, a taller tree than others, has to protect the roots he grows by. Unlucky chances attack the tree, and Marina's parentage is "rooted out" by time. Should disaster overtake them, a humble councilor says, all will mingle their blood in the earth, "from whence we had our being and our birth." This is the music of *Pericles,* non-intellectualizing and claiming little for man the measure of all things.

John Gower, Chaucer's friend, versified the story for the English Middle Ages. This fourteenth-century poet combined teaching with delighting, and *Pericles* brings him on to apply his didactic truth in oldfashioned couplets. He lived in the priory of St. Savior's, Southwark, and the church preserves his tomb with its recumbent effigy, near the monument to Shakespeare and the grave of his brother Edmund. Engaging Shakespeare's mind from his first days in theater, Gower's account of the much-buffeted hero furnished hints for *The Comedy of Errors,* farce leavened and sobered with a medieval sense of man's fate. "After so long grief," husband, wife, and children meet again "accidentally" at Diana's temple in Ephesus. The conclusion of *Pericles,* "by miracle" too, goes back to their reunion.

Not a meditated reunion engineered by the happy parties, it isn't contrived either but pays its respects to the natural cycle, sunshine after hail and the other way round. Spring follows winter, day follows night, and King Antiochus and Daughter, wicked ones both, must yield to Simonides and his daughter Thaisa. In the new generation, Philoten yields to Marina, dove against crow. Partly, Shakespeare wants us to distinguish good from bad, but like the seasons his play returns on itself, blurring distinction. "Womb" and "tomb" have their fellowship, and the cat with burning eyes is a guest at the wedding. Life asserts itself in the birth of the child but maidenhead is lost. High points for the play, "a tempest, / A birth, and death" bristle with difference but make a composition, vivid in Shakespeare's heroine. She's born in a tempest when her mother dies.

Modern perceptions of decorum, gaining ground in Shakespeare's age, insist that like must pair with like, but his art reflects the old "coincidence of opposites," left over from the age before him. A "glorious casket" and "fair viol," his bad daughter "looks like" the good one. Thaisa has her casket too, and when they wrench it open the viol sounds once more. Diana's nun includes her opposite, Thaïs the courtesan. But Diana, patroness of virgins, is a moon goddess too, on the side of Eros. Lucina, gentle midwife "to those that cry by night," is one of her aspects.

In the brothel, that den of iniquity, Marina invokes the chaste goddess. But "what have we to do with Diana?" Answers are in the offing as Shakespeare winds up his play. The Bawd, an herb woman, sets seeds and roots of shame whose quickening is unexpectedly wholesome. Mother and daughter quicken when they put off Diana's livery, gladdening licentious ears. This begets the happy ending, predicted long before in the emblem that stands for Pericles, a withered branch but green at the top. Unguessed at resemblances give us the theme, not the same as the moral. It doesn't suggest that we should turn libertine, rather that good and bad, life and death, have their connection.

Like some other mythy stories, Mozart's *Magic Flute,* for instance, Shakespeare's dramatizes a ritual testing. In 1.1 the hero, a bold champion, bids for the hand of an incestuous daughter. (2.2, another tournament, replicates this scene.) A riddle tests his powers as he enters the lists: Who am I? "mother, wife, and yet his child." He and we think we know what this means, but the question is thorny and a sufficient answer isn't disclosed till the end. For resolving the riddle, the one thing the hero doesn't want is address, like that of Oedipus confronting the Sphinx.

The last scenes supply the answer, embodied in Marina, "like something," no doubt her mother, but that isn't it. Saluting his long-lost child, Pericles hits on the answer: "Thou that beget'st him that did thee beget." So the ending returns us to the beginning, and the fair but foul mistress, mother, wife, and child. Incest, open in the beginning, is potential in the end when the beautiful maid of Mytilene is thrust at her father. But alpha and omega aren't just the same in *Pericles,* more than simple replication.

Losses are restored as Shakespeare's play concludes, nature seeing to it that dead flowers "blow" or bloom again. This playwright is himself, though, still the author of *King Lear* where art redresses nature. For completeness' sake, *Pericles* needs its intervention. Art "sisters" nature when dead Simonides turns into a star, light in darkness. A "goddess argentine," not flesh and blood but silvered, points our way out of the maze. Precious stones and gold enameling, the cunning work of hands, transform mother and daughter, retrieved from the sea. Those are pearls that were their eyes.

"Virtues," meaning accomplishments like weaving, dance, and versing, glorify the heroine. With her needle and thread, she composes "nature's own shape of bud, bird, branch, or berry," close to the real thing but at a remove. Schooled in music, she betters the nightingale and gives life to the mortified man. A melancholy bird, the nightingale "records with moan," remembering the rape of Philomela. But old sorrows invigorate, transformed by art, like the "still and woeful music" that rekindles life in Thaisa. Pericles, nearing the end of his journey, is "wild" to look at, and first must clip his beard "to form." But the form, though "artificial," is felt as natural too, like the "molding" of the babe Marina, "framed" or shaped by nature's hand.

A COMMONPLACE OF CRITICISM pictures late Shakespeare sailing into calm waters, finally at peace with himself. But evil darkens his last plays, and you could say he wrote them to still his beating mind. Politics, the study of men and women in society, always attracted him; now it sharpens to personal grievance. *Cymbeline* is a bully pulpit and getting up there he gives us an earful.

No play more rife with improbabilities and none less romantic in the way it inspects them. Shifting his scene from Britain to Rome, Shakespeare finds deformity wherever he looks. "The city's usuries" put him out of temper or the poison seeping from "place of greater state." Monsters breed in this place, a version of King James's Court, but the playwright cuts off their heads. Villainous Cloten, shortened by a head and flung to the waters, can "tell the fishes he's the Queen's son," brutality that makes us blink. Solemn events need solemn music, Shakespeare's character says, but he has his own priorities, and interrupting a death scene puns bizarrely on rich heirs whose fathers lack a monument to cover their bones. How this bears on the play is less important than the playwright's need to get it in. Potting away at gilded honor or closefisted men who squeeze their broken debtors, he seems his own best target, "armigerous" Shakespeare, the buyer-up of tithes.

Sexual infidelity, morbidly anatomized, sets a cuckold before us, relishing the act that undoes him. Who knows what strange fowl light on neighboring ponds? *Cymbeline* asks the question and *The Winter's Tale* pursues it. Holding his wife by the arm, the pestered man little thinks she's been "sluiced" and his pond fished in his absence. Late Shakespeare has some sick offense on his mind, hung with fantastic pictures, men vaulting or mounting women, longing for garbage, slavering with whores. Boiled or sodden, they might poison poison.

An invidious proposition says that all women are like that. Though you buy their flesh at a million a dram, you can't preserve it from tainting. A villain is our speaker but in *Cymbeline* the gap narrows between the playwright and his players. Nausea floats free, recalling the Sonnets and *Troilus and Cressida,* "exhumations" first published in the year of the play. Both *Cymbeline* and *The Winter's Tale,* written close together in 1609–10, surprise us with outbursts that seem more "lyric" than dramatic. This lyric poet is beside himself.

His characters from the beginning often act inexplicably, as if subject to some greater power, but in the plays posterity most favors the agnostic strain is muted. *Macbeth* and *King Lear* are more dramatic and less cursory than the romances. Estimating villains and heroes impartially, a more generous eye dowers them with glamor. Tragic Shakespeare so loved the world. The last plays give much of this excitement away, and a certain nervelessness goes with their magnanimities. (*The Two Noble Kinsmen* illustrates best.) Heroes have an affliction "on" them, or if they are guilty, theirs is the crime of birth. Posthumus in *Cymbeline* stands for them all. Ripped from his mother's womb as she died, he comes "crying 'mongst his foes, / A thing of pity."

Melancholy, breaking in on the day's walk and night's slumber, is Pericles' sad companion. Not a punishment for crime but the condition of his being, it drops on him and us unbidden. Late Shakespeare calls this burden the "imposition hereditary ours." In the romances, he undertakes to shift it.

Like old Henry James, returning in *The Ambassadors* to his earlier novel, *The American,* Shakespeare toward the end reconnoitered the past. Looking once more at *Othello* and *King Lear,* he imagined another reading of the tragic life. The romances, translating this to theater, show him experimenting with all a young man's vitality. Perhaps fellow feeling played a part in his experiments. Likelier, technical questions absorbed him, viz., how without fudging to make the data of tragedy add up to a different sum.

Where the tragedies, like fallen lances, intersect the curve of earth, the romances travel farther, completing the broken arc. *Pericles,* dramatizing the chance that redeems all sorrows, completes the broken arc of *King Lear.* In *The Tempest* the banished king is restored to his kingdom, less to rule than to meditate on last things. *Cymbeline* and *The Winter's Tale* revisit *Othello,* the former evoking memories of *Titus Andronicus* and *The Rape of Lucrece.* Back in the beginning, Sinon brought in betrayal with his Trojan Horse, and here it is at the end, still working our confusion. Prurient Iachimo thinks of Tarquin the ravisher, Imogen has been reading the sad tale of Tereus. (She turns down the page where Philomel "gave up.") Assimilating so much misery challenged all Shakespeare's skills, and addressing the task must have pleased him.

He had a working pattern in the Greek Romances, bittersweet stories of love lost, then found again. Modern readers will recognize "Daphnis and Chloe," familiar from Ravel's ballet. Characters in these ancient tales stumble on misery, but learning their error find their way out of the maze. Or they learn nothing and the gods "chalk forth" the way. Shakespeare in *Twelfth Night* likens his Duke Orsino to one of them, the "Egyptian thief at point of death." Both are distracted and mean to murder where they love. This reminiscence of "The Ethiopian History" is worth a footnote. Shakespeare's roots in antiquity go deeper than that, however, telling less of "influence" than a common reading of the world.

Written down in the early Christian centuries, the Romances look back to a remoter past, preserving its riddling truth for the future. Shakespeare's subplot in *King Lear,* the story of blinded Gloucester and his bastard son, came to him at second hand from Greek Heliodorus. Farther back lies a version of the Oedipus story. He didn't know Sophocles but two thousand years later had his subterranean connection.

Before his hero was Pericles he was Apollonius, whose adventures got into all the European tongues. Sidney in the *Arcadia* sponsored his change of name. Literary students still read his story in Anglo-Saxon and Greek shepherds still recite it. Jonson saw a "moldy tale," no more, Shakespeare a pilgrim's progress through lasting storms to safe harbor.

A voyage by sea or land supplies the plot of the Romances. Loss is the given, and Psyche, losing her lover Cupid, must cross "unpathed waters, undreamed shores" to find him. Elizabethan novel writers uncovered a rich lode in these peregrination tales and playwrights ransacked them to furnish the theaters. At Harrow they entertained/edified schoolboys. Even in the Shakespeare Country, where literature wasn't itself unless morally stultifying, a local vicar owned "The Voyage of a Wandering Knight."

This hero (or heroine), footloose in Bohemia, Cambria, etc., is Shakespeare's. Already *The Comedy of Errors* suggests him: "Known unto these, and to myself disguised!" Sensational incident enlivens his wanderings, the stuff of dreams "or else such stuff as madmen / Tongue" and can't interpret. But whatever it is, says the hero in *Cymbeline,* "the action of my life is like it."

Sidney, a major artist, domesticated Greek Romance, only he and Shakespeare probing below its melodramatic surface. (Greene and the others were satisfied with visceral tickling.) The product of a bad style, his *Arcadia* mixes too much sweet, too little sour, and reading it today needs *Sitzfleisch.* Shakespeare, brought up on this style, didn't mind. The end goes far to redeem the means, however.

Tempests and shipwreck tutor Sidney's heroes, and a riddle whose deeper sense is unexpected stretches thought. Disguise, often sexual, asks them to find out who they are. Ridding the country of "cruel monsters and monstrous men," they act out a "skirmish between reason and passion." The country isn't "Phrygia" but closer to home, and sometimes the skirmish defeats them. These knightly heroes aren't "sans peur et sans reproche" but live beneath a shadow, our muddy vesture of decay. Fortune directs their course in all matters "natural or accidental." Ruing this, Sidney likens them to tennis balls, "tossed by the racket of the higher powers." Their ordeal transforms them, though, and in the end they "rather appear governors of necessity than servants to fortune."

Sidney's conclusion gives hostages to the new and more hopeful world he had one foot in. Shakespeare has reservations but his archetypal voyage runs on parallel lines. Months or years go by en route to the end, twenty years in *Cymbeline,* sixteen in *The Winter's Tale.* Collapsing time, the playwright makes "a child, now swaddled," grow to manhood or old age. An "ill custom," Jonson called this, but Shakespeare's eye is less on clock time than ripeness.

Like old painters before perspective came in, he treats all his scenes as foreground. Careless of distinction, *Cymbeline* moves from Caesar's Rome to ancient Britain and Renaissance Italy. New Calvinist theology is on their minds in Britain, and at Court they talk easily of "grace" and "election." Meanwhile the wandering knight, "past hope and in despair," pursues his dreary round. But breaking this tragic circle is Shakespeare's business and the voyage ends in harmony, the diminished kind that goes with age. It isn't composed by the hero, however, but tuned by the powers above.

VARYING THEIR COMMON THEME, his romances try out different melodies, not equally pleasing. *Cymbeline,* anyway, has its longueurs. Will the fifth act never end? Can't the playwright speak his mind without torturing our English language? Erring on the other side, he lapses in oldfashioned "fourteeners," no verse more naive. Apothegms from someone's sampler do duty for wisdom, and the old proverb monger, always potential in Shakespeare but emancipated in *Cymbeline,* demands a hearing.

> Weariness
> Can snore upon the flint when resty [lazy] sloth
> Finds the down pillow hard.

Bromides sound better in Latin than English, and Shakespeare's English sounds better than ours.

Early Shakespeare, laboring exposition, hopes to tuck it in without our noticing; late Shakespeare hardly bothers to try. Wanting to convey things, he burdens a nameless Gentleman with some such phrase as "You don't mean to tell me?" King Cymbeline echoes the first line of old *King John:* "Now say, what would Augustus Caesar with us?" Stagy asides point the action, complemented by whimsicalities appropriate to farce. How do we know the lost child Guiderius except by a mole on his neck? Imogen has one too, and the villain, telling about it, persuades the not-so-bright hero that she's guilty. This reminiscence of *The Comedy of Errors* is sinister.

Evidently pastiche, Shakespeare's play recycles other work of his, but the echoes that might cue us to meaning die in air. Perhaps self-critical Shakespeare wonders what he meant in the first place. The bloody handkerchief, supposed evidence of murder, is a) Desdemona's, b) left over from Pyramus and Thisbe. Posthumus, consumed with jealousy, reminds us of Othello but coarsens the resemblance, meditating an anti-feminist tract. He'll write against women, "detest them, curse them." Tragic heroes won't want to do this.

Xenophobic Shakespeare doesn't like Italians but his Italian villain repents in Act V. This conversion strains belief, suggesting an old playwright whose hand has lost its cunning. (Or maybe "propter hoc" is what he no longer believes in.) Some patriotic rhetoric, recalling *Richard II's,* does him credit, but a Wicked Stepmother delivers his lines. Considering their source, we might look askance but aren't meant to. Perhaps women are like that, full of surprises. Who can read them? King Cymbeline inquires.

This woman makes a bad end but not because evil recoils on itself, and no "great perturbation in nature" draws the moral. A wicked Cardinal in *Henry VI,* Part One models her death scene, Shakespeare going all the way back to his earliest history. Both Queen and Cardinal are dead as the curtain falls, but more than this the playwright can't say.

So which Shakespeare is before us in *Cymbeline,* a half-bored-to-death one, going through the motions? a latecomer to romance, still in search of his style? He had the style down pat, however, and most of his early comedies mix hornpipes and funerals. Only the "ligatures," explaining things, are gone now. Shaw's "stagy trash" laughs the problem out of court; other readers, more indulgent, resolve it by citing the "golden inconsequences of romance." Shaw, wrong about Shakespeare, was right about the facile playwright often hypothesized by his defenders.

This reader thinks late Shakespeare is holding up the mirror to nature. But nature isn't nicely reticulated any more. It shows him a vexed image, so blurs the relation of cause and effect. Imitating this mysterious world, the dominion of age, is risky business for drama, and he doesn't always carry it off.

The "imbecilic" plot of *Cymbeline* provoked some of Johnson's most majestic periods, but that is only Shakespeare thumbing his nose at realistic theater where God, no Anglophile, favors the big battalions and girls don't dress up as boys. Johnson to the contrary, the trouble is with Shakespeare's poor players. All keep a low profile, even those with names, and distinguishing one from another isn't easy.

Old Belarius, a banished lord, is known also as Morgan. The King's sons, Guiderius and Arviragus, tongue-twisters both, turn into Polydore and Cadwal, supposed sons of this Morgan, while the King's daughter Imogen reappears as the Roman page Fidele. Aggravating our difficulty, Shakespeare fashions parallels in character and incident, converting his play into a house of mirrors. Two men make a wager, Cloten losing his "upon an upcast" or chance. You expect that of a fool. But the hero, foolishness incarnate, loses his wager too. In the event, chance restores him, Shakespeare having mercy on whom he will have mercy. False report takes in the hero, also the

King. British villains in other days, getting the King's ear, bely a guiltless man, Morgan-Belarius. Imposing on the hero, the Italian villain reenacts this scene in the present. Old Cymbeline, a "dullard" deceived by his wife, pleads "nolo contendere." None of these gulls, though gifted with eyesight, can make "partition" between fair and foul. Victorians, liking plucky young women, excepted the heroine, but she isn't more acute than the rest.

A shocking scene tells us this. Confronting a headless corpse dressed in her husband's garments, Imogen knows that leg and hand, foot Mercurial, Martial thigh. For savage humor, if that is what it is, nothing in Shakespeare compares. Is it possible after all that clothes make the man? They come up often in *Cymbeline,* inclining us to wonder. Riddles and visions ask attention too, but one is so cryptic that reason can't "untie" it. The other, the Roman soothsayer's, doesn't pose a problem to this professional. On the first try, however, he gets it wrong.

Late Shakespeare, hoping to make sense of what his characters say or do, invokes a formal topos, Nature, as in "the sparks of," a "noble strain," an "invisible instinct." Once manners made the man; now he isn't so sure. "Blood," imperious in his unfledged juveniles, says they are princes born. This token of what they are isn't earned but innate, though, and the valor that sets them off is charismatic. Maybe villainy is like that.

Flowers, trees, and birds, including the Phoenix, adorn the margins of *Cymbeline,* and Shakespeare's pallid characters take their definition from this natural context. One of them, Belarius, used to be a fruitful tree, its boughs bending with "mellow hangings," but a storm shakes them down, leaving him bare to the weather. The King is like this bad weather, blighting the buds around him, also like a cedar whose branches have been lopped. His sons present the branches. Opposing states of mind mingle their roots in Imogen, no different from Posthumus except that the others can't "delve" him to his root. He has a great line, addressed to the wife he loses and recovers: "Hang there like fruit, my soul, till the tree die." This image from the natural world, gathering up so many others, offers an ultimate reading of character, not moral-ethical but physiological. Diminishing for freedom, it acquits us of blame.

A "golden chance" for Posthumus, the riddle that saves him drops in his lap. Its terms are natural, however, and nature participates in the resolution. "Dead many years," the stately cedar that figures the King greens again at the top when its branches are rejoined to the old stock. Thanks aren't owing to King or hero, however, and neither, left to himself, can undo the wrong he's done.

Is it enough for wretched Posthumus to say he's sorry? The question answers itself. But the end, a "gracious season," finds the gods full of mercy, and pardon's the word to all. Signaling the end, the Thundermaster creaks down from the heavens, pleasing the boys, Jonson said. But old Shakespeare's taste for spectacle is neither here nor there, and the last plays depend on theophanies like this one. Without the god's intervention, his little people are certainly doomed.

Not aware of this, they spend themselves in action, earning the playwright's approval. Shakespeare thinks the cloistered life is less good than going out on the roads. Imogen, like Helena, meditates a pilgrimage to some "other place," opening herself to all that time will give her. Shakespeare's four male leads gain much glory in battle. Two of them, the young princelings, resemble young men in his earliest comedies, eager to "see the wonders of the world abroad." Quitting the nest exposes them to misery, but knowledge, even painful, "is as our earing," that is, it ploughs us up. Shakespeare likes this old truth of his, ringing changes on it.

He doesn't say that knowledge is power. The famous battle gets nothing done, and when the last trumpet sounds all go back to the status quo ante. Imogen's wandering, unless ratified by time, has no point but itself. Something gets done in *Cymbeline,* independent of our questing and striving, however. A benediction ends the play, falling like dew from heaven. Shakespeare's characters, relying on this "donation," strike a submissive posture. Spelling it out, saws and sayings partake of the wisdom of the folk, placatory and not open to intellectual constructions.

How does the hero arrive at answers? Shakespeare's Philharmonus, a lover of harmony, tells him how: "without seeking find." Living under a cloud, Posthumus must abide "the change of time," hoping in winter that warmer days will come. Maybe they won't come or answers that don't please await him. But whatever the gods ordain, he's blest as he obeys.

If you believe late Shakespeare, our chances improve when we're "guiltless of election" or choosing. This unforthputting psychology always attracted him and in *The Taming of the Shrew* he previews the last plays. His story of the shrewish woman who learns happiness when she sinks her knee came to him in outline from Gower's tale of "Florentius' love." (Sex, male or female, is off the point of the story, and Chaucer's Wife of Bath, reciting her own version, chooses as protagonist an ego-ridden man.) Beset with questions like Shakespeare's hero, an erring knight has to tell them what women most desire. The old hag who knows the answer exacts a price, his hand in marriage. Closing his eyes, the hero capitulates and ugliness turns into beauty. The tone deepens in *Cymbeline* but the intransitive voice still governs, making little of our fribbling intervention. If fortune favors us, it brings in some boats that aren't steered.

THE LAST PLAYS, assimilating discord, are often labeled tragicomic, a two-for-the-price-of-one art. Refreshing the audience with a good cry, it discloses a different face in Act V. This art isn't Shakespeare's, and in his romances tears and laughter harmonize like the rose and thorns that belong to our youth. The bloody corpse in *Cymbeline* needs the flowers that deck it, but not to hide or deny the violence. One figures the world's care, the other its pleasures. Within the "infant rind" of the flower itself, poison and medicine live together. This ambiguous compound, locking up our mortified spirits, revives them. Some think the opposition works out for the best, good canceling evil, but Shakespeare's point is less to happiness than rightness. A line of Chaucer's, the poet he was closest to, gives the sense of his integer: "Joy after woe, and woe after gladnesse."

Beaumont and Fletcher dropped the second clause, and teasing us with woe, exclude it from the ending. Tragicomedy, flourishing side by side with Shakespeare's lifelike amalgam, begins with them. Fifty-two plays make up the Beaumont and Fletcher canon but this is syndicate work, "B-F et cie," and others had a hand in the writing. Most of the plays are of a piece, homogenized by "theory." Tragicomedy, Fletcher said, wasn't so called because it mixed "mirth and killing"—Shakespeare's hybrids do that—"but in respect it wants death, which is enough to make it no tragedy, yet brings some near it, which is enough to make it no comedy." You could have your cake and eat it.

An odd couple, one a trifler touched with genius, the other a professional who burned the midnight oil, Beaumont and Fletcher lived together on the Bankside. Sharing the same clothes and cloak, they "had one wench in the house between them." Francis Beaumont, of Oxford and the Inner Temple, survives to posterity for his *Knight of the Burning Pestle,* Cervantes purged of feeling to suit an upscale clientele. After five years with Fletcher, the sweat and moil of theater business no longer pleased, and finding a rich heiress he left the wench and the writing of plays to his friend.

A bishop of London was John Fletcher's father, and two cousins wrote moral allegories imitating *The Faerie Queene*. Fletcher, overlaying his sexy stories with a moral patina, paid them lip service. When the King's Men leased Blackfriars, he joined the company, later succeeding Shakespeare as its "ordinary poet." At least twice the two worked together on plays, not a congenial partnership. Standard Beaumont and Fletcher suggests this.

James on the art of the puppet show gives its quiddity: "Such economy of ends!" Character, only a vehicle, changes as the plot requires, and a vacuum yawns where the heart used to be. "The appearing are fantastic things, mere shadows," Fletcher said. He was that kind of Platonist. In the pastoral play, a spinoff from tragicomedy, he managed our escape to the Garden of Eden. The Garden has a serpent, but like the pretend one in *The Magic Flute,* and a Faithful Shepherdess crushes its head with her heel. Italian Guarini, the pastoral's first begetter, called it a "natural" compound (hot blending with cold, "the dry humor with the moist"), but Fletcher's version of the golden world prefers art to nature. No bitter sky freezes and the chastely erotic heroine plucks the trees for bread. Artificial toads in a real garden, his play is like the masque enclosed in its picture frame. Pepys in the next age said people went to see him "for the scene's sake."

Exploiting cross-dressing, he and his collaborator hope to please everyone, giving offense to none. *Hamlet,* offending some, wrings our withers, but their revision of Shakespeare's play, appropriating the melancholy, turns it to laughter. In *Philaster,* or *Love Lies a-Bleeding,* the blood is wiped up in Act V. One of their kingly heroes falls in love with his sister. *Respice finem,* though: that wasn't his sister and the hero wasn't really a king. Mistaken identity occupies late Shakespeare too, and his sad but happy plays look like Beaumont and Fletcher in outline. Readers who don't discriminate between means and ends set him at the feet of his junior colleagues, an old dog learning new tricks.

IN *The Winter's Tale,* for example. Leontes, King of Sicilia, sure that his wife Hermione has been false with Bohemia's King, threatens this friend with destruction. Mamillius, Leontes' son, is a victim of his wrath, like the Queen and the daughter she carries. In the end, however, woe yields to joy. Monstrous to reason, the dead wife quickens and the lost daughter Perdita journeys homeward across unpathed waters. An old tale or fairy tale, this one has a rare Italian master who hopes to improve on nature. Julio Romano, Shakespeare calls him, the only artist he mentions by name. Analogs to the play include the lying ballads handed round by a peddler poet, Autolycus, and partly the setting is Bohemia's seacoast, "no sea near by some 100 miles." (Shakespeare counted on Jonson to point this out to him.) Were his story recited, all would hoot at it, says Paulina, another type of the artist.

But plot, certifying meaning, assigns first place to nature, and Shakespeare's fiction, different from the peddler's, lies like truth. He knew about Pygmalion whose statue comes to life, but his own art has limits and his sculptor can't cut breath with his chisel. Like a wave of the sea, moving still, "still so," Shakespeare's heroine Perdita vindicates life. We'd have her do it ever. But even as the rhetoric declares poise and stasis, the wave breaks and is gone.

Shakespeare's pastoral records our expulsion from Eden, and his characters, "postlapsarian," live in history, outside the walls. "A sad tale's best for winter," this one leaving a residue of pain. True, the hero's fury burns itself out, but the wrongs he commits are too grievous to expiate. Penance coming too short, the evil-doer has to forgive himself. Unchaste behavior, not Hermione's but someone's, loses the Garden. As rank as any flax-wench, a woman we never meet "puts to" before her troth-plight. What can that mean if it doesn't mean that she lay with her spouse out of wedlock? Permissive modern readers will wonder at Shakespeare's agitation, but there it is.

In the more or less happy ending, Leontes and the others find their way back (most, not all). But the landscape has altered, winter flowers like rue belonging to age. Sorrow alters youth's complexion, wrinkling Hermione's, and though youth won't believe it, it subdues the heart as well. For Shakespeare's mature protagonists, men and women like himself, the best isn't to come but behind.

A pastoral interlude, set in "Eden" and lively with song and dance, contrasts with Sicilia's Court where the King's heart dances, "but not for joy, not joy." Shakespeare's heroine, like unsullied Eve, embodies the goodness potential but wrecked in our fallen estate. Classical myth (where he learned his "anthropology") engages him too, and Eve is also Proserpine, Queen of the Shades. Gloomy Dis in the background waits to take her.

Peaking in the disclosure of the hero's stunning aberration, the play's great second scene focuses on that cloudless time when unreflecting boys imagined no more in prospect "but such a day tomorrow as today." Looking on his son's face, Leontes sees himself in his own boyish habit, green velvet coat, dagger sheathed lest it bite him. But dawn goes down to day, the dagger is unmuzzled, and the hero's tragedy begins.

Saying how it begins, Shakespeare offers a menu of reasons, astrological determinism, palpitations like Lear's climbing sorrow, cataracts ("the pin and the web"), an infection that addles the brain. So many readings of "the doctrine of ill-doing" cancel each other, and the injured wife and son look around for "bugs" or goblins. Solicitous courtiers, hoping to purge the King, come forward with "physic." One, Camillo, is "clerklike experienced," but his learning isn't helpful and when they ask him what the trouble is, he stands mute. Later he gets a new job as physician to Polixenes, another patient who won't or can't be cured.

In the novel Shakespeare drew on, the trouble builds slowly, not in the play. Rational-minded critics, supposing that nobody hates at first sight, think the King must be abused by some "putter-on" or plotter. It was like that in *Othello* where a "villainous knave" abuses the Moor. But no knave or plotter rationalizes behavior in *The Winter's Tale*. Dispensing with excess baggage, it seems more realistic than the tragedy it remembers.

Leontes has his own reading, like *Cymbeline's*. (Montaigne and other apologists for natural man winced when they heard it.) He says "natural goodness" engineers his ruin. Unexpectedly, the play's heroine supports this. In her the "affection" of nobleness, an inborn disposition, governs for behavior, and nature in Perdita triumphs over nurture. Lucky for her, unlucky for Leontes, this reading of what we are leaves little room for volition.

The reasoning faculty, to which we appeal on our volitional side, isn't heard from in *The Winter's Tale*. All depend for answers on dreams or a voice from the whirlwind. No wife more virtuous than the hero's but he sees her, just that, meeting noses with a paramour, kissing with inside lip, and though his shame is nothing he can "relish" or taste it. Intensely physical imagery merges "Homo sapiens" with "the rest of the herd." Woman is less herself than a horse, heifer, or dam. Unfledged in girlhood, later fat and tame, crammed with the food of praise, she holds up her neb like a bird. Copying his father (as like him "as eggs"), the little boy is a calf or bawcock, also a collop (slice of meat), cut from the same flesh. Supers are choughs or jackdaws who can't hear or feel. One is remarkable for "pettitoes" or pig's toes.

Falling but doomed to fall, Shakespeare's characters are guilty and not guilty. Perdita, a prisoner of the womb like Posthumus, is "condemned to loss" from the moment of her birth. Sinful she isn't, not so far as the story takes us, but her innocence is only formal. Like Hermione in the Trial Scene, she can plead "Not guilty" if she wants to. "Infirmities" disgrace the wisest in Shakespeare's fallen world, asserting their humanity. *Othello* and *Macbeth* draw the same equivalence but Shakespeare's tragedies seem more hopeful, and the good man, "franchised" or autonomous, disputes the "cursèd thoughts" nature sends his way. In the romances, Shakespeare's final assaying of our tragic condition, his "settled senses" defer to his madness.

Dense with premonitory signals, *The Winter's Tale* hints at what's to come from its opening lines. As we begin, malignant chance is uppermost, and difference between the royal friends is predicted. Our speakers, jollying each other, look forward to "sleepy drinks," overthrowing the reason. Like Leontes, they speak as understanding instructs them, too bad for them and him. A beautiful boy is their loving topic and they "note" how he makes old hearts fresh. Already this King's son is marked for death, however, but their senses, "unintelligent," don't know that.

Recurrences echo everywhere in a play as thickly textured as music. Back before the beginning, Hermione gives her white hand to Leontes, his forever. Time passes, scarred with betrayal, and Florizel, another suitor, takes Perdita's hand, soft like swan's down "and as white as it." These two, pairing like turtle doves, "never mean to part." But Paulina, "an old turtle," comments on their vow. Parted from Antigonus, she laments this husband who's never to be found again.

Losses are restored when Hermione is found and the news, says a tearful Gentleman, "angled for mine eyes." But this figure remembers Perdita, "the angle" or fishhook "that plucks our son hither," and brings us back to the beginning where Leontes the fisherman, "angling now," reels in his wife and friend. Violent like Leontes repudiating a daughter, the friend, another deluded parent, throws his son from him, "farre [farther] than Deucalion off." Horribly, what's past is prologue, and this web is what we never get free of.

But under the fury a surprise has been preparing, and the play's remorseless circularity, though not intermitted, has its hopeful-impersonal side, like the seasons. Waves break but reform, endlessly recurring, and Proserpine, dead to the world all winter, rises again in the spring. A pregnant woman "rounds apace," spreading to a "goodly bulk," then drops her burden, and a new cycle begins. Deucalion, another Noah, confronts a barren land, destroyed by the Deluge. But tutored by the oracle, he covers his head, throwing the bones (i.e., stones) of his mother earth behind him. Softened by time, the stones lay aside their hardness, and the sowing of seeds, unmeditated, not purposive, refreshes the land.

Shakespeare's cyclical pattern, assimilating tragedy to a grander scheme, isn't providential and doesn't require that we awake our faith. No godlike presenter brings a statue to life. Newborn things meet and succeed things dying, a natural conjunction, and this is how the red blood reigns again in the winter's pale.

Expositors in the first scene remember our two kings, "trained together" in childhood, maybe like vines espaliered or trained on the wall. Affection, "rooted" between them then, "cannot choose but branch now." This branching is exfoliating and first of all it means separation. Lastly, though, it means growing to an organic whole. Time's progress, leading us from innocence to sad experience, ripens us too, fortifying "our weak spirits." Rearing them higher is Shakespeare's ambiguous phrase.

The meeting of endings and beginnings in his story invigorates an old paradox, first claiming his attention in *The Taming of the Shrew.* The child is father to the man ("gets" or begets a sire), says a scheming servant in Shakespeare's farce comedy. Now jest turns to earnest, or rather its implications emerge. The spring fathers the year, and by analogy the child repairs the parent. King Cymbeline says this but repairing seems wasted on an Old Pantaloon. The stakes are higher in *The Winter's Tale,* incomparably the greater play, and Leontes, big enough to be damned, is worth saving. His rage is more violent "as his person's mighty."

Let us stipulate a rule for late Shakespeare, however, making him occupied less with persons than types. Changing and passing, his special is absorbed in the general. The heroine, transformed or you could say metamorphosed, queens it in "borrowed flaunts," prince and peddler exchange garments, and we hear how the gods undergo transformations to bull, ram, or humble swain. This last presents Apollo who puts on mortality and fills up the grave of Alcestis. (Euripides, whose play Shakespeare knew at second hand, wants an incarnate god, not a deus ex machina.) But Alcestis changes too, like Proserpine or Shakespeare's Hermione, bequeathing her numbness to death. Virgins, likened to plants, belong in this company. Branches bear their growing maidenheads, then loss or rapine blights them. Flowers and maidenheads are a dime a dozen, though.

Shakespeare has a metaphor for this change from life to death and the other way round, "discasing" or "dismantling." For once, however, he isn't thinking of St. Paul and his injunction to put on the new man. A false clue for *The Winter's Tale,* the moral-ethical idea suggests that we quicken when the sins of our youth are forgiven us. Shakespeare's Clown, not a wise one, promotes this idea, and Camillo imagines Leontes asking the son's forgiveness. A grace note, it becomes the young. But sins and their remission have little to do with the brightening world of Act V.

Sanctioning the future, Shakespeare's recurrences don't intimate a better future, only a bringing round again. The hero's son is dead but his daughter survives, "the whole matter / And copy of the father." Polixenes' son mirrors his father too, prints him off, Leontes says, resuming Shakespeare's bookish figure. Paulina, a supplicant, wants the copy corrected, no "yellow" (jealousy) in it. But Shakespeare has no power to order the mind, and whether this prayer will be answered no one knows.

Opposing art to nature, the future to the past, Polixenes, like famous Julio Romano, hopes to improve on nature. He thinks we can inoculate our old stock, making it bear a bud of nobler race. All for grafting in principle, he won't have it in practice, however. Shakespeare, pleased with ironies, gives him an antagonist who might be improved by marriage to a gentler scion. But Perdita holds out for unadulterated nature, not licked or amended by art. The debate between these two is ticklish, provincial Shakespeare honoring his old rubric, "respect" or context. The play's drift suggests where he stands, though.

Looking wryly at proposals for genetic engineering, he has the Clown tell us that marriage between the young couple would enrich his father's blood, dearer "by I know not how much an ounce." This raises a laugh, glancing not only at the Clown but the King, and generally in *The Winter's Tale* laughter greets the considering man who takes thought for tomorrow. "Every 'leven wether tods, every tod yields pound and odd shilling," etc. But Shakespeare's Clown gets his pockets picked and vagrant Autolycus comes away with the spoils. When he wanders, he mostly goes right.

Purging their melancholy, Shakespeare's characters put to sea, not a "determinate" (meditated) voyage. Their dedication to "unpathed waters, undreamed shores" looks wild but plot approves it. Feathers or flies for each wind that blows, they ought to make us tremble, remembering Macbeth, the reckless man who struts to his confusion.

This part of the forest has its own rules, however, and a lucky wind blows them to good. Sometimes, not always, our indiscretion serves us well.

Lifting the curse on "issue" or generation, Shakespeare's wayward children expel the fetid air that hangs over the kingdom. Years go by before that happens, however, not a "post hoc" relation but contingent. Time, critical for all the last plays, achieves character status in this one. Entering in 4.1, the tickle point between death and life, it claims power to plant and overwhelm custom, staling fresh things, then making them glister. Longer than art, this "king of men" orders the future, unguessed at until Time brings it forth.

Men and women, like growing things, are shadowed by Time's presence, sustained by it too. Puppets in a comedy not scripted by themselves, all must answer to their part, "performed in this wide gap of time." A modest part, it doesn't set them up, but attenuating loss, makes possible its restoration. Though Mamillius is in his grave and Hermione might be, new life peers through the hollow eyes of death, like the flowers the young hero sees, "peering in April's front."

Many think that Time, passing, refines us (more Judeo-Christian ideology). On this reading, Leontes, the villain of the first three acts, is broken, i.e., mended, when he reappears in Act IV. Broken he is and perhaps he repents. Perhaps the sorrows they lead him to are refreshing, like rain. But change in Leontes doesn't mandate the outcome and nothing gets done at his bidding. Years have to pass but not to school the old man, to allow the new scion to grow. All the while Leontes' Queen is hidden from sight, Time does its work of renewing. Hermione, waiting on the event, descends when "'tis time," a great coup of theater but this is incidental.

Shakespeare the marriage broker, cold as always, arranges the final scene. Paulina needing a spouse, Camillo too, happiness is thrust on both. Never mind their pretension, if any, to romantic love, who are they that we should be mindful of them? So take the woman, says Leontes, having "noted" her honesty (chastity) himself. Words, not ideas, compose Shakespeare's play, and playgoers alert to nuance will prick up their ears at this "noting."

Already in King and courtier, the tale of the foundling, "a daughter of most rare note," elicits "very notes of admiration" or wonder. But Leontes is no stranger to this "notable passion" and in Act I it stirs him to frenzy. Did Camillo not "note" it, the crazy man wants to know, all that whispering and kissing, "a note infallible / Of breaking honesty," i.e., chaste behavior turned to lust. As Shakespeare's characters make their adieux, what's past is still prologue, and the King of Act V, justifying what he thinks he knows, resumes the role he played in the beginning.

ACCORDING TO THE MYTHOS, Shakespeare said farewell in *The Tempest,* at the same time providing an allegorical key to his career. E.g., misshapen plays ("Caliban") held the stage before him but he liberates the spirit of poetry ("Ariel"). Then, having done what he set out to do, he retires to Milan/Stratford to live with Miranda/Susanna. This account omits the opportunist, however. Devoid of intention but uncommonly curious, he wrote over his lintel, "on s'engage, puis on voit." First he got involved with something, then considered where it might lead. When he lodged on Silver Street with the tiremaker Mountjoy, the Widow Digges and her teenage sons lived close by on Philip Lane. Shakespeare came to know them, consequential for him and us.

Years later Leonard Digges remembered his "wit-fraught book" in a pair of commendatory verses. He said the inspired playwright took nothing from others, finding plot, language, etc., in himself. An epitaph in St. Mary's, Aldermanbury remembers Thomas Digges, the father, two parts credentialed scientist, one part crank. This friend of Tycho Brahe's owned the great astronomer's portrait, engraved with the names of Danish forebears. Two got Shakespeare's notice, Rosencrantz and Guildenstern. Digges, a student of "the ancient disciplines of war," served with Leicester in the Low Countries. The "new discipline" he found there wasn't up to the pristine art of Greeks and Romans. Committing this opinion to print, he took his stand with Alexander and Pompey. Richard Field of Stratford published his "arithmetical-military" treatise, and Shakespeare, leafing through it, saw pedantic Fluellen come into focus.

Helping the Mountjoys and their daughter arrange a marriage, he likely did as much for the Diggeses. Mistress Anne, well left, attracted fortune-hunting suitors, including his friend Thomas Russell. Subsequently the overseer of Shakespeare's will, Russell had a part in the erotic tangle *Willobie His Avisa* tells of. This cryptic poem of the 1590s stars the "old player W. S.," tutor to another protégé in the art of love. Russell, with or without a hand up, married Widow Digges in August 1603, Shakespeare's colleague Heminges signing the book as witness. After the wedding, bride and groom moved to Alderminster in the Shakespeare Country, depositing young Leonard at Oxford.

Dudley, the elder son, got the house on Philip Lane. *The Tempest,* whatever tangent it goes off on, begins with this matter-of-fact.

Dudley Digges's ambition ran to public affairs, and he schemed to explore and colonize the New World. William Leveson was his neighbor on Philip Lane. Trustee in 1599 for Shakespeare and the Chamberlain's Men, this former church warden of St. Mary's, Aldermanbury promoted the Virginia Company, soon a pet project of Digges's. Other friends or acquaintance of Shakespeare's sat with Digges on the Council that ran the Company's business, among them the earls of Southampton and Pembroke. These connections gave Shakespeare a passport to lands beyond the sea.

Sometimes the Council convened at Southampton House, bringing old enemies together. Politics made strange bedfellows and Shakespeare's former patron found himself playing host to Chief Justice Popham, the same who passed sentence on Southampton's friend Essex. Odious in person but standing high at Court, Popham helped the Company secure its royal patent. Where others aimed to line their pockets or plant the flag abroad, he meant to rid the kingdom of riffraff. Aubrey said "he first set afoot the Plantations, e.g., Virginia, which he stocked and planted out of all the jails in England." This swarming of jailbirds guaranteed faction, "idleness and bestial sloth," and most never got a penny from Virginia. Shakespeare's Gonzalo, a would-be colonizer, doesn't make the connection.

Over the water things went from bad to worse and in 1609 the Council sent out reinforcements, a fleet of nine ships and five hundred new settlers. But a "cruel tempest," like the one in *Othello,* scattered the fleet and it limped into Jamestown minus the *Sea-Venture,* its "admiral" or flagship. Virginia's new governor, presumed lost with the flagship, couldn't command the elements to silence. Within a year, however, news of a miracle reached England. Driven on the island of Bermuda, uninhabited but full of noises, the *Sea-Venture* survived its wreck without the "perdition" or loss of a hair. Some, drunk when it foundered, ought to have drowned but came ashore "by Providence divine." Customarily, Providence helps those who help themselves, not in this story. Shakespeare, working up his own version, has a drunken crewman float to safety on a butt of sack. Shipped at sea in the "rotten carcass of a butt," Prospero gets there before him. Shakespeare's parallel seems to say that drunk and hero have something in common.

The men of the *Sea-Venture,* wintering on the island, sailed for Jamestown next spring, returning to England that September. They brought with them a full-dress account of the wreck, William Strachey's. One of Henry Evans' partners in the boys' company that played Blackfriars, Strachey went out to the New World as Secretary of Virginia. He got the post John Donne had hoped to get before making his peace with ambition. A friend of Ben Jonson's, Strachey praised this friend's tragedy, *Sejanus,* in lines Shakespeare stooped to plunder. But his unvarnished account of life in Paradise, offputting to investors, went unpublished.

Morose reading for Council members and their private friends, it came to Shakespeare via Thomas Russell and his stepson. In November 1610, Digges, visiting his mother at the manor house in the Cotswolds, found a semi-retired Shakespeare, come over from Stratford to see an old friend. Or maybe the two met in London. One way or another, Shakespeare heard a good yarn.

Next year he wrote *The Tempest,* one Englishman's tribute to a sea-haunted age when his countrymen explored the round earth's imagined corners. Setting his scene in the Mediterranean, he had his eye on places farther from home, Patagonia, for instance, where savage natives adored their great devil Setebos. Like Henry James, he rifled his reading for uncommon names, jotting them down in his tables. He followed Ralegh to the New World and circled the globe with Drake and Magellan, courtesy of travel writers like the great Purchas. Hudson's last voyage in the *Discovery* coincided with the *Sea-Venture's,* and he saw how it reproved happy endings. Preservation was the miracle, hardly the rule, and "few in millions" can speak like the persons of his play.

Sidney and the Greek Romances lie below its surface, at a deeper level his boyhood reading in the Bible. The Acts of the Apostles (ch. 27) supplied an archetypal tempest, almost the death of St. Paul. En route to Italy, this apostle and his companions, driven off course, run aground "upon a certain island." The violence of the waves threatening destruction, they cast themselves in the sea, some on boards, some on broken pieces of the ship. God's arm sustains them, though, and "it came to pass that they escaped all safe to land."

But where St. Paul's story, moralized, reduces to size, Shakespeare's keeps widening out. Like his long-ago "story of the night," building "from strange to stranger," it grows to something of great constancy. An apparition, the harpy, suggests the figure the play makes, incidentally pointing the moral. Precepts seem thin, however, against the palpable thing that declaims them. Snatching away the banquet, the harpy is loathsome but has a "devouring" grace, i.e. absorbing. Bad ones in the play are like that, "all knit up" in their distraction, both captive to madness and composed. Perhaps this is the difference between the playwright's art and the teacher's.

More than reportage or the random pillage of books, *The Tempest* has its occulted side, of moment only to Shakespeare. But it gives the play a new dimension and an elegiac tone, bassing the happy ending. Like its companion plays, this one features a perfect woman, Shakespeare's stay against the disgrace age is heir to. Different heroines present his nonpareil but though one is married, all are felt as virginal, types of the pale primrose that grows in shade and spring. "Bright Phoebus," rising in his strength, hasn't touched them.

Some think Shakespeare's grandchild gave her likeness to the heroines of the romances. She was Elizabeth, born in 1608, the year of *Pericles,* to his daughter Susanna. Others point to a godson, William Walker, his friend Henry's child, born the same year and remembered eight years later in Shakespeare's will. But old memory and desire quicken in the last plays, and Shakespeare's girl-heroines evoke his own son Hamnet, long dead like the son of Leontes. In the person of Alonso, Shakespeare asks the dead child forgiveness. Sovereign in Naples and elsewhere, this petty despot rejoices in "the name of king." But his temporal power is no help in last things, and meditating suicide he seeks his son in the ooze, "deeper than e'er plummet sounded." Prospero says he must be patient.

A great magus, Shakespeare's hero sits "on the top," directing events like the God of Creation. Graves open at his command and through his intervention the lost son Ferdinand receives a second life. But his power, like an artist's, is circumscribed by the play, lasting only for its few hours' traffic. In the end he drowns his book, "deeper than did ever plummet sound." The lost child, called Flavina, appears once more in Shakespeare's last work for the stage. His heroine in *The Two Noble Kinsmen* describes her, dead when both were eleven.

THOUGH *The Tempest* isn't Shakespeare's swan song, he comes close to us in Prospero, the man who looks through experience. First of all, however, his play is impersonal, not capitulating to life's chaos but blessing it with form. Zeroing in on the heart of the matter—no sixteen-year hiatus, no beginning "ab ovo"—*The Tempest* acts out its story in one place, to one end, and in little more time than it takes to play the play. "Here" Prospero meets his victims, wrecked "three hours since" upon the shore of this island, a crucible where attitudes are tested. Late Shakespeare, summoning the famous Unities of time, place, and action, goes back to the classical structure he aped in *The Comedy of Errors*. He wanted to make a perfect fist. Also he lets us see how his endings are in his beginnings.

Once again, regeneration gives him his theme. When did the hero "lose" his daughter? "In this last tempest," Prospero tells them, resuming the triple sequence familiar from *Pericles,* "a tempest, / A birth, and death." His travelers, moving from death to birth, undergo a sea change, arriving at last on the other side of the storm. Salt water, drenching their garments, doesn't stain but new-dyes them. This is metamorphosis.

Giving its terms, Shakespeare reascends the moralist's podium, vacated for a while. On one side, his story suggests that we learn and prosper (merging with the hero) when we whip out the old Adam. This story records the triumph of light over darkness. It begins with imprisonment, our natural condition, ending with freedom, at least partly earned. Duress being our way to freedom, we bend like Ariel to appointed tasks, not interrupting them "before the time" is out, submit ourselves to study without which we're "sots," allay the "fire in the blood." Ferdinand damps it down with "white cold virgin snow," abating the ardor of his liver, passion's seat. (Highfalutin talk, it makes us wonder at Shakespeare.) Also the young hero bears logs, a metaphor for schooling. "Some kinds of baseness / Are nobly undergone," pointing the way to rich ends.

As the play nears its climax, Prospero comes to himself. He, who didn't know himself, discovers what belongs to him, virtue, within a good man's achieving, not vengeance. Others participate in this voyage of self-discovery, finding themselves "when no man was his own." The active voice describes them. All have to court their fortune, and Shakespeare puts a premium on voluntary behavior. (You can do it if you want to.) This means, for erstwhile villains, turning over a new leaf. Even the monster Caliban seeks for grace.

Schoolmasterly Prospero, cast in Shakespeare's likeness, does his best to lend the monster a hand. Humane care doesn't stick on Caliban, though, and by and by his thwarted tutor confines him in a rock. Colonists in Virginia could have predicted this outcome. One, Sir Thomas Gates, said you had to wield the lash, seeing "how little a fair and noble entreaty works upon a barbarous disposition." Friends of this governor's were Shakespeare's friends too, and hearkening to Gates's counsel, his Prospero finds it good. "Stripes" do better than kindness.

Modern readers of *The Tempest* go up in flames at this. Their "Eurocentrist" Shakespeare, putative racist and sexist, also speaks for the new imperialism, mewing its youth in his time. Prospero, no hero, looks like its advance man. Dispossessing the too-trustful native, he threatens his rival Ferdinand with irons, even bullies sweet-tempered Miranda. "This island's mine," they hear Caliban say, noting how the late arrival "usurps" a name he doesn't own. Is he any different from the wicked brother who boots him out of Milan? Not a frivolous question, Shakespeare supposes, and his play hopes to resolve it.

Some in his time sketch the modern point of view, Montaigne, for example, englished by a tutor of Southampton's. Prospero's friend Gonzalo has been reading this French essayist. In his ideal "plantation," stripes are out, permissiveness is in. Magistrates have no place, while pieties deal with felony and treason. All are idle, and nature, left to itself, brings forth abundance, feeding an innocent people. So don't sophisticate nature, say Montaigne-Gonzalo. Wild fruit tastes better than the hothouse variety, altered by "artificial devices." Artificial means civilized.

Shakespeare thinks about this. Reconvening the debate already joined in *The Winter's Tale,* he poses the claims of nurture against the alfresco life where whatever pleases is lawful. Or rather plot, his old arbiter, stands in for the playwright. Drawn swords that threaten murder follow Gonzalo's tale of Utopia. This courtier means well but most at Court are time-servers. Taking bad suggestion "as a cat laps milk," they look the other way when Prospero loses his dukedom. The past predicts the sorry present, and "bloody thoughts," enough to go round, seem to assure the death of Alonso. Someone had better raise Hue and Cry.

A clown, funny but only partly this, engineers a coup d'état, imitating his betters. Things are free gratis in the "brave kingdom" he means to inherit. This drunken Stephano takes Gonzalo's talk to heart. Caliban, all for "freedom," i.e., license, is Gonzalo's faithful disciple. "Letters" are an insult and book burning comes first on his agenda.

A common idiom aligns the monster and ingenuous Miranda, twin studies in naivete. Though she is our heroine, others, some worse than devils, let us know that her goodness is rare. Caliban is our villain, a "natural" or halfwit. Vividly appetitive, he has killing on the brain. This Caliban = cannibal. Pieced together from books and old plays, he takes color from Kenilworth's Wild Man, a scary presence recollected from boyhood. One of the plays Shakespeare drew on puts the Wild Man before us, "a lean and hungry negro cannibal / Whose jaws swell to his eyes with chawing malice." The thing of darkness isn't out there but part and parcel of ourselves. Shakespeare's romance, sending up warning signals, looks like a cautionary tale.

But this account of *The Tempest,* though tenable, is foreshortened. Stand back a little and "Alps on Alps arise." Associating high- and lowborn, villains and heroes, ingenue and demi-devil, Shakespeare menaces demarcation, and his morality play, clear in outline, begins to shimmer. Caliban, intending mischief, thinks of "wicked dew" brushed with a raven's feather from some unwholesome fen. But Ariel, oddly like the monster, fetches dew from the "still-vexed" Bermudas, and a goddess in the wedding masque diffuses its honey drops. Her wings are saffron.

Though events on Shakespeare's island tell against naive Gonzalo and his vision of the Golden Age, unregenerate men, not to our liking, impeach the vision and ridicule the nice old man who entertains it. Later, plot unfolding, these skeptics are confounded. Murder is in the offing when villainous Antonio sees in his mind's eye a crown drop on the head of Sebastian. But Gonzalo sees this crown too, only it figures happiness, and dreaming Caliban imagines riches "ready to drop upon me." Shakespeare's analogies, moving the play forward, put its destination in doubt.

Perhaps he wants us to look twice at his ill-assorted pairings. A famous speech of Caliban's, recalling "sounds and sweet airs that give delight and hurt not," pairs with shocking cruelty: "batter his skull . . . paunch him with a stake." Beauty and a bestial nature go together in the monster, perhaps they make a sequence. A fertility goddess without whom love freezes graces the masque, her life-giving presence chiming with frigid talk of abstention. No sooner do "our revels" end than a brutish trio takes over the stage. Shakespeare says their feet stink.

Different from convention's either/or world, his mingles spongy April and the end of harvest, the dismissed bachelor and the wedded pair, "pole-clipped vineyards" (embraced by their poles) and the sterile margin of the sea. Dusky Dis, allowed a place, devises the rape of Proserpine-Miranda, and outside the charmed circle "foul conspiracy" gathers head. In Ariel's song, a touchstone for poetry, dogs bark, the rooster crows. This discordant music allays the storm's fury, also our grief.

Not an enclosed garden, *The Tempest* abuts on savage country,

Shakespeare's tragic world. His old wit vs. will play is still there vestigially and his villains, making love to their wicked employment, get just deserts. Antonio, Prospero's brother, recapitulates the fortunes of knavish Macbeth. Stolen garments fit better the longer he wears them. Putting them on, this villain self-destructs. But intimations of constraint cut across the familiar pattern. Though repentance is urged on the evil-doer and his crony of Naples, the two of them won't/can't repent. Officially a redemption play, *The Tempest* leaves some on the outside.

Others are saved but all wander in a "maze," extricated if lucky by "some heavenly power." Or they put to sea in an "unstanched" (leaky) vessel, and need some presider to bring them safely in. "All is but fortune," says the reckless butler, so "let no man take care for himself." This saying seems withershins to the purposive bias of the play.

Madness, charming the senses, afflicts Shakespeare's characters. Ignorant fumes darken reason, "mantled" like the "filthy mantled pool" where lowbrows dance up to their chins. Evil's onset appears involuntary, possibly natural, as when good wombs bear bad sons, and natural process, not wishing and willing, insures the triumph of goodness. Morning succeeds darkness or the tide comes in again, more efficient than when we back our "nobler reason." As for reason, who is so firm or constant that this "coil"—our mortal coil—would not infect it? Shakespeare's hero, supremely rational, has to ask this.

Though Caliban, the "salvage and deformed slave" of the cast list, supports its description, we can't "miss" or do without him. Intensely physical, he knows about natural things. This "earth," not dross but alloy, is also our best poet. Perhaps he tells of our creative side, the light that shines out of darkness. Encountering in sleep his vision of a golden world, Caliban is the dreamer, and waking cries to dream again.

Shakespeare's last plays discover great gain in sleep and dream, perhaps more replenishing than the purposive life. Thick slumber hangs on Pericles' eyes, and giving way he learns his salvation. Sleep, a grandsire, recreates Posthumus, the unfathered man, and Shakespeare's Bo'sun in *The Tempest,* dead asleep, wakes to freedom. Meanwhile, back on Gonzalo's plantation, indolent men dream pipe dreams. A hard-eyed critic says they mistake the truth but Shakespeare's romance courts another reading. Perhaps, like Amphion's miraculous harp, they raise walls and houses from nothing. Artists have this faculty too.

In the old spirit war, reason and fury fight it out to the death. But Prospero's metamorphosis isn't all in all, and coercing his passion he still "relishes" or tastes it. Sheltering from the storm beneath a single "gaberdine," Trinculo and Caliban have their weird symmetry, four legs and two voices. Back in England, says the jester, the monster would make a man, i.e., make his fortune. "Any strange beast there makes a man." This tilts at the audience and they loved it. But Shakespeare's line says also that you make a man when you join opposing ends of the spectrum. In the play's important crisis, deferred to the end, the hero vindicates himself, not as he dwindles but as he takes in the dark other.

Resolving the debate between nurture and nature, Shakespeare on a second hearing declines to vote for either. Like Greek Aeschylus, a playwright he didn't know but resembles profoundly, he thinks we have to have both. Atop the hill of Mars are the law courts, embodied reason. Any world worth living in is binary, though, and below them in darkness are the Furies. At the end of his career, the rational poet of the Psychomachia, climbing out on the ledge that overhangs the abyss, takes truce with the dark chthonic powers.

9

Journeys' End

"ALL ON A SUDDEN," said one of Shakespeare's first editors, "he left the stage and returned without éclat into his native country." This was in 1610–11. Some writers, beset by demons, never lay down the pen, for example Henry James. His hands still performing the act of writing when he died, he wondered at Shakespeare, forsaking "his muses dear." But Shakespeare was like his Ariel who longed to be free, and after 1613 wrote no more.

James, the prose Shakespeare, comes up often in this narrative, worthy to stand comparison with an artist even greater than himself. Also, better than any other, he illuminates the difference between old-fashioned Shakespeare and the modern mandarin. "It is art that *makes* life, makes interest, makes importance . . . and I know of no substitute whatever for the force and beauty of its process." Mundane Shakespeare could never have said this, but more assured than James, didn't have to.

New Place, fitted out a long time ago, waited on his retirement. For years he had let it wait, allowing Thomas Greene, his wife and two children, to live there. In 1609 this Stratford cousin got leave to stay another year. Then Shakespeare changed his mind. "I am old," the Queen tells them in his last history play, though no more than forty-three. Nearing fifty himself, he decided to drown his book and go back where he came from. Or perhaps, in his lines for Prospero, he wasn't speaking from the heart but embroidering a well-known passage in Ovid. One way or another, Greene moved out, no later than June 1611, making way for Shakespeare.

Settled down in the country, he pulled his own fruit in his own orchards, fed his sheep and beeves, honored his household gods. But though *rus* was delightful, *urbs* beckoned seductively. In the poem by Horace, among Shakespeare's masters, the usurer who retires to rural peace and quiet itches to reinvest his money. Shakespeare was like this too. Journeying up to town in 1612, he testified before the Court of Requests, returning in 1613, again a year later. He hoped for yet another box office success, not least for the elusive thing, perfection.

London in 1612–13 abandoned itself to revels, celebrating the marriage of Princess Elizabeth and Frederick, the Elector Palatine or Count of the Rhine. Pageants and processions moved through the streets, the Thames blazed with fireworks, and plays and masques, working the King's Men hard, diverted the young couple. Bright metal on a sullen ground, the Palatine marriage made English happy. James's only surviving daughter and her brother Henry, Prince of Wales, filled the place in popular affection the ungainly King and Queen had left empty. But in November 1612 Prince Henry died of typhoid, and joy turned to mourning.

Mourning had its term, however, the wedding taking place on St. Valentine's Day, February 14, 1613. To grace it, the King's Men put on fourteen plays at Whitehall, including *The Winter's Tale* and *The Tempest*. Many think Shakespeare revised *The Tempest* to suit the occasion but his Act IV masque salutes a betrothal, not a wedding, also making a perfect join with the play. He wasn't behindhand in paying compliments, though, entered in another entertainment, *Henry VIII*. Festivities still going strong a month later, he added an allegorical painting.

Shakespeare's "impresa" honored the King's Accession Day, March 24, 1613. Emblazoned on a paper shield, it illustrated a motto in Latin or Italian. Richard Burbage, accomplished both as player and painter, executed Shakespeare's design. Francis Manners, Earl of Rutland, paid each of them 44 shillings in gold. Shakespeare, who didn't find the work demeaning, perhaps found it amusing. Other poets, notably Jonson, hired out their talents for employment like his, meant to glorify Jacobean times with the afterglow of chivalry. The more the monarchy verged on decay, the more it did homage to things past.

In the tilting that signaled the King's anniversary, young Rutland took the field with Shakespeare's device carried before him. A servant hung it up with other *imprese* on posts below the pavilion where the royal Scot enjoyed the mock combat. Across the tilt or *toile,* a barrier running fore and aft down the center of the lists, mounted combatants fought each other with swords or blunted spears. Clothes made the man, more telling than deportment. Robert Carey, the same who galloped to Holyrood with news of the Queen's death, spent "above £400" on another Accession Day, balanced against an income of £100 a year. In Shakespeare's age they didn't count the cost. Twenty-four yards of "watchet," sky-blue silver velvet, caparisoned Rutland's horses, and he and his grooms dripped with gold and silver lace. Some of the grooms, disguised, looked "like savages or like Irishmen."

A chronicler of the age remembered pasteboard shields like Shakespeare's, painted with their emblems "very pretty and ingenious," and in *Pericles* Shakespeare describes them. Parading before the King, the hero bears "a withered branch, that's only green at top." The Latin inscription spells out his meaning, saying that he lives in this hope. Sometimes sense deferred to ingenuity, and at the tilting in 1613 an eyewitness found the devices "so dark" that he couldn't understand their meaning. He wondered if that wasn't the meaning.

No one knows how Shakespeare came to Rutland's notice but guesses aren't out of the way. A patron of actors and playwrights, the Earl was fast friends with Shakespeare's patron, Southampton. Rutland's career and Southampton's intersect from their nonage onward, both wards of Lord Burghley and students of St. John's, Cambridge. Rising with Essex, both went to prison after his fall. Shakespeare's official tie to his patron begins and ends with the love poems. But "ripples," moving outward from his long-ago dedications, suggest that the connection persisted. His single purchase of London property, evoking memories of Southampton, sets the Earl and the past he figured in before us.

In March 1613, coinciding with the King's Accession Day, Shakespeare bought a house and yard on Puddle Dock Hill, a few hundred feet from Blackfriars. He knew it as the Gatehouse, once part of the old Dominican priory and notorious or hallowed as a hideaway for papists. A nineteenth-century biographer lays out the site: "At the bottom of the hill was Puddle Dock, a narrow creek of the Thames which may yet be traced, with its repulsive very gradually inclined surface of mud at low water, and, at high, an admirable representative of its name." Men watered their horses in this smelly place.

Built over a great gate and converted to a shop and tenements, Shakespeare's London property faced the King's Wardrobe, housing "the ancient clothes of our English kings." From the Wardrobe in 1604, Shakespeare got the scarlet cloth he wore for the new King's coronation. Priesthunters kept an eye on the Gatehouse, honeycombed with "places of secret conveyance," some leading down to the Thames. In the fall of 1605, Father John Gerard looked for sanctuary there, hoping to meet with Robin Catesby and the men of Gunpowder Treason. "Have you no one to ruin but me and my family?" his despairing hostess asked him.

A kinswoman of the earls of Southampton, she was Ellen Fortescue, married to a nephew of the Master of the Wardrobe. The Bannisters, Mary and Edward, shared the house with the Fortescues, recusants all. Government agents, patrolling Farringdon Ward, a hotbed of popery, reported Mary Bannister's visits to Southampton House, just across Holborn Bars. The dowager Countess took in missionary priests, among them Mary's brother, Robert Southwell. Shakespeare's Blackfriars purchase adds another link to the tenuous but intriguing chain that binds him to his "cousin" and Southampton's.

Henry Walker, a London minstrel, not the same as Stratford's mercer, sold him the Gatehouse, March 10, 1613, for £140. He never lived in the house, leasing it to John Robinson, a common name to hang a tale on. Names echo oddly in Shakespeare's story, like the Antonios and Sebastians who keep reappearing in his theater of the mind. A John Robinson, Catholic, served the Master of the Wardrobe, and in 1596 petitioned Privy Council to block the opening of the Blackfriars playhouse. Dead by 1613, he left two sons, one intended for the priesthood. Perhaps the second son, unnamed, was Shakespeare's John, lessee of the Gatehouse. In 1616 this tenant or a namesake signed Shakespeare's will.

Most think Shakespeare the rentier meant to make his money breed. An unlikely investment, the Gatehouse cost him dear, however, almost a third more than the previous owner had paid. Also the site, like the whiff of popery, raises eyebrows. Close to Shakespeare's private theater, it was only a wherry's ride from the Globe on Bankside, no quarters more convenient for a working playwright. Having turned his back on London and the stage, did he entertain second thoughts? Perhaps he was reliving a past still enveloped in shadows.

Three nominal partners signed the purchase agreement with him, John Jackson, William Johnson, and John Heminges of the King's

Men. Two remember the Mermaid Tavern, home to the wits and once a rendezvous for traitors. Jackson, "loving friend" of Shakespeare's Globe trustee, Thomas Savage, belonged to the worshipful fraternity that met each month at the Mermaid. Verses of his appear in Coryat's *Crudities* (1611), mixed in with other work of the wits. Coryat reported their goings-on at the Mermaid, presided over by William Johnson. This London vintner served them meat, not fish, on Fridays, bringing down the law on his head. Eight years before Shakespeare bought the Gatehouse, Johnson hosted the Gunpowder Plotters.

So eager was the purchaser to push the transaction through that he mortgaged £60 of the agreed-upon price, buying the property one day and leasing it back the day after at the annual rent of a peppercorn, i.e., nothing. The mortgage deed commits him to liquidate his debt by Michaelmas next (September 29); otherwise his purchase, "null and void and of none effect," reverts to the seller. Had he paid up on his death three years later? Some say no, others that he must have, still others that the Halls pitched in to help him. Putting the future at risk, he did what he could to secure it. The year before he died, he joined with neighbors in litigation meant to clear the title to his property and theirs. Murky in particulars, the Blackfriars transaction shows a tenacious Shakespeare defending his own. Only the way he went about it seems peculiar.

Shakespeare's joint tenancy, a legal fiction, deprived his wife of her widow's dower right to a third share of the estate. In 1618 his three trustees, obeying "the true intent and meaning" of his will, handed over the property to representatives of his daughter Susanna. Normally a third of it would have come to Anne the widow, but only if her spouse were sole possessor. Sin and Satan in a poem by George Herbert play this game. God, cast as a harried relict, is pinched and straitened by the two of them, artful conspirators who seek to gain the widow's "thirds." Herbert's poem, ending happily, vindicates poetic justice, but Shakespeare left no loophole and the Gatehouse went to his daughter as planned.

LIKE SOME professional athletes, he couldn't stop saying goodbye. Sounding the elegiac note in *The Tempest,* he reappeared in 1612 with a new play, *Cardenio,* shared between him and Fletcher. Roughly half of all Elizabethan and Jacobean plays represent the work of more than a single hand, but for most of his career Shakespeare worked alone. Toward the end he collaborated, less a comment on him than his fellows. Old-fashioned, they must have thought him, in need of a sprightlier pen. Perhaps "the overflowings of Mr. Fletcher's wit" might help enliven Shakespeare's? Their shared effort doesn't survive and no one knows how well Fletcher met the need.

Shakespeare's company acted *Cardenio* before the Court at Whitehall in the Christmas season of 1612–13, again on June 8 at Greenwich. Both occasions were festive and an ambassador of the Duke of Savoy attended the second performance. Forty years later, the publisher Humphrey Moseley advertised the play as "by Fletcher and Shakespeare," but if an edition followed, all trace of it vanished in the Great Fire of 1666. Some downgrade Moseley's testimony—at least once he gave Shakespeare credit for a play that wasn't his—and *Cardenio* doesn't appear in his Beaumont and Fletcher Folio of 1647. (Perhaps he hadn't yet acquired a copy.) In the eighteenth century it surfaced again, "revised" by Lewis Theobald, Shakespeare's editor and a great *bête-noir* of Pope's. Theobald's *Double Falsehood* or *The Distressed Lovers* (1728) claims to adapt an original play of Shakespeare's, "built upon a novel in *Don Quixote*." This introduces Shakespeare to Cervantes, a newcomer to the story and one of his genuine peers.

They died the same year, like those mighty opposites St. Thomas and St. Bonaventura, tradition says on the same day. Among the major artists few look more different, though, one the veteran of Lepanto and a prisoner of the Moors, the other a civil citizen living mostly in the mind. But under the skin, resemblances are striking. Each, born in an iron age, resuscitates the age of gold. Cervantes assigns this function to his knightly hero, two parts foolish with a mysterious third, and some of Shakespeare's heroes, chasing chimeras, are like that. Neither Shakespeare nor Cervantes is romantic, however, and though both write romance, they entertain a double vision, looking at life with the eyes of the dreamer—he apprehends a world of figures—and the unillusioned man who corrects him.

Cardenio recorded the pooling of their talents, not less than Shakespeare's and Fletcher's. Reason in madness is a theme both like to play on, each vindicating folly against the wisdom of the world. Mad Lear, crowned with fumiter and furrow weeds, is Shakespeare's version of Don Quixote. "What is more dangerous than to become a poet?" Cervantes' character inquires. Raising the question too, Shakespeare answers it equivocally. Perhaps cocksure men who know what they know stand in greater jeopardy than poets. "Keep your foot still and rest quiet at home," the old ladies urge him, but he quits the bosom of discretion and sets out on his travels. The stories he returns with seem incredible to sense, like the lies Falstaff tells and Don Quixote believes in. Not decorating the truth, however, they transcend it. "I speak of Africa and golden joys," says Ancient Pistol, a fantastic, exiting to stormy applause.

Thomas Shelton's translation of *Don Quixote,* Part I, published in 1612 but completed "five or six years" before this, gave Shakespeare the story of Cardenio and his lost love Lucinda, an island in the stream of Cervantes' loosely articulated fiction. A councilor for the Virginia Company was Shelton's dedicatee and Edward Blount was one of the printers. Earlier, this friend of Marlowe's printed Florio's Montaigne, among Shakespeare's quarries, and later had a hand in the Folio of 1623. Possibly Shakespeare, trading on his connections, read *Don Quixote* before it went to the press. Readers intent on reconstructing the play ought to begin with Shelton's translation. In an age of great ones, his ranks with the greatest.

What Theobald made of Cardenio's story only comments on cultural history, however, and many dismiss his lost Shakespeare play as a fraud. But he didn't know that *Cardenio* had ever been acted—he reports to the contrary—and wasn't aware of the Moseley entry that certifies its existence. The ghost of Shakespeare stalks the play as we have it, and readers of *The Double Falsehood* will hear his voice beneath the lines. Sometimes it echoes weirdly, the lunatic hero sounding less like King Lear than Titus Andronicus. Blame for the mad scenes rests with Cervantes, whose distressed lover commits "all the pranks of rage and madness," tearing his clothes, howling through deserts, and filling the air with lamentations. Fletcher would have liked this, or possibly Theobald saw his chance to try out the high wire.

His tragicomedy pleased many when it opened at Drury Lane, though some thought the coloring, diction, and characters nearer the style and manner of Fletcher. Acknowledging Fletcher's contribution might have bolstered Theobald's case but he won't allow it, and paradoxically this supports his bona fides. Later, however, he excluded *Cardenio* from his edition of Shakespeare (1734), so perhaps had second thoughts. Friends of his arch-enemy Pope led the attack against him, but Pope himself never supposed the play to be Theobald's. "He gave it as Shakespeare's and I take it to be of that age."

Old manuscript copies get star billing in his account, one purchased from a "noble person," another in the hand of the prompter John Downes. The Restoration actor Betterton, famous for mad scenes, once owned this manuscript and intended to usher it into the world but "accident" prevented his purpose. Others, "great judges," had a look at it too, but Theobald doesn't say who they were. In 1770 one of his Shakespeare copies still survived in the library of Covent Garden playhouse. But fire, a lurid presence in Shakespeare's last years, destroyed the playhouse, taking the library with it. "Yes, it has perished," said John Philip Kemble, "gone with all its treasures."

From the unnamed noble person, Theobald heard a tale of Shakespeare's play, "given by our author as a present of value to a natural daughter of his, for whose sake he wrote it in the time of his retirement from the stage." All know Shakespeare's two daughters, Susanna and Judith, but Rowe, his first biographer, says he had three. Though scholars brush aside this addition to the family, maybe Rowe and the noble person knew whereof they spoke. Like Anne Whately, the lost love of Shakespeare's youth, his illegitimate child remains a nebulous presence on the life's periphery, investing matter-of-fact with romance.

Cervantes' tale of Cardenio is like that, stuffed with surmises, some pretty wild. But Shakespeare, like the canon in *Don Quixote,* found one good in this novella, "a large and open plain," both epic and lyric, tragic and comic, through which the pen might run unencumbered. Letting it run, he fashioned another image of our mingled yarn. Though the given he had to work with is melodramatic, analogy to his other romances suggests that he renewed it with emotion personal to himself, a Medea's bath and transforming. The theme is Shakespearean, even compulsively. Occupying him first in *The Two Gentlemen of Verona,* the story of the false friend who betrays a friend and steals his woman never lost its sinister appeal. It still haunts him in his last play, *The Two Noble Kinsmen.* The arbitrary ending looks like Shakespeare too, an act of reconciliation that cancels all crimes but leaves important questions unanswered. How quickly, perhaps willfully, in Shakespeare and Cervantes do characters forgive and forget.

ON JUNE 29, 1613, the Globe Theater burned to the ground. That afternoon, a play of Shakespeare's represented "some principal pieces of the reign of Henry VIII." Unluckily, realism glamorized the play, a Jacobean version of *son et lumière.* Early in the action two chambers—small cannon—heralding the King's entrance, razed the "glory of the Bank." Hot wadding from the cannon set the thatched roof ablaze, but spectators, mesmerized by Shakespeare's extravaganza, kept their eyes on the show while the fire ran round the house like a train. Though this was an S.R.O. day, all escaped to safety with the loss of "a few forsaken cloaks." One of the spectators might have been broiled, his breeches catching fire, but "by the benefit of a provident wit" he put it out with a bottle of ale.

A "relic of the stews," Puritans called the playhouse, laying its destruction to the hand of God. Braving divine wrath, it rose again in the new year, this time roofed with tiles, at a cost to the shareholders of £1,400. They got their money back, and the new playhouse, "far fairer than its predecessor," stood for thirty years. But an epoch ended with the burning of the Globe.

Fittingly, Shakespeare marked it in a last history play, climaxed by an exultant vision that promised the end of history. This met the mood of the time. Buoyed by hopes of the Palatine marriage, English in these early years of the seventeenth century prepared to enter God's kingdom on earth. Many hailed the Elector as the pledge of Christian union against the Antichrist, and pamphleteers and poets identified the young princess with "that now triumphant saint, our late Queen." Shakespeare, not his usual grudging self, heaps praise on the Queen, "a gem / To lighten all this isle," and Cranmer's prophecy, glorifying Elizabeth and her successor, catches up the language of contemporary marriage tracts and sermons. If you take the play at face value, "prosperous life, long, and ever happy," was just over the horizon.

Woe followed soon enough, though. Frederick, the Winter King, lost his kingdom to the armies of the Counterreformation. Fighting on but in vain, Elizabeth long outlived him. Men, moved by her sorrows, called her the Queen of Hearts. When she died in the Restoration years, Shakespeare's age and the hopes it fed on were dust. His play, though a celebration, is inflected deeply with sadness, and perhaps, discounting the heady rhetoric, he read the future.

Shakespeare wrote *Henry VIII* late in 1612 or early in 1613. "New," a letter writer called it in July 1613, "acted not passing 2 or 3 times." It isn't listed among the plays presented at Whitehall the February before this, but "much expectation" greeted an untitled play, possibly *Henry VIII*, set for the sixteenth of the month. Hundreds waited in the Great Hall on its performance "but it lapsed," giving way to a masque. According to old tradition, Shakespeare oversaw his play, tutoring a colleague, John Lowin, in the part of

King Henry. This retired playwright, one foot in Stratford, another in London, kept busy.

But "Who Wrote Shakespeare's *Henry VIII?*" James Spedding, Bacon's nineteenth-century editor, asked the question first, whipping up a storm of scholarship that hasn't petered out yet. Two distinct styles confronted him in the play, one dense, fresh, and vigorous, the other "diffuse and languid," and he gave more than two-thirds of it to Fletcher. Bits of extraneous vulgarity—e.g., the Old Lady who means to screw more money out of the King—ring depressingly like Fletcher, and long before Spedding some readers thought they saw another hand than Shakespeare's. Malone in the eighteenth century quotes an earlier critic who detected a surprising number of verses closed by "a redundant syllable," i.e., feminine endings. This was Spedding's argument, founded mostly on metrical tests. Deep down, however, he disliked the play's design, unworthy of Shakespeare, and his conclusion, though appealing to "science," seems a priori.

The argument from metrics isn't heard much today, superseded by a new touchstone, linguistic evidence. One recent scholar turns with relief from literary matters to its "statistical security." For many, perhaps most, the data still supports Fletcher, but his hand isn't so obtrusive as it used to be and his share reduces to less than a third. Some, rejecting collaboration, have him working over an unfinished play of Shakespeare's, left with the company when he retired to Stratford. But peculiarities in language forms and spelling, though they seem to indicate two hands, needn't reflect the author. In other plays of Shakespeare's, they reflect the compositor or the company's scribe. Turning up in the "Fletcher" scenes, they turn up elsewhere in late Shakespeare (along with Spedding's languid style). The disintegrators' case, however weighty, rests on internal evidence, while all external evidence points to Shakespeare. Included with his histories in the First Folio, *Henry VIII* brings up the rear. In the absence of matter-of-fact that might give the play or part of it to Fletcher, this reader is from Missouri and stands with Heminges and Condell.

A skilled hand directs Shakespeare's last plays but the skill goes into different things than it once did. Opening the box and puppets isn't among them, and late Shakespeare is bored out of his head with stage "business." Like the old-fashioned "presenter" in Senecan plays and morality plays, he leaves it all to words. In the primitive tropes and rituals out of which the drama emerged long before, onstage action is only a gleam in the eye. "Whom do you seek?" the Angel guarding the tomb asks the Three Marys and they tell him. Later, the drama throws off its shackles, action flourishes, and the play's the thing. All the while, however, there lives within its flame "a kind of wick or snuff" that will abate it.

Beginning with a question, varied at need, *Henry VIII* begs important questions. "What news abroad?" etc. Though Shakespeare's well-bred interlocutors are only being polite, his audience wants to know, a reason for playgoing, or rather, like Thomas, the Doubting Apostle, it asks him for tangible proof. Events on the Field of the Cloth of Gold, at Buckingham's trial, Anne Bullen's coronation, are "well worth the seeing," Third Gentleman thinks. But Shakespeare skimps on his old commitment to language plus gesture. A line of King Henry's reproves him: "words are no deeds."

The words are worth listening to but teach no political lesson. You can't use them to underprop faith and morals, though some try. Anticipating grand opera, they go back to old declamation. Buckingham's aria on "the long divorce of steel" evokes exiled Mowbray saying goodbye in *Richard II,* ancient history. Action stops while these characters fill the silence with music. Like the oboes beneath the stage in *Antony and Cleopatra,* Shakespeare's resonant commonplaces echo in a vacuum.

> Men's evil manners live in brass; their virtues
> We write in water.

This is like and unlike *Julius Caesar,* where we hear how the evil that men do lives after them, a certain text and the play bears it out.

By 1613 Shakespeare had mastered the noblest rhetoric ever fashioned in English. Sometimes, though, dowering his victims with praise or pity, it seems automatic. Tennyson could write blank verse in his sleep, Shakespeare too, not wholly a virtue. His heroes dance to the same tune when the last fit of their greatness is on them. Making this play's music, the old organ grinder cranks up at bidding or at will.

"All Is True," the play's alternative title, doesn't mean true-to-life but truth in the surface, inviting comparison to the tiltyard or masque. The man in his habit as he lived belongs to yesterday, and in this art of cosmetology much interest goes to the habit. Stage directions, a lot of them in *Henry VIII,* mean to see that the costumier gets it right. Despite its appeal to verisimilar theater, possibly because of it, Shakespeare's play is less mimetic than processional. The cast is his largest, needed for a pageant play, and choristers, a lute, and trumpets swell the procession. One contemporary said that his superficial truth made "greatness very familiar, if not ridiculous."

Conventions and some turns of phrase, remembered for old times' sake, assimilate the play to the rest of his repertory. Taking a decisive part in *Julius Caesar, Hamlet, Coriolanus,* the mutable rank-scented many mills about in the background. All will agree that Shakespeare's mob has color. Smitten King Henry, in love at first sight, recalls Romeo, and the King and his companions, disguised as shepherds for the banquet scene, recall the foolish "Muscovites" of *Love's Labor's Lost.* Cranmer, pious or pietistic (but who knows for sure), harks back to Duke Humphrey and Henry VI. What stronger breastplate than his untainted heart. Shakespeare's romances are still fresh in mind and Queen Katherine, "a most poor woman and a stranger," has something in common with cast-off Hermione. Devotees of generic resemblance think *Henry VIII* belongs with the romances, its new generation allaying the pain of the old. In the last act, Shakespeare, the King's good servant, says this happens. Some point to a common theme, patience in adversity, and a waiting woman called Patience appears in the play.

Times and titles alter in *Henry VIII* but action is stealthy, no battles, insurrections, or murders. Shakespeare used to like the bustle of the panoramic play—York and Lancaster's "long jars"—but turns away from all that, disdaining "noise of targets," "fool and fight." Possibly he thought it vulgar or empty of meaning. He who crowded the stage with so many volcanic figures has lost his enthusiasm for their powerful gesticulating, and his dramatis personae pass before us like figures in a painted cloth.

Structure there is but not Aristotle's cause-and-effect one. Against the sad fate of "old" Queen Katherine, he poses the happy fate of young Queen Anne. Wolsey falls but Cranmer rises. In a first part, Buckingham et al. oppose the Cardinal; in a second a new faction, led by Gardiner, opposes his successor. Point counterpoint gives the scheme of Shakespeare's earlier histories and many lay it over his last one. Katherine's vision of a better life must reprove the worldly glitter of the coronation, just preceding, and so on. But Shakespeare's scenes are freestanding, and though they face each other vividly, make no moral comment on what goes before or follows.

A self-protective playwright keeps mum on point of view, or life looked like that at fifty, thesis meeting antithesis, with no synthesis unless by fiat. Promoting a debate between Katherine and her Gentleman Usher, Shakespeare updates old "stichomythia," open-ended, however, like poetry itself. First disputant puts down the Cardinal, second disputant sings his praises, a rhetorical competition allowing the playwright to speak on both sides. He isn't irresolute, only giving the whole story, and if the theater needs point of view, that is the theater's lookout. But his structure that won't divulge it lands innocent and guilty on one level. Queen Anne's coronation is about to begin and two gentlemen remember how, at their last encounter, the Duke of Buckingham came from his trial. "But that time offered sorrow; / This, general joy." So for a moment joy displaces sorrow, but sorrow comes round again, and replication is the rule for *Henry VIII.*

All for sequential form where things depend on things, moderns liken Shakespeare's history to a Bildungsroman. In their education-of-the-hero play, King Henry, deluded at first, grows into his role at the end. But Shakespeare's hero only veers round. Poke him and he cries "Ha!" like beef-witted Ajax. Directors, fishing for clues, often merge this cartoon with Holbein's imperious fat man. Too lavish of clues, Shakespeare leaves the possibility open. His Henry is a) conscientious, b) hulls in the wild sea of his conscience, c) has a "soft cheveril conscience," pliable like kidskin. Though courtiers ironize at his expense, perhaps a due sincerity governs his behavior. Perhaps Buckingham, who looks innocent, is guilty.

Answers don't come easy in *Henry VIII,* its characters being shallow or deeper than thought. You can invoke collaboration to explain away their inconsistencies but readers of late Shakespeare, often concessive in the face of behavior, may not wish to do this. Nothing in the wicked Cardinal predicts his affecting self-awareness in decline. Like some giant tree, he puts forth leaves and bears his honors thick upon him. But a frost nips his root and he falls. "This is the state of man." Some persuasive analogies liken the frost to evil, a voluntary commitment, and in the Lear World evil doers "sliver and disbranch" themselves. Here at the end, things ripen, then rot. Shakespeare's earliest plays are like that, and his dying Katherine, her legs like loaded branches bowing to earth, recalls the dying Mortimer in the first *Henry VI* play, drooping his sapless branches to the ground.

Not poisoned by guilt or palliated by goodness, the moment has come for both. Natural process brings them to this exigent, as when fire heats the vessel and the liquor within it. Mounting until it spills over the rim, the liquor wastes itself, another figure for life, "consumed with that which it was nourished by." A hopeful councilor, reciting the analogy, goes on to apply it. He says how virtuous men quench passion's fire with the "sap" or fluid of reason. Shakespeare's tragedies sustain the analogy, off the point in *Henry VIII.*

Dr. Johnson put it in the second class of the histories, with *King John* and *Richard III.* This seems right. Except in suavity, *King John* is the better play. But *Henry VIII* shows us the playwright near the end of the journey, altogether more compelling. Performing an act prescribed by instinct or racial memory, he looks at the end for the source of his being, and finishes where he began.

In *Henry VIII* "phylogenetic" Shakespeare recapitulates the history of drama in his time. He writes a Fall of Princes play, *de casibus virorum illustrium,* "of the falls of famous men." When he was young and the drama with him, his countrymen saw tragedy under the aspect of Fortune's Wheel. A man of stature, mounting the wheel, is carried to the apogee, then he falls, never rising again. Wolsey, Fortune's eldest son, acts out the up-and-down. This priest is frail like the rest of us, all "capable" of the flesh, i.e., incapacitated by it. Shakespeare's phrase, not indicting our faults, only tells of the human condition.

An exemplary pattern for drama at its simplest, the revolution of the wheel came to him via *A Mirror for Magistrates,* first published five years before he was born. Rising and falling, the princely heroes who ride the wheel owe little to the Psychomachia. Henry, Duke of Buckingham, arrived at the last hour of his weary life, speaks his own valediction:

> My rule, my riches, royal blood and all,
> When Fortune frowned, the feller [more fell] made my fall.

This is how the *Mirror,* cruder than Shakespeare's play, otherwise not much different, reports him. In Shakespeare and his model text, the hero's life describes a pattern. But it doesn't corroborate Johnson's "modern" idea that if you thought causally you had to think morally.

Already Shakespeare's Henriad implies this pattern beyond morality. Marlowe makes it explicit, and reading him we feel that temptation and all that is merely formal. The hero-villain in his greatest play waxes, then wanes:

> Base Fortune, now I see that in thy wheel
> There is a point to which, when men aspire,
> They tumble headlong down.

In *Henry VIII* Shakespeare returns to this involuntary sequence, aloof from wishing and willing like the clenchings of the heart.

"Think you see them great," the Prologue instructs us. "Then, in a moment, see / How soon this mightiness meets misery." Buckingham on the scaffold, a little happier than his wretched father, knows that both are the same in their fortunes. Wolsey, dogging this victim, follows him in death, and is followed by his adversary Katherine. A little after the curtain falls, Wolsey's successor Thomas More goes to the block, then his successor Cromwell. Surviving the plot against him in *Henry VIII,* Cranmer dies at the stake in Oxford's High Street. Anne, enjoying her moment, gives way to another queen.

> Like as the waves make toward the pebbled shore,
> So do our minutes hasten to their end.

Young Shakespeare, unconcerned as yet to complicate the marching of the waves, reserves this to the tragedies. Many causes contribute to the deaths of Lear and Antony, not least willful behavior, and both these heroes must say "mea culpa." In the beginning, however, blame hardly plays a part. Warwick the Kingmaker, a cedar stooping to his base, surveys his trophies in the last Henry VI play. "Even now" they forsake him, but not for cause.

> Why, what is pomp, rule, reign, but earth and dust?
> And, live we how we can, yet die we must.

Shakespeare in the great years discovers many things his chronicle histories have no inkling of. But he discovers nothing that supersedes what he knew at the beginning. At the end, composing a farewell for the last of his colossal heroes, he puts away the immense erudition the tragedies record and settles for the knowledge of earlier days.

> I have touched the highest point of all my greatness,
> And from that full meridian of my glory,
> I haste now to my setting. I shall fall
> Like a bright exhalation in the evening,
> And no man see me more.

STRATFORD was a good place to come from and go back to, but Shakespeare didn't care to live there and in his last days looks like Ovid among the Goths. Rowe on the other hand says that "the latter part of his life was spent, as all men of good sense will wish theirs may be, in ease, retirement, and the conversation of his friends." He had a large fund of tolerance, also a great capacity for quiet, and perhaps these two views of him aren't mutually exclusive.

Tradition sits him down on a wooden bench "at his house in Warwickshire," drinking from an earthen half-pint mug. Like the fabulous head in his enemy Greene's old play, he brooded on times past and faroff places, chalk downs on the Channel coast, the heaths of Surrey, swamps and fens of Norfolk, primeval forests north of Trent. Annalists like Leland in his grandfather Richard's time charted this country, familiar to an itinerant player. He himself was an "inland" or citified man, not by birth but election. "I'll view the manners of the town," says his early hero, come to "Ephesus,"

> Peruse the traders, gaze upon the buildings,
> And then return and sleep within mine inn,
> For with long travel I am stiff and weary.

Carrying his mug to "a certain public house in the neighborhood of Stratford," he took his draughts of ale there every Saturday afternoon. Locals at the public house, versions of Dull the Tharborough, spoke home truths and quoted prices. "How [much] a good yoke of bullocks?" "The whole week's not fair if any day it rain." No Boswell made a record of his conversation and odds on he said little. "As old as Sibylla" and wearied with all he knew, he kept to jocularities, omitting poetry, doggerel excepted. John Shakespeare, hoping to be persuaded, said you dared "crack a jest with him at any time." But coldness went with his trade, first of all impersonal. Ruskin says somewhere that the artist's function, contemplating the dying soldier, is not to grieve but to estimate the color of his eyes. Faithful to this function, Shakespeare must have seemed a man from Mars.

The friends of his youth remained friends in his age, getting on, but that was true of him too. One was Alexander Aspinall, Oxford M.A. and Stratford's grammar-school master. Until his death, eight years after Shakespeare's, he lived in the Pedagogue's House, piecing out his income by trading in wool and yarn like Shakespeare's father. Respectful townsfolk knew him as "an ancient master of art and a man learned." Some, less respectful, called him Great Philip Macedon, a type of the domineering pedant. Arriving on the scene too late to tutor young Shakespeare, Aspinall served as the butt of his wit, "a natural wit," said one approving Stratfordian, "without any art at all." In 1594 he married the Widow Shaw, and Shakespeare wrote a posy "upon a pair of gloves that master sent to his mistress":

> The gift is small
> The will is all:
> Alexander Aspinall.

The gloves, they say, came from John Shakespeare's shop. The posy is obscene, "will" meaning sexual desire. In Shakespeare's latter years, old Aspinall, promoted to deputy town clerk, sat on Stratford's council. Piping up often ("his continual advice"), he kept the council minutes.

The brothers Nash, Anthony and John, had a head for business, commending them to Shakespeare. Both witnessed his purchase of land in Old Stratford and twice Anthony managed his tithes. Except for the Combes, no one in Stratford paid a larger subsidy. Dying rich, he left his son Thomas the Butt Close by the Avon where patriotic burghers used to shoot at butts or targets. Later Shakespeare's granddaughter, Elizabeth Hall, married young Thomas Nash, another lawyer in litigious Stratford.

Anthony's brother John owned the Bear in Bridge Street, one of Stratford's two principal inns. In 1606 Constable Dogberry booked his wife Dorothy for permitting unlawful games in the house. Frequenters of the Bear or Swan played chess and backgammon, Shovel-Board or Shove-ha'penny, using a silver counter, the broad shilling of Edward VI. This gave offense in Stratford, every year more austere. Rev. Thomas Wilson spoke for the killjoys, and Shakespeare's friend John Nash, leading an anti-Puritan riot, threatened to flay the vicar in church. "Hang him," he cried, "pull out his throat." William Reynolds, another old acquaintance, played a part in the riot. In Shakespeare's last year, he married Francis de Bois "of London in Philip Lane, French," evoking memories of the Diggeses, the Virginia Company, and *The Tempest.*

In the country, however, Shakespeare heeded country matters. When Robert Johnson, vintner and one of his debtors, died in 1611, he got £20 from the post-mortem inventory of this neighbor's estate. It represented payment for the lease of an old brick barn behind the Birthplace on Henley Street. The same year, he and seventy others helped defray the cost of lobbying Parliament "for the better repair of the highways." A shrewd countryman like the others, he wanted government to foot the bill. This matter-of-fact, humdrum but consequential to him, helps complete his portrait.

Predacious neighbors like the Combes, Sir Edward Greville, and Lord Carew of Clopton troubled his peace but got as good as they gave. Flouting the law, they withheld the lease rent obligated to Henry Barker, owner of Stratford's tithes. This jeopardized Shakespeare's investment. (Barker, leasing the tithes to others, reserved the power of reentry if the full sum due him weren't forthcoming.) Egged on by their betters, smaller tithe-holders couldn't or wouldn't agree "how to pay the residue of the said rent," and Shakespeare had to make up the difference. That was "against all equity and good conscience," the man of property said. Bringing suit in Chancery, he brought the delinquents to heel.

"A king among the meaner sort," he took his company where he found it. In 1614 a companionable preacher bent his ear. Visiting Stratford to deliver a "foundation" sermon, mandatory listening for the bailiff and council, he put up at New Place, across from the chapel. Piety was growing on Shakespeare's wife Anne, or he himself wanted news of the world he once moved in. The corporation paid him for refreshments, a quart of sack and another of claret. Sack, better than claret, manured the blood.

Preachers in his vicinity liked to trace the hand of God in our everyday business, but the fire of July 9, 1614 struck them dumb. In his younger time, "Stratford upon Avon was twice on the same day twelvemonth (being the Lord's Day) almost consumed with fire." A local clergyman said it came from heaven, God's judgment for profaning the Sabbath. The fire of 1614 broke out on Saturday, however, burning fifty-four houses worth £8,000. Thatch, roofing the houses, was the principal culprit, a familiar story to Shakespeare, shareholder in the Globe. But he didn't scoff at portents and prodigies, moralizing them often in plays.

His brother Gilbert, who took delivery for him of the Old Stratford yardlands, died in February 1612, in his forty-fifth year. Next year, almost to the day, Richard Shakespeare followed, not yet forty. With this death Shakespeare's male line became extinct. His sister Joan, married to William Hart, a maker of hats, still lived in the west wing of the Birthplace. She was her brother's pensioner and got the Henley Street house for the annual rent of a shilling. A Shakespeare Hart was living there in 1694 but in the nineteenth century the Birthplace passed from the family. Hart the hatter died in 1616, having fathered three sons, also a daughter, dead before him. His funeral took place the same month as Shakespeare's, and his wife outlived them both by thirty years.

Shakespeare and Anne, living apart for most of their marriage, renewed acquaintance before it ended. The battlefield is nothing "to the dark house and the detested wife," says an unwilling husband in *All's Well That Ends Well,* and already in the first Henry VI play forced wedlock is likened to "an age of discord and continual strife." Elsewhere we hear that a mad dog's tooth poisons less than "the venom clamors of a jealous woman." Shakespeare's writing isn't personal but dramatic, however, and appealing from the work to the life carries risks. In 1613 his daughter Susanna made page one news in gossipy Stratford, slandered by John Lane, the scion of neighborhood gentry. Three years later his second daughter Judith married in haste, repenting at leisure. As to daughters, said old Capulet, "one is one too much." He was a heavy-handed parent, and in this case at least life imitated art.

Susanna, said young Lane, "had the running of the reins [kidneys] and had been naught with Rafe Smith at John Palmer," evidently at his house. Smith was a local haberdasher, Palmers lived in Snitterfield and Wilmcote, and running of the reins is gonorrhea. Defending her character, Susanna brought an action against her accuser, July 15, 1613. Worcester's ecclesiastical court heard the case. Shakespeare, many years before, had gone down to Worcester for his license to wed, and his favorite child retraced this journey. Robert Whatcott, his servant or Dr. Hall's, appeared for the plaintiff, later witnesssing Shakespeare's will. Lane didn't appear and the court sentenced him to excommunication. He went from bad to worse, meeting our sense of fitness, and in 1619 the wardens of Holy Trinity had him up for drunken behavior. A modern chronicler of the Shakespeare family, quoting *Hamlet,* sympathizes with Susanna's troubles: "Be thou as chaste as ice, as pure as snow, thou shalt not escape calumny." James Joyce, however, read this tale of sexual impropriety under the heading, like father, like daughter.

Judith Shakespeare was thirty-one, in the time's opinion well past her prime, when she married Thomas Quiney, going on twenty-seven. Disapproving Shakespeare appears in their story as the hoodwinked parent in one of his plays. "See, to beguile the old folks, how the young folks lay their heads together!" Judith and Thomas spoke their vows February 10, 1616. They lacked a license and married in Lent, out of bounds for weddings. Summoned by the court in Worcester, both were fined and expelled from the Church. Young Quiney ignored the summons but got off with a slap of the wrist. Excommunication wasn't what it used to be, lapsing when he and Judith christened their firstborn in November.

Ink was hardly dry on the contract, however, when news leaked that Thomas had got another woman pregnant. Worse followed and Margaret Wheeler died with her infant in childbirth. Stratford's ecclesiastical court—the "bawdy court," they called it, an index of its business—sentenced the offender to wear a white sheet in church on three successive Sundays. He had a glib tongue and evading the sentence, paid a fine and confessed in his street clothes. But he still had to reckon with his father-in-law.

The day after Quiney pleaded guilty in court, Shakespeare changed his will. In a revised version he gave Judith £100 for her marriage portion, plus another £50 provided that she surrender Shakespeare's cottage in Chapel Lane to Susanna. If she or a child of hers were still living after the date of the will, they could expect the interest on an additional £150. The interest, not the principal. Until Quiney settled lands on his wife in the same amount, the testator, taking no chances, withheld it.

Thomas Quiney, one of the nine children of Shakespeare's loving friend Richard, ran his vintner's business out of the Cage on the High Street. Once, Stratford lodged its prisoners in the dark vaulted chamber under the house. Upstairs, Quiney sold wine and tobacco. A small-scale transgressor in Puritan Stratford, he adulterated his wine, let tipplers use the house, and took the Lord's name in vain. Fines penalized these transgressions. Also, emulating his father the bailiff, he held office as burgess, constable, and chamberlain. A couplet in French from the poet Saint-Gelais heads his second chamberlain's account and might have endeared him to Shakespeare.

The Quineys left no heirs. In 1617 the "great bell" in Holy Trinity tolled for their first child, called Shakespeare. Two brothers, Richard and Thomas, lived longer, the first dying at twenty-one, the second at nineteen. Judith lived to seventy-seven but when Thomas died isn't recorded.

One by one, Shakespeare's friends dropped away, John Combe going in 1614, three days after Stratford's great fire. Storytellers reported that Shakespeare mocked this grasping man in satirical verses, stinging him "so severely that he never forgave it." However, he left Shakespeare £5 in his will, also leaving ten black gowns to poor folk who came to the funeral. Taking up where the usurer left off, his nephews William and Thomas planned to enclose the common fields north of town. Four to six hundred acres made up the lot, two hundred of it arable land. William Combe estimated the worth of this land at £250 after enclosure. Having "improved" it, he proposed to sell at a profit. One man's meat was another's poison, however, and Stratfordians, no doubt saying so, rose in fury.

William Combe had a well-placed ally, Arthur Mainwaring, steward and kinsman of England's Lord Chancellor. Owning farm land in Welcombe, Mainwaring wished to convert it to pasture. (Sheep brought more money than tillage.) His kinsman Ellesmere, the Chancellor, favored enclosures—for the public's good, he said. This far-sighted view put Stratford on the defensive, a point not lost on Combe. "The company [Stratford's corporation] had by stirring in this business got, he would not say the greatest, but almost the greatest men in England" to oppose it. Using the Chancellor's name as a bugbear, he threatened to enlist his support against the town. First, however, he needed Shakespeare's, a problem for both.

In the reign of Henry VIII, eight million sheep lived on the land, something less than three million people. This ratio worsened, and as Shakespeare's fortunes rose, many he knew went under. In the Midlands "of very late" (said the rebels of 1607), "there were three hundred and forty towns decayed and depopulated." Peasants and yeoman farmers cleared out, replaced by flocks of sheep, some numbering 7,000 head. Local landlords helped along this process, one converting 300 acres of farmland to a huge rabbit warren. The conies he bred fetched a good price up in London. Shakespeare's Warwickshire, dairying and grazing country today, was once the heartland of the common-field system, among the great corn-growing regions of the Midlands. Already in his boyhood this was ceasing to be true, one reason he took flight for the city.

His plays, especially the late ones, bear angry witness to this upheaval, and everyone will notice how, breaking off the play to indulge private animus, he reproves "the tyrants of his native fields." For instance, this from *Pericles:*

> the blind mole casts
> Cooped hills towards Heaven to tell the earth is thronged
> By man's oppression, and the poor worm doth die for 't.

But Shakespeare's social conscience had to contend with a potent sense of meum and tuum.

Though enclosure didn't threaten his Old Stratford and Welcombe freehold, it undercut the value of his tithes. This might have allied him with Stratford's corporation, dependent on tithes for its income. Fearing the decay of tillage, the corporation rallied commoners and local gentry to its cause. "All three fires were not so great a loss to the town as the enclosures would be," said one alderman, canvassing supporters. Most took the town's side, only Sir Thomas Lucy, Charlecote's master, siding with Combe. A letter went to Shakespeare, December 23, 1614, endorsed by "almost all the company's hands." But he had a piece of paper protecting his rights, though the men of the company didn't know this.

Stratford's officialdom wrote Mainwaring too, entreating him "to call to mind the manifold great and often miseries this borough hath sustained by casualties of fires fresh in memory." Almsfolk, seven hundred of them, "have ever been much relieved by the works of husbandry" but the provision stored in Stratford's barns and stables, having gone up in flames, left the town "in the ashes of desolation." Nothing came of this entreaty. Shakespeare, guessing at the outcome, didn't hold his breath but struck his own deal with the enclosers. On October 28, an agreement with Mainwaring's cousin William Replingham, local agent for the Combes, promised him compensation "for all such loss, detriment and hindrance . . . by reason of any enclosure or decay of tillage."

His cousin Thomas Greene found himself included in the agreement. Some see Shakespeare's thoughtful hand in this, but more likely the lawyers hoped to quiet his tongue. Later Combe offered Greene £10 "to propound a peace," enough to buy him a gelding. Though holding a reversionary interest in tithes, he didn't bite, so didn't ride. On November 12 he carried the fight to Privy Council in London. Four days after this, Shakespeare came to town with Dr. Hall, his son-in-law, and Greene "went to see him how he did." A memorandum of his, dated November 17, reports on their meeting. The Combes had assured him, Shakespeare told Greene, that "they meant to enclose no further than to Gospel Bush," i.e., a petty matter, commencing in April "and not before." In Shakespeare's own opinion, echoed by his son-in-law, "there will be nothing done at all."

But digging of ditches began when the frost broke in December. Early in the new year, two of Stratford's aldermen "went together in peaceable manner to restrain" it. Assaulted by Combe's men, they lay on the ground while "the said Mr. Combe . . . sat laughing on horseback." Good football players, he called them, bidding the diggers get on. A comic version of the benevolent servant in *King Lear,* one of his men interposed on behalf of the townsfolk. He was Stephen Sly, "reckoned up" by the drunken tinker in *The Taming of the Shrew.* Quickening with a life of his own, he stepped from Shakespeare's pages to wag a reproving finger at the playwright.

Next day reinforcements, a troop of women and children, sallied out from Stratford and Bishopton. Carrying spades, they filled in the ditches and leveled the hedge-mounds. A stiffer challenge came from Attorney-General Coke, in Warwick to conduct the Lenten assizes. On March 27, 1615, he issued a restraining order, advising Combe with mock solicitude to "set his heart at rest." While the Attorney General served the King, "he should never enclose nor lay down his common arable land."

Chastened but obdurate, Combe tried a softer line. He needed grass land in place of tillage, not to build his fortunes but for "maintenance of hospitality and good husbandry." Even so, he was willing to reduce the area marked off for enclosure. Sand might still be dug by the town's "better sort," etc. Stratford not budging, he appealed to force.

Buying up land and houses in Welcombe, he depopulated the village, reserving a single house for himself. In the summer of 1615, again the year later, he turned a flock of sheep into Welcombe Meadow, destroying the hay crop. Tenants who protested were beaten or went to jail. One, Arthur Cawdrey, heard from the landlord "that if he sowed his said wheat land," Combe "would eat it up with his sheep." When Alderman Barber, in debt to Thomas Combe, petitioned for relief, he "willed his brother to show Mr. Barber no favor." Thomas needed no willing. "Dogs and curs," he called Stratford's protesting councilmen, also beating and kicking a local shepherd who wanted his wages. Alderman Barber could expect to be "served up" to London within a fortnight. There the Marshalsea waited, as it had for Shakespeare's friends years before.

A cryptic entry in Greene's diary, the last concerning Shakespeare, notes his "telling J. Greene [Thomas's brother] that I was not able to bear the enclosing of Welcombe." This news seems gratuitous and hopeful commentators argue that instead of "I" Shakespeare's cousin meant to write "he." Whatever Shakespeare's inmost feelings, the old ways triumphed one last time, and Stratford won its fight with the Combes. Though William, the county's high sheriff, felt safe in defying Attorney-General Coke, he couldn't get round Privy Council. In 1619 it instructed him to throw open his enclosures and restore the ancient greensward to tillage. By then Shakespeare was dead. Living to a great age, Combe died fifty years later. A monument on the south side of Holy Trinity church preserves his memory.

SHAKESPEARE still had one play in his scrip, *The Two Noble Kinsmen,* less drama than ritual but not a dying gasp. Art, a sedentary trade, is also the work of hands, and though this work of art may tell of tedium vitae, it tells nothing of an old man's fatigue. In the year 1612–13, three plays engaged Shakespeare, almost a throwback to the arduous commitment of earlier days. Coping with them needed address.

Likely his last play dates from the summer of 1613, opening that fall at Blackfriars. Once again he collaborated, the play's first edition (1634) assigning the work to "the memorable worthies of their time, Mr. John Fletcher and Mr. William Shakespeare, Gent." Their joint labor, says the title page, won "great applause," much of it at a guess saluting Fletcher's blend of comedy and pathos. More of the play is his than Shakespeare's, inclining Heminges and Condell to omit it from the Folio. Who wrote what isn't recorded, but *The Two Noble Kinsmen,* divided as if with calipers, separates irresistibly in parts. Shakespeare initiates, providing the basic outline and introducing the major characters, Fletcher follows. The tragicomic underplot, reciting the tribulations of a Jailor's Daughter, mad for love, belongs almost wholly to him. Readers who annotate the play will find themselves underscoring heavily in Acts I and V (ignoring the second scene), also in the opening scene of II and III. The rest of it won't much detain them.

This is too bad, for Shakespeare's contribution shows him at the top of his bent. "The first and the last acts . . . of *The Two Noble Kinsmen,* which in point of composition is perhaps the most superb work in the language . . . would have been the most gorgeous rhetoric, had they not happened to be something far better" (De Quincey). Were all the play Shakespeare's, it would take place with the great ones. To one reader it seems credible that the age after ours will call the last plays the crown of his achievement.

Fletcher snaps at his heels, though, or makes moues behind his back, bringing on *Hamlet's* Gertrude when the heroine consults her lovers' pictures, Ophelia for the mad scenes, the bed trick from *Measure for Measure* and *All's Well.* A country schoolmaster, preparing his entertainment, remembers Holofernes, while the witless entertainers remember his fellow Worthies, also the "mechanicals" of *A Midsummer Night's Dream.* In this spurious context, echoes of *King Lear* and *Macbeth* raise a laugh, perhaps by design. Shakespeare's noble kinsmen, Palamon and Arcite, undergo a drastic change when Fletcher gets hold of them. Vowing eternal friendship, they split on the rock of love, diverting, this playwright thinks.

P. I saw her first.
A. That's nothing.
P. But it shall be.
A. I saw her too.

Second-rate but vastly talented, Fletcher was no fool, and his reprise of Shakespeare sounds like self-conscious parody, the acolyte getting back at the master. His Jailor's Daughter, in love with Palamon but taking an anonymous Wooer to bed, lets us in for vulgar rib-tickling (it never came amiss). Some think the mad girl is meant to parallel Shakespeare's heroine, accepting the lover appointed her by fate. Endlessly the sport of fate, Emilia can do no other, though. Her plight evokes tears or thoughts too grave for tears, and Shakespeare's play is at daggers' points with Fletcher's.

Standing on Chaucer's shoulders, Shakespeare found his story in *The Knight's Tale,* where joy and woe chase each other in an endless round. Their fellowship is the burden of his four romances, resumed and completed in this dying fall. A day or two we look sad, gracing Arcite's funeral, then smile with Palamon, for whom "but one hour since" we were as dearly sorry. But sadness is a kind of mirth, mingled in the luckless-lucky man, "as if mirth did make him sad . . . sadness merry." Arcite's ambiguous victory is like that, "right joyful, with some sorrow," and the news of his overthrow, uplifting a fallen friend, brings tidings "most dearly sweet and bitter." Two songs point the play, pairing quick-eyed pleasure with "sad and solemn shows." Marigolds bloom on deathbeds, and though the path some grieving women take leads to their household's grave, joy waits to seize them tomorrow.

These pairings make a whole, like our mingled yarn, and Shakespeare, having no option, contemplates it equably, more or less that. But he isn't saying that the best is yet to be. Theseus and Hippolyta, their nuptials preparing in *A Midsummer Night's Dream,* are still about to marry as his final play begins. Enter to this happy scene three queens all in black, triangulating the stage with their hearses. They have a tale to tell of once mighty sovereigns who endure the beaks of ravens in the foul fields of Thebes, and Theseus, hearing them out, is wise as he thinks of himself.

> King Capaneus was your lord. The day
> That he should marry you, at such a season
> As now it is with me, I met your groom.
> By Mars's altar, you were that time fair.

But grief and time consume this virgin's beauty, and "will all devour."

"Strange ruins" meet the eye in Thebes, changed mightily since Shakespeare's heroes went to school. The man who loved cities is out of love with them now, this one, stained with vice, resembling London under "Creon." Bereavement gives the tenor of his autumnal play.

> There's many a man alive that hath outlived
> The love o' the people, yea i' the self same state
> Stands many a father with his child.

Better to die, late Shakespeare continues, so prevent

> The loathsome misery of age, beguile
> The gout and rheum that in lag hours attend
> For gray approachers.

Reporting little that's good of the way we live in the present, *The Two Noble Kinsmen* regrets the happier past, before "the crimes of nature" sullied our gloss of youth. Better when we were boys, says Polixenes in *The Winter's Tale,* better, says Emilia, "when our count / Was each eleven." Sans marriage and adulthood, the state of innocence lives again in the mind of a rueful playwright. Age is yet to come when the dust is over all and heterosexual love replaces the "true love" between maid and maid, boy and boy. Reaching back to his beginnings, Shakespeare writes another friendship play, this time "The Two Gentlemen of Thebes." The sexual prize his heroes contend for doesn't match what it costs, and buying it they lose what's dearest to them. Their story remembers Valentine's, buying the love of Silvia and losing the friendship of his sworn brother Proteus, except that Shakespeare's early comedy, felt as merely personal, leaves us discontented with the figure it makes. *The Two Noble Kinsmen,* heartfelt but controlled, offers a reading of life.

"Is it all forgot?" schooldays' friendship, childhood innocence, Helena asks her friend in another comedy taking off from *The Knight's Tale. A Midsummer Night's Dream* answers Yes to this question, and Hermia, joining with men, puts away childish things. Narcissus, though fair, was a fool to love himself, and adult love, more maturely seasoned, is buckled with stronger judgment than a child's. But reservations, edged with bitterness, are entered.

Love's "yoke," though worn like roses, is heavier than lead, stings more than nettles. Our blood being our fate, Emilia, a single rose, will be gathered. Diana's votaress murmurs against this but love is the argument, allowing no appeal. Shakespeare's hero knows a man of eighty winters who wed a lass of fourteen:

> the agèd cramp
> Had screwed his square foot round,
> The gout had knit his fingers into knots,
> Torturing convulsions from his globy eyes
> Had almost drawn their spheres. . . .

But this "anatomy" (skeleton) begets a child on his mate, Shakespeare's details insuring revulsion. Not a ribald anecdote, not "January and May," his stunning tribute to the power of love seems more concessive than joyful.

Reigning in mortal bosoms from eleven to ninety, too potent sexuality takes the world for its "chase" or hunting ground. "We in herds" are the game. Where is character in all this? For late Shakespeare, perhaps it reduces to convention. In two of his romances, now again in the last play, he sets his scene in ancient Hellas where the gods come close to men. In all five plays, divinity leans over the action. Shakespeare's characters, histrionic but passive, don't much affect it, and distinguishing between or among them is labor lost. (One noble kinsman is taller than the other.) The diminishing of character, already well along in *Timon of Athens,* is flagrant in the last plays, directed by Fortune or some lunar deity, "general of ebbs and flows." A nautical figure, very different in its import from Henley's famous lines ("Master of my fate! Captain of my soul!"), likens Shakespeare's generic hero to a ship at sea. Hoisting the sails that must bring it to port, the master doesn't know where he's going, only "where / The heavenly limiter pleases." His vessel, unaware of a hand at the tiller, waits for the surge that next approaches.

Though, in Act V, some ships come safely in, the sequence Shakespeare dramatizes is anti-dramatic, not from complication to its unraveling but from start to finish and then to start again. Plot looks dynamic, not the theme it presents, however, and action signifies less than meditation on action. Shakespeare's handling of incident reflects this. Battles and tournaments enliven the story but mostly we aren't permitted to see them. Shakespeare's soldier-protagonists bow down their stubborn bodies, "dove-like" in the best case, not a phrase for heroes. One of them prays for victory, seeking to bind the future, but gets his cruel comeuppance. Shakespeare's play has a moral, inauspicious for theater: Don't just do something, stand there.

Style matches subject, a perfect fit for the play but hard on playgoers. Shakespeare's rhetoric, though of great power, is often elliptical, sometimes opaque. Abiding our questions, he answers them in gnomic couplets, easy to memorize, otherwise unhelpful:

> This world's a city full of straying streets,
> And death's the market place where each one meets.

"Transported" or "troubled," Duke Theseus looms over the darkening scene, a dimly majestic presence muttering difficult truths. "Vaticinatory" they are, like the old Greek *vates* dressed in his singing robes, or the riddles Shakespeare puts at the heart of the romances.

Blank verse, the ideal instrument of the discursive or reasoning intelligence, gives way to rhyming tetrameters, four-foot lines like Gower's in *Pericles* or Prospero's Epilogue in *The Tempest.* Some of Shakespeare's verse, modulating from short lines to shorter, recalls his cryptic *Phoenix and Turtle.* Drama is going back to its cradle.

Shakespeare's judgment of men and women, insofar as he ventures it, is muted and reserved. Devotees of philosophy will still find solid nutriment in *The Two Noble Kinsmen,* like all his plays a vision of experience. Shakespeare's comments drop from him casually, however. Here are his last lines for the stage:

O you heavenly charmers,
What things you make of us! For what we lack,
We laugh; for what we have, are sorry; still
Are children in some kind. Let us be thankful
For that which is, and with you leave dispute
That are above our question. Let's go off,
And bear us like the time.

Straining old friendships, *The Two Noble Kinsmen* taxed understanding. A contemporary remarked Shakespeare's "old-fashioned wit, which walked from town to town in turned hose," a little threadbare and long since outmoded. "Shakespeare to thee was dull," said this poet, addressing Fletcher. It isn't hard to imagine a deputation from the King's Men waiting on their famous colleague. After a long and illustrious career, perhaps he should rest on his laurels.

SHAKESPEARE died on his birthday, April 23, 1616. The story goes that he and his friends, Michael Drayton and Ben Jonson, "had a merry meeting and it seems drank too hard." Death followed from "a fever there contracted." Some jib at this—"no ground for imputing to him an excessive indulgence in 'hot and rebellious liquors'"—but the story originates with a student of medicine who became Stratford's vicar while Shakespeare's kin still lived there. Drayton, of Warwickshire, wrote at least one great poem, Jonson more than a few, and Shakespeare, if drink killed him, was lucky in his companions.

Though his contemporaries lived shorter lives than we do, at fifty-two he wasn't all that old, inclining biographers to guess at a lingering illness. Opulence and squalor lived together in his age—Chapel Lane, running beside his Stratford mansion—harbored stray pigs and a pigsty until the council put its foot down—and perhaps for him the conjunction was fatal. His son-in-law the doctor came along on his London visit in 1614, and to many the hand that signed his will looks infirm. Perhaps Judith's imprudent marriage lowered his strength. (About time she got married, though, and it might have set him up again.) Perhaps, like his weary philosopher Macbeth, he had lived long enough, knowing how nature overtakes us.

A clergyman from nearby Gloucestershire, the same who told of Shakespeare, the youthful poacher of venison, says he died a papist. Buried from his home two days later, he went to the grave in a wooden coffin. Poorer folk, wrapped only in a shroud that sometimes left the face uncovered, were laid in the churchyard, but his interment took place within the chancel rail of the church. The great bell of the Gild Chapel, broken but fixed in time for the funeral, tolled his passing.

His will, dated March 25, 1616, covered one side of three sheets. Ready for signing in January, the will was altered in March, its first page replaced by a new one, reflecting Judith's recent marriage. Interlinings and cancellations, blotting the whole, might have called for a fair copy, but this was dispensed with, perhaps suggesting need for haste. Shakespeare lived on nearly a month, however, and the will describes him as "in perfect health and memory."

He signed each sheet at the bottom, spelling his name indifferently "Shakspere" or "Shakspeare." Spelling, grammar too, had yet to acknowledge the "adamantine net." Five witnesses signed with him, Francis Collins of Warwick, his lawyer, Julius Shaw, Stratford's bailiff that year and his next-door neighbor but one on Chapel Street, John Robinson, Gatehouse tenant or Stratford laborer, his boyhood friend Hamnet Sadler, and Robert Whatcott, servant. Solicitor Collins and Thomas Russell, the London friend from Philip Lane and earlier days, acted as overseers. In a preamble, no doubt formulaic but who knows what it meant to the man who endorsed it, Shakespeare commends his soul into God's hands, "hoping and assuredly believing through the only merits of Jesus Christ my savior to be made partaker of life everlasting." Then, having property and £350 in cash to dispose of, he turns to business.

First satisfying himself in the matter of Judith, he leaves his sister £20, a lifetime tenancy of the Birthplace, "and all my wearing apparel." Her three sons get £5 each, his godson William Walker a 20 shilling goldpiece, and his granddaughter Elizabeth—"niece," he calls her, an old form—all his plate except "my broad silver and gilt bowl." This he reserves to Judith. Elizabeth Hall, eight years old when Shakespeare died, married Thomas Nash, living with her husband in Nash House, next to New Place. She took a second husband on Nash's death, John Barnard, a wealthy widower, subsequently Sir John. He had a large family, *satis quod sufficit,* and Shakespeare's granddaughter died without issue.

Remembering Stratford's poor (£10), Shakespeare remembered his rich friend Thomas Combe, brother of the terrible William. This Thomas gets his sword. Cash bequests to the overseers compensate their labor, the lawyer, who didn't come cheap, getting an impressive sum, 20 marks. Old Thomas Combe, father of the enclosers, employed this solicitor, and John the usurer stood godfather to his son. Shakespeare's last testament says something of the circle he moved in.

His fellows Heminges, Condell, and Burbage, survivors of the company he joined in his youth, receive bequests of 26s., 8d., the same amount going to four Stratford acquaintance, the Nashs, Anthony and John, Hamnet Sadler, and William Reynolds. Shakespeare meant them all to buy rings in his memory, a rare personal touch in this sandy patch of legalese. Susanna and her husband, his executors, get the bulk of the estate, New Place, the two Henley Street houses, "my barns, stables, orchards, gardens, lands, tenements and hereditaments" in Stratford and thereabouts, the London Gatehouse, and "all the rest of my goods." Likely this blanket phrase covered Shakespeare's shares in the Globe and Blackfriars. Some of his fellows, e.g., Pope, Heminges, and John Underwood, willed their shares in writing, some, like Phillips, Burbage, and Condell, did this orally, leaving no record. After Shakespeare's death, Heminges increased his shares in both theaters and perhaps, via the executors, Shakespeare's came to him.

Few wills of the time show such concern, poignant, even desperate, to keep the estate intact. Shakespeare's will entails it down to the seventh son of Susanna's body, beyond this to the sons, if any, of her daughter and her sister Judith. Always the son, if only he be lawful issue. Like his noble kinsman, the unlucky one, Shakespeare sought to prescribe for the future. (The playwright, different from the householder, saw how this was idle.) He hoped that his house, dignified by armorial bearings, would stand against time. But Susanna left no male children, her only daughter died childless, and her sister Judith, though producing sons, outlived them. Shakespeare's direct line came to an end with the death of Lady Barnard in 1670, and he has no lineal descendants.

Anne Shakespeare needed no special provision, common law entitling her to residence in New Place and her dower of a life-interest in one-third of the estate, unless legally barred like the Gatehouse. An insertion in the will, possibly an afterthought made at her request, gives "unto my wife my second best bed with the furniture," i.e., the hangings and bed clothes. Though the bed came from her old house at Hewlands, singling it out for special mention seems peculiar, some say invidious. But Thomas Combe the elder, who lived in the priests' College, dying there in 1609, left his widow the use of all his bedsteads, "except the best bedsteads," willed to his son the encloser. Perhaps the second-best bed meant more to Anne than Shakespeare or it meant very little, a point in itself. Anne died at sixty-seven in 1623, the year of the First Folio. In her Latin epitaph, near Shakespeare's grave in Holy Trinity, her older daughter Susanna regrets that her mother, giving her life, got in return only a tombstone.

More than a hundred years after Shakespeare's death, a Stratford antiquarian turned up a transcript of his will. "Dull and irregular," he thought it, "so absolutely void of the least particle of that spirit which animated our great poet, that it must lessen his character as a writer to imagine the least sentence of it his production." All will feel the force of this, not least Shakespeare's admirers. His impersonal tone, but a chillier phrase is needed, sets the will apart from most then and later. Convention, sentiment too, dictate mention of the spouse "with whom I have by the goodness of God lived a long time." This is the language contemporaries favored and Shakespeare's fellows in the King's Men employ it, Condell saying goodbye to a "well-beloved wife," Heminges wanting to be buried near his Rebecca. Shakespeare's will concedes almost nothing to flesh and blood. "Carved in alabaster" describes the man who made it.

But every reader knows better, knowing how this most vital of great poets kindles with a warmth like life itself. Posterity's judgment, hardly wrong, appeals to the plays and poems, no impeaching what they tell us. "The character of the man is best seen in his writings," said Shakespeare's first biographer. But more than this needs to be said.

While he lived, friends of his or the friends of friends wrote down their impressions, fifty or sixty of them. Most salute the artist but some speak of the man, and the way he comes through is worth noting. Praise belongs to the man, couched in general terms, however. Nothing prickly about him, he bears little resemblance to Marlowe, Jonson, or Donne. "Sweet Master Shakespeare" lacks edges.

Honest, open, and free, they call him, nimble of brain and "pregnant" of wit (the insipid prose of the will notwithstanding), friendly, good company, "so dear loved a neighbor." He was all these things, even to excess, wanting only one thing, definition, his gift to others. Like his Holofernes, the wordmongering schoolmaster, he had an extravagant spirit, full of forms, figures, and shapes. Crowding his brain, they left little room for the indigenous man, "I William Shakespeare."

His most credentialed portraits, the Janssen bust in Stratford church and Droeshout's copperplate engraving for the First Folio, sketch an inoffensive but anonymous man, his belly lined with good capon, such a one as his father aspired to be. Clothes help define him, and Shakespeare wears the rich costume of a well-to-do burgher of Stratford. In the bust the auburn-colored hair, fluffed out at the sides, tells of careful grooming, the hazel eyes, though open wide, look at nothing. Droeshout's Shakespeare, valenced like Janssen's with light-colored hair, shows less beard and moustache. Suggesting, but only that, the friendly man of the encomia, the lips are touched by the hint of a smile. Hair curls around the ears but recedes from the huge egg-shaped forehead. "A stupider face I never beheld," said Gainsborough, contemplating this portrait. Beeston, the son of a Chamberlain's man, said he was "handsome, well-shaped," however. A bare name and no essential thing except as the art invests him, protean Shakespeare is always slipping away. All art aspires to the condition of autonomy, and he typifies the artist at his highest pitch. "What particular habitude or friendships he contracted with private men," Rowe had been unable to learn. He noted Shakespeare's "good nature," though.

He lies before the altar in the chancel of Holy Trinity, on his left his wife Anne, on his right Thomas Nash, John Hall, and an epitaph that remembers Susanna. Only a few feet from his grave stood Stratford's charnel house, adjoining the church and "almost filled with human bones, skulls, etc.," sufficient, said a visitor, to load a great number of wagons. "Rattling bones," Shakespeare called them in *Romeo and Juliet,* imagining the reeky shanks and the foul mouth of death. No healthsome air breathed in there. The dead decaying in earth (but there was never enough of it), their bones went to the charnel house to make room for late-comers. In the age after Shakespeare, Sir Thomas Browne, who wanted urn burial, shuddered at the "tragical abomination" of this, "knaved out of our graves . . . our skulls made drinking bowls and our bones turned into pipes." Some such fate overtook Susanna, buried, she thought forever, until, in the next century, a tithe-holder claimed her place and sextons moved her remains to the bonehouse. Later, too late, posterity restored the inscription.

Shakespeare, disrobing himself of art, provided against this. His doggerel epitaph, crude enough to suit "the capacity of clerks and sextons, for the most part a very ignorant set of people," admonishes times to come:

> Good friend for Jesus' sake forbear
> To dig the dust enclosèd here:
> Blest be the man that spares these stones,
> And curst be he that moves my bones.

"Deep six" did for most, in Stratford and elsewhere, but sextons, fearing to draw Shakespeare's curse on themselves and their descendants, "laid him full seventeen feet deep," enough, said an early tourist, to secure him. The river Avon flows beside the church and his dust has long since mingled with its waters.

Sometime before the publication of the Folio, friends or relations erected the white marble monument that overlooks his grave. Painted to resemble life, then repainted in the eighteenth century—"like a popish saint," Garrick said—whitewashed by Malone and painted once more a hundred years ago, it still holds its ambiguous place on the north wall of the chancel. Two black Corinthian columns, gilded at top and bottom, flank Shakespeare's memorial, its panels inlaid with black "touch." Applying "touch" or touchstone was how you found out truth, but truth, being itself, didn't need this, said Jonson, simpler in his psychology than Shakespeare. On the cornice above the columns sit a pair of male cherubs, one, with a spade, standing for Labor, the other, with a skull and inverted torch, for Rest. Between them on a square stone block, Shakespeare's arms, helm, and crest honor the Stratford man who prospered. Another skull, chap-fallen, crowns the whole.

Below the entablature, a central recessed arch encloses the half-length figure of the poet, carved from soft Gloucestershire limestone. Shakespeare is composing, a quill pen in his right hand, his left clasping a scroll. A sleeveless black gown partly covers his doublet, scarlet for the livery worn by the King's Men. Beneath the doublet, the cuffs and turned-down collar are white. At the base of the recess, a panel inscribed in Latin and English compares Shakespeare to Nestor, Socrates, and Virgil. "Quick nature died" when he did.

Gheerart Janssen (englished to Gerard Johnson) made Shakespeare's monument in his London studio near Southwark Cathedral, a few minutes' walk from the Globe. John Combe's elaborate tomb on the east wall is his and in 1619 he and his family prepared the tomb in Leicestershire for that Earl of Rutland who commissioned Shakespeare's *impresa*. Old tradition reports that Janssen worked from a life mask or death mask. Droeshout, still a boy when Shakespeare died, had a model before him too, perhaps a painting by Shakespeare's colleague Burbage. Family and friends raised no objection to either bust or engraving, and must have thought them an adequate likeness. Later in the century, a traveler visiting Stratford heard from an ancient clerk that Shakespeare's "wife and daughters did earnestly desire to be laid in the same grave with him." Mindful of the curse, not one of the sextons dared touch his gravestone, however, and Shakespeare is buried alone.

Notes
(By Page Number)

ABBREVIATIONS of Shakespeare's works, given here, are standard, as is the order in which the works appear, that of the Folio. Citations follow the Riverside edition (1974), to which the Harvard Concordance is keyed.

TMP	The Tempest
TGV	The Two Gentlemen of Verona
WIV	The Merry Wives of Windsor
MM	Measure for Measure
ERR	The Comedy of Errors
ADO	Much Ado About Nothing
LLL	Love's Labor's Lost
MND	A Midsummer Night's Dream
MV	The Merchant of Venice
AYL	As You Like It
SHR	The Taming of the Shrew
AWW	All's Well That Ends Well
TN	Twelfth Night
WT	The Winter's Tale
JN	King John
R2	Richard II
1H4	Henry IV, Part One

2H4	Henry IV, Part Two
H5	Henry V
1H6	Henry VI, Part One
2H6	Henry VI, Part Two
3H6	Henry VI, Part Three
R3	Richard III
H8	Henry VIII
TRO	Troilus and Cressida
COR	Coriolanus
TIT	Titus Andronicus
ROM	Romeo and Juliet
TIM	Timon of Athens
JC	Julius Caesar
MAC	Macbeth
HAM	Hamlet
LR	King Lear
OTH	Othello
ANT	Antony and Cleopatra
CYM	Cymbeline

Not Collected:

PER	Pericles
TNK	The Two Noble Kinsmen
STM	Sir Thomas More
VEN	Venus and Adonis
LUC	The Rape of Lucrece
PHT	The Phoenix and Turtle
SON	The Sonnets
LC	A Lover's Complaint

1. Two-Headed Janus

1. Sonnets: Drawing on nos. 62, 63, 66, 138.

2. "out of act": AWW, 1.2.30.

2. "old" murderer: ROM, 3.3.94.

2. the provident ant: In *Groatsworth of Wit*, 1592.

2. ten plays: According to this biography: 1–3H6, R3, ERR, TGV, SHR, LLL, TIT, JN.

2. Henslowe . . . wrote Alleyn: Sept. 28, 1593; E. K. Chambers, *William Shakespeare*, 1930, 2.314.

3. two plays: TIT and *Taming of a Shrew*, probably a corrupted version of SHR.

3. three . . . plays: TIT, *The First Part of the Contention between York and Lancaster* (2H6), *Taming of a Shrew.*

3. as a poet: First noticed in *Willobie His Avisa.*

3. the modern Catullus: Richard Carew, *The Excellence of the English Tongue*, c. 1596.

3. "master-mistress": SON 20.2.

4. pastoral-comical: HAM, 2.2.396–99.

4. "tide of times": JC, 3.1.257.

5. Nashe called him: In *Pierce Penniless*, 1592.

5. "thou dost act": "To Edward Allen."

5. warrant licensing . . . travels: May 6, 1593.

5. bed was sown: G. L. Hosking, *The Life and Times of Edward Alleyn*, 1952, pp. 51–53.

6. he "Burbage" cried: Richard Corbet, *Iter Boreale*, c. 1618.

6. a prohibition: Nov. 6, 1589.

6. "so to do": J. Q. Adams, *A Life of William Shakespeare*, 1923, p. 190; E. K. Chambers, *The Elizabethan Stage*, 1923, 4.316.

6. actors went elsewhere: EKC, *WS*, 1.63 and App. D; 2.312–16.

6. Romeo won . . . "plaudities": John Marston, *The Scourge of Villainy*, 1598.

6. to Gray's Inn: The story is in *Gesta Grayorum*, dating from this time but not pub. until 1688.

7. "and modern instances": AYL, 2.7.156.

7. at Court: EKC, *ES*, 4.164–69 lists LCMs performances at Court under Elizabeth. See also 2.192.

7. theater season: Sidney Lee, *A Life of William Shakespeare* (1898), 1916, pp. 68–69, 372–73.

7. "for the masque": EKC, *ES*, 1.87. Details on "The Revels Office" are, unless noted otherwise, from EKC, ch. III, 1.71–105. A good account is Marchette Chute, *Shakespeare of London*, 1949, pp. 139–43.

8. A royal proclamation: May 16, 1559. Lee, *WS*, pp. 127–29; Irving Ribner, *William Shakespeare An Introduction to His Life, Times, and Theatre*, 1969, pp. 163–64.

8. the time's chronicles: HAM, 2.2.524–26.

8. "allowed": JQA, *WS*, pp. 502–9.

9. the censor's attention: Excepting *Sir Thomas More*, not wholly Shakespeare's.

10. Court Calendar: EKC, *ES*, 4.75–130.

10. "into the hazard": H5, 1.2.263.

10. Performances at Court: Details in EKC, *ES*, 3.1–46.

10. "the tables up": ROM, 1.5.29.

10. At the other . . . the stage: Recent scholarship disputes this, locating the stage in the middle of the playing space (like a boxing ring), or against one of the side walls: Herbert Berry, *The Boar's Head Playhouse*, 1988, pp. 98–108, 163–68.

11. rule was simplicity: T. J. King, *Shakespearean Staging, 1599–1642*, 1971, musters the evidence.

11. acts or scenes: Most of the traditional divisions in Shakespeare's plays are those established by W. G. Clark and W. A. Wright in the 1863 Cambridge ed., and most survive in modern texts. Recent scholarship has attempted to modify or overturn them, e.g., James E. Hirsch, *The Structure of Shakespearean Scenes*, 1981. T. W. Baldwin in several books argues for a five-act convention in the mind of the playwright but can't really adduce examples (*On Act and Scene Division in the Shakespeare First Folio*, 1965; *On the Compositional Genetics of "The Comedy of Errors,"* 1965; *William Shakespeare's Five-Act Structure*, 1947). Wilfred T. Jewkes (*Act Division in Elizabethan and Jacobean Plays, 1583–1616*, 1958), examining 236 plays, finds act division relatively rare before 1616, decidedly rare in public theater plays.

11. "yonder coppice": LLL, 4.1.9–10.

11. "about the stage": ROM, 1.4.114. S.d.s from Qto 1.

12. "without the town": MND, 1.1.165.

12. like Romeo: In 3.5 and 5.1.

12. "scene is Rhodes": 4.3.17.

12. "in Mantua, / Here": ROM, 5.1.51–52.

12. "where he is": *Apology for Poetry*, c. 1583.

12. "and universal theater": AYL, 2.7.137.

12. "great curtains": EKC, *ES*, 3.31.

12. Sans intermission: Intervals weren't standard in the public theater until relatively late in Shakespeare's career. Jewkes, *Act Division*, pinpoints the transition and gives the statistics.

13. as they consume: ROM, 2.6.11.

13. "division none": PHT, 1.27.
13. "to burn bright": ROM, 1.5.44.
13. "would not dance": 1.5.128–38.
13. "womb" and "tomb": 2.3.9–10.
13. "the everlasting flint": 2.6.16–17.
13. Youth . . . "gapes": 2.PRO.1–2.
14. "limping winter": 1.2.27–28.
14. "it lightens": 2.2.119–20.
14. a Restoration playwright: Thomas Otway, *Caius Marius*, 1679–80.
14. "Ancient" . . . "mutiny": 3 PRO. and 1.1.104.
14. "gored state" . . . "ranged empire": LR, 5.3.321; ANT, 1.1.34.
14. "a glooming peace": ROM, 5.3.305.
14. "things came about": HAM, 5.2.380.
14. "form of death": ROM, 5.3.246.
14. "of more woe": 5.3.309.
14. "exchange of joy": 2.6.4.
15. "Triumphant" . . . "lantern": 5.3.83–86.
15. as the sea: 2.2.133.
15. "O happy dagger!": 5.3.169.
15. of holy nuns: 5.3.156–57.
15. "that run fast": 2.3.94.
15. "commission": 4.1.64–65.
15. he doesn't feel: 3.3.64.
15. remembers Phaeton: 3.2.2–3.
15. one . . . said: William Painter, introducing his *Palace of Pleasure*, 1565–67.
15. A narrative poem: Arthur Brooke, "Romeus and Juliet," 1562.
15. "purposes mistook": HAM, 5.2.382, 384.
15. "we can contradict": ROM, 5.3.153.
16. our weary bark: 5.3.117–18.
16. not "traded": TRO, 2.2.64.
16. "sectary astronomical": LR, 1.2.150.
16. "or evil luck": SON 14.3.

16. "fortune's fool": ROM, 3.1.141.

16. fool of fortune: LR, 4.6.191.

16. "Wedded to calamity": ROM, 3.3.3.

16. unmade grave: 3.3.70.

16. mouth of outrage: 5.3.216.

16. "sour misfortune's book": 5.3.82.

16. "an envious worm": 1.1.151.

16. not yet "ripe": 1.2.11.

16. "on Lammas Eve": 1.3.21.

16. "come to confusion": MND, 1.1.149.

17. "man of wax": ROM, 1.3.76.

17. "boy": 5.3.70 and 3.1.66.

17. culling simples: 5.1.40.

17. poor compounds: 5.1.82.

17. up that plant: 2.3.27–30.

17. "Of men's impossibilities": LR, 4.6.73–74.

17. famous schools: John Stow, *Survey of London*, 1598 (Everyman's Library, 1945), pp. 66–67.

18. "Crossed" lovers: MND, 1.1.150.

18. "engilds" . . . blood: ROM, 2.2.15–22, 3.5.59; MND, 3.2.187–88, 96– 97.

18. "trooping with crows": ROM, 1.5.48.

18. "at first sight": ROM, 1.5.52; MND, 3.1.141.

18. "parted their fathers": MND, 5.1.351–52.

18. this blessed life: 1.1.74.

18. "cold fruitless moon": 1.1.72–73.

18. "fair vestal": 2.1.156–64.

18. "Cupid's flower": 4.1.73.

19. "to be blamed": 5.1.356–57.

19. "mortal grossness": 3.1.160.

19. "new-bent": 1.1.10.

19. "lips at all": 5.1.201.

19. "jaws of darkness": 1.1.134, 141–48.

19. of her burden: 2.1.123–35.

19. harelip, and scar: 5.1.411.
19. "enforced chastity": 3.1.200.
19. "with love's wound": 2.1.167.
19. with his sword: 1.1.16.
19. Centaurs . . . Bacchanals: 5.1.44–49.
20. these mortals be: 3.2.115.
20. "weak and idle": 5.1.427–28.
20. of great constancy: 5.1.23–26.
20. like a dream: 5.1.386.
20. "and new jollity": 5.1.370.
20. "or carol blest": 2.1.102, 115–16.
20. the bride-bed: 5.1.401–6.
20. cool reason's ascendancy: 5.1.6.
20. "themselves in night": 1.1.7.
20. "you by that": *Plays Confuted in Five Actions*, 1582.
20. "and stranger companies": MND, 1.1.219.
20. "as a god": 1.1.47.
21. Titania's lord: 2.1.63.
21. the triple Hecate: 5.1.384.
21. "exposition of sleep": 4.1.39.
21. core or skein: TGV, 3.2.53.
21. Transported or "translated": MND, 4.2.4, 3.1.119.
21. "dream it was": 4.1.200–19.
21. music of discord: 4.1.117–18, 122.
21. the tangled chain: 5.1.125–26.
21. "with bristled hair": 2.2.31.
21. "crawling serpent": 2.2.146.
21. "Enthralled": 3.1.139.
21. "changeling" boy: 2.1.20–27.
21. "call them generally": 1.2.2.
21. love won't alter: 2.2.61.
22. a million fail: 3.2.92–93.
22. "doting": 1.1.230 (repeated with variations 5 times).
22. "adamant": 2.1.195.

22. A horse beguiled: 2.1.45–46.

22. "his mare again": 3.2.461–63.

22. don't need night's: 3.2.386–87.

22. own fool's eyes: 4.1.84.

22. "of voluntary choosing": MV, 2.1.16.

22. "in the eyes": 3.2.67.

22. "more the pity": MND, 3.1.145–47.

22. a watery eye: 3.1.198.

22. a "vain boast": OTH, 5.2.264.

22. "all be changed": 2 Corinthians 15:51.

23. Subsidies: E. K. Chambers, *Sources for a Biography of Shakespeare*, 1946, pp. 31–32, gives the rates and details.

23. drank deep: H5, 1.1.20.

23. "lazy yawning drone": 1.2.187–204.

23. "desire they were": ADO, 3.5.10–12.

23. "the King's tavern": 1H4, 2.2.57–59.

23. the tax rolls: For the facts and documents: EKC, *WS*, 2.87–90; B. Roland Lewis, *The Shakespeare Documents*, 1940, 1.262–71; N. E. Evans, *Shakespeare in the Public Records*, 1964.

24. "odd yard-land": Abraham Sturley reports this: Lee, *WS*, pp. 291–93; Charles Isaac Elton, *William Shakespeare His Family and Friends*, 1904, pp. 218–20. A yardland averaged bet. 30 and 40 acres.

24. "houses for merchants": Stow, pp. 148–57, surveys Bishopsgate ward.

24. "minds of usurers": Stephen Gosson, *The School of Abuse*, 1579.

24. "of his friend": MV, 1.3.134.

24. on John Shakespeare: D. L. Thomas and N. E. Evans, "John Shakespeare in the Exchequer," *Shakespeare Quarterly* 25 (Autumn 1984), 315–18; Lewis, *Documents*, 1.65.

24. his first printer: James Roberts, entering MV in the Stationers' Register, July 22, 1598.

24. a coup d'état: R3, 1.3.344.

25. "two-headed Janus": MV, 1.1.50.

25. he lived in: Thomas F. Ordish, *Shakespeare's London*, 1904, p. 218.

25. London's livery companies: A. Prokter and R. Taylor, *The A to Z*

of Elizabethan London, 1979; G. Unwin, *The Gilds and Companies of London*, 1927.

25. "not for meed": AYL, 2.3.58.

25. "covetous, and crafty": William Underhill the younger (Mark Eccles, *Shakespeare in Warwickshire*, 1961, p. 88; hereafter ME).

26. "soil and country": In his preface to the *Survey*.

26. in MND: 1.1.165–67.

26. "in hideous darkness": TN, 4.2.30.

26. Bedlam beggars: LR, 2.3.14–20.

26. Winchester House: Henry T. Stephenson, *Shakespeare's London*, 1905, p. 198.

26. in H8: 2.1.132–33.

27. full of water: R2, 4.1.184–87.

27. "may not be": 2.3.144–45.

27. "our English merchants": Stow, p. 31.

27. he works them: WIV, 4.3 and 5.

28. for human slaughter: MV, 4.1.133–34.

28. an otter: 1H4, 3.3.127–28.

28. "dove-feathered raven": ROM, 3.2.76.

28. "poor naked wretches": LR, 3.4.28.

28. "a heart untainted": 2H6, 3.2.232.

28. "branch, or berry": PER, 5.CHO.5–6.

29. "as the world": MV, 1.1.77.

29. Stratford . . . fire: Details from Edgar I. Fripp, *Shakespeare Man and Artist*, 1938, 1.419.

29. "ladies of esteem": ROM, 1.3.69–71.

29. of the time: Peter Alexander (*Shakespeare's Life and Art*, 1939, p. 111) dates in 1595; Hazelton Spencer (*The Art and Life of William Shakespeare*, 1940, p. 241) and EKC (*WS*, 1.373) in 1596. Some recent scholarship (e.g., the New Cambridge ed.) argues for a later date, in the theatrical season of 1597–98.

29. stands for sacrifice: MV, 3.2.55–57.

29. Southampton: Details from Fripp, *WS*, 1.420.

30. the best times: MV, 2.6.8–19.

30. love's disasters: 5.1.1–14.

30. fleece is Portia's emblem: 3.2.244 (and 1.1.170–72).
30. sunny locks: 1.1.169 (and 3.2.92).
30. entrapping men's hearts: 3.2.92, 100–1.
30. gnats in cobwebs: 3.2.121–24.
30. many cowards: 3.2.83–85.
30. a dangerous sea: 3.2.97–99.
30. "sand-blind": 2.2.36–37.
30. "varnish" or "garnish": 2.5.33, 2.9.49; 2.6.45, 3.5.69.
30. "a gracious voice": 3.2.75–77.
30. "of a devil": 1.2.130.
30. "make incision": 2.1.6.
31. a blinking idiot: 2.9.54.
31. vice so "simple": 3.2.81–82.
31. "of the flock": 4.1.114.
31. he isn't merry: 1.1.47–48.
31. "and smiles not": 1.2.47–48.
31. "at a bagpiper": 1.1.51–56.
31. "i' the nose": 4.1.49–50.
31. "affection": 4.1.50–53.
31. consulting their wit: 2.9.80–81.
31. rolls the dice: 2.1.32.
32. "goes by destiny": 2.9.83.
32. drops manna: 5.1.294–95.
32. dropping like rain: 4.1.184–86.
32. "Jacob served for": 1.3.77–93.
32. hero is fortunate: 3.2.207–8.
32. "a good wench": 2.2.166–67.
32. "choose as true": 3.2.131–33.
32. "God sort all": 5.1.132.
32. fair, and true: 2.6.53–56.
33. "as 'tis valued": TRO, 2.2.52.
33. "seasoned": MV, 5.1.107–8.
33. rose in winter: LLL, 1.1.105.

33. disappoints them both: MV, 4.1.214–17.

33. "good without respect": 5.1.99.

33. "badge of Hell": LLL, 4.3.250.

33. wine and Rhenish: MV, 3.1.41–42.

33. in manners: 2.3.19.

33. that doesn't glister: 2.7.65.

2. The Revolution of the Times

34. on every tomb: AWW, 2.3.137–41.

34. tale of me: R2, 5.1.44.

34. "sapless age": 1H6, 4.5.4.

34. "gentler scion": WT, 4.4.93.

35. a new Aeneas: 2H6, 5.2.62–65.

35. "killed his son": 3H6, 2.5.54, 78.

36. "a gentleman born": WT, 5.2.139.

37. "no other heralds": *Poetaster*, 1601, 1.2.53–55.

37. "Not without mustard": *Every Man Out of His Humor*, 1599, 3.4.86.

37. "charge, and countenance": William Harrison, *Description of England*, 1577; EKC, *WS*, 2.26.

37. "his own merit": H8, 1.1.59–64.

37. the vulgar heart: 2H4, 1.3.90.

38. them like necessities: 3.1.92–93.

38. "and dally now": 1H4, 5.3.55.

38. "born in't": ANT, 2.2.9–10.

38. tilt with lips: 1H4, 2.3.91–92.

38. the Shakespeare Apocrypha: Ed. C. F. Tucker Brooke (1908), 1967. Not included in this collection is *Edmund Ironside*, recently proposed as Shakespeare's. An anonymous history that reads like work of the late 1580s, it "echoes" Sh. or draws on conventions in language and gesture inherited by him. *Sh's Lost Play Edmund Ironside*, ed. Eric Sams, 1985; E. B. Everitt, *The Young Shakespeare: Studies in Documentary Evidence* (*Anglistica* II), 1954. Charles Hamilton, like Everitt, identifies Shakespeare's hand in the BL MS. *In Search of Shakespeare: A Reconnaisance into the Poet's Life and Handwriting*, 1985.

38. star lived greatly: H5, Ep.5–6.

38. on his sword: 5 Pro.32.

38. one . . . in five: Louis B. Wright, *Middle Class Culture in Elizabethan England* (1935), 1958, p. 621.

38. "house of thought": H5, 5.Pro.23.

39. feeds "contention": 2H4, 1.1.155–60.

39. "warlike Blunt": 1H4, 4.4.30.

39. "ever valiant": 1.1.53–54.

39. "all the world": 2.4.479–80.

39. *Edward III*: Ed. and repr. in Brooke's *Sh. Apocrypha.*

39. "worse than weeds": SON 94.14.

39. Subdue myself: *Edw. III*, 2.2.94–100.

39. "unto a stake": 5.1.143–45.

39. in *Henry V*: 1.2.105–14; 2.4.53–62; 4.2.29–31.

40. *Sir Thomas More*: R. C. Bald, "Book of Sir TM and Its Problems," *Sh. Surv.* 2 (1966), pp. 44–61, accepting Hand D as Sh's, summarizes the scholarship. Giles E. Dawson brings the case up to date: "Sh's Handwriting," *Sh. Surv.* 42 (1990), pp. 119–28. Scott McMillin, *The Eliz. Theater and "The Book of Sir TM,"* conflates Hands C and D in the MS.

40. "Clubs!" or "Stones!": H8, 5.3.51; AYL, 5.2.41.

40. bloody-pated servingmen: 1H6, 3.1.76, 89–90.

40. "our best plotter": Francis Meres in *Palladis Tamia*, 1598.

41. "a lucifer match": Edward Maunde Thompson, *Sh's Handwriting*, 1916, p. 53.

41. "overpeering" its banks: HAM, 4.5.100.

41. "of the deep": LR, 4.2.49–50.

41. doesn't follow today: R2, 2.1.195–97.

41. "damned commotion": 2H4, 4.1.36.

42. comedy plus history: *Cambises*, c. 1561.

42. history plus tragedy: *Gorboduc*, 1561.

42. Standard accounts: The most comprehensive is Irving Ribner, *The Elizabethan History Play* (1957), 1965, esp. pp. 98–103.

42. like the Hydra: 2H4, 4.2.38.

42. by the beard: H5, 5.2.206–10.

42. in our will: OTH, 1.3.325–26.

42. With being nothing: R2, 5.5.38–41.

42. all the water: 3.2.54–55.

43. "proportion of subjection": H5, 4.1.144–46.

43. an angry arm: R2, 1.2.37–41.

43. "specialty of rule": TRO, 1.3.78.

43. on the honeybees: H5, 1.2.187–204.

44. in *King Lear*: 1.4.244.

44. "a viperous worm": 1H6, 3.1.72–73.

44. "low and lower": H5, 1.2.180–81.

44. "piles of ruin": COR, 3.1.205–6.

44. "Alarum . . . Exeunt": 3H6, 5.4.82 s.d.

45. "is a swan": EKC, *ES*, 2.360–62.

45. Shakespeare's fellows [at] . . . Swan: Leslie Hotson's supposition, *Shakespeare Versus Shallow*, 1931, pp. 13–19.

45. "plays in it": EKC, *Sources*, pp. 35–36.

45. Pembroke's Men . . . there: Wm. Ingram, *A London Life in the Brazen Age Francis Langley, 1548–1602*, 1978, pp. 154–56. Details about Langley, unless otherwise cited, come from this biography.

45. "sink or swim": 1H4, 1.3.194.

45. London's Corporation: Hotson, pp. 13–14.

45. "in or about": Letter in Ingram, p. 169.

46. Privy Council ordered: JQA, *WS*, pp. 270–72; Ingram, p. 173.

46. "speedily perform": Ingram, p. 185.

46. lodger on Bankside: First placed there (without surviving evidence) by Edmund Malone in 1796. Evans, *Records*, p. 12.

46. into the country: EKC, *ES*, 2.196, records his travels.

46. "immoderate use": Lee, *WS*, p. 338.

46. far as Aberdeen: A. W. Pollard, *Shakespeare's Folios and Quartos*, 1909, p. 73.

46. "better both ways": HAM, 2.2.329–31.

47. "tedious dead vacation": Thomas Nashe's letter is quoted in Hotson, p. 16.

47. "lord of the castle": 1H4, 1.2.41–42.

47. died a martyr: 2H4, Ep.32.

47. "to youthful sin": *Sir John Old-castle* (by Munday, Wilson, Drayton, Hathaway), 1599.

47. dragons . . . at large: After Ingram, p. 162.

47. "time and state": *The Staple of News*, 1626.

47. bill of particulars: Quoting Wm. Ames, *Cases of Conscience*, 1639; Wm. Prynne, *Histriomastix*, 1633; I. G., *Refutation of the Apology for Actors*, 1615. R. A. Fraser, *The War Against Poetry*, 1970.

47. "parrots [and] puppets": John Melton, *A Six-Fold Politician*, 1609.

48. what he paid: M. M. Reese, *Shakespeare His World and His Work*, 1980, pp. 141–45.

48. for his plays: Peter Thomson, *Shakespeare's Theatre*, 1983, pp. 58, 82– 83; Reese, pp. 142, 201; EKC, *WS*, 1.84, 96.

48. more than £1,000: Reese, p. 251.

48. "thousand a year": John Ward in EKC, *WS*, 2.249.

48. his yearly earnings: JQA, *WS*, pp. 428–29, 441–45; Reese, p. 252; G.E Bentley, *The Profession of Dramatist in Shakespeare's Time* (1971), 1986, ch. V; Bernard Beckerman, *Shakespeare at the Globe 1599–1609*, 1962, p. 22.

48. Dekker made: Thomson, *Shakespeare's Theatre*, p. 58.

48. "vouchers, his recoveries": HAM, 5.1.104–6.

49. Distinguish form: R2, 2.2.18–20 (and H5, 5.2.320).

49. against the word: R2, 5.3.122.

49. "in all things": H5, 4.7.33.

49. "salmons in both": 4.7.31.

49. Falstaff, "sealing": 2H4, 4.3.131.

49. prelate, "sealing": 4.1.91.

49. an honest man: 2H4, 5.1.48–49.

49. "disciplines of war": H5, 3.2.140.

50. "ceremonies": 4.1.72.

50. "Unto the breach": 3.1.1.

50. "choice-drawn cavaliers": 3.Pro.24.

50. "to the breach": 3.2.21.

50. "find no partition": 2H4, 4.1.194.

50. but he lives: H5, 2.1.127–28.

50. "God knows": 2H4, 4.5.183.

50. a "blunt monster": Ind.18–19.

50. is bait: 3.2.331–32.
50. bloodsucking: H5, 2.3.56–58.
50. "the orphans' cries": 2.4.106.
50. throats are cut: 4.1.193–94.
50. "a hot day": 2H4, 1.2.207–8.
51. "Bouncing Bess": In *The Famous Victories of H5*, before 1588.
51. "A Lamentable Tragedy": *Cambises.*
51. "leaping houses": 1H4, 1.2.9.
51. "in one sphere": 5.4.65.
51. "crescive" Hal: H5, 1.1.66.
51. bating and dwindling: 1H4, 3.3.2.
51. curtsy to kings: H5, 5.2.268–69.
52. Falling like Phaeton: R2, 3.3.178.
52. need friends: 3.2.175–76.
52. than his name: 4.1.255.
52. "is like thee": 1H4, 2.4.246.
52. shillings an ell: 3.3.71–72.
52. powers to death: 2H4, 1.3.31–33.
52. to brave deeds: 2.3.19–21.
52. of Christian kings: H5, 2.Pro.6.
52. fears and desires: 4.1.99–112.
52. in the stews: R2, 5.3.16–19.
52. into the grave: 2H4, 5.2.123.
52. small beer: 2.2.10–11.
52. "plodding": H5, 1.2.277.
53. "his good judgments": 4.7.46–47.
53. "veil of wildness": 1.1.64.
53. Imitating the sun: 1H4, 1.2.197.
53. sonnets: Nos. 33, 34.
53. "in admiring eyes": 1H4, 3.2.76–84.
53. "sullen ground": 1.2.212.
53. "litter but one": 2H4, 1.2.11–12.
53. "little kingdom, man": 4.3.102–32.
53. "grand jurors": 1H4, 2.2.91.

53. "hate us youth": 2.2.85.
53. tun of vices: 2.4.493.
53. gross and palpable: 2.4.225–26.
53. "mockeries": H5, 4.Pro.53.
54. give battle "tonight": 1H4, 4.3.1.
54. a dull fighter: 4.2.79–80.
54. part of valor: 5.4.120.
54. "Within the center": HAM, 2.2.158–59.
54. "our dull workings: 2H4, 4.2.22.
55. "manure" the ground: R2, 4.1.137.
55. "fall of leaf": 3.4.49.
55. new-come spring: 5.2.46–47.
55. with wit's regard: 2.1.27–28.
55. fool of time: 1H4, 5.4.81–83.
55. "eyes of death": R2, 2.1.270–71.
56. "new world": 4.1.78.
56. "will break out": 2H4, 4.4.118–20.
56. "farewell": R2, 3.2.160–64.
56. "journeyman to grief": 1.3.274.
56. way of nature: 2H4, 5.2.4.
56. "and after holiday": R2, 3.1.44.
56. Subject to Time: 2H4, 1.3.110.
56. along the stream: 4.1.70.
56. to the sea: 5.2.129–31.
56. pox . . . gout: 1.2.230–31, 243–44.
56. it outlives performance: 2.4.260–61.
56. "of our kingdom": 3.1.38–40.
56. a pustulous boil: R2, 5.1.58–59.
57. recollecting it: In 2H4, 3.1.76–77.
57. "are all diseased": 4.1.54.
57. God a death: 3.2.235.
57. come peascod time: 2.4.382–83.
57. lifting-up of day: 4.4.91–93.

57. chimes at midnight: 3.2.214.

57. "of the times": 3.1.45–56.

57. "in his nightgown": I.e., dressing gown. 3.1.s.d.

57. "whoreson tingling": 1.2.112–14.

57. "cup of alteration": 3.1.52.

58. "ruin and decay": J. O. Halliwell-Phillips, *Outlines of the Life of Shakespeare*, 1889, 1.131.

58. "his own mind": Theobald's Preface to Shakespeare; Malone, 1.25.

58. In fewer offices: 2H4, 1.3.41–47.

59. boxes, and inkstands: Lee, *WS*, p. 289*n*.

59. an early biographer: H-P, 1.131–36.

59. William Bott: ME, p. 88.

59. the deed records: I.e. the "foot of fine," EKC, *Sources*, p. 14.

60. clear the title: ME, pp. 88–89.

60. "diverse books, boxes": EKC, *Sources*, pp. 41–43.

60. Shakespeare litigated: H-P, 1.149, 185-86, 212, 225; 2.77–80; S. Schoenbaum, *William Shakespeare: A Compact Documentary Life*, 1977, pp. 28, 40 hereafter SS); JQA, *WS*, p. 256. (Most who mention the Clayton suit suppose another Wm. Shakespeare.) The Court of Record suits vs. Rogers and Addenbrooke are described in EKC, *WS*, 1.84–85 and App. A; Lee, *WS*, pp. 321–22; ME, pp. 107–10; Halliday, *Shakespeare*, p. 206.

61. summoned John Shakespeare: Mrs. Charlotte Stopes' discovery, recapitulated in Peter Alexander, *Shakespeare*, 1964, pp. 25–26. Hotson, discoverer of Wayte's petition, describes the case in *Sh. v. Shallow*.

61. something dangerous: HAM, 5.1.261–62.

61. "reckoning or value": Hotson, p. 24. A loan of Wm. Wayte's, "if he be living at my decease," is remitted in the will of Shakespeare's Stratford friend and business acquaintance John Combe, Jan. 28, 1612/13 (Lewis, *Documents*, 2.328; Shakespeare Birthplace Trust reference number BRU 15/7, no. 254). Combe died July 10, 1614. Wayte makes no other appearance in Stratford documents but Dr. Levi Fox (letter to the author, March 17, 1989) refers to the marriage record of Wm. Wayte and Elizabeth Gardiner, Jan. 4, 1554 in Bisley, Gloucestershire.

61. William Gardiner: Thomas Russell, Shakespeare's friend and overseer of his will, is connected to Gardiner through the Stepkins, Rus-

sell's kin. John Stepkin, a legatee of Russell's, is probably grandson of Gardiner's son-in-law John, who lamented his father-in-law's "persecution." Hotson, *I Wm. Sh.* (1937), 1970, pp. 134–35, 277–78.

61. on his coat: WIV, 1.1.16–21.

62. troupe of fairies: 5.5.61–76.

62. Whitehall Palace housed: SS, pp. 197–98.

62. in Shakespeare's memory: WIV, 5.1.25; 1.1.89–90.

62. young "William": In 4.1.

63. Jokes on Shallow's: 1.1.7–8.

63. "Armigero": 1.1.10.

63. to the future: Beckerman, *Shakespeare*, gives the case for dating WIV in 1600–1.

63. Jonson . . . began: *Every Man in His Humor.*

63. "through the realm": WIV, 5.5.144–45.

63. with fat meat: 2H4, Ep.26–27.

63. early tradition: Elaborated by John Dennis, ded. to *The Comical Gallant* (a rewriting of WIV), 1702; and Rowe in 1709.

63. "make not monks": H8, 3.1.23.

64. "upon ill employment": WIV, 5.5.126–28.

3. Sailing to Illyria

65. mending the pavement: Sturley to Quiney, Jan. 24, 1598, in Lewis, *Documents*, 1.227.

66. "where, and how": Nov. 4, 1598 (Lewis, 1.230–32). Quiney's letter is lost but Sturley "imported" its contents.

66. E. K. Chambers: *ES*, 1.370.

66. another historian: Ellis Powell, *The Evolution of the Money Market*, 1915, p. 33.

66. unskilled laborers: The Elizabethan Age saw steady inflation, with prices rising out of all proportion to wages. Between 1590–1630, real wages declined by 50 to 60 percent. B. A. Holderness, *Pre-Industrial England*, 1976, p. 204.

66. the proper multiple: Drawing on William Ingram, *The Business of Playing*, forthcoming from Cornell, 1992.

66. "to your occasions": MV, 1.1.127–30, 138–39.

66. "nature's riches": SON 94.6.

67. "disburse some money": Sturley (quoting Adrian Quiney) to R. Quiney, Jan. 24, 1598; Lewis, 1.227.

67. "that bred it": ADO, 3.1.9–11.

67. cried Essex: Sir Walter Ralegh, "A Relation of the Cadiz Action . . . 1596," *Works*, ed. Thomas Birch, 1829, 8.668.

67. Donne, recalling it: In "The Calm."

68. "of a lion": ADO, 1.1.13–15.

68. name he used: Hesketh Pearson's suggestion, *A Life of Shakespeare*, 1949, p. 84.

68. "this is all": ADO, 5.1.94–99.

68. "merry war": 1.1.62.

68. "honest kersey noes": LLL, 5.2.413.

68. melts in "blood": ADO, 2.1.180.

68. "best becomes her": 2.1.331–32.

68. An obstinate heretic: 1.1.234–35.

68. "A notable argument": 1.1.256.

68. "all are full": Leonard Digges, commendatory verses to Shakespeare's *Poems*, 1640.

68. Claudio "notes": ADO, 1.1.162.

68. blame the music: 2.1.69–70.

69. "out of measure": 1.3.2.

69. "good sharp fellow": 1.2.18.

69. "white-bearded fellow": 2.3.118–19.

69. make the man: 3.3.118–19.

69. "a deformed thief": 3.3.124.

69. "which is Beatrice": 5.4.72.

69. "sign and semblance": 4.1.33.

69. "full of proof": 5.1.104–5.

69. "may avoid him": 5.1.260–61.

69. "misprision": 4.1.184.

69. truth to light: 5.1.232–34.

69. "note" of things: 3.3.28.

70. least deserving man: 3.3.9–16.

70. "as a king": 3.5.21.

70. "our whole dissembly": 4.2.1.

70. "bent" or "humor": 2.3.222, 4.1.186, 1.1.131.

70. plain-dealing villain: 1.3.32–37.

70. stuffed: 1.1.56–57.

70. Turning a spit: 2.1.252.

70. kindred . . . "wayward marl": 2.1.62–65.

70. "transgressed": 2.1.252.

70. "suffer salvation": 3.3.3.

70. "in the garden": 5.1.179–80.

70. "of the lady": 4.1.158.

70. connects to "travail": 4.1.212.

70. "Die to live": 4.1.252.

70. graves "utter": 5.3.19–20.

71. the same "semblance": 5.1.251–52.

71. "mistaking": 5.1.273–74.

71. "what they do": 4.1.20; Luke 23:34.

71. necessity will make . . . forsworn: LLL, 1.1.149.

71. "approved wanton": ADO, 4.1.44.

71. "approved" a villain: 4.1.301.

71. Taking "infection": 2.3.121.

71. the greatest note: 3.2.54–55.

71. dinner bell: 2.3.210 (and 2.1.171).

71. the smallest twine: 4.1.250.

71. "flesh and blood": 5.1.34.

71. "fit": 1.1.318 (and 1.1.319, 1.3.28, 2.1.57–58, 2.3.42, 3.2.111 and 115–16, 3.3.22–23).

71. fox . . . fowl . . . fish: 2.3.42, 92, 108–9.

71. "Limed": 3.1.104.

71. lapwing . . . fish . . . haggard: 3.1.24, 26–28, 35–36.

72. blood and wisdom: 2.3.163–65.

72. sounds of woe: 2.3.68–69.

72. gulled or "converted": 2.3.22 (and 3.4.90).

72. worth the noting: 2.3.55.

72. bad parts: 5.2.60.

72. guess what he is: 1.1.109–10 (and 3.4.86–87).

72. "Put down": 2.1.283–84.

72. "Dotage": 2.3.211–12 (and 2.1.309, 2.3.96).

72. "must be peopled": 2.3.242.

72. Rebecca to Isaac: Genesis 24:65.

72. "meaning well suited": ADO, 5.1.225.

72. "wolves have preyed": 5.3.25.

72. until tomorrow: 5.4.127.

72. Stratford's Court Leet: Ed. R. Savage and E. I. Fripp for the Dugdale Society, Stratford, 1921, 1.94; J. R. Brown, "The Presentation of Comedy," p. 19 in *Shakespearian Comedy*, ed. M. Bradbury and D. Palmer, 1972.

73. "are an ass": ADO, 4.2.73.

73. another playwright: John Day, *The Travels of the Three English Brothers*, 1607.

73. Hamlet . . . bids the players: 3.2.

73. Kempe: Details from Fripp, *WS*, 1.207*n*., 208; *The Pilgrimage to Parnassus*, 1597; TGV, 4.4.22; David Wiles, *Shakespeare's Clown*, 1987, p. 105.

73. "tickle o' the sere": HAM, 2.2.323–24.

73. of Dick Tarlton: Nashe, dedicating *An Almond for a Parrot*, 1590.

73. Shakespeare's wise fools: After John Davies, *Scourge of Folly*, 1610.

73. dance with Death: R. Braithwaite, *Remains after Death*, 1618.

73. fixed at twelve: After 1603.

74. "and kind fellows": Reese, pp. 162–63.

74. "thou winter wind": AYL, 2.7.174.

74. "the present time": 5.3.30.

74. daughter or widow: T. W. Baldwin, *The Organization and Personnel of the Shakespearean Company*, 1927, p. 148.

74. "old stuttering Heminges": From a "sonnet" on the burning of the Globe, 1613.

75. a Restoration annalist: Richard Flecknoe, *A Discourse of the English Stage*, 1664.

75. whetstone of wit: AYL, 1.2.56.

75. developed a "line": Baldwin, *Shakespearean Company*, esp. chs. VIII and IX.

76. sixteen players: Wm. A. Ringler, "The Number of Actors in Sh's Early Plays," *The Seventeenth Century Stage*, ed. G. E. Bentley, 1968, pp. 110–34.

76. in one play: *The Seven Deadly Sins.*

76. A popular play: Preston's *Cambises.*

76. This argued versatility: T. J. King demonstrates, "The Versatility of Sh's Actors," pp. 144–50 in *Sh. and Dramatic Tradition Essays in Honor of S. F. Johnson*, ed. W. R. Elton and Wm. B. Long, 1989.

76. a traveler: Thomas Platter.

76. "a beard coming": MND, 1.2.47–48.

76. "of Margaret Chambers": Thomson, *Shakespeare's Theatre*, p. 11.

76. "overlusty at legs": LR, 2.4.10.

76. John Manningham: Entry for March 13, 1602.

76. Five of them: R. Burbage, Heminges, Cowley, Pope, Phillips.

76. Condell . . . Heminges: Charles Connell, *They Gave Us Shakespeare*, 1982.

77. "Pope the Clown": Samuel Rowlands, *The Letting of Humor's Blood in the Head-vein*, Satire IV, 1600.

77. providing a legacy: H-P, 1.317.

77. One eulogist: Thomas Middleton.

77. "this deponent's nose": Andrew Gurr, *Shakespearean Stage*, 1970, p. 67.

78. One theater historian: Beckerman, pp. 6–7.

78. "about the church": Stephenson, pp. 312–13.

78. "dull" . . . "disgrace": COR, 5.3.40–42; SON 23.1–2 (after Ivor Brown, *Shakespeare*, 1949, pp. 222–23).

78. a "plot": Thomson, p. 116; W. W. Greg, ed. *Dramatic Documents from the Elizabethan Playhouses*, 1931, 1.2–4, 73; Hosking, p. 63; G. E. Bentley, *The Profession of Player in Shakespeare's Time* (1984), 1986, 2.211.

78. the "part": EKC, *WS*, 1.123–24; Ribner, *WS*, p. 169; Thomson, p. 117; Reese, p. 201; Beckerman, p. 9.

78. a German visitor: Johannes Rhenanus, 1611. Quotations from Da-

vid Klein, "Did Shakespeare Produce His Own Plays?" *MLR* 57 (1962), 556–60.

79. directing . . . in *Hamlet*: JQA, *WS*, pp. 311–12.

79. "augmented, and amended": The bookseller Cuthbert Burby, promoting a new ed. of ROM, 1599.

79. "the town here": Jonson, *Poetaster*, 3.4.367.

79. internal evidence suggesting: Bentley, *Profession of Dramatist in Shakespeare's Time* l. 262–63; EKC, *WS*, 1.211–42.

80. a second play: "*The Division of the Kingdom Shakespeare's Two Versions of "King Lear,"* ed. Gary Taylor and Michael Warren, 1983. Sidney Thomas refutes, "Sh's Supposed Revision of LR," *SQ* 35, no. 4 (Winter 1984), pp. 506–11.

80. "to the matter": MM, 5.1.90.

81. writer of epigrams: John Weever, "Ad Guilielmum Shakespeare," *Epigrams*, 1599, IV.2.

81. his "comparative discourse": *Palladis Tamia.*

81. a later edition: the fourth, in 1598.

81. "old Robin Hood": AYL, 1.1.116.

82. "good in everything": 2.1.17.

82. "to the smother": 1.2.287.

82. liberty, not banishment: 1.3.138.

82. winter wind . . . bitter sky: 2.7.174, 184.

82. uncouth desert: 2.6.6, 2.7.110.

82. faint with hunger: 2.7.132.

82. the melancholy foliage: 2.7.111.

82. "a better place": 2.4.17.

82. town vs. country: *Narrative and Dramatic Sources of Shakespeare*, ed. Geoffrey Bullough, 1963, 2.188.

82. "in respect of": AYL, 3.2.13–21.

82. "of the world": 3.2.420.

82. "compact of jars": 2.7.5.

83. doesn't know why: 1.1.155–58.

83. pair of baboons: 2.5.26–27.

83. he cultivates "extremity": 4.1.5–6.

83. "Signior Love": 3.2.291–92.

83. men are "humorous": 1.2.266.
83. never schooled: 1.1.166–67.
83. "are you virtuous": 2.3.5.
83. daughter who gives: 1.2.19–21.
83. loving . . . overcomes her: 1.3.32–34.
83. "is not inherited": 1.3.61.
83. a general curse: LR, 4.6.206.
83. borne bad sons: TMP, 1.2.120.
83. a "humorous sadness": AYL, 4.1.19–20.
83. full of briers: 1.3.12.
83. a sad one: MV, 1.1.79.
83. "Is 't possible": AYL 5.2.1 (and 2.2.1).
83. "at first sight": 3.5.82.
83. "fantasy": 2.4.31.
83. like rams: 5.2.30–31.
83. strange "capers": 2.4.54–55 (and 3.3.7–9).
83. Like snails: 4.1.54–57.
83. crest is ancient: 4.2.14–15.
84. "country copulatives": 5.4.55–56.
84. "of their estate": 1.2.15.
84. "piace, ei lice": Tasso, *Aminta*, Act I, sc. 2, l.26.
84. "atones" them: AYL, 5.4.110.
84. "his mother earth": 1.2.200–1.
84. "dead and buried": 1.2.117.
84. "Breaking of ribs" . . . "sport for ladies": 1.2.138–39.
84. "Yonder they lie": 1.2.129.
84. try a fall: 1.1.126.
84. "My trial": 1.2.186–87.
85. "let Time try": 4.1.199–200.
85. isn't a traitor: 1.3.63.
85. "poverty of grace": 3.5.100.
85. "of this forest": 5.4.34.
85. "main harvest reaps": 3.5.101–3.
85. Book of Ruth: 2:2–3.

85. "into the fire": AYL, 1.2.43–44.
86. a "venerable burden": 2.7.167.
86. St. Paul's injunction: Colossians 3:9.
86. the old news: AYL, 1.1.98–100.
86. "o'ergrown with hair": 4.3.106.
86. whip him out: H5, 1.1.28–29.
86. remembers Esau: Genesis 25:23.
86. "his just occasion": AYL, 4.3.129.
86. "miserable slumber": 4.3.132.
86. St. Luke's gospel: 15:11–32.
86. his "poor allottery": AYL, 1.1.73.
86. a rotten tree: 2.3.63.
87. "extermined": 3.5.89.
87. armor of God: Ephesians 6:11.
87. flood, like Noah's: AYL, 5.4.35–36.
87. convert to graces: HAM, 4.7.21.
87. "a giddy thing": ADO, 5.4.108.
87. giddiness in question: AYL, 5.2.5.
87. "old religious man": 5.4.160.
87. patience, and endurance: 5.4.170–93.
87. fruit . . . falls unbidden: 3.2.232–35.
87. "heaped in joy": 5.4.178.
87. "virtue in If": 5.4.99–103.
87. can't relinquish [honor]: 1.2.76–78.
87. Shaw . . . has them: *Shaw on Shakespeare*, ed. E. Wilson, 1962, p. 1.
87. "wiser, the waywarder": AYL, 4.1.161.
88. "bountiful blind woman": 1.2.35–36.
88. our natural wits: 1.2.52–53.
88. of Shakespeare's schoolbooks: Marcellus Palengenius, *Zodiacus Vitae*.
88. the Latin tag: J. Q. Adams, *Shakespearean Playhouses* (1917), 1960, p. 248 and *n.* (citing Malone, *Variorum*, 3.67), gives the motto from John of Salisbury.
88. In *Hamlet*: 2.2.361–62.

88. "in the occupation": JQA, *WS*, p. 287 (quoting from the inquest on the Brend estate, 5/16/1599).

88. a Swiss traveler: Thomas Platter.

88. Old maps: Francis Delaram's "View," bet. 1615–24, represents London in James's Coronation year, 1603; Hollar's is later, c. 1647.

88. excavations in our time: Reported in *TLS*, Nov. 10–16, 1989; and Andrew Gurr, *SQ* 41, no. 1 (Spring 1990), pp. 97–100; and substantially anticipated in John Orrell, *The Quest for Sh's Globe*, 1983.

88. "called the Globe": JQA, *WS*, p. 285.

88. "of the yard": J. C. Adams, *The Globe Playhouse* (1942), 1961, p. 90.

88. Corporation was winning: Andrew Gurr, *Playgoing in Shakespeare's London*, 1987, pp. 23–26.

89. wrote Thomas Dekker: *The Gull's Hornbook*, 1609.

89. located their playhouse: W. W. Braines, *The Site of the Globe Playhouse*, 1924.

89. "long straggling place": John Strype's ed. (1720) of Stow's *Survey of London*.

90. Jonson described it: In "An Execration upon Vulcan."

90. "her own dirge": Ordish, *Shakespeare's London*, p. 303.

90. as Paris Garden: Stephenson, pp. 304–6.

90. in *Henry VIII*: 5.3.1–2.

91. Malone: Citing a lost memorandum of Alleyn's.

92. indulgence to sin: 1H6, 1.3.35.

92. Token-books: Ordish, p. 298.

92. "to and fro": 2H6, 4.8.24–25, 55–56.

93. "these two months": H8, 5.3.85–86.

93. "of a limekiln": WIV, 3.3.78–79.

93. "edge of husbandry": HAM, 1.3.77.

93. like our grandmothers: After Shaw in his rev. of CYM, 9/22/1896.

93. Kempe had . . . departed: "About the time of the building of the Globe," said Heminges and Condell (Alexander, *Shakespeare's Life and Art*, p. 131).

93. Some identify: E.g., E. A. G. Honigmann, *Sh: The 'lost years,'* 1985.

94. "at Malvolio's suit": TN, 5.1.276.

94. of fair behavior: 1.2.47.

94. an "inland man": AYL, 2.7.96, 3.2.345.

94. Barents . . . Shirley: TN, 3.2.26–28, 2.5.180–81, 3.4.278–79.

94. play of 1600: Recent scholarship (e.g., Elizabeth Story Donno's New Cambridge ed., 1985), dates TN in 1600 or 1601.

94. "of the Indies": TN, 3.2.78–80.

94. "for a while": PER, 1.2.106.

94. "mere extravagancy": TN, 2.1.12.

94. immediate source: Barnaby Riche, "Apolonius and Silla," the second story in Riche's *Farewell to Military Profession*, 1581.

95. "voice, one habit": TN, 5.1.216.

95. inquisitive, confounds himself: ERR, 1.2.35–38.

95. "cleft in two": TN, 5.1.223.

95. "to her bias": 5.1.260.

95. "should I do": 1.2.3–4.

95. "what I am": 3.1.141.

95. cakes and ale: 2.3.114–18.

95. in their brain: 1.5.57.

95. "of 'we three'": 2.3.17.

95. the "natural perspective": 5.1.217.

95. Some think: E.g., JQA, *WS*, p. 292 (1/6/1600); Leslie Hotson, *The First Night of TN*, 1954 (1/6/1601).

96. Pepys complained: Jan. 6, 1663.

96. "and bulk unprizeable": TN, 5.1.55.

96. three sovereign thrones: 1.1.37–38.

96. legs and thighs: 1.3.139–41.

96. Olivia thinks this: 1.5.310–11.

96. Sebastian . . . the same: 2.1.3–4.

96. thanking his stars: 2.5.178.

96. Fortune . . . "golden Time": 5.1.251–52, 382.

96. perdition of souls: 3.4.317–18.

96. a "happy wreck": 5.1.266.

96. "was a sailor": 3.2.16–17.

96. darkness more puzzling: 4.2.45–47.
96. envy calls fair: 2.1.29.
97. trout . . . woodcock: 2.5.22, 30–31, 83.
97. sexual entendres: E.g., 2.5.89.
97. Witchcraft: 5.1.76.
97. "an ordinary man": 1.3.83–84.
97. makes the monk: 1.5.56.
97. "in other habits": 5.1.387–88.
97. "upon his brow": 5.1.249.
97. an "impressure": 2.5.92–93.
97. "set their forms": 2.2.30.
97. "truly blent": 1.5.239.
97. "at your gate": 1.5.268.
98. "estate" or condition: 1.2.44.
98. of this estate: 5.1.393.
98. a drowned man: 1.5.135–36.
98. in his pocket: 5.1.32–33.
98. her damask cheek: 2.4.111–12.
98. a cloistered nun: 1.1.27–31.
98. hers to reserve: 1.5.187–89.
98. "patched with virtue": 1.5.47–49.
98. like standing water: 1.5.159.
98. "grossly clad": 5.1.238.
98. a "pregnant enemy": 2.2.28.
98. "taint of vice": 3.4.356.
98. will turn out: 2.2.33.
99. "a proper man": 3.1.133.
99. "sowed a grizzle": 5.1.165.
99. growing "mellow": 1.2.43.
99. "before 'tis ripe": 5.1.154.
99. "whirligig" of time: 5.1.376.
99. "intent" or purpose: 1.2.53–55.
99. "voyage of nothing": 2.4.75–78.

99. "to the world": 1.2.42.
99. is only "perchance": 1.2.5–7.
99. "you with chance": 1.2.8.
99. watery tomb: 5.1.234.
99. "in grain": 1.5.237.
99. taint . . . cited often: 3.1.68, 3.4.13 and 131, 5.1.138 and 357.
99. waves and surges: 5.1.229.
99. fresh in love: 3.4.384.
99. "eye-offending brine": 1.1.29.
99. "Present" love: 2.3.48.
100. their driving boat: 1.2.11.
100. flood of fortune: 4.3.11.
100. Reason . . . fetters itself: 3.1.155.
100. hard a knot: 2.2.40–44.
100. they "wrangle": 4.3.14.

4. Fools of Nature

101. *Phoenix* . . . Antonio: TN, 5.1.60–61, 69.
101. breach of the sea: 2.1.23.
101. "sanctity of love": 3.4.361.
101. "and bravely rigged": TMP, 5.1.224.
102. "let it be": HAM, 5.2.37–38.
102. nicely mixed: JC, 5.5.73–74.
102. "not more twin": TN, 5.1.223.
102. "make one twain": SON 39.13.
103. *Love's Martyr*: Ed. Alexander B. Grosart, 1878.
103. over the years: A "long expected labor" (says Robert Chester), the PHT section of *LM* was written more than a decade before its publication in 1601. Pp. lxix–lxx in *Poems by Sir John Salusbury and Robert Chester*, ed. Carleton Brown, 1914.
104. "thy good report": SON 36.14.
104. Other poets: Ignoto, a fourth poet, is often assumed to stand for Jonson too.

105. in her blood: SON 19.4.

105. "nest of spicery": R3, 4.4.424.

105. and things newborn: WT, 3.3.114.

105. their medicinal gum: OTH, 5.2.350. The trees are myrrh trees, aromatic like amomum.

105. the Arabian bird: ANT, 3.2.12.

105. Timon and Imogen: TIM, 2.1.32; CYM, 1.6.17.

105. "at this hour": TMP, 3.3.22–24.

105. The salt flood: TIM, 5.1.216–18.

105. ending is despair: TMP, Ep.15–16.

106. of their chance: ANT, 5.2.173–74.

106. his own sword: JC, 5.3.95–96.

106. "like himself": 5.4.25.

106. has more glory: 5.5.36–38.

106. "dint of pity": 3.2.194.

106. pioneered by him: E.g., in MND, 3.2.171.

106. "steely bones": AWW, 1.1.103.

106. "an ordinary pitch": JC, 1.1.73.

106. of this envy: 2.3.13–14.

106. debt is paid: 3.1.83.

106. "as I myself": 1.2.95–96.

106. "petty men": 1.2.136.

106. "and master spirits": 3.1.163.

107. it will come: 2.2.34–37.

107. to silence: 1.2.286.

107. "mighty yet": 5.3.94.

107. "'with just cause'": *Timber or Discoveries* (pub. 1641), ed. Herford and Simpson, 8.584.

107. ironed out: As by revising to read: "Know, Caesar doth not wrong, nor without cause / Will he be satisfied" (JC, 3.1.47–48).

107. "'freedom, and liberty'": 3.1.110.

107. "in the theater": 1.2.259–61.

108. in his way: 1.1.48–50.

108. drenched in blood: Following 3.1.

108. hides bad deeds: 5.1.30.

108. "a savage spectacle": 3.1.223.

108. for the gods: 2.1.173–74.

108. a lofty scene: 3.1.111–13.

108. Blood drizzles: 2.2.21.

108. stars but ourselves: 1.2.140–41.

108. "another Caesar": 5.1.54.

108. let money stick: 4.3.23–26.

108. bowl of wine: 2.2.126 (and Brutus, 4.3.141).

108. spurns a . . . petition: 3.1.44–46 (and Brutus, 4.3.5; see also, for "spurn," 2.1.11–12).

108. on last things: 2.2.32–37 (and Brutus, 4.3.190–92).

108. Cassius . . . Caesar's: 4.3.100–1; 1.2.264–66.

108. Octavius . . . Caesar: 4.1.48; 3.1.204.

109. "more days": 4.1.18 and 5.1.19–20.

109. "older in practice": 4.3.30–32.

109. "seen more years": 4.3.132.

109. Antony is "pricked": 3.1.216.

109. pricks out others: 4.1.1.

109. at Pompey's Theater: 1.3.152.

109. in this theater: 3.1.115, 3.2.188–89.

109. Pompey at Pharsalia: 5.1.74.

109. tag-rag people: 1.2.258.

109. blocks and stones: 1.1.35.

109. wood or stones: 3.2.142.

109. "the glories": 5.5.81.

109. at their heels: H5, 5.Pro.26–31.

110. "High noises": LR, 3.6.111.

110. "like a fray": JC, 2.4.18.

110. in his nightgown: 2.2.1 s.d.

110. can't bear children: 1.2.7–9.

110. takes a walk: 3.3.3–4.

110. has a birthday: 5.1.72.

110. of a friend: 5.5.29.

110. "own too much": HAM, 4.7.118.

110. the untrod state: JC, 3.1.136.
110. "by reflection": 1.2.51–53.
110. Phoenix and Turtle: Ll.33–36.
110. like an alchemist: JC, 1.3.159–60.
110. "quarrel" won't bear: 2.1.28–30.
110. "Roman actors": 2.1.226.
110. Honor and Brutus: 3.2.14–16.
110. playing on . . . "honor": 1.2.92.
110. portents and prodigies: 1.3, 2.1.
110. tide in men's affairs: 4.3.217–24.
110. "govern us below": 5.1.106–7.
111. the "general wrong": 3.1.170.
111. "fell down": 3.2.191.
111. "private griefs": 3.2.213–14.
111. "things done undone": 4.2.9.
111. he can't sleep: 2.1.62.
111. labors to attain: 5.5.41–42.
111. "only proper": 1.2.39–41.
111. "Some sick offense": 2.1.268.
111. phrase of Casca's: 1.3.101–2.
111. "an exorcist" . . . "sick men whole": 2.1.323, 327.
111. come at the spirit: 2.1.169–70.
111. drives out pity: 3.1.171.
111. cruel to be kind: HAM, 3.4.178.
111. Nothing "personal": JC, 2.1.11.
111. the unkindest cut: 3.2.183.
111. "nicely mixed": 5.5.73–75.
111. leap in himself: 5.5.24–25.
111. against self-slaughter: 5.1.100–8.
111. "swallowed fire": 4.3.156.
111. true to him: 5.5.35.
112. using his "countenance": 1.3.159.
112. appealing to "necessity": 4.3.227.

112. "end is known": 5.1.122–25.

112. "it will come": HAM, 5.2.220–23.

112. "is come round": JC, 5.3.23.

112. "my country's friend": 5.4.5.

112. very valiant rebel: 1H4, 5.4.62.

113. not in love: TRO, 1.3.287–88.

113. "must manage it": S. T. Bindoff, *Tudor England*, 1950, p. 297.

113. "appointed for death": Stow, *Annals*, 1631, sigs. Xxx, Ir.

114. "in my death": ANT, 4.14.99–100. Perhaps another reminiscence evokes Claudio in MM, 3.1.82–84. R. Fraser, *Young Shakespeare*, 1988, p. 179.

114. to an oyster-wench: R2, 1.4.31.

114. a contemporary said: Everard Guilpin, *Skialethia*, a book of satires written 1597–98.

114. the "vulgar heart": 2H4, 1.3.89–90.

115. "Rough rugheaded kerns": R2, 2.1.156.

115. "caterpillars": R2, 2.3.166. H-P, *Outlines*, 1.199 (quoting a "hitherto unpublished" MS), and C.C. Stopes, *The Life of . . . Southampton*, 1922, p. 193.

115. Augustine Phillips: JQA, *WS*, pp. 317–18, gives his testimony at the trial.

116. king of snow: R2, 4.1.260.

116. "for a friend": JC, 5.5.29.

117. "he found it": 1H4, 5.1.28.

117. tragedy of 1601: Dating follows Philip Edwards in his New Camb. ed., 1985.

117. landless "resolutes": HAM, 1.1.98.

117. "this three years": 5.1.139.

117. "*se offendendo*": 5.1.9; EKC, *WS*, 2.3–4.

117. grant of impalement: Lewis, *Documents*, 1.299–306.

118. "of known honor": HAM, 5.2.248.

118. that earlier duel: A homonymic echo links the two duels, Osric's "carriages" or sword hangers (5.2.151) recalling the "comart and carriage" (1.1.93–94) that stipulates the terms of the original wager.

118. "law and heraldry": 1.1.87.

118. Like his lawyer: 5.1.98–112.

118. has bad dreams: 2.2.254–56.

118. Shakespeare's Stratford neighbors: Halliday, *Shakespeare*, pp. 156–57.

118. Sadler . . . Walker: ME, pp. 60, 143.

118. Sh's godson William: Baptized Oct. 16, 1608. ME, pp. 110, 142; H-P, 1.225.

118. loads of willows: M. Chute, p. 242.

118. Thomas Greene: ME, pp. 127–30.

119. "distracted multitude": HAM, 4.3.4.

119. In England: 5.1.150–52.

119. state is rotten: 1.4.89.

119. an "imposthume": 4.4.27.

119. corpse . . . ear: 3.4.64–65, 5.1.166.

119. the King's table: 5.2.86–87.

119. "pregnant hinges": 3.2.61.

119. their "wisdoms": 1.2.15–16.

119. land and fertile: 5.2.84–85.

119. "'a sucked it": 5.2.187–88.

119. "buyer of land": 5.1.104.

119. can shape them: 3.4.89–91, 3.1.121–26.

119. eyes upon himself: R2, 4.1.247–48.

119. "earth and heaven": HAM, 3.1.126–28.

119. drossy age: 5.2.189.

119. "leprous distillment": 1.5.64.

119. an unweeded garden: 1.2.135–37.

120. "the nasty sty": 3.4.93–94.

120. exceeds the facts: After T. S. Eliot's essay, "Hamlet and His Problems."

120. for the source: HAM, 3.2.337–38.

120. "delight and dole": 1.2.13.

120. a heart "unfortified": 1.2.95–97.

120. assail his ears: 1.1.31–32.

120. "custom": 5.1.65–68.

120. "proof and bulwark": 3.4.36–39.

120. "pursy" (bloated) time: 3.4.153.

120. An antic disposition: 1.5.172.

120. "splenitive and rash": 5.1.261.

120. drinks hot blood: 3.2.390–92.

120. the croaking raven: 3.2.253.

121. "and Hell": 2.2.584.

121. gore-encrusted . . . "malicious sport" . . . "cue": 2.2.461–62, 513–14, 560–61.

121. "Eat a crocodile": 5.1.276.

121. "spirit" . . . guilty . . . Christmas: 1.1.154, 148, 157–64.

121. "in the best": 1.5.27.

121. rash and bloody: 3.4.27.

121. Marching . . . warlike . . . parleys . . . Smote . . . slay: 1.1.49, 47, 62, 63, 86.

121. born the day: 5.1.143–44, 147.

121. Hercules: 1.2.152–53, 1.4.82–83, 2.2.361–62, 5.1.291–92.

121. puttings things right: 1.5.188–89.

121. than the weed: 1.5.32–33.

121. offenses in question: 4.5.214.

121. "of the ulcer": 4.7.123.

121. cure the "hectic": 4.3.66–67.

121. "by desperate appliance": 4.3.9–11.

122. will and . . . matter: 2.2.481.

122. without tainting: 1.5.85.

122. "the chief end": *Shakespearean Criticism*, ed. T. M. Raysor, 1930, 2.181–98.

122. "conscience" makes cowards: HAM, 3.1.82–84.

122. "gross" . . . "event": 4.4.46, 50.

122. at the stake: 4.4.53–56.

122. "have no bounds": 4.7.128.

122. "Within the center": 2.2.158–59.

122. of their own: 3.2.213, 215.

122. shoots his arrow: 5.2.243–44 (and Claudius, 4.7.21–24).

122. weekdays aren't divided: 1.1.75–78.

122. weasel or whale: 3.2.376–82.

122. from his horse: 4.7.82–88.

123. "they change rapiers": 5.2.303 s.d.

123. flesh and blood: 1.5.6, 15, 21–22.

123. "fools of nature": 1.4.54.

123. "stamp" . . . "mole" . . . "stock" . . . "relish": 3.4.168, 1.4.24, 3.1.116–18.

123. "particular fault": 1.4.36.

123. "of one defect": 1.4.23–38.

123. "contagious blastments": 1.3.39–42.

123. "pales and forts": 1.4.28.

123. "readiness": 5.2.221–22.

123. "I'll do't": 3.3.74.

124. "ourselves is debt": 3.2.192–93.

124. after their deserts: 2.2.528–29.

124. "his true nature": 3.3.61–62.

124. "relative" grounds: 2.2.603–4.

124. falls without shaking: 3.2.190–91.

124. a "heavy burden": 3.1.53.

124. "double business bound": 3.3.41.

124. and will not: MM, 2.2.33.

124. Polonius enumerates: HAM, 2.2.396–99.

124. a "limèd soul": 3.3.68–69.

124. vesture of decay: MV, 5.1.64.

124. beyond his reach: HAM, 1.4.54–56.

124. "thoughts of love": 1.5.29–31.

124. "nothing worth": 4.4.66.

125. "thieves" . . . "naked": 4.7.43–44.

125. "like a soldier": 5.2.396.

125. of the Theaters: Josiah H. Penniman, *The War of the Theatres*, 1897; Roscoe Addison Small, *The Stage-Quarrel between Ben Jonson and the So-Called Poetasters*, 1899; EKC, *WS*, 1.71–72; and *ES*, 1.381, 3.293, 365, 428.

125. "about of brains": HAM, 2.2.358–59.

125. "that terrible Poetomachia": Thomas Dekker's phrase.

125. "win upon 'em": "Apologetical Dialogue" appended to Jonson's *Poetaster*, lst printed in 1616 Folio.

125. "the two houses": Dekker in *Raven's Almanac*, 1609.

125. Berattled by "goosequills": HAM, 2.2.341–44.

125. "his load too": 2.2.360–61.

125. "old cracked trumpet": *Poetaster*, 1601, 3.4.

125. "the late innovation": HAM, 2.2.332–33.

125. "humors of children": Following Q1, 1603.

125. Earl of Worcester's: J. Q. Adams, *Shakespeare's Playhouses*, pp. 157–59, 294–309 (for their tenure at the Red Bull).

126. the "prose Shakespeare": Charles Lamb's phrase.

126. Shakespeare's Ajax: TRO, 1.2.20–30.

127. "in many poets": *Conversations with WD.*

127. "this side idolatry": Jonson in *Timber.*

127. "wit and invention": *Worthies*, 1662.

127. in *Twelfth Night*: 3.1.59.

127. "all lamp oil": Marston on Jonson in *What You Will*, 1600.

128. "*Poetaster* on him": *Conversations with WD.*

128. "dresser and plagiary": *Poetaster*, 5.3.

128. says Rosencrantz: HAM, 2.2.342–43.

128. Jonson called them: In *Cynthia's Revels*, pub. 1601.

128. "forty shillings": 3.4.

128. back to jail: For his part in *Eastward Ho* (1604), a collaboration with his former enemies Marston and Chapman.

128. of the Thames: The t.p. of the lst ed. (1602) of *Satiromastix or The Untrussing* says it has "been presented publicly by . . . the Lord Chamberlain his servants and privately by the children of Paul's."

128. "mastic" jaws: TRO, 1.3.73. "Mastic" is "abusive."

128. "books lying confusedly": *Satiromastix*, scene 2.

128. "that vile line": "Apologetical Dialogue."

128. A year later: Following the New Arden TRO (ed. Kenneth Palmer, 1982, pp. 17, 19), which dates the play in 1602.

129. ignorance . . . down himself: TRO, 3.3.312; 2.3.175–87.

129. outlandish words: E.g., "propension" (2.2.133), "propugnation" (2.2.136), "impare" (4.5.103).

129. "proud full sail": SON 86.1.

129. "hit me dead": TRO, 4.5.249–51.

129. Agamemnon's battle piece: 5.5.6–16.

129. not fool's play: 5.3.43.

130. the cormorant: 2.2.6.

130. daily with blood: 1.1.90–91.

130. for a "placket": 2.3.20.

130. daws after eagles: 1.2.243–44.

130. cheese . . . dog fox: 5.4.10–11.

130. a louse: 5.1.65–66.

130. "seven-times-honored": 3.3.277.

130. brains as earwax: 5.1.52–53.

130. "blood and honor": 5.4.27.

130. more to say: 5.10.21–22.

130. "fell as death": 4.5.268.

130. worth a blackberry: 5.4.11–12.

131. love's pains earned: Leslie Hotson's suggestion, rejected by most but plausible to me: *Shakespeare's Sonnets Dated and Other Essays*, 1949, pp. 37–56.

131. ruin of oblivion: TRO, 4.5.166–67.

131. only to calumniate: 5.2.120–24.

131. "a fountain stirred": 3.3.308.

131. "proves this god": TN, 3.4.365.

131. "world of charge": TRO, 4.1.58.

131. "in the doing": 1.2.287.

131. "take her cliff": 5.2.10–11.

132. "go from Troy": 4.2.109.

132. "of the game": 4.5.63.

132. with ribald crows: 4.2.9.

132. inside and outside: 1.1.2–3.

132. a soldier's arm: 1H4, 5.2.72–74.

132. an enemy's bearing: 2H6, 5.2.20–21.

132. heart of Aufidius: COR, 4.5.115–18.

132. whore . . . "brach": TRO, 5.1.15–17, 2.1.114.

132. longing . . . "limb": 3.3.237–41, 4.5.231–33, 238.

132. passion . . . "bolster": OTH, 3.3.386, 396.

132. this were she: TRO, 5.2.134–35.

132. "rule in unity": 5.2.141.

132. "alms for oblivion": 3.3.146.

132. "by reflection": 3.3.115–16, 99.

133. "bifold authority" . . . "inseparate": 5.2.144, 148.

133. reason panders . . . will: HAM, 3.4.88.

133. the will dotes: TRO, 2.2.58–59.

133. deceived and deceiving: 5.3.90.

133. "enchanted": 3.2.19-20.

5. Treason in the Blood

134. love you better: Speech to Parliament, Nov. 30, 1601.

135. the "maiden Phoenix": H8, 5.4.40–47.

135. an anonymous versifier: Quoted JQA, *WS*, p. 356.

135. James at thirty-seven: Following Anthony Weldon, *The Court and Character of KJ*, 1817 ed.; J. Dover Wilson, *The Essential Shakespeare*, 1932, p. 114; H. Pearson, p. 146; M. C. Bradbrook, *Shakespeare*, 1978, pp. 170–72; Halliday, *Shakespeare*, p. 175; A. L. Rowse, *Sh's Southampton*, 1965, pp. 175–77, 193, 221.

135. lights, and sonties: EKC, *WS*, 1.238–42; *ES*, 4.338–39.

136. said Clarendon: *History*, 1888 ed., 1.74.

136. tavern or brothel: LR, 1.4.243–47.

136. "insubstantial pageant": TMP, 4.1.155.

136. furnish a masque: Bradbrook, p. 179.

136. hanged a cutpurse: SS, pp. 249–50; Hosking, p. 98.

136. "in the seat": MM, 1.2.160–62.

136. to stage himself: 1.1.68.

137. get rid of: Rowse, *Southampton*, p. 221 (quoting S. R. Gardiner, *History of England, 1603–1642*, 1899 ed., 2.251).

137. "of the fields": F. P. Wilson, *The Plague in Sh's London*, p. 88

(quoting T. M., *The True Narration of the Entertainment of His Royal Majesty*, 1603).

137. Plague afflicted London: F. P. Wilson, pp. 90–93, 114–15, 130–33.

137. "Philosophical persons": AWW, 2.3.1–3.

137. "my right hand": *Epigrams*, XLV; *Conversations with Drummond.*

137. a panegyric: Herford and Simpson ed., 2.262–63.

137. its traditional pageantry: Thomas Dekker, *The Magnificent Entertainment*, 1604, sigs. B4–C2; *London in the Age of Shakespeare: An Anthology*, ed. Lawrence Manley 1986, pp. 343–44.

138. Shakespeare . . . in the procession: EKC, *WS*, 1.73; Lewis, *Documents*, 2.367–68.

138. playwrights he knew: Dekker, Drayton, Jonson.

138. Shakespeare's company traveled: F.P. Wilson, pp. 54, 110–13; EKC, *WS*, 1.78, 2.328–29.

138. players [at] . . . Wilton: EKC, *WS*, 2.329. (The letter mentioning Shakespeare is lost.)

139. Generosity like this: Details from F. P. Wilson, pp. 111–12; EKC, *WS*, 1.77–78; Rowse, *Shakespeare the Man*, 1973, p. 201.

139. Letters patent: Lewis, *Documents*, 2.363–66.

139. James told them: EKC, *WS*, 1.72.

139. "by God's sonties": MV, 2.2.45.

139. Court performances: M. M. Reese, *Sh. His World and His Work*, pp. 156– 57; EKC, *WS*, 1.77 and App. D, 2.329–45; SS, p. 252 (a different tally).

139. the Spanish Ambassador: JQA, *WS*, pp. 364–70.

139. in later days: As headquarters of England's Probate Registry.

140. the other grooms: By this time 12 in number, the new fellows being John Lowin (from Worcester's Men), Alexander Cooke, Samuel Crosse, d. 1605 and replaced by Nicholas Tooley.

140. said an eyewitness: JQA, *WS*, pp. 367–69 (quoting a Spanish pamphlet, printed 1604).

140. the "continent": ANT, 4.14.40.

140. "particular grief": OTH, 1.3.55.

140. "to the Senate": 3.2.2.

140. royal "siege": 1.2.22.

140. outsize "mirrors": ANT, 5.1.33.

140. the "hollow Hell": OTH, 3.3.447.

140. his "sooty" skin: 1.2.70.

140. "and wheeling stranger": 1.1.136.

140. beneath their shoulders: 1.3.143–45.

140. "hair-breadth scapes": 1.3.136.

140. *Masque of Blackness*: Produced Jan. 6, 1605.

141. ambassadors from Barbary: Details from Eldred Jones, *Othello's Countrymen The African in English Renaissance Drama*, 1965; Bernard Harris, "A Portrait of a Moor," *Sh. Survey* 11 (1958), pp. 89–97.

141. A popular proverb: Turning up, e.g., in *Edmund Ironside* (2.1.811), an anon. play of the late 1580s sometimes given to Shakespeare.

141. "lips" . . . "ram" . . . Devil: OTH, 1.1.66, 88, 91.

141. the hero wonders: 3.3.263.

141. "a lascivious Moor": 1.1.126.

141. Shakespeare's immediate source: Giraldi Cinthio, *Hecatommithi*, Venice, 1565; French trans., Paris, 1584.

142. "in the extreme": OTH, 5.2.346.

142. making "incision": MV, 2.1.6.

142. in his mind: OTH, 1.3.252.

142. makes me ugly: 5.1.19–20.

142. "Free and bounteous": 1.3.265.

142. "must be found": 1.2.30.

142. will rust them: 1.2.59.

142. makes ambition virtue: 3.3.347–50.

142. "horribly stuffed": 1.1.13–14.

142. "paragons" fame: 2.1.62.

142. "just equinox": 2.3.123–24.

143. "exsufflicate" or windy: 3.3.182.

143. "ordinary pitch": JC, 1.1.73.

143. "is thy work": OTH, 5.2.364.

143. "placed and possessed": ADO, 3.3.150–51.

143. "are a senator": OTH, 1.1.118.

143. "practice": 5.2.292.

143. the Pontic Sea: 3.3.453–54.
143. "treason" . . . in his blood: 1.1.169.
143. "please his fantasy": 3.3.299.
143. to Othello's fantasy: 3.3.88–89.
143. wrong side out: 2.3.52.
143. dawn comes up: 2.3.378.
143. from their "propriety": 2.3.175–76.
143. "she shall be": 4.1.73.
144. has to speak: 5.2.184.
144. rules in Cyprus: 5.2.332.
144. "Once so good": 5.2.291.
144. "general" (universal) enemy: 1.3.49.
144. mines of sulphur: 3.3.329.
144. all his tribe: 5.2.243–44 (following H. Spencer, *Art and Life*, 1940, p. 324).
144. "in Aleppo once": OTH, 5.2.352.
144. in a vault: 3H6, 5.2.44.
144. poisons sight: OTH, 5.2.364.
144. "wretched fortune": 4.2.127.
144. "and most unfortunate": 5.2.283.
144. "dart of chance": 4.1.267.
144. "modern seeming": 1.3.108–9.
144. dull or abused: 5.2.225, 4.2.139.
144. some are saved: 2.3.103–4.
144. a huge eclipse: 5.2.99.
144. knocking to get in: 4.3.53.
144. like a "grange": 1.1.105.
144. lack "composition": 1.3.1.
144. reason . . . can't sift: 1.3.18.
144. city on fire: 1.1.76–77.
144. why they fear: 5.2.38–39.
145. "Is't possible": 2.3.285–87.
145. night's dull watches: 1.1.123.

145. appeals to "proof": And variations ("approved," "approve"), recur at 1.1.28, 1.3.77, 2.1.44 and 49, 2.3.62 and 312, 4.3.19, 5.1.26 and 66.

145. A sacrificer: 5.2.65.

145. where he loves: 5.2.22.

145. without witchcraft: 1.3.64.

145. of the moon: 5.2.109.

145. by some planet: 2.3.182.

145. Trifles ensnare him: 3.3.322.

145. "web of it": 3.4.69.

145. by the "pestilence": 2.3.356.

145. in a trance: 4.1.43.

145. begotten on itself: 3.4.162.

145. not easily jealous: 5.2.345.

145. "fruits of whoring": 5.1.116.

145. best sometimes forget: 2.3.241.

145. "and law days": 3.3.138–40.

145. in the dark, "abuse": 4.3.67, 62.

145. a strumpet: 5.1.78, 121.

145. what she says: 5.1.122–23.

145. "with moe men": 4.3.57.

145. "a proper man"; 4.3.35.

145. supersubtle Venetian: 1.3.356.

145. prays for forgiveness: 4.2.88.

145. "us our sins": 2.3.111–12.

145. and not guilty: Like Bertram, AWW, 5.3.289.

146. "I am sorry": OTH, 4.1.282.

146. *Crudities*: 1611. Reprinted 2 vols., Glasgow, 1905.

146. caught Falstaff's eye: In WIV, 3.3.56–58.

146. furnished Queen Anne: Halliday, pp. 178–79.

146. an old map: Ralph Agas, *Civitas Londinum A Survey of . . . London . . . Westminster . . . Southwark and parts adjacent*, about 1560, repr. London, 1874.

146. A legal document: Discovered in the PRO by C. W. Wallace, "Sh.

and His London Associates," *Studies of the Univ. of Nebraska*, 10, no. 4 (Oct. 1910), 261–304. Lewis, *Documents*, 2.426–33; A. L. Rowse, *William Shakespeare*, pp. 337–39; *Shakespeare the Man*, pp. 196–98; JQA, *WS*, pp. 378–95.

146. "is *en France*": H5, 5.2.218–19.

147. Shakespeare's Dark Lady: Edward Fisher, *Love's Labour's Won* (a novel), 1963. Hugh Calvert, *Shakespeare's Sonnets and Problems of Autobiography*, 1987, p. 202, summarizes and dismisses EF.

147. quarter he lived in: Details from Stow, *Survey*, "Cripplegate Ward."

147. Jonson . . . noticed: In *The Silent Woman*, 4.2.94–95.

147. "unprofitable burdens": The consensus opinion, e.g., Robert Bolton, *Some General Directions for a Comfortable Walking with God*, 1625, p. 151 (quoted Fraser, *War Against Poetry*, 1970, p. 86).

148. the "sweating tub": MM, 3.2.57.

148. "French crown": 1.2.52.

148. "houses of resort": 1.2.95–102.

148. their "metal" breed: 2.4.48.

148. Pompey said: 3.2.5–9.

148. "pity and mercy": John Aubrey, *Brief Lives*, 1898 ed., 2.158–60; Pearson, *Shakespeare*, p. 115.

148. "mealed": MM, 4.2.83.

148. Donne . . . said: "Poetical Epistle to Ben Jonson," Jan. 6, 1603 (attributed verses).

148. "this man live": MM, 3.1.232–33.

148. "quits" him well: 5.1.496.

148. the Counter: Or Compter, a generic term for prisons accommodating debtors or common trespassers (Stow).

148. "the Lord's sake": MM, 4.3.19.

148. Simon Forman: Details from A. L. Rowse, *SF: Sex and Society in Shakespeare's Age*, 1974.

149. "congregated College": AWW, 2.1.117.

149. Barbican: I.e., "burgh-kenning."

149. their slanderous tongues: MM, 3.2.188.

150. Coryat . . . saluted: Michael Strachan, *The Life and Adventures of TC*, 1962, pp. 144–48.

150. an anecdotal clergyman: Bp. Thomas Fuller, *Worthies*.

151. said their . . . apprentice: JQA, *WS*, p. 393.

151. By 1607: According to Edmond Malone (whose *Inquiry*, p. 215, is quoted by JQA, *WS*, p. 395).

151. "feather" . . . "face" . . . "ladies": H8, 1.3.25, 7, 39–41.

151. corruption bubbles: MM, 5.1.318–19.

152. are all frail: 2.4.121.

152. "of his trade": 2.1.256.

152. Pompey the Great: 2.1.217–19.

152. "steely bones": AWW, 1.1.103.

152. pair of shears: MM, 1.2.27–28.

152. "a sinful fact": AWW, 3.7.47.

152. properties of government: MM, 1.1.3.

152. the summer before: Following J. W. Lever, New Arden ed., 1965, pp. xxxi–xxxv.

152. a year later: Following my New Cambridge ed., 1985, pp. 1–5. Most see AWW as preceding MM. Malone (*Life of Shakespeare*, 1.295) puts it in 1606 and suggests that the play is the same as a lost comedy, *An Ill Beginning Has a Good End*, assigned to John Ford in S. R. and played by the King's Men in 1613. See A. Harbage (revised S. Schoenbaum), *Annals of English Drama 975–1700*, 1964; W. W. Greg, *A Bibliography of the English Printed Drama to the Restoration*, 1962, 2.173.

152. with current events: Willem Schrickx fleshes out the political background, "AWW and Its Historical Relevance," pp. 257–74, in *Multiple Worlds, Multiple Words, Essays in Honour of Irene Simon*, Liege, 1988.

152. "peace concluded": AWW, 4.3.40.

153. says a letter: March 28, 1605, quoted Schrickx, p. 272.

153. fruitdish of threepence: MM, 2.1.90–93.

153. by the nose: 3.1.108 (and 1.3.29).

153. "untrussing" . . . tick-tack . . . "tun-dish" . . . trouts: 3.2.179, 1.2.190-91, 3.2.172, 1.2.90.

153. is congealed ice: 3.2.110–11.

153. "most noble father": 2.1.7.

153. "fornicatress": 2.2.22.

153. "thing on thing": 5.1.62.

153. Showing defers to telling: Partly adapting the intro. essay to my New Camb. ed.

153. "things are we": AWW, 4.3.19–20.

154. "delivering": 1.1.1.

154. "haggish age": 1.2.29.

154. "up against mortality": 1.1.31.

154. he's a beggar: Ep.1.

154. "Embowelled": 1.3.241.

154. "flaws": MM, 2.3.11.

154. grace can reprieve: AWW, 3.4.27–28.

154. "skill in grace": 4.5.20–21.

154. hope is coldest: 2.1.144.

154. Grace lends grace: 2.1.160.

154. quicken . . . stone: 2.1.73–74.

154. heavenly actor: 2.3.23–24.

154. ever conduct of: TMP, 5.1.244.

154. latter-day Solomon: Schrickx, p.259.

154. "in dismal thinkings": AWW, 5.3.128.

154. "yet seems well": 5.3.333.

154. "idolatrous fancy": 1.1.97.

155. into another man: 4.3.3–5.

155. its just occasion: AYL, 4.3.129.

155. "privily": MM, 1.1.67.

155. deputy his terror: 1.1.19.

155. "in some sort": 3.2.28.

155. stop the air: 2.4.24–30.

155. "detected for women": 3.2.121–22.

155. "dart" . . . "bosom": 1.3.2–3.

155. a stricter restraint: 1.4.4.

155. been sick for: 2.4.102–4.

155. "fated sky": AWW, 1.1.217–19.

156. "Philosophical persons": 2.3.1–6.

156. "babe" . . . "minister": 2.1.137–39.

156. lie in herself: 1.1.216.

156. no "stars": JC, 1.2.140.

156. on his will: OTH, 1.3.325–26.

156. Edmund . . . sounds like: E.g., LR, 1.2.118–21.

156. the cold roads: AWW, 3.4.6.

156. intentions being "fixed": 1.1.229.

156. evils are "fixed": 1.1.102.

156. Than our foregoers: 2.3.135–37.

156. tell them apart: 2.3.118–20.

157. "of the blood": OTH, 1.1.169.

157. "fill a place": AWW, 1.2.69 (and 4.3.339).

157. language echoes . . . incidents recur: Detailed in my New Cambridge ed., pp. 13–14.

157. touch of nature: TRO, 3.3.175.

157. All are frail: MM, 2.4.121.

157. Caesar . . . couldn't cope: AWW, 3.6.52–54.

157. Heaven delights: 3.4.27–28.

157. "goodly clew": 1.3.182.

157. "getting" of children: 3.2.41–42.

157. "of nature's truth": 1.3.131–34.

157. "Natural rebellion": 5.3.6.

158. "control his fate": OTH, 5.2.265.

158. "the destined livery": MM, 2.4.138.

158. "of the world": AWW, 4.5.49.

158. live . . . drives: MM, 2.1.223; AWW, 1.3.29–30.

158. "good angel": MM, 2.4.16.

158. "enskied and sainted": 1.4.34.

158. "of my vice": 3.1.137.

158. a little bad: 5.1.439–41.

158. Helen of Troy: AWW, 1.3.68–71.

158. counselor and traitress: 1.1.167–70.

158. "composition": 1.1.203–4.

158. "by our virtues": 4.3.71–74.

159. "incensing": 5.3.23–25.

159. "had you rather": MM, 2.4.52–54.

159. "gravel heart": 4.3.64.

159. "the unfolding star": 4.2.203.

159. "desperately mortal": 4.2.145.

159. "his straw rustle": 4.3.35–36.

159. "well-balanced form": 4.3.100.

159. "scope of justice": 5.1.234.

159. bruises to death: 2.1.6.

159. law a scarecrow: 2.1.1–4.

159. the people scope: 1.3.35.

159. turns into restraint: 1.2.127–28.

159. mercy . . . [seasons] justice: MV, 4.1.197.

159. makes him live: AWW, 4.3.334.

159. verifies the Duke: MM, 5.1.356.

159. bad instruments: AWW, 5.3.201–2.

159. burr will stick: MM, 4.3.179.

6. The Wine of Life

160. Thomas Hart: ME, pp. 141–43.

160. Thomas [and Katherine] Rogers: ME, p. 46; Halliday, *Shakespeare*, p. 192.

161. "heel of pastime": AWW, 1.2.57.

161. Augustine Phillips: JQA, *WS*, pp. 387–88.

161. "mouth-honor": MAC, 5.3.27.

161. Plague [in 1605]: EKC, *WS*, 2.333; Thomson, *Shakespeare's Theatre*, pp. 75, 78; H-P, 1.219.

161. "dreadful trade": LR, 4.6.14–15.

161. sold this property: A fictitious action at law, supplementing the deed of conveyance, confirmed the title. Purchaser brought suit against vendor in the Court of Common Pleas, the suit ending with vendor's admission that the property belonged to purchaser. The court recorded this admission in a decision known as a "fine," i.e., *finis* or end of the suit. For unknown reasons, eight years passed

before the fine was entered in the Common Pleas records, confirming Sh's purchase. The £100 he is said to have paid for his confirmation is probably also a fiction, though some take it as a genuine payment. EKC, *Sources*, pp. 14–15; ME, p. 101; Tucker Brooke, *Sh. at Stratford*, 1926, pp. 39–42, 63.

161. Thomas and Lewis Hiccox: SS, pp. 245–46.

162. Chapel Lane [cottage]: ME, p. 92; H-P, 1.204–5; EKC, *WS*, 2.111–13; Halliday, p. 173.

162. "copyhold" land: EKC, *Sources*, pp. 13–14, explains.

162. "Ratifiers and props": HAM, 4.5.106.

162. buying up "tithes": JQA, *WS*, p. 388; Lewis, *Documents*, 1.227; Chute, p. 279; EKC, *WS*, 2.118–27 and App. A; SS, pp. 246–47; Halliday, p. 192.

163. in 1605 . . . *King Lear*: K. Muir in his New Arden ed., 1952, musters the evidence.

163. lake of darkness: LR, 3.6.7.

163. "and turn again": 1H6, 3.3.85.

163. that's true too: LR, 5.2.11–12.

163. "pelican" daughters . . . fangs: 3.4.75, 3.7.58.

163. to the stake: 3.7.54.

164. "send in time": 5.3.248.

164. hold the chair: 3.7.65–67.

164. "of their deservings": 5.3.303–5.

164. of his Leviathan: Charles Lamb on Nahum Tate's revision of LR.

164. "the tragedy good": *Revenger's Tragedy*, 3.5.198.

164. "will not, so": MM, 1.2.123–24; Romans 9: 15–18.

164. against than sinning: LR, 3.2.60.

164. the worst fortunes: 5.3.4.

164. Gloucester's "flawed" heart: 5.3.197–200.

164. strings of life: 5.3.217–18.

164. heave her heart: 1.1.91.

164. heart of a fool: After Proverbs 12:23, 14:33.

164. her father's business: LR, 4.4.24.

165. pity . . . "rebel-like": 4.3.10–16.

165. "Visible" spirits: 4.2.46.

165. wrong side out: 4.2.9.
165. "tailor made thee": 2.2.55.
165. soul . . . in his clothes: AWW, 2.5.43–44.
165. forms of justice: LR, 3.7.25.
165. to lead it: 4.4.18–19.
165. "Slivered and disbranched": 4.2.34.
165. a joint stool: 3.6.52.
165. Gloucester learns to see: 4.6.149.
165. "and feeling sorrows": 4.6.222.
165. "love us most": 1.1.51.
165. "garments on him": 4.7.20–21.
165. putting off/putting on: Ephesians 4:22–24.
166. We come wailing: LR, 4.6.178–80.
166. "grossly clad": TN, 5.1.236–37.
166. smells of mortality: LR, 4.6.133.
166. "wheel of fire": 4.7.46.
166. medieval accounts: Muir lists in Arden ed., p. 190*n*.
166. "in that kind": LR, 4.6.162.
166. the "forfended place": 5.1.11.
166. "civet": 4.6.130.
166. out of "plackets": 3.4.96–97.
166. "be cut shorter": 1.5.52.
166. "scalding, stench, consumption": 4.6.114–29.
166. "and vicious place": 5.3.173.
166. "smell a fault": 1.1.16.
166. "general curse": 4.6.206.
167. "tender-hefted": 2.4.171.
167. Natural "bias": 1.2.111.
167. "rub" or deflect: 2.2.154.
167. to natural "law": 1.2.1.
167. nature's bias: TN, 5.1.260.
167. like the cuckoo: LR, 1.4.215–16.
167. filial ingratitude: 1.4.259–61.

167. "forked" or two-legged: 3.4.107–8.
167. furrow-weeds and nettles: 4.4.3–5.
167. "need" . . . "need": 2.4.263, 270.
167. "Who am I": 1.4.78.
167. "what are you": 4.6.220.
167. "What art thou?": 1.4.9–10, 3.4.45.
167. "lion in prey": 3.4.92–94.
168. the thing itself: 3.4.106–9.
168. "fitness": 4.2.63.
168. redeem our sorrows: 5.3.267.
168. like the time: 5.3.30–31.
168. "plague" . . . nice distinctions: 1.2.3–4.
168. himself alone: After 3H6, 5.6.83.
168. "as I fathered": LR, 3.6.110.
169. "fields near Dover": 4.6.s.d.
169. "side-piercing sight": 4.6.83–85.
169. "inch a king": 4.6.107.
169. hawthorn . . . straw: 3.4.47, 45.
169. "superflux": 3.4.35.
169. "should undo excess": 4.1.70.
169. "houseless poverty": 3.4.26.
169. obey his blood: 4.2.64.
169. "hot-blooded" France: 2.4.212.
169. anger . . . its privilege: 2.2.70.
169. "true things": H5, 4.Pro.53.
169. "respects of fortune": LR, 1.1.249.
169. "pregnant" to pity: 4.6.223.
169. no knave: 2.4.84–85.
169. "mystery of things": 5.3.16.
170. blessing of Heaven: 4.6.225.
170. yield to age: 4.1.6–12.
170. "freedom": 1.1.181.
170. "wind and rain": 3.1.11.

170. of Dover Cliff: 4.6.11–22.

170. our lives' sweetness: 5.3.185.

170. riot and excess: Harington on the audience assembled for the masque of *Solomon and the Queen of Sheba*, 1606, at Salisbury's Hertfordshire house, Theobalds. Halliday, p. 197; Pearson, *Shakespeare*, p. 140.

170. Cyril Tourneur: Discussion of him and Ford, Chapman, and Webster, also the medieval drama and the masque, draws on my *Dark Ages and the Age of Gold*, 1973, and my introduction to *English Renaissance Drama*, 1976.

171. *'Tis Pity*: Probably 1620s; lst pub. 1633.

171. of a shadow: 1.1.18–19. *Bussy* dates from c. 1604.

171. "passion's fumes": 3.1.64–66.

172. way please them: *Duchess of Malfi* (1613–14), 5.4.53–54.

172. "in a mist": 5.5.94.

172. form and matter: 5.5.113–17.

172. "no essential thing": 3.2.74–75.

173. The Red Bull: George F. Reynolds, *The Staging of Elizabethan Plays at the Red Bull Theater 1605–1626*, 1940, esp. pp. 7–11 and ch. VIII.

173. *White Devil*: 1609–12. Quotations that follow come from Webster's preface to the reader.

173. Heywood: In *The Brazen Age*, 1610–13.

173. Dr. Forman: At the Globe April 20, 1611.

173. "history of Holy Scripture": Stow, *Survey*, p. 16, reporting Fitzstephen.

173. "were in nature": Following Sidney in his *Apology for Poetry*, 1595.

173. "open and black": Preface to the reader.

173. a disgruntled poet: Samuel Daniel.

174. "graceful discourse": Following the designer Joseph Furtenbach, 1628.

174. "light and motion": Aurelian Townshend, the new Court favorite.

174. "they were real": Conflating Castiglione and Vasari.

174. "lost in wonder": Sebastiano Serlio, *Architettura* (1545), tr. Robert Peake, 1611.

175. "womanly defense": MAC, 4.2.78.

175. ill-weaved ambition: 1H4, 5.4.88.

175. "in the cause": After Fr. John Gerard in Hugh Ross Williamson, *The Gunpowder Plot*, 1951, p. 164.

175. "iniquity of Catholics": Quoted Philip Caraman, *Henry Garnet 1555–1606 and the Gunpowder Plot*, 1964, p. 376.

175. a provocation: John Gerard, *What Was the Gunpowder Plot?*, 1897 (countered by Samuel R. Gardiner, *What Gunpowder Plot Was*, 1897, repr. 1969).

175. Catesby: Following Leslie Hotson, "Gunpowder Treason," ch. VIII, in *I, William Shakespeare*, 1937.

175. be a rebel: MAC, 1.2.10.

175. confusion's masterpiece: 2.3.66.

175. "one fell swoop": 4.3.219.

176. Clopton House: Windle, *Sh's Country*, 1899, p. 57; Halliday, pp. 193–95; Rowse, *WS*, p. 9.

176. with man's act: MAC, 2.4.5–7.

176. a Scots voice: Bradbrook, *Shakespeare*, p. 181.

176. "hands, not hearts": OTH, 3.4.47.

177. George Badger: Rowse, *WS*, p. 24; ME, p. 47.

178. "dire combustion": MAC, 2.3.58.

178. distant relatives: Hotson, *WS*, p. 197; and the genealogical tables in H. Mutschmann and K. Wintersdorf, *Sh. and Catholicism*, 1950, p. 422.

178. the women waited: Rowse, *Sh. the Man*, p. 4.

178. net or lime: MAC, 4.2.34.

178. Throckmortons . . . Southwell: Christopher Devlin, *The Life of Robert Southwell Poet and Martyr*, 1956, pp. 18, 58, 263–64.

178. "equivocate": Peter Milward, *Sh's Religious Background*, 1973, pp. 61–67; Devlin, pp. 300–1.

178. Catholic pamphleteers: The 1598 pamphlet war pitted Catholic secular priests against Jesuits, whose spokeman, Fr. Robert Persons, defended equivocation (*A Brief Apology or Defense of the Catholic Ecclesiastical Hierarchy*, 1602).

178. "will undo us": HAM, 5.1.136–37.

179. "Master W. S.": Devlin, pp. 260–64, 355.

179. the fiend's equivocation: MAC, 5.5.42.

179. "Against the word": R2, 5.5.13–14.

179. upon their pikes: From Campion's "Brag," reprinted Evelyn Waugh, *Edmund Campion*, 1946, pp. 235–39.

179. study . . . at Rheims: SHR, 2.1.79–80.

179. Dibdale . . . Harsnett: Milward, pp. 39, 52–54; Bradbrook, p. 194; K. Muir, "Sh. and 'King Lear,'" *R.E.S.*, 1951, pp. 11–21. No one, so far as I know, has ever noted Dibdale's presence in Harsnett.

179. Shakespeare a witness: T. W. Baldwin in his ed. of ERR, 1928, pp. xii– xv; and in *Wm. Shakespere Adapts a Hanging*, 1931.

180. the abbey here: ERR, 5.1.120–22.

180. punishment . . . sacramental test: Godfrey Davies, *The Early Stuarts 1603–1660*, 1959, pp. 207–9; Williamson, pp. 245–46; SS, pp. 286–87.

180. Thomas Reynolds: ME, p. 123.

181. equivocate to Heaven: MAC, 2.3.4–11. Equivocation is treated in Caraman, pp. 377, 407, 410, 416, 447–48; Williamson, pp. 138–39; Hotson, *WS*, pp. 178, 194; Devlin, pp. 333–34.

181. "must be hanged": MAC, 4.2.46–50.

181. to be saved: Garnet quoted in Caraman, p. 438.

181. "Two truths": MAC, 1.3.127–29.

181. "and filthy air": 1.1.12.

181. first half of 1606: Following Muir, Arden ed., 1951. Henry N. Paul, *The Royal Play of "Macbeth,"* 1950, seeks to establish when, why, and how the play was written.

181. a Court performance: Probably at Hampton Court, Aug. 7, 1606.

182. scales against either: MAC, 2.3.8–9.

182. Macbeth . . . catches up: 1.3.38.

182. bearded . . . "corporal": 1.3.46–47, 81.

182. "Lesser" . . . "greater": 1.3.65–66.

182. can't be good: 1.3.130–31.

182. lost and won: 1.1.4.

182. Promising comfort: 1.2.27–28.

182. to our hope: 5.8.20–22.

182. each other's strength: 1.2.7–9.

182. "arm 'gainst arm": 1.2.56.

182. Insurrection: 1.3.136, 140; 2.1.35–44; 1.4.52; 1.5.26.

182. dreams: 3.2.18–19.

182. "pestered" senses: 5.2.23–25.
182. "Perturbation" . . . violent hands: 5.1.9, 5.9.36.
182. "success" . . . "surcease": 1.7.4.
183. "in the instant": 1.5.58.
183. "latch" the ear: 4.3.195.
183. "wine of life": 2.3.95–96.
183. done . . . undone: 3.2.12, 5.1.68.
183. Memory . . . a fume: 1.7.65–66.
183. sorrows, "rooted": 5.3.41–42.
183. "unfixes" . . . "unfix": 4.1.95–96, 1.3.135.
183. "Known . . . to speak": 3.4.122.
183. "root" of kings: 3.1.5–6.
183. "scorched": 3.2.13.
183. the "mortified" man: 5.2.3–5.
183. "man would die": 3.4.77–78.
183. name in hell: 5.7.6–7.
183. "degrees . . . going": 3.4.1, 118.
183. the timely inn: 3.3.6–7.
184. state . . . "measure": 3.4.4–6, 11; 5.9.39.
184. of the table: 3.4.86–89.
184. nature's second course: 2.2.36.
184. has no children: 4.3.216.
184. "dearest chuck": 3.2.45.
184. bond is canceled: 3.2.49.
184. The martlet: 1.6.3–10.
184. purged of disease: 5.3.51–52.
184. shake his bark: 1.3.24–25.
184. his bosom "franchised": 2.1.27–28.
184. heals . . . maladies: 4.3.141–59.
184. "physic" to the dogs: 5.3.47.
184. in God's hand: 2.3.130.
184. dogs are dogs: 3.1.92–100.
184. "an imperial charge": 4.3.19–20.

185. "grace makes destiny": R3, 4.4.219.

185. "ambition" . . . spurs: MAC, 1.7.25–27.

185. a "spur": 1.6.23.

185. the pauser, reason: 2.3.110–11.

185. "grace of Grace": 5.9.38.

185. newly planted: 1.4.28–29.

185. sear and yellow: 5.3.23.

185. borrowed garments: 1.3.109, 145–46.

185. the dyer's hand: SON 111.7.

185. "rooky wood": MAC, 3.2.51.

185. moon . . . candles: 2.1.2, 5.

185. takes them off: 2.3.33.

185. drugged "possets": 2.2.6.

185. "insane root": 1.3.84–85.

185. "Metaphysical aid": 1.5.29.

185. "vaporous drop": 3.5.23–31. This passage (and some others: 4.1.39–43, 125–36) is generally read as interpolated from Middleton's *The Witch*, n.d., ?1616. Maybe Middleton is borrowing from Shakespeare.

185. the magic potion: MND, 2.1.165–72.

185. in a moment: MAC, 2.3.108–10.

186. servant to defect: 2.1.17–18.

186. and violent sea: 4.2.18–21.

186. "in the extreme": OTH, 5.2.346.

186. "rancors": MAC, 3.1.66.

186. poisoned chalice: 1.7.11.

186. "dwarfish thief": 5.2.22.

186. "usurper's cursèd head": 5.9.21.

186. on their battlements: 1.2.23.

186. in harness: 5.5.51.

186. "reeking wounds": 1.2.39.

186. like old Aeson: MV, 5.1.14.

187. "guilt" . . . "gilds": MAC, 2.2.53–54.

187. a "similitude": Notes in 1765 ed.

187. "an earthly crown": Marlowe's Tamburlaine.

187. "great doom's image": MAC, 2.3.78.

187. Golgotha: 1.2.40.

187. Lord's anointed temple: 2.3.67–68.

187. the brightest angel: 4.3.22.

187. fall of man: H5, 2.2.142.

187. "modest wisdom": MAC, 4.3.119.

187. "fiend-like queen": 5.9.35.

187. "Struts": 5.5.25.

7. Bravest at the Last

188. Tavern: Later called the Crown, No. 3 Cornmarket St. EKC, *WS*, 1.572–76; H-P, *Outlines*, 1.214–15; SS, pp. 224–27 (who suggests that Sh. may have stayed at the Cross Inn, now the Golden Cross, contiguous to Davenant's Tavern on the north). EKC, vol. 2, frontispiece, gives the wall inscription.

188. Playing Oxford: EKC, *WS*, 2.329, 333. Plausibility requires Sh's presence there not later than June 1605 (9 months before Wm. Davenant's christening).

188. state visit: Details from H. N. Paul, *The Royal Play of "Macbeth,"* "Shakespeare at Oxford," pp. 15–24.

188. their "practiced accent": MND, 5.1.93–97.

189. editor of the Poems: Bernard Lintot, 1709. JQA, *WS*, pp. 376–77, cites the missing correspondence.

189. John Davenant: Following Anthony à Wood, *Athenae Oxoniensis*, 1692; JQA, *WS*, p. 389.

189. a youthful ode: H-P, 1.218.

190. John Aubrey: In a MS before 1680.

190. Shakespeare's Oxford affair: William Oldys, quoted SS, pp. 225–26. The anecdote turns up in non-Shakespearean contexts, e.g., in John Taylor the Water Poet, *Wit and Mirth*, 1629.

190. "open countenance": Wm. Rufus Chetwood, a former Drury Lane prompter. Davenant's portrait is in H-P collections, Folger Library.

190. a complacent diarist: John Evelyn, Nov. 26, 1661.

190. Davenant . . . made them "fit": Hazelton Spencer, *Shakespeare Improved* (1927), 1963, pp. 66–82; A. H. Nethercot, *Sir William D'Avenant*, 1938, ch. XIX. Lee, *WS*, p. 592*n* lists the plays.

190. Shadwell's *Timon*: 1678; Spencer, *Shakespeare Improved*, p. 282; Spencer, *Art and Life*, pp. 354–55.

191. not one allusion: Perhaps 3.3.33–34 refers to the Powder Plot: "Like those that under hot ardent zeal would set whole realms on fire."

191. "man of war": After Fuller, *Worthies*.

191. Timon's story: Chiefly Lucian's satiric dialog, *Timon the Misanthrope*, written in Greek in the second century A.D. A French trans. (1582) was available to Sh., and perhaps he read Lucian's dialogs, trans. into Latin by Erasmus, as a grammar school student: H. J. Oliver, New Arden ed., 1959.

191. "the very hem": TIM, 5.1.215–16, 5.4.66.

191. "my lands extend": 2.2.151.

191. "unwisely, not ignobly": 2.2.174.

191. "altogether a fool": 2.2.115.

191. him all things: After 5.1.188.

191. until he feels: 2.2.7.

192. summoning "confusion": 4.1.21.

192. "outlives incertain pomp": 4.3.242–43.

192. the gored state: LR, 5.3.321.

192. with the olive: TIM, 5.4.82.

192. "an illness followed": After EKC.

192. "and flying off": LR, 2.4.90.

192. engine . . . battery: COR, 5.4.18–21.

192. "after vibration": Coleridge on its relation to LR.

192. "beneath world": TIM, 1.1.44.

193. "Senators" . . . "Athenian" . . . Lords: 1.1.38 s.d., 109 s.d., 255 s.d.

193. Strangers: 3.2.1 s.d.

193. Apemantus: 1.2.1 s.d.

193. "sweep of vanity": 1.2.132.

193. "kinds of natures": 1.1.65.

193. "the world's soul": 3.2.64.

193. "figure of us": MM, 1.1.16.

193. "may be true": TIM, 4.3.456–57.

193. "rich are fair": 1.2.13.

193. "monstrousness of man": 3.2.72.

193. like molten lead: LR, 4.7.47.

193. allegory of Fortune: TIM, 1.1.63–94.

193. "of all erection": 4.3.157-58, 162–64.

194. "o' th' brothel": 4.1.13.

194. "the golden fool": 4.3.17–18.

194. "usuring" . . . "usury": 3.5.109, 98.

194. "than you rob": 4.3.431–33.

194. "thing's a thief": 4.3.436–49.

194. "and compounded thee": 4.3.271–73.

194. Honor is cudgeled: H5, 5.1.84–89.

194. "set him clear": TIM, 3.3.28–31.

194. "Multiplying bans": 4.1.34.

195. "now a fool": 4.3.221.

195. becomes a man: MAC, 1.7.46.

195. only its extremes: TIM, 4.3.300–1.

195. Dr. John Hall: Following Harriet Joseph, *Shakespeare's Son-in-law: John Hall, Man and Physician*, 1964; C. Martin Mitchell, *The Shakespeare Circle A Life of Dr. John Hall Sh's son-in-law with glimpses of their intimate friends and relations* (1947), 1977; JQA, *WS*, pp. 395–97.

195. "antidotes are poison": TIM, 4.3.432.

195. scorning "physic": MAC, 5.3.47.

196. Lear's fumiter: LR, 4.4.3.

196. "in the profession": JQA, *WS*, p. 396.

196. back in Oxford: H-P, 1.220–21; EKC, *WS*, 2.334.

196. a recent biographer: Peter Levi, *The Life and Times of William Shakespeare*, 1988. Levi gives the argument (with a text of the poem) in *A Private Commission New Verses by Shakespeare*, 1988. Louis Marder summarizes (*The Shakespeare Newsletter* XXXVIII:1, no. 197, Spring 1988), and James Knowles controverts (*TLS*, April 29-May 5, 1988, pp. 472, 485).

196. eulogizing an acquaintance: Donald W. Foster, *Elegy by W.S. A Study in Attribution*, 1989. (Some circumstantial evidence, not enough, connects Sh. with the elegy.)

197. price of bullocks: 2H4, 3.2.38.

197. *Coriolanus*: Dated by me in late 1607, just after TIM and just before ANT (which must follow no later than May 1608). Philip Brockbank, New Arden ed. (1976, pp. 24–29) marshals the facts that bear on dating; and Geoffrey Bullough, *Narrative and Dramatic Sources of Shakespeare*, vol. 5, 1964, reprints possible sources.

197. the Midlands Revolt: Details from Roger B. Manning, *Village Revolts Social Protest and Popular Disturbances in England, 1509–1640*, 1988, esp. ch. 9; E. C. Pettet, "COR and the Midlands Insurrection of 1607," *Shakespeare Survey* 3 (1950), 34–42; Fripp, *WS*, 2.706; John Stow, *Annales*, continued by Edmund Howes, 1631; letters bet. the earls of Shrewsbury and Kent; and Wm. Combe to the Earl of Salisbury, i.e., Robert Cecil (June 2, 1608); Bullough, 5.457, 553–58.

197. "yet distinctly ranges": COR, 3.1.205.

197. "bolting" or sifting: 3.1.320.

198. "poor suitors": 1.1.60.

199. "all other counties": Abraham Sturley to Richard Quiney, Jan. 24, 1598, in Lewis, *Documents*, 1.227.

199. "crammed with grain": COR, 1.1.80–81, 17.

199. statistics: Leading to different conclusions in Lee, *WS*, pp. 291–92; and SS, p. 237.

199. "rank-scented many": COR, 3.1.66.

199. them in awe: 1.1.186–88.

199. channel . . . flat: 3.1.93–97, 197–98.

199. "of the people": 1.1.7–8.

199. crying "Hoo-oo": 3.3.137 and s.d.

199. children . . . pieces: 5.6.51–52, 120.

199. fins of lead: 1.1.179–80.

199. "the graver bench": 3.1.105–6.

199. have strong arms: 1.1.60–61.

200. "full of vent": 4.5.223.

200. in Camden: *Remains*, 1605. COR, 1.1.96–112.

200. is a buttocks: 2.1.52.

200. flour and bran: 1.1.100, 136, 144–46.

200. Ulysses . . . Falstaff: TRO, 1.3.109; 2H4, 4.3.117–21.

200. "cranks and offices": COR, 1.1.135–38.

200. "sink" or sewer: 1.1.115–30.

200. "bosom": 3.1.131–32.

200. rebellion's great toe: 1.1.155–58.

200. foot . . . knee: 3.1.304–6 (and 4.3.8–9), 3.2.75, 117–20.

200. "metonymic" habit: Described in my essay, "Elizabethan Drama and the Art of Abstraction," *Comparative Drama*, 2,2 (Summer 1968), 73–82.

201. men suffocate degree: TRO, 1.3.125.

201. at the morning: COR, 5.1.50–56.

201. god . . . sword: 5.4.23–24, 13 (and 4.1.30), 5.2.111, 1.6.76.

201. "every man himself": 3.1.263–64.

201. butterflies: 1.3.57–66, 4.6.94.

201. "counterpoised": 2.2.86–87.

201. "thing of blood": 2.2.89–122.

201. its slippery turns: 4.4.12.

202. forms and customs: 2.2.142–44.

202. "rotten" custom: 1.10.23, 2.2.136.

202. author of himself: 5.3.35–36.

202. "dull actor": 5.3.40–41.

202. "than one thing": 4.7.41–42.

202. man he is: 3.2.15–16.

202. pride . . . "nature": 4.7.35–49.

202. "best of it": 5.6.145–46.

202. remember his name: 1.9.90.

202. "it's twenty-seven": 2.1.153–55.

202. breasts of Hecuba: 1.3.40–42.

202. Enter cursing: 1.4.29.

202. he carries noise: 2.1.158–60.

202. leaving widows behind: 4.4.2.

202. "he were flayed": 1.6.21–22.

202. "with coagulate gore": HAM, 2.2.462.

203. in its interstices: Dissenting from the orthodox reading, as expressed, e.g., in Bullough, 5.494; and notably by T. S. Eliot, essay on HAM.

203. "here at home": COR, 2.1.188.

203. hates his . . . country: 4.4.23.

203. "common file": 1.6.43.

203. "right-hand file": 2.1.23.

203. "I banish you": 3.3.123.

203. "a man's wife": 4.3.32–33.

203. "everyone he meets": Robert J. Stoller, "Shakespearean Tragedy: COR," *Psychoanalytic Qtly* XXXV (1966), 263–74.

203. "wars with him": COR, 1.1.234–35.

203. rival and mistress: 4.5.109–11, 195.

203. "dead with nothing": 4.5.121–26.

203. "boy of tears": 5.6.100.

203. "comes his mother": 4.2.8.

203. "gracious silence": 2.1.175.

203. recent biography: Anthony Burgess'. Bradbrook, *Shakespeare*, p. 213, connects Volumnia and Mary Arden, buried Sept. 9, 1608.

203. "of his bed": COR, 1.3.2–5.

204. "Clucking": 5.3.163.

204. Bitter cold: Details from *The Great Frost*, ?Thomas Dekker, 1608; *Letters of John Chamberlain*, ed. N. E. McClure, 2 vols., 1939 (1.253); Bullough (citing Stow and Dekker), 5.559–63.

204. "upon the ice": COR, 1.1.173–74.

204. him in death: Aug. 12, 1607.

205. Moving back: Malone cites a (lost) document putting him in Southwark in or before 1608. JQA, *WS*, p. 395.

205. plays at Whitehall: EKC, *WS*, 2.335; *ES*, 4.174.

205. "old lecher's heart": LR, 3.4.112.

205. the boy actors: Chronicled in EKC, *ES*, 2.8–61.

206. Quiney . . . addressed: 10/25/1598.

206. "by the church": TN, 2.3.117; 3.1.5.

206. upper-class residents: EKC, *ES*, 2.501; Ordish, p. 62; Stow, pp. 61–66.

206. a petition: EKC, *ES*, 2.508.

206. "little eyases": HAM, 2.2.339.

207. got together: In *Eastward Ho!*

207. John Day: *The Isle of Gulls*, Feb. 1605. Details in Albert A. Tricomi, *Anticourt Drama in England 1603–1642*, 1989, esp. ch. 4.

207. against her husband: EKC, *ES*, 1.325, quotes a letter of the French ambassador, March 29, 1608. The play, untitled and no longer extant, is attributed to Marston. Tricomi describes, pp. 46–47.

207. Chapman: *The Conspiracy and Tragedy of Charles Duke of Byron*, 1608.

207. Expelling the boys: James's anger against them evidently cooling, they were back at BF for the Christmas season 1608–9, and possibly in occupancy (not the same as performing) as late as Sept. and Oct. Wm. Ingram builds on lawsuits instituted by tenants evicted to make room for the new arrivals: "The Playhouse as an Investment, 1607–1614; Thomas Woodford and Whitefriars," *Medieval and Renaissance Drama in England*, 1985, 2.214. Some boys joined the KM, others moved in 1609 to Whitefriars, west of BF on the Thames. Installed in their new theater, they received a renewal of their patent (Jan. 4, 1610) under the name of the Children of the Queen's Revels: Ingram, p. 213; Bradbrook, *Shakespeare*, p. 206; EKC, *ES*, 2.56; H. N. Hillebrand, *The Child Actors* (1926), 1964, p. 237. This matter-of-fact complicates standard accounts of their expulsion and dissolution.

207. five other sharers: Cuthbert Burbage, Heminges and Condell, Wm. Sly, and Thomas Evans, presumably kin to Henry Evans.

207. "on the Bankside": Edward Kirkham, testifying in 1612.

207. asked the city: June 1619. JQA, *WS*, pp. 406–7.

208. the city's jurisdiction: Confirmed Sept. 20, 1608.

208. tenements replaced . . . theater: Lee, *WS*, p. 66*n*.

208. siege of plague: Bradbrook, p. 250, *n*. 2, cites the plague orders closing the theaters from July 1608 to Dec. 1609. EKC, *WS*, 2.335–36, records the KMs travels in the provinces and performances at Court, 1608–9.

208. caused a shift: The "classical" statement is G. E. Bentley's, "Sh. and the BF Theatre," *Sh. Survey* 1 (1948), pp. 38–50; rephrased in *Sh. and His Theatre*, 1964, ch. IV.

208. at Blackfriars: Richard Hosley describes the theater (building partly on inference) in *The Revels History of Drama in English 1576–*

1613, ed. C. Leech and T. W. Craik, 1975, vol. 3, pt. 3, ch. 4. See also John Orrell, *The Human Stage English Theatre Design 1567–1640*, 1988, ch. 12.

208. Maps: Esp. W. Hollar's Long Bird's-Eye View of London, 1647.

209. in CYM: 5.4.122 s.d.

209. in ANT: 4.3.12 s.d.

210. Dr. Forman: His *Book of Plays* notes performances of MAC, WT, and CYM in 1611, the first two specified as at the Globe.

210. with equal ease: A. M. Nagler, *Shakespeare's Stage*, 1958, pp. 101–2.

210. "strong necessities": ANT, 3.6.83–85.

210. landlord . . . hair: 3.13.72, 1.1.21.

210. pair of jaws: 3.5.13–15.

210. "slippery people": 1.2.185–87.

210. "quick comedians": 5.2.214–21.

210. the common liar: 1.1.60–61.

211. might darken him: 3.1.22–24.

211. swan's-down feather: 3.2.48–50.

211. No midway: 3.4.19–20.

211. "lackeys" the water: 1.4.44–47.

211. everything happens twice: After Louis Auchincloss, *Motiveless Malignity*, 1969, "The Tragedy of Antony," esp. p. 58.

211. more gaudy night: ANT, 3.13.182.

211. gap of time: 1.5.5.

211. spring, 1608: An entry in the Stationers' Registers (Arber's *Transcript*, 3.167b), May 20, 1608, cites both ANT and PER.

211. other men's work: New Arden (ed. M. R. Ridley, 1956, and based on the ed. of R. H. Case, 1906), points to Daniel's revised *Cleopatra*, 1607, and three other plays of the period: pp. xxvi–xxxi.

211. "at the last": ANT, 5.2.335.

212. "of his reason": 3.13.2–4.

212. Overflowing all measure: 1.1.2.

212. foison it promises: 2.7.20–21.

212. "Grates me": 1.1.18.

212. *broaches . . . shines*: 1.2.173, 1.3.45.

212. *breeds . . . kisses*: 1.2.192, 3.10.7.

212. kissing revives him: 4.15.38–39.

212. "high order": 5.2.366.

212. heaven and earth: 1.1.17.

212. "Behold this man": 4.8.22.

212. great snare uncaught: 4.8.17–18.

212. Ajax: 4.13.1–2.

212. "wide arch": 1.1.33–34.

212. Young Clifford: 2H6, 5.2.40–45.

212. the wild flood: 2H4, 1.1.153–54.

213. "till destruction sickens": MAC, 4.1.60.

213. "melt" in Tiber: ANT, 1.1.33.

213. his ancestor Hercules: 4.3.16–17.

213. "diminution": 3.13.196–98.

213. van against him: 4.6.8–10.

213. upbraid: MAC, 5.2.18.

213. "becomes" . . . his flaw: ANT, 3.12.34.

213. "poor Antony": 4.1.16.

213. greatness going off: 4.13.5–6.

213. Wine . . . midnight bell: 3.13.184–91.

213. dead butcher: MAC, 5.9.35.

213. own "particular": ANT, 4.9.20.

213. where he lives: 4.15.38.

213. Reason . . . story: 3.10.35–36, 3.13.41–46.

213. "turpitude": 4.6.30–33.

213. "beguiled": 4.12.29.

213. "witch" or "charm": 4.12.47, 25.

213. "poisoned hours": 2.2.90.

213. a cold morsel: 3.13.116–17.

213. "his sword Philippan": 2.5.23.

213. shirt of Nessus: 4.12.43.

213. "of her magic": 3.10.18.

213. "wounded chance": 3.10.35.

213. "he cannot change": 1.4.12–15.

214. "pity of him": 1.4.71.

214. "by night's blackness": 1.4.12–13.

214. "fetters": 1.2.116–17.

214. Samson and Delilah: Judges 16–21.

214. "bolt up" change: ANT, 5.2.6.

214. "boggler" . . . fragment: 3.13.110, 117.

214. "salt": 2.1.21.

214. defect . . . "riggish": 2.2.231, 239.

214. Others: E.g., Chaucer.

214. toil of grace: 5.2.347.

214. hearts are waxen: TN, 2.2.30.

214. like an opal: 2.4.75.

214. her burnished throne: Following ANT, 2.2.

214. "aspic": 5.2.293.

214. "serpent of old Nile": 1.5.25.

214. never be saved: 5.2.255–57.

214. discredited his travels: 1.2.152–55.

215. the same cradle: As in the medieval *Secunda Pastorum*.

215. Lucifer and Christ: As in Rhabanus Maurus' ninth-century *Allegory on Holy Scripture*.

215. "a strange serpent": ANT, 2.7.42, 48.

215. "world" . . . "nature": 1.2.192, 1.3.16.

215. "won and lost": 3.11.70.

215. "huge sphere": 2.7.14–15.

215. best preserves it: 3.4.21–22.

215. "well-divided": 1.5.53.

215. "Taints" and "honors": 5.1.30–31.

8. Unpathed Waters, Undreamed Shores

216. *Pericles*: Evidence for dating in New Arden PER, ed. F. D. Hoeniger, 1963; EKC, *WS*, 2.335. Inference suggests that Sh's play was written and staged bet. 1606–8, probably early in the latter year, just prior to the first datable reference.

216. uncommonly popular: Reprinted five times between 1609–35. Arden ed., p. lxvi, quotes an anon. pamphlet of 1609 on the crowds that flocked to see it, their "civil throats stretched out so loud."

217. Scholarly opinion: Philip Edwards, "An Approach to the Problem of PER," *Sh. Survey* 5 (1952), pp. 25–49, has Sh. responsible for the entire play, laying its different levels of merit to different "reporters." Karen Csengeri, *English Studies*, Netherlands, 71, 3 (June 1990), 230–43, argues for Sh's sole authorship and offers a convenient summary of opinion pro and con. G. W. Knight's PER is a "thoroughly organic" play, marked by "running coherences of idea, image, and event" (*The Crown of Life*, 1948). H. Dugdale Sykes, *Sidelights on Sh.*, 1919, p. 176, bases PER on Wilkins' novel. Most opinion splits the play bet. Acts I and II, substantially not Sh's, and III–V, substantially his.

217. "With bloody veins": PER, 1.4.92–94.

217. Eighteenth-century editors: E.g., George Steevens, Malone.

217. Wilkins: Sykes, pp. 143–203, locates in his acknowledged work the same ellipsis of the relative pronoun in the nominative case that distinguishes PER. The ellipsis occurs in other writers, notably Thos. Heywood, even Sh. (e.g., H8, 3.2.103, 5.4.75; TNK, 1.2.50, 5.1.6), but Wilkins made it his trademark.

217. lived in the parish: Mary R. McManaway, "Poets in the Parish of St. Giles, Cripplegate," *Sh. Qtly* IX, no. 4 (1958), 561–62.

217. Wilkins . . . testifying: Lewis, *Documents*, 2.432; C. W. Wallace, "Sh. and His London Associates," pp. 261–304.

217. gave them lodgings: JQA, *WS*, pp. 386–87, 399.

217. The minor playwright: Details from Roger Prior, "The Life of George Wilkins," *Sh. Survey* 25 (1972), pp. 137–52; and "GW and the Young Heir," *Sh. Survey* 29 (1976), pp. 33–39; Willem Schrickx, "'Pericles' in a Book-List of 1619," *Sh. Survey* 29 (1976), pp. 21–32.

218. a prose romance: *The Painful Adventures of Pericles Prince of Tyre.*

218. another version: Laurence Twine, *The Pattern of Painful Adventures*, entered S. R., 1576, pub. c. 1594, repr. 1607.

218. One recent commentator: Edwards, "An Approach," pp. 37–38.

218. a "carpet": PER, 4.1.16.

218. "infirmities of men": 2.1.49.

219. "Motes and shadows": 4 CHO. 21.

219. "She here": ANT, 3.13.98.

219. "lass unparalleled": 5.2.316.
219. wanton nag: 3.10.10.
219. "the mean knight": PER, 2.2.58 s.d.
219. "a murderer": 4 CHO. 52.
219. Two or Three Gentlemen: 3.2.10 s.d., 4.5.1 s.d., 5.1.7 s.d.
219. "new seafarer": 3.1.41.
219. wind was north: 4.1.51.
219. oppressed with cold: 2.1.71–73.
219. with simple shells: 3.1.59–64.
219. "winds of heaven": 3.3.36–37.
219. a "visor": 4.4.44.
219. the "triumphs": 5 CHO. 16–17; 5.1.17.
219. powers above him: 3.3.9–10.
220. to play upon: 2.1.59–61.
220. perish at sea: 1.3.28.
220. out the tempest: 4.4. CHO. 30–31.
220. parent and grave: 2.3.46.
220. "Infirmities": 1 CHO. 3.
220. her "eaning time": 3.4.5–6.
220. a taller tree: 1.2.30 (and 1.1.114–15).
220. "rooted out": 5.1.92.
220. "and our birth": 1.2.113–14.
220. John Gower: *Confessio Amantis*, VIII.271–2008.
220. "so long grief": ERR, 5.1.407.
220. "accidentally": 5.1.362.
220. "by miracle": 5.1.265.
220. sunshine after hail: AWW, 5.3.33.
220. dove against crow: PER, 4 CHO. 32–33.
220. "Womb" and "tomb": ROM, 2.3.9–10; PER, 2.3.46.
220. cat with burning eyes: 3 CHO. 5–6.
220. maidenhead is lost: 3 CHO. 10–11.
220. "A birth, and death": 5.3.33–34.
220. her mother dies: 4.1.18.

221. "casket" and "fair viol": 1.1.77, 81.

221. sounds once more: 3.2.88–90.

221. "cry by night": 3.1.11–12 (and 1.1.9). Sh. found Lucina in one of his sources, Twine's *Painful Adventures* (ch. V), where Thaisa is called by this name.

221. "do with Diana": 4.2.149–50.

221. seeds . . . wholesome: 4.6.85–86, 24.

221. gladdening licentious ears: 5.3.30.

221. a withered branch: 2.2.42–43.

221. "yet his child": 1.1.69.

221. "like something": 5.1.102–4.

221. "did thee beget": 5.1.195.

221. "blow" or bloom: 3.2.94–95.

222. Art "sisters" nature: 5 CHO. 7.

222. "goddess argentine": 5.1.250.

222. dance, and versing: 4.6.183–84.

222. "branch, or berry": 5 CHO. 6.

222. Schooled in music: 4 CHO. 7–8.

222. "records with moan": 4 CHO. 26–27.

222. "and woeful music": 3.2.88.

222. "wild": disheveled; ecstatic in what he sees. 5.1.222.

222. beard "to form": 5.3.74.

222. "artificial": 5.1.72.

222. "molding": 3 CHO. 11.

222. "framed": 4.2.139.

222. his beating mind: TMP, 4.1.163.

222. "The city's usuries": CYM, 3.3.45.

222. "of greater state": 3.3.77–78.

222. Monsters breed: 4.2.35.

222. "the Queen's son": 4.2.153.

222. need solemn music: 4.2.191–92.

222. lack a monument: 4.2.224–27.

222. gilded honor: 5.5.4.

222. their broken debtors: 5.4.18–21.

223. strange fowl: 1.4.89.

223. his pond fished: WT, 1.2.193–96.

223. vaulting or mounting: CYM, 1.6.134, 2.5.15–17.

223. longing for garbage: 1.6.50.

223. slavering with whores: 1.6.105.

223. might poison poison: 1.6.125–26.

223. million a dram: 1.4.134–36.

223. written close together: Evidence for dating in New Arden CYM, ed. J. M. Nosworthy, 1955, pp. xiii–xvi; New Arden WT, ed. J. H. Pafford, 1963, pp. xxi–xxiv; Bullough, *Sh's Sources*, 8.117.

223. some greater power: ROM, 5.3.153.

223. affliction "on" them: WT, 1.2.110.

223. "thing of pity": CYM, 5.4.47.

223. Melancholy: PER, 1.2.2.

223. "imposition hereditary ours": WT, 1.2.74–75.

224. redeems all sorrows: LR, 5.3.267.

224. Trojan Horse: CYM, 3.4.59–60.

224. Philomel "gave up": 2.2.12–13, 44–46.

224. the Greek Romances: Ben Edwin Perry, *The Ancient Romances*, 1967, surveys the territory without mentioning Sh. (but readers who know him will find him everywhere in this account).

224. "chalk forth": TMP, 5.1.203.

224. "point of death": TN, 5.1.118.

224. from Greek Heliodorus: By way of Sidney's *Arcadia*. Samuel Lee Wolff, *The Greek Romances in Elizabethan Prose Fiction*, 1912, p. 366*n*.

224. Sidney . . . sponsored: Pericles = Pyrocles, Sidney's hero.

224. a "moldy tale": "Ode to Himself," after 1629.

224. "waters, undreamed shores": WT, 4.4.567.

225. playwrights ransacked them: Said Gosson in *Plays Confuted*.

225. At Harrow: Where Heliodorus's "Ethiopian History" was part of the currriculum.

225. a local vicar: John Marshall, vicar of Bishopton, d. 1607, left an inventory of his books, including this romance.

225. "to myself disguised": ERR, 2.2.214.

225. "is like it": CYM, 5.4.148–49.

225. "reason and passion": Epilogue to Bk. II.

225. tennis balls . . . "servants to fortune": Bk. V.

225. Jonson called this: Prologue to a later version of *Every Man In*, 1605–6?

225. "grace" and "election" . . . in despair: CYM, 1.1.136–37, 1.2.26–27.

226. the powers above: 5.5.466–67.

226. down pillow hard: 3.6.33–35.

226. "Caesar with us": 3.1.1.

226. on his neck: 5.5.364–65.

226. The bloody handkerchief: 5.1.1 s.d.

226. "them, curse them": 2.5.32–33.

227. can read them: 5.5.48.

227. "perturbation in nature": MAC, 5.1.9.

227. bored-to-death: Lytton Strachey's suggestion, "Sh's Final Period," pp. 51–69 in *Books and Characters*, 1922.

227. Shaw's "stagy trash": Rev. of Irving's CYM, *The Saturday Review*, 1896.

227. "inconsequences of romance": Nosworthy, New Arden, p. xxvi.

227. The "imbecilic" plot: Johnson, *General Observations on the Plays of Sh.*, 1756.

227. "upon an upcast": CYM, 2.1.2.

228. a guiltless man: 3.3.66–68.

228. a "dullard": 5.5.265.

228. can make "partition": 1.6.36–38.

228. leg and hand: 4.2.308–11.

228. can't "untie" it: 5.4.148.

228. the Roman soothsayer's: 4.2.346–52.

228. Nature: 4.2.170–71.

228. "the sparks of": 3.3.79.

228. a "noble strain": 4.2.24.

228. an "invisible instinct": 4.2.177.

228. are princes born: 4.4.53–54.

228. to the weather: 3.3.60–64.
228. King is like this: 1.3.36–37.
228. like a cedar: 5.4.140–41, 5.5.453–55.
228. can't "delve" him: 1.1.28.
228. "the tree die": 5.5.263–64.
228. A "golden chance": 5.4.132.
228. "Dead many years": 5.5.437–40.
228. at the top: As in PER, 2.2.43.
229. say he's sorry: CYM, 5.4.11.
229. a "gracious season": 5.5.401.
229. full of mercy: 5.4.13.
229. pardon's the word: 5.5.422.
229. the Thundermaster: 5.4.92 s.d.
229. pleasing the boys: Prol. to *Every Man In*.
229. some "other place": CYM, 3.4.141.
229. all that time: 3.4.181–82.
229. "the world abroad": TGV, 1.1.6.
229. Quitting the nest: CYM, 3.3.27–29.
229. "as our earing": ANT, 1.2.109–11.
229. dew from heaven: CYM, 5.5.351.
229. this "donation": 5.5.367.
229. "without seeking find": 5.5.436.
229. "change of time": 2.4.4–6.
229. as he obeys: 5.1.16–17.
229. "guiltless of election": TNK, 5.1.154.
229. "Florentius' love": SHR, 1.2.69; *Conf. Amantis*, I. 1, 407–1861.
230. that aren't steered: CYM, 4.3.45–46.
230. rose and thorns: AWW, 1.3.129–30.
230. care . . . pleasures: CYM, 4.2.296–97.
230. "infant rind": ROM, 2.3.23–24.
230. revives them: CYM, 1.5.42.
230. "woe after gladnesse": *The Knight's Tale*.
230. Beaumont and Fletcher: Two good books survey their achievement:

Eugene M. Waith, *The Pattern of Tragicomedy in B and F*, 1952; Philip J. Finkelpearl, *Court and Country Politics in the Plays of B and F*, 1990. Cyrus Hoy says who wrote what, "The Shares of Fletcher and His Collaborators in the B and F Canon," *Studies in Bibliography*, 1962, 15.85–88.

230. Fletcher said: Pref. to *The Faithful Shepherdess*, 1610.

230. "house between them": Said John Aubrey, *Brief Lives*.

231. At least twice: In TNK and the lost play *Cardenio*.

231. "mere shadows": *The Wild Goose Chase*, performed 1621.

231. Guarini . . . first begetter: In *Pastor Fido*, pub. 1589. Quotation from *Il Verso*, 1588.

231. Pepys . . . said: Commenting on *The Faithful Shepherdess* in 1663.

231. One of their . . . heroes: *A King and No King*, perf. 1611.

231. at the feet: E.g., F. R. Ristine, *English Tragicomedy* (1910), 1963, esp. p. 113; A. H. Thorndike, *The Influence of B and F on Sh.*, 1901.

231. Monstrous to reason: WT, 5.3.117.

231. An old tale: 5.2.28, 61.

231. rare Italian master: 5.2.97.

232. "some 100 miles": Jonson's *Conversations with Drummond*, Herford and Simpson, 1.132.

232. hoot at it: WT, 5.3.116.

232. with his chisel: 5.3.78–79.

232. wave of the sea: 4.4.135–42.

232. "best for winter": 2.1.25.

232. grievous to expiate: 3.2.208–10.

232. forgive himself: 5.1.5–6.

232. "puts to": 1.2.277–78.

232. like rue: 4.4.74–79.

232. Sorrow alters: 4.4.572–77.

232. wrinkling Hermione's: 5.3.28–29.

232. "joy, not joy": 1.2.110–11.

232. "tomorrow as today": 1.2.62–65.

232. his son's face: 1.2.153–57.

233. astrological determinism: 1.2.1, 201–2; 2.1.105; 2.2.28.

233. palpitations: I.e., tremor cordis, 1.2.110; LR, 2.4.57.

233. "and the web": WT, 1.2.291.

233. an infection: 1.2.145.

233. "doctrine of ill-doing": 1.2.70.

233. "bugs" or goblins: 2.1.25–26, 3.2.91.

233. "clerklike experienced": 1.2.392.

233. learning isn't helpful: 1.2.200.

233. the trouble is: 1.2.432–33.

233. novel Sh. drew on: Greene's *Pandosto*, 1588.

233. "putter-on": WT, 2.1.141.

233. a "villainous knave": OTH, 4.2.139.

233. "natural goodness": WT, 2.1.164–65.

233. "affection": 5.2.36–37.

233. meeting noses . . . kissing: 1.2.285–86.

233. "relish" or taste: 2.1.167.

233. "of the herd": 4.4.608–9.

233. horse, heifer, or dam: 1.2.124, 137.

233. Unfledged . . . fat . . . bird: 1.2.78, 91–96, 183.

233. "as eggs": 1.2.130.

233. calf . . . bawcock . . . collop: 1.2.124, 121, 137.

233. choughs: 4.4.616–17.

233. "pettitoes": 4.4.607.

234. prisoner of the womb: 2.2.26, 57.

234. "condemned to loss": 2.3.192.

234. "Not guilty": 3.2.25–26.

234. "Infirmities": 1.2.250–64.

234. "cursèd thoughts": MAC, 2.1.8–9.

234. "settled senses": WT, 5.3.72–73.

234. "sleepy drinks": Following 1.1.

234. Recurrences: For more, see Richard Proudfoot (and other essays cited by him), "Verbal Reminiscence and the Two-Part Structure of 'The WT,'" *Sh. Survey* 29 (1976), pp. 67–78.

234. her white hand: WT, 1.2.103–5.

234. "white as it": 4.4.362–63.

234. "mean to part": 4.4.154–55.

234. be found again: 5.3.132–35.

234. "for mine eyes": 5.2.82.

234. "our son hither": 4.2.45.

234. "angling now": 1.2.180–81.

234. "than Deucalion off": 4.4.430–31.

234. past is prologue: TMP, 2.1.253.

234. "goodly bulk": WT, 2.1.16–20.

235. Deucalion: Following Ovid, *Metamorphoses*, 1.240–415, Sh's source.

235. awake our faith: WT, 5.3.95.

235. succeed things dying: 3.3.113–14.

235. the winter's pale: 4.3.4.

235. "our weak spirits": 1.2.72–73.

235. "gets" or begets: SHR, 2.1.407–11.

235. repairs the parent: CYM, 1.1.132.

235. "his person's mighty": WT, 1.2.453–54.

235. "borrowed flaunts": 4.4.23 (and 4.4.1).

235. gods undergo transformations: 4.4.25–30.

235. fills up the grave: 5.3.101.

235. Sh. knew [Euripides]: Whose play was trans. into Latin before 1611; George Pettie tells the story in his *Petite Palace of Pleasure*, 1576.

235. numbness to death: WT, 5.3.102.

235. Virgins: 4.4.115–20.

236. "discasing" or "dismantling": 4.4.633, 652.

236. sins of our youth: 3.3.119–20.

236. the son's forgiveness: 4.4.547–50.

236. "of the father": 2.3.99–100.

236. prints him off: 5.1.125–28.

236. no "yellow": 2.3.105–7.

236. inoculate our old stock: HAM, 3.1.117.

236. of nobler race: WT, 4.4.93–95.

236. "respect" or context: MV, 5.1.99.

236. "much an ounce": WT, 4.4.703–6.

236. "and odd shilling": 4.3.32–33.

236. mostly goes right: 4.3.17–18.

236. Purging their melancholy: 4.4.762–64.

236. a "determinate" . . . voyage: TN, 2.1.11.

236. "waters, undreamed shores": WT, 4.4.566–67.

236. Feathers or flies: 2.3.154, 4.4.539–41.

237. serves us well: HAM, 5.2.8.

237. curse on "issue": WT, 2.1.147–50, 5.1.168–70.

237. making them glister: 4.1.7–14.

237. "king of men": PER, 2.3.45.

237. brings it forth: WT, 4.1.25–27.

237. "gap of time": 5.3.153–55.

237. eyes of death: R2, 2.1.270–71.

237. "in April's front": WT, 4.4.2–3.

237. sorrows they lead him to: 3.2.242–43.

237. "'tis time": 5.3.99.

237. "noted" her honesty: 5.3.144–45. Some editors make Camillo the referrent, surely wrong.

237. "most rare note": 4.2.41–42.

237. "notes of admiration": 5.2.10–11.

237. "notable passion": 5.2.15–16.

237. not "note" it: 1.2.214.

237. "note infallible": 1.2.287–88.

238. justifying: 5.3.144–46.

238. an allegorical key: After the Romantic poet, Thomas Campbell.

238. commendatory verses: Prefaced to F1, 1623, and *Poems*, 1640 (in EKC, *WS*, 2.231–34). LD (remembering WT?) also did a verse trans. of Claudian's "Rape of Proserpine," 1617. Hotson tells Digges's story in *I Wm. Sh.*, ch. X.

238. An epitaph: Destroyed, but recorded by Stow. TDs career is summarized in Hotson, pp. 116–17, 124–25.

238. "disciplines of war": H5, 3.2.129.

238. "arithmetical-military" treatise: *Stratioticos*, 1590.

238. Thomas Russell: His career and relation to Sh. are summarized in

Donald W. Foster, *Elegy by W. S.*, 1989, pp. 191–92; and in Hotson, ch. XI.

239. Dudley [Digges]: Hotson, ch. IX, "Sir DD and 'The Tempest.'"

239. William Leveson: Hotson, pp. 160–62, 168, 231.

239. acquaintance of Sh's: Charles M. Gayley, *Sh. and the Founders of Liberty in America*, 1917, ch. II; Arden TMP, 1954, pp. xxvii–xxviii.

239. convened at Southampton House: Rowse, *Sh's Southampton*, pp. 247–48.

239. Aubrey said: *Brief Lives*. But Popham established his plantation in Maine.

239. "and bestial sloth": Conflating Wm. Strachey, *A True Repertory of the Wrack*, 1610, pub. 1625; *A True Declaration of the Estate of the Colony in Virginia*, 1610. Other pamphlets Sh. used are described in Arden TMP, pp. xxvi–xxx; and Gayley, ch. III (whose Appendix, pp. 225–30, lists pamphlets, letters, and miscellaneous data relating to the expedition).

239. elements to silence: TMP, 1.1.21–22.

239. "perdition": 1.2.30.

239. "by Providence divine": 1.2.159.

239. butt of sack: 2.2.121.

239. "of a butt": 1.2.146.

240. Strachey praised . . . *Sejanus*: In a prefatory sonnet, picked up by Sh. in LR. Strachey's career is summarized by Foster, *Elegy*, App. B, pp. 276–88. His *True Repertory*, a long letter dated July 15, 1610, is addressed to an anon. lady, perhaps evoking Sh's much-glossed reference to "the Lady of the Strachey" who married "the Yeoman of the Wardrobe" (TN, 2.5.40).

240. he wrote TMP: After Sept. 1610 (when the Strachey letter became available to him) and before Hallowmas, Nov. 1, 1611 (first recorded performance at Whitehall). EKC, *WS*, 1.491, 2.342. Perhaps the masque was added for a subsequent performance at Court, bet. the betrothal (Dec. 27, 1612) and marriage (Feb. 14, 1613) of Princess Elizabeth to the Elector Palatine.

240. his reading: Summarized in Bullough, *Sources*, 8.240–61, 268*n.*; Arden TMP, pp. xxx–xxxix, lix.

240. Hudson's last voyage: Dudley Digges helped underwrite Hudson's voyages to find the Northwest Passage, also serving as a governor of the NWP Co. (with Wm. Leveson and Richard Hakluyt).

240. "few in millions": TMP, 2.1.3–8.

240. "strange to stranger": 5.1.228.

240. of great constancy: MND, 5.1.23–26.

240. a "devouring" grace: TMP, 3.3.84.

241. "all knit up": 3.3.89–90.

241. "Bright Phoebus": WT, 4.4.122–25.

241. asks . . . forgiveness: TMP, 5.1.197–98.

241. "name of king": 1.1.17.

241. "e'er plummet sounded": 3.3.101.

241. must be patient: 5.1.140–41.

241. "on the top": 3.3.17 s.d.

241. Graves open: 5.1.48–49.

241. a second life: 5.1.194–95.

241. "ever plummet sound": 5.1.56.

241. both were eleven: TNK, 1.3.54.

241. "three hours since": TMP, 5.1.136.

242. "this last tempest": 5.1.153.

242. a sea change: 1.2.401.

242. new-dyes them: 2.1.62–65.

242. "before the time": 1.2.246.

242. "sots": 3.2.93.

242. "in the blood": 4.1.53.

242. liver, passion's seat: 4.1.55–56.

242. to rich ends: 3.1.2–4.

242. virtue . . . not vengeance: 5.1.28.

242. "was his own": 5.1.213.

242. court their fortune: 1.2.181–84.

242. seeks for grace: 5.1.295–96.

242. in a rock: 1.2.343, 361.

242. Colonists in Virginia: The Council's *True Declaration*, 1610, one of Sh's primary texts, finds "no trust in the fidelity of human beasts."

242. "a barbarous disposition": Bullough, 8.245.

242. "Stripes": TMP, 1.2.345.

243. "This island's mine": 1.2.331.

243. "usurps" a name: 1.2.454–55.
243. his ideal "plantation": 2.1.148–69.
243. "artificial devices": Florio's Montaigne, Bk. I, ch. xxx.
243. "cat laps milk": TMP, 2.1.287–88.
243. "bloody thoughts": 4.1.220–21.
243. Things are free . . . inherit: 2.2.175, 3.2.144–45.
243. "freedom": 2.2.186.
243. worse than devils: 3.3.35–36.
243. goodness is rare: 3.1.74–75.
243. a "natural": 3.2.33.
243. and old plays: E.g., *Mucedorus*, c. 1598, Epilogue, ll. 35–36.
244. thing of darkness: TMP, 5.1.275.
244. some unwholesome fen: 1.2.321–23.
244. "still-vexed" Bermudas: 1.2.228–29.
244. its honey drops: 4.1.78–79.
244. head of Sebastian: 2.1.208–9.
244. Gonzalo sees . . . crown: 5.1.202.
244. "drop upon me": 3.2.142.
244. "and hurt not": 3.2.136.
244. "with a stake": 3.2.90.
244. their feet stink: 4.1.184.
244. of the sea: 4.1.65–69.
244. Dusky Dis: 4.1.89.
244. "foul conspiracy": 4.1.139.
244. storm's fury . . . our grief: 1.2.382–93.
245. Stolen garments: MAC, 1.3.145; TMP, 2.1.272–73.
245. in a "maze": 5.1.242 (and 3.3.2).
245. "some heavenly power": 5.1.105–6.
245. "unstanched": 1.1.48.
245. "is but fortune": 5.1.256–57.
245. Madness, charming . . . senses: 5.1.115–16, 53–54 (and 31–32).
245. "mantled": 5.1.64–68, 4.1.182–83.
245. bear bad sons: 1.2.120.

245. Morning . . . tide: 5.1.65–66, 79–82.

245. "nobler reason": 5.1.26–27.

245. not infect it: 1.2.207–8.

245. we can't "miss": 1.2.311.

245. natural things: E.g., 2.2.172.

245. "earth": 1.2.314.

245. to dream again: 3.3.139–43.

245. Thick slumber: PER, 5.1.234–35.

245. Sleep, a grandsire: CYM, 5.4.123.

245. dead asleep: TMP, 5.1.230–35.

245. mistake the truth: 2.1.58.

245. Amphion's miraculous harp: 2.1.57, 87–88.

246. reason and fury: 5.1.26.

246. "relishes" or tastes: 5.1.23–24.

246. "gaberdine" . . . voices: 2.2.37–38, 91–92.

246. "makes a man": 2.2.28–32.

9. Journeys' End

247. "his native country": George Steevens in Malone, *The Plays and Poems of WS*, 1821, 1.468.

247. "of its process": James to H. G. Wells, July 10, 1915.

247. "I am old": H8, 3.1.120.

248. Greene moved out: ME, pp. 127–30.

248. a year later: Perhaps once more in spring 1615 to litigate *re* London Gatehouse.

248. plays at Whitehall: EKC, *WS*, 2.343.

248. Sh's "impresa": So-called in Italian; in French *devise*. Details from Alan Young, *Tudor and Jacobean Tournaments*, 1987 (itemizes Rutland's expenses for 1616 tilting); EKC, *WS*, 1.87, 2.153; and *ES*, 1.140–48; Lee, *WS*, pp. 453–56; JQA, *WS*, pp. 429–31; H-P, 2.88.

249. A chronicler: Aubrey.

249. "green at top": PER, 2.2.43–44.

249. an eyewitness: Sir Henry Wotton in L. P. Smith, *Life and Letters of Sir HW*, 1907, 2.16–17.

249. bought a house: Lewis, *Documents*, 2.435–48.

249. hideaway for papists: Devlin, *Robt. Southwell*, pp. 215–17; EKC, *WS*, 2.165–69; Lee, *WS*, pp. 456–59.

249. "of its name": H-P, 1.240.

250. "our English kings": Fuller, *Worthies*.

250. Father John Gerard: Hotson, *I Wm. Sh.*, pp. 180–82.

250. Mary Bannister's visits: Devlin, p. 109.

250. a London minstrel: H-P, 1.238–41; EKC, *WS*, 2.168–69.

250. A John Robinson: EKC, *ES*, 4.319–20.

250. signed Sh's will: EKC, *WS*, 2.174. JR, laborer of Stratford, had a son John, born 1589, and men of this name appear in Stratford records bet. 1579–1613 (ME, p. 142).

250. Jackson: Hotson, *Sh's Sonnets Dated*, pp. 111–40, 207–17.

251. meat, not fish: Halliday, *Life of Sh.*, p. 180.

251. mortgaged: H-P, 1.239; Hotson, *Sh's Sonnets Dated*, p. 212.

251. paid up: Lee, *WS*, p. 457, asserts without evidence that he left his debt unpaid; Lewis, 2.448, that he discharged it; H-P, 2.345, that the Halls did this for him.

251. in litigation: Summarized SS, pp. 274–75.

251. representatives of his daughter: John Greene, Clement's Inn lawyer and Thomas's brother; Matthew Morris, Dr. Hall's servant.

251. poem by Geo. Herbert: "Decay."

251. in 1612: First acted winter season 1612–13. EKC, *WS*, 1.539, 2.343; G. Harold Metz, *Sources of Four Plays Ascribed to Sh.*, 1989, pp. 257–59.

251. more than a single hand: *Sh., Fletcher, and "The TNK,"* ed. Chas. H. Frey, 1989, discusses collaboration.

252. "Mr. Fletcher's wit": Conflating John Aubrey and Wm. Cartwright on Beaumont's relation to Fl.; quoted JQA, *WS*, p. 432.

252. acted *Cardenio*: Metz, p. 257, dates second performance June 13, 1613, presumably an error; JQA, *WS*, p. 433, confuses date of Court payment to Heminges (May 1613) with date of first performance.

252. Moseley advertised: *SR*, Sept. 9, 1653. Metz, pp. 257, 260.

253. "and golden joys": 2H4, 5.3.100.

253. he didn't know: Some, quoted Metz, p. 260*n*, dispute this.

253. hear his voice: I "hear" 1H4, TRO, ROM, OTH, LR, MM, AWW. Kenneth Muir, *Sh. as Collaborator*, 1960, ch. VIII, amplifies, esp. pp. 154–58.

253. "of that age": Letter of 1738, quoted Metz, p. 264*n*.

254. In 1770: A newspaper account this year reports the MS; playhouse burned 1808. Metz, p. 280; *WS A Textual Companion*, Wells et al., 1987, p. 133.

254. "from the stage": Theobald's preface.

254. Rowe: *Life of Sh.*, 1709.

254. Globe Theater burned: Conflating letters by Thomas Lorkin to Sir Thomas Puckering (June 30), Sir Henry Wotton to Sir Edw. Bacon (July 2), Henry Bluett to Rich. Weekes (July 4), John Chamberlain to Sir Ralph Winwood (July 8); also Edmund Howes's continuation of Stow's *Annals* (1618), Jonson's "Execration upon Vulcan," written 1623, and a contemporary ballad, repr. *TLS*, June 20, 1986, pp. 689–90.

255. "all this isle": H8, 2.3.78–79.

255. "and ever happy": 5.4.2.

255. in 1612 or . . . 1613: Dating and discussion follow New Arden ed., R. A. Foakes, 1957; and New Cambridge ed., John Margeson, 1990.

255. "but it lapsed": EKC, *WS*, 2.342.

255. tutoring . . . John Lowin: According to John Downes, Davenant's prompter at Lincoln's Inn Fields, in *Roscius Anglicanus*, 1708. EKC, *ES*, 2.329; *WS*, 2.264.

256. James Spedding: *Gentleman's Magazine*, Aug. 1850, pp. 115–24; Oct. 1850, pp. 381–82. New Camb. ed., p. 5, gives Spedding's division.

256. the Old Lady: H8, 5.1.171–76.

256. "a redundant syllable": *Life of Sh.*, 2.400.

256. "statistical security": Cyrus Hoy, "The Shares of Fletcher and His Collaborators in the B and F Canon (VII)," *Studies in Bibliography*, ed. Fredson Bowers, 1962, 15.71–90 (citing p. 77).

256. Some, rejecting collaboration: E.g., A. C. Partridge, *The Problem of H8 Reopened*, 1949.

256. compositor or . . . scribe: New Arden, p. xxi; F. Bowers, Cambridge ed. of *The Dramatic Works in the B and F Canon*, vol. 7, 1989, esp. pp. 6, 9.

257. "wick or snuff": HAM, 4.7.114–15.

257. "What news abroad?": H8, 3.2.391.
257. "worth the seeing": 4.1.61.
257. "are no deeds": 3.2.154.
257. "divorce of steel": 2.1.76.
257. exiled Mowbray: R2, 1.3.154–73.
257. Like the oboes: ANT, 4.3.12s.d.
257. write in water: H8, 4.2.45–46.
257. *Julius Caesar*: 3.2.80.
257. fit of their greatness: H8, 3.1.77–78.
257. One contemporary said: Wotton letter, July 2, 1613.
258. love at first sight: H8, 1.4.75–76.
258. "and a stranger": 2.4.15.
258. and titles alter: 4.2.112.
258. "noise" . . . "fight": PRO., 15, 19.
259. "This, general joy": 4.1.6–7.
259. conscientious: 2.2.142–43.
259. the wild sea: 2.4.200–1.
259. "soft cheveril conscience": 2.3.32.
259. "state of man": 3.2.350–58.
259. "sliver and disbranch": LR, 4.2.34.
259. like loaded branches: H8, 4.2.2.
259. his sapless branches: 1H6, 2.5.12.
259. heats the vessel: H8, 1.1.144–45.
259. "was nourished by": SON 73, l.12.
259. fluid of reason: H8, 1.1.148–49.
260. Fortune's eldest son: 2.2.20–21.
260. "capable" of the flesh: 5.3.10–12.
260. his weary life: 2.1.133.
260. tumble headlong down: *Edward II*, 5.6.59–61.
260. in their fortunes: H8, 2.1.120–21.
261. to their end: SON 60, ll.1–2.
261. die we must: 3H6, 5.2.27–28.
261. see me more: H8, 3.2.223–27.

262. stiff and weary: ERR, 1.2.12–15.

262. every Saturday afternoon: Steevens, 1780, in EKC, *WS*, 2.295–96.

262. Tharborough: Dull's conflating of the titles farborough and thirdborough.

262. "yoke of bullocks": 2H4, 3.2.38.

262. "day it rain": TNK, 3.1.65–66.

262. "old as Sibylla": MV, 1.2.106.

262. "crack a jest": John Shakespeare's observation, according to a seventeenth-century reminiscence. EKC, *WS*, 2.247.

262. Alexander Aspinall: ME, pp. 57–58; T. W. Baldwin, *Wm. Shakspere's Small Latine & Lesse Greeke*, 1944, 1.481; Edgar I. Fripp, *Master Richard Quyny*, 1924, p. 62.

262. "a natural wit": John Ward in EKC, *WS*, 2.249.

263. The brothers Nash: ME, pp. 101, 104, 121–24.

263. William Reynolds: ME, p. 123.

264. suit in Chancery: Probably in 1611 (Sh's complaint is undated). Thomas Greene (who had reversionary title to the Combe family holdings) and Richard Lane (uncle of the John Lane who slandered Susanna) joined with him as complainants. Tucker Brooke, *Sh. of Stratford*, 1926, pp. 59–63; ME, pp. 104–6; H-P, 1.227–28, 2.19–31; EKC, *Sources*, p. 15, and *WS*, 2.126–27.

264. "among the meaner sort": John Davies of Hereford, 1610; EKC, *WS*, 2.214.

264. a companionable preacher: ME, p.135; SS, pp.280–81; H-P, 1.244.

264. manured the blood: 2H4, 4.3.119.

264. "consumed with fire": ME, pp. 135–36.

264. His sister Joan: Pp.142–43.

264. of a shilling: So Sh's testament.

264. "the detested wife": AWW, 2.3.291–92.

264. "and continual strife": 1H6, 5.5.62–63.

264. "a jealous woman": ERR, 5.1.69–70.

265. "one too much": ROM, 3.5.166.

265. Robert Whatcott: ME, p. 142.

265. Lane didn't appear: EKC, *WS*, 2.12–13; ME, p. 113; Reese, pp. 250–51; SS, pp. 289–90.

265. "their heads together": SHR, 1.2.138–40.

265. Judith and Thomas: EKC, *WS*, 1.88, 2.7–8; Bradbrook, pp. 222–23; H-P, 1.254–57; ME, pp. 139–41; B. C. A. Windle, *Sh's Country*, 1899, p. 17; Reese, pp. 251–53; SS, pp. 292–96.

266. John Combe: His family described in Reese, p. 242*n*; E. I. Fripp, *Sh's Stratford* (1928), 1973, pp. 61–66.

266. Sh. mocked [Combe]: So Rowe, 1709; EKC, *WS*, 2.138–41.

266. ten black gowns: Fripp, *Sh's Stratford*, pp. 63–64.

266. enclose the common fields: Details from EKC, *WS*, 2.141–46, and Appendix A, #1; ME, pp. 121, 137–38; *Victoria History of the County of Warwick* (1904), 1945, 3.266–68; JQA, *WS*, pp. 454–57; H-P, 2.36.

267. "his native fields": Tucker Brooke's phrase, *Sh. of Stratford*, p. 62.

267. die for 't: PER, 1.1.100–2.

267. enclosure didn't threaten: Greene (diary entry, Sept. 5, 1614) notes "no common" on his lands. EKC, *WS*, 2.143–44, reprints the entries.

268. Stephen Sly: SHR, Induction 2.94–95; Charles I. Elton, *WS: His Family and Friends*, 1904, p. 127.

269. "Barber no favor": Barber dying August 14, 1615, Wm. Combe sent a servant to his executors, hoping to acquire B's interest in Welcombe. Lee, *WS*, p. 478*n*, followed by Fripp, *Sh's Stratford*, p. 9, thinks it was Sh. who dispatched the servant, meaning through the executors to relieve the deceased's children. See, however, EKC, *WS*, 2.149.

269. last play dates: Writing postdates Court performance, Feb. 20, 1613, of Beaumont's *Masque of the Inner Temple and Gray's Inn*, whence the morris dance in 3.5. TNK's Prologue, l.32, refers to King' Men's losses, i.e., burning of Globe, June 29, 1613; and *Bartholomew Fair*, lst produced Oct. 31, 1614, glances twice at Palamon. Metz, *Sources*, p. 376, and Bowers, ed. *B and F*, 7.147–48, date 1613, perhaps near summer. TNK is most recently ed. by E. M. Waith, Oxford Shakespeare, 1989.

269. first edition: SR, April 8, 1634 to J. Waterson.

270. Who wrote what: Peculiarities in spelling probably reflect scribe and two compositors, so don't help determine authorship (Bowers, 7.150–56); but critics for once are largely agreed in discriminating bet. Sh. and Fletcher. Hoy (*Stud. in Bibliog.* XV [1962], 71–76), relying on Fl's linguistic eccentricities, gives more than most to Sh. K. Muir, "Sh's Hand in 'The TNK,'" *Sh. Survey* 11 (1958), invokes metrical tests, vocabulary, image clusters; and cites work of previ-

ous investigators. Paul Bertram, *Sh. and the TNK*, 1956, argues for Sh's sole authorship.

270. De Quincey: *Essays on Style, Rhetoric, and Language*, ed. F. N. Scott, 1893, p. 166*n*.

270. echoes: Metz, p. 425, cites 28 Sh. plays and poems.

270. saw her too: TNK, 2.2.160–61.

271. as dearly sorry: 5.4.125–30.

271. "sadness merry": 5.3.51–53.

271. "with some sorrow": 5.3.135.

271. "sweet and bitter": 5.4.46–47.

271. on deathbeds: 1.1.11.

271. seize them tomorrow: 1.5.7–12.

271. fields of Thebes: 1.1.40–42.

271. that time fair: 1.1.59–70.

271. "Strange ruins": 1.2.13–15.

272. For gray approachers: 5.4.1–9.

272. "crimes of nature": 1.2.2–5.

272. "Was each eleven": 1.3.53–54.

272. "true love": 1.3.81–82.

272. dearest to them: 5.3.112.

272. "it all forgot": MND, 3.2.201–16.

272. to love himself: TNK, 2.2.119–21.

272. than a child's: 1.3.56–57.

272. more than nettles: 5.1.95–97.

272. will be gathered: 5.1.170.

272. is the argument: 5.1.70.

272. drawn their spheres: 5.1.110–16.

273. eleven to ninety: 5.1.130–33 (and 1.4.4–6).

273. "ebbs and flows": 5.1.163.

273. "heavenly limiter pleases": 5.1.28–30.

273. that next approaches: 5.4.82–83.

273. "dove-like": 5.1.11–13.

273. each one meets: 1.5.15–16.

273. "Transported" or "troubled": 1.1.55, 77.

274. "in turned hose": Wm. Cartwright in a verse letter to JF.

274. imagine a deputation: After Theodore Spencer, "The TNK," Signet TNK, 1966, p. 241.

274. "drank too hard": Diary or notebooks of John Ward, vicar from 1662; EKC, *WS*, 1.89, 2.249.

274. "'and rebellious liquors'": Lee, *WS*, p. 481.

274. and a pigsty: H-P, 2.141–42; ME, p. 134.

275. hand . . . looks infirm: EKC, *WS*, 1.507.

275. died a papist: Richard Davies, before 1708; EKC, *WS*, 2.255–57.

275. spelling: EKC, *WS*, 2.371, collects 83 spellings of Sh's name; and discusses his surviving autographs in *Sources*, pp. 43–44.

275. Julius Shaw: JS signs as July/Julynes/Julyns/Julyne; in Latin Julianus and Julinus. Son of Ralph Shaw, wool-driver, who left Ann S. a widow in 1592, he was alderman in 1613, bailiff 1616. ME, pp. 126–27, 142.

276. Thomas Combe: Perhaps the same TC who trans. a French emblem book introducing Machiavelli to English readers. Some of the emblems seem to reflect passages in Sh. John Doebler, "TC's 'The Theater of Fine Devices': A Renaissance English Emblem Book," *The Early Drama, Art, and Music Review*, vol. 12, no. 2 (Spring 1990), pp. 34–44; Fripp, *Sh's Stratford*, p. 62; EKC, *WS*, 2.135.

276. 20 marks: 13s. 4d. = 20 marks.

276. came to him: Lee, *WS*, p. 492.

277. "the best bedsteads": EKC, *WS*, 2.136.

277. "it his production": Joseph Greene in 1747; SS, pp. 297–98.

277. "a long time": An uncle of the playwright Thos. Heywood in his will, 1624; JQA, *WS*, p. 466.

277. "in his writings": Rowe in EKC, *WS*, 2.269.

277. of the man: Conflating 2 *Parnassus*, Jonson, Thos. Freeman, Wm. Camden, Anthony Scoloker, Wm. Beeston, Wm. Barksted. EKC, *WS*, 2.App.B and C; J. Munro, ed. *The Shakspere Allusion Book*, 1932.

278. figures, and shapes: LLL, 4.2.65–77.

278. said Gainsborough: In JQA, *WS*, p. 541.

278. Beeston . . . said: To John Aubrey; EKC, *WS*, 2.253.

278. "good nature": EKC, *WS*, 2.267.

278. "human bones, skulls": An anon. tourist in 1777; EKC, *WS*, 2.290.

278. number of wagons: Wm. Hall in 1694; EKC, *WS*, 2.260–61.

278. "Rattling bones" . . . healthsome air: ROM, 4.1.81–83, 4.3.33–34.

279. "set of people": Wm. Hall.

279. to secure him: Hall.

279. "a popish saint": EKC, *WS*, 2.184.

280. or death mask: H-P, 1.281; *Life and Letters in Tudor & Stuart England*, ed. L. B. Wright and V.A. Lamar, 1962, p. 83.

280. Burbage: Or Jos. Taylor, an actor with the KM; or John Taylor, a contemporary artist.

280. "grave with him": Mr. Dowdall in 1693; EKC, *WS*, 2.259.

Index

Accession Day celebrations, 248–49
Actors, 72–76; boy, 7–8, 74–75, 125, 205, 206–7; in Southwark, 92; as theater owners, 90–91
Actresses, 74
Acts of the Apostles, 240
Adam (O.T. character), 70, 71–72, 86
Addenbrooke, John, 61
Admiral's Men (acting company), 3, 6, 46, 139
Advancement of Learning, The (Bacon), 80
Aeschylus, 246
Allen, Giles, 88, 89
Alleyn, Edward, 2, 5, 6, 50, 138, 149
"All Is True," *see Henry VIII*
All's Well That Ends Well, 118, 151–59
Almshouses, 147
Ambassadors, The (H. James), 223
American, The (H. James), 223
Analogies (in Shakespeare), 200
Androgyny (in Shakespeare), 132; *see also* Cross-dressing
Animals: in MND, 21; in LR, 167
Anne of Denmark, Queen, 136, 139, 140, 146, 207
Antony and Cleopatra, 192, 209, 210–15
Apocrypha, Shakespeare, 38
Apprentice actors, 74–75
Arcadian tradition 81–82
Arcadia (Sidney), 138, 224, 225
Architecture (in 2H4), 58
Arden family, 117, 178
Arden, Mary, 60, 203
Aristotle, 169, 258
Armin, Robert, 73
Armorial bearings, 36–37, 176, 248–49
Aspinall, Alexander, 262–63
Astrology, 16, 18, 96; *see also* Fate
Astrophel and Stella (Sidney), 113
As You Like It, 81–88; ADO and, 70; at Christmas revels (1603), 138–39; generosity theme in, 66; Lodge and, 4; music in, 74; TN and, 96
Aubrey, John, 93, 190, 239

Bacon, Francis, 44, 54, 80, 116
Badger, George, 177
Bankcroft pasture, 118

Bannister family, 250
Barber of Seville, The, 98–99
Barber, Thomas, 269
Barents, Willem, 94
Barker family, 162
Barker, Henry, 263
Barlow, William, 177
Barnard, Elizabeth, 276
Barnard, John, 276
Barrymore, John, 77
Bear pits, 90
Beaumont and Fletcher Folio, 252
Beaumont, Francis, 149, 230–31
Bedlam, 26
Beeston, Kit, 73
Beeston, William, 278
Behaviorism (in LR), 168
Belott, Stephen, 150, 151
Benefit performances, 48
Betrayal: as theme, 104
Betterton, Thomas, 253–54
Bible, 85, 86, 92, 179; *see also* Paul, St.
Bildungsroman (and Shakespeare's histories), 53, 56, 259
Billingsley, Henry, Mayor of London, 45
Bishopsgate Street, 27
Blackfriars (playhouse): audience of, 206; Burbages and, 89; Chamberlain's Men and, 91; Children of the Queen's Revels and, 205, 207; closed, 208; construction of, 209–10; Court performances and, 10; John Robinson and, 250
Blacks (and OTH), 141
Blank verse, 274
Blount, Charles, Baron Mountjoy, 115
Blount, Edward, 253
Boaz (O.T. character), 85
Bodleian Library, 113
Bois, Francis de, 263
Bott, William, 59
Boy actors, 7–8, 74–75, 125, 205, 206–7
Bracciano, Virginio Orsino, Duke of, 96
Brahe, Tycho, 238
Brend, Nicholas, 93
Bridewell Prison, 205
Brooke, William, Lord Cobham, 47
Browne, Thomas, 278
Bryan, George, 73
Buck, George, 8
Buckingham (in H8), 26
Buckingham, John Sheffield, Duke of, 189
Burbage, Cuthbert, 89
Burbage, Mrs. Cuthbert, 74
Burbage, James, 66, 88, 89, 206
Burbage, Richard: Blackfriars and, 89, 206, 207; career of, 77; Droeshout and, 280; private life of, 76; in R3, 6; Shakespeare and, 248, 276
Burghley, William Cecil, first Baron, 9, 45, 112
Burning Babe, The (Southwell), 178
Bussy D'Ambois (Chapman), 171

Camden, William, 200
Campion, Edmund, 179
Cardenio (Fletcher and Shakespeare), 251–54
Carew, George, Baron of Clopton, 176, 263
Carey, George, Lord Hunsdon, 47, 62, 206
Carey, Henry, Lord Hunsdon, 3, 6, 46, 47
Carey, Robert, first Earl of Monmouth, 135, 249
Carr, Robert, Earl of Somerset, 136
Catesby, Robert ("Robin"), 175, 177, 250
Catholics, 175, 176, 178, 179, 180, 250
Cawdrey, Arthur, 269
Cecil, Robert, first Earl of Salisbury, 112, 116, 175, 177, 180
Cecil, William, *see* Burghley
Censorship, 2, 8–9, 40, 173
Cervantes, Miguel de, 230, 252–53, 254
Chamberlain's Men (acting company): in Court performances, 10; at Cross Keys Inn, 6; before Elizabeth Tudor, 117, 134; *Every Man in His Humor* and, 126; James I and, 139; members of, 73–74; Shakespeare's stake in, 3, 91; as theater owners, 91; Theater War and, 125; *see also* King's Men (acting company)
Chambers, E. K., 66

Chance, as theme, *see* Fate, as theme
Chapman, George, 104, 126, 129, 171, 207
Chastity, as theme (in WT), 237
Chaucer, Geoffrey, 229, 230, 271
Cheke, John, 148
Chester, Robert, 104
Children of the Chapel (acting company), 126
Children of Her Majesty's Revels (acting company), 139, 205
Chronicles of England, Scotland, and Ireland (Holinshed), 189
Church attendance, 25
Clarendon, Edward Hyde, Earl of, 136
Clayton, John, 60
Clink Liberty district, 91–92
Clopton, George Carew, Baron of, 176, 263
Clopton, Hugh, 57, 176
Clopton, Joyce, 176
Clopton Manor, 58, 60, 176, 177
Clutterbook, Ferdinando, 23
Coats of arms, 36–37, 176, 248–49
Cobham, William Brooke, Lord, 47
Coke, Edward, 118, 119, 177, 268, 269
Coleridge, Samuel Taylor, 141
College of Arms, 117, 206
Collins, Francis, 275
Combe family, 263, 266
Combe, John, 161, 266, 280
Combe, Thomas (the elder), 276, 277
Combe, Thomas (the younger), 266, 269, 276
Combe, William, 161, 198, 263, 266–69
Comedy of Errors, The: classical structure of, 242; CYM and, 226; execution in, 180; Gower and, 220; at Gray's Inn, 6–7; Greek romances and, 225; TN and, 94, 95, 96
Compters, *see* Prisons
Condell, Henry: family of, 76; H8 and, 256; PER and, 216; residence of, 150; TNK and, 270; on Shakespeare's manuscripts, 79; Shakespeare's will and, 276, 277
I Corinthians (N.T. epistle), 22–23
Coriolanus, 197–204; ANT and, 210, 211, 213; at Blackfriars, 209; inspiration for, 118; TIM and, 192
Coryat, Thomas, 146, 150, 251
"Counters," *see* Prisons
Court performances: of *Cardenio*, 252; features of, 10–11; in Great Frost (1607), 205; of LR, 170; length of, 77–78; of R2, 115–16; schedule of, 7; of TN, 95–96
Covent Garden (playhouse), 254
Coverdale, Miles, 92
Cowley, Richard, 76, 77
Cranmer, Thomas, 255
Crime and punishment, 136
Cripplegate district, 147–49
Crosby Place, 24–25
Cross-dressing, 94, 231; *see also* Androgyny
Cross Keys Inn, 6, 88, 205
Crown (royal government), 8, 45–46, 175, 198
Crows (in PHT), 102
Crudities (Coryat), 146, 251
Cuffe, Henry, 113
Curtain (playhouse), 5, 6, 89
Curtains (in Court plays), 12
Cyclical patterns, 192, 220, 235; *see also* Time, as theme
Cymbeline, 209, 222–30, 235

Dante Alighieri, 214
Danvers, Charles, 113
"Daphnis and Chloe," 224
Daughter characters in Shakespeare, 29, 33, 221, 222
Davenant family, 189
Davenant, William, 189–90
Day, John, 207
Debates (as dramatic mode), 17–18
De Bois, Francis, *see* Bois, Francis de
Debtors' prisons, *see* Prisons
Dekker, Thomas, 48, 79, 89, 128
Delilah (O.T. character), 214
De Quincey, Thomas, 270
De Velasco, John, *see* Velasco, John de
Devereux, Robert, *see* Essex, Robert Devereux, second Earl of
De Witt, Johannes, see Witt, Johannes de
Dibdale, Robert, 179
Diggers, 197
Digges, Dudley, 239, 240
Digges family, 238

Directors (and Shakespeare's plays), 78–79
Discovery (ship), 240
Disease, as theme, 56–57; *see also* Mortality, as theme
Distressed Lovers, The (Theobald), 252
Dr. Faustus (Marlowe), 182, 186
Don Giovanni (Mozart), 75
Donne, John, 67, 105, 148, 149, 240
Don Quixote (Cervantes), 252–53, 254
Double Falsehood (Theobald), 252, 253
Dover Cliff, 170, 174
Downes, John, 253
Dramatic unities, 12, 242
Drayton, Michael, 59, 195–96, 274
Dreams, as theme, 245
Droeshout, Martin, 278, 280
Drummond of Hawthornden, William, 126–27
Dryden, John, 190, 215
Duke, John, 73

Eastward Ho! (Jonson), 176
Economic changes, national, 25, 66, 197–99, 267
Edward III, 39, 40, 56, 260
Egalitarianism, as theme, 156–57
Egerton, Thomas, Baron Ellesmere, 266
Egregious Popish Impostures (Harsnett), 179
Eliot, T. S., 207
Elizabeth Stuart, Princess, 175, 248, 255
Elizabeth Tudor, Queen: blacks and, 141; Chamberlain's Men and, 10; death of, 134–35; Essex and, 114, 115, 116–17; flattery and, 43, 44; Master of the Revels and, 8–9; WIV and, 63, 64; MND and, 18; Spanish War and, 67; taxation by, 23
Ellesmere, Thomas Egerton, Baron, 266
Enclosures, land, 118, 197–98, 266–69
Enslow Hill rising, 198
Equivocation, 178, 181
Eros, *see* Sexuality
Esau (O.T. character), 86
Essex, Robert Devereux, second Earl of, 112–17; death of, 103, 116, 134; Gunpowder Plot and, 177; H5 and, 38, 55; JC and, 109; London mobs and, 40; Lopez and, 28; Popham and, 148; R2 and, 42; Southampton and, 249; in Spanish War, 67; TRO and, 129
Euripides, 97, 235
Evans, Henry, 206
Every Man in His Humor (Jonson), 126
Every Man Out of His Humor (Jonson), 127

Faerie Queene, The (Spenser), 231
Farce, 94, 95, 121, 194
Fate, as theme: in ANT, 213; in AYL, 85; in H8, 260; in late plays, 273; in MAC, 183; in MV, 31–32; in OTH, 144; in TN, 96, 99; in WT, 234; *see also* Astrology
Father characters, 29, 33, 35, 118, 221
Fawkes, Guy, 176, 177; *see also* Gunpowder Plot
Ferres, Edward, 81
Field, Nathaniel, 74–75
Field, Richard, 103, 147, 149, 206, 238
Figures of speech, 168–69, 200–1
First Folio: actors listed in, 73–74; COR and, 202; dedicatees of, 136; editors of, 77, 79, 216; H8 and, 256; Hugh Holland and, 149–50; Salisbury on, 103; TNK and, 270
Fletcher, John, 230–31; *Cardenio*, 251–54; H8 and, 256; at Mermaid Tavern, 149; TNK, 223, 241, 254, 269–74
Fletcher, Laurence, 139
Flood, Humphrey, 150
Ford, John, 171
Foreigners, *see* Blacks; Frenchmen; Germans; Italians; Jews; Xenophobia
Forman, Simon, 148–49, 173, 210
Fortescue, Ellen, 250
Fortune (playhouse), 88
Fortune, as theme, *see* Fate, as theme
Foxe, John, 149
Frederick V, Elector Palatine, 248, 255
Frenchmen, 27, 151
Fuller, Thomas, 127

Gainsborough, Thomas, 278
Gardens (in R2), 55; (in Fletcher), 231
Gardiner, William, 46, 61

Garnet, Henry, 179, 180–81
Garrick, David, 279
Garter Feasts, 62
Gastrell, Francis, 58
Gatehouse, 249–51
Generosity, as theme, 66–67, 98, 182
Geographical discoveries, 94, 240
Gerard, John, 250
Germans (in WIV), 27, 62
Globe (playhouse): Blackfriars and, 207, 208, 209; burns down, 254–55; construction of, 88–89; history of, 90–91; Poets' War and, 125; Shakespeare's investment in, 91, 93, 207
Golding, Arthur, 105
Gorboduc, 7
Gosson, Henry, 217
Gosson, Stephen, 20, 47
Government, royal, 8, 45–46, 175, 198
Gower, John, 220, 229
Gowry, 175
Grace, as theme, 85; *see also* Redemption, as theme; Sin, as theme
Gray's Inn, 6-7
Great Frost (1607), 204–5
Greek romances, 224, 225, 240
Greene, Robert, 2, 4, 78
Greene, Thomas, 118–19, 247, 248, 268, 269
Gresham, Thomas, 25
Greville, Edward, 118, 263
Grooms of the Chamber, 138
Guarini, Giovanni Battista, 231
Gunpowder Plot, 175–78; aftermath of, 180; Gatehouse and, 250; Jesuits and, 179; William Johnson and, 251
Gwinn, Dr. Matthew, 189

Hakluyt, Richard, 94
Hall, Elizabeth, 241, 263, 275–76
Hall family, 60
Hall, John, 195–96, 268, 278
Hall's Croft, 195
Hall, Susanna (Shakespeare): epitaph of, 278; John Hall and, 195, 196; John Lane and, 264–65; on mother's tombstone, 277; nubility of, 29; religion of, 180; remains of, 279; Shakespeare's will and, 251, 276
Hamlet, 117–25; Beaumont and Fletcher and, 231; COR and, 202; equivocation in, 178; Hamnet Shakespeare and, 35; Kyd and, 4; length of, 77; PER and, 218; ROM and, 15, 16; Tourneur and, 171; TRO and, 132
Hamlet, Katherine, 117
Hampton Court, 10
"Hand D," 40, 41, 79
Harington, John, 170
Harper, John, 59
Harsnett, Samuel, 179
Hart, Joan (Shakespeare), 118, 264, 275
Hart, Thomas, 160, 162
Hart, William, 264
Harvard family, 160
Hathaway, Anne (Shakespeare), 35, 251, 264, 277, 278
Hawkins, John, 141
Hayward, John, 114
Heliodorus, 224
Heminges, John: burial of, 277; business affairs of, 77; family life of, 76; Gatehouse and, 250; H8 and, 256; Knell and, 74; as marriage witness, 238; PER and, 216; residence of, 150; Shakespeare's bequest to, 276; on Shakespeare's manuscripts, 79; TNK and, 270
Henrietta Maria, consort of Charles I, 57-58
1 *Henry IV*, 23, 38–44, 47, 49–57, 67
2 *Henry IV*, 38–44, 49–57; architecture and, 58
Henry, Prince of Wales, 248
Henry V, 38–44, 49–57; Baron Mountjoy and, 115; Christopher Mountjoy and, 146; Essex and, 55; JC and, 109; PER and, 218
1 *Henry VI*, 227, 259
3 *Henry VI*, 35, 261
Henry VIII, 255–61; Buckingham and, 26; Cripplegate plays and, 153; Elizabeth Stuart and, 248; Elizabeth Tudor and, 43; French manners and, 151; James I and, 135; Lancastrian plays and, 54; Paris Garden and, 90

Henslowe, Philip, 2, 90, 126
Heraldry, 36–37, 176, 248–49
Heralds' College, 117, 206
Herbert family, 138
Herbert, George, 251
Herbert, Mary, Countess of Pembroke, 138
Herbert, Philip, Earl of Montgomery, 135–36
Herbert, William, Earl of Pembroke, 136, 140, 206
Hesketh, Thomas, 93
Heywood, Thomas, 20, 126
Hiccox, Lewis, 118, 161
Hiccox, Thomas, 161
Holbein, Hans (the younger), 259
Holinshed, Raphael, 35, 38, 41, 189
Holland, Hugh, 149–50
Holy Trinity Church (Stratford), 163, 278–79
Homer, 129
Honor, as theme, 118
Horace (Quintus Horatius Flaccus), 3, 214, 248
Horneby, Thomas, 61
Hospital of St. Mary of Bethlehem, 26
Huband, Ralph, 162
Hughes, Mrs. Margaret, 74
Humorous characters in Shakespeare, 63, 75
Hunsdon, George Carey, Lord, 47, 62, 206
Hunsdon, Henry Carey, Lord, 3, 6, 46, 47
Hunt, Simon, 179
Hyde, Edward, Earl of Clarendon, 136

Ibsen, Henrik, 156
Iliad (Homer), 129
Impresas, *see* Heraldry
Incest, as theme, 221
Infidelity, as theme, 222–23
Inganni, 94
Inner Temple, 7
Inns in Bishopsgate, 24
Insanity, *see* Madness
Ireland, William Henry, 60
Isle of Dogs, The (Jonson and Nashe), 45
Italians, and Shakespeare, 226
Ixion (mythological character), 166

Jackson, John, 250, 251
Jacob (O.T. character), 32
Jaggard, William, 149
James, Henry, 49, 184, 223, 231, 240, 247
James I of England, King, 135–40; accession anniversary of, 248–49; accession of, 137–38; AWW and, 154; censorship by, 8; flattery and, 3–44; foreign negotiations of, 152; Long Parliament and, 208; MM and, 155; MND and, 11; MV and 7; in Oxford, 188–89; "Poetical Essays," 147; satirized, 207
James IV of Scotland, King, 147
Janssen, Cornelius, 206
Janssen, Gheerart, 278, 280
Jenkins, Thomas, 62
Jesuits, 179
Jew of Malta (Marlowe), 5
"Jew of Venice, The," *see Merchant of Venice, The*
Jews, 27, 32, 149
Johnson, Gerard, *see* Janssen, Gheerart
Johnson, Robert, 263
Johnson, Samuel: on AWW and MM, 152; on CYM, 227; on equivocation, 181; on H8, 259; LR and, 163; on MAC, 187; on moral thought, 260; on Shakespeare's language, 80; on TN, 95
Johnson, William, 176, 250, 251
Jones, Inigo, 136, 149, 173, 174, 189
Jonson, Ben: on Alleyn, 5; Anne of Denmark and, 136; character of, 4, 126–28; on directors, 79; *Every Man in His Humor*, 126; *Every Man Out of His Humor*, 127; on Globe, 90; Greek romances and, 224; Gunpower Plot and, 176; humor of, 63; Isle of Dogs, 45; at James's coronation, 138; on JC, 107; *Masque of Blackness*, 140, 174; masques and, 173–74; at Mermaid Tavern, 149, 150; Nathaniel Field and, 74–75; at New Place, 59; "Ode to Himself," 127; PHT and, 103, 104; in plague (1603), 137; *Poetaster*, 128; in Poets' War, 125; satire by, 62, 207; *Sejanus*, 240; Shakespeare and, 126, 128, 150, 274; Shakespeare's coat of arms and, 37 Southwell and, 178; in Spanish War, 67; Spencer and, 44; on theater,

47; on truth, 279; TN and, 94; on wigmakers, 147; WT and, 232
Joyce, James, 141, 265
Julius Caesar, 106–12; cast of, 76; Essex rebellion and, 117; at Globe, 88; HAM and, 119; H8 and, 257; OTH and, 144; TRO and, 130

Kemble, John Philip, 254
Kempe, Will, 2, 73, 75, 91, 93
Kenilworth Castle, 243
King John, 35, 226, 259–60
King Lear, 163–70; AWW and, 156; AYL and, 83; Heliodorus and, 224; James I and, 44; MAC and, 182; madness theme in, 26; romances and, 223; ROM and, 16; TIM and, 191–92, 193; variants of, 80
King's Men (acting company): at Blackfriars, 209; at Elizabeth Stuart's wedding, 248; Fletcher and, 231; in Great Frost (1607), 205; James I and, 139, 208; *Revenger's Tragedy* and, 170; *see also* Chamberlain's Men (acting company)
King's Wardrobe, 250
Knell, William, 74
Knight of the Burning Pestle (Beaumont), 230
Knights of the Garter, 62
Knight's Tale, The (Chaucer), 271, 272
Knox, John, 147
Kyd, Thomas, 2, 4, 12, 120

Lamb, Charles, 80
Lambert, Edmund, 60
"Lamentable Tragedy, A," 51
Lammas, 16
Lane, John, 265
Langley, Francis, 44–45, 46, 61, 89
Latimer, Bp. Hugh, 28
Lawrence, D. H., 211
Lee, Anne, 61
Leland, John, 262
"Lendings," 167–68
Levellers, 197
Leveson, William, 93, 239
Life and Reign of King Henry IV, The (Hayward), 114
Lodge, Thomas, 4, 81, 85
London: districts of, 91–93, 147–49; Great Frost (1607) in, 204–5; mayors of, 24–25; mobs of, 40; plague in, 2, 46, 137, 161, 204, 208; schools of, 17
London Corporation, 8, 45–46, 47, 88
Long Parliament, 208
Lopez, Roderigo, 27–28, 33, 181
Lord Chamberlain's Men (acting company), *see* Chamberlain's Men (acting company)
Love Lies a-Bleeding (Beaumont and Fletcher), 231
Love's Labor's Lost: H8 and, 258; ADO and, 68, 70, 72; staging of, 11; TRO and, 131; variants of, 79
Love's Martyr, 103–4
Lowin, John, 255–56
Lucy, Thomas, 61–62, 267
Lyly, John, 4

Macbeth, 181–87; ANT and, 213; Davenant and, 190; Garnet and, 179, 181; Gunpower Plot and, 175, 178; JC and, 109; romances and, 223; TIM and, 192; WT and, 236
Madness, 26; as theme, 167, 245, 252, 253
Magic Flute, The (Mozart), 221, 231
Maidenhead (inn), 118
Mainwaring, Arthur, 266, 267
Malone, Edmond, 91, 216, 256, 279
Manners, Francis, sixth Earl of Rutland, 248, 249, 280
Manningham, John, 76, 94, 95
Marlowe, Christopher, 4, 5, 182, 186, 260
Marriage of Figaro, The (Mozart), 98
Marston, John, 104, 126, 127, 128, 207
Masque of Blackness (Jonson), 140, 174
Masques, 173–74
Master of the Revels, 7–8, 40
Mayors of London, 24–25
Maypoles, 26
Measure for Measure, 148, 151–59, 193, 218
Megalopsychia (and LR), 169
Melancholy, as theme, 223
Merchant of Venice, The, 29–33; AYL and, 83; generosity theme in, 66; Gresham's crest in, 25; as hybrid, 13; James I and, 7; *Jew of Malta* and, 5;

Merchant of Venice, The (cont'd)
John Shakespeare and, 24; Lopez and, 28; MND and, 22; OTH and, 141
Meres, Francis, 81
Mermaid Tavern, 149–50
Merrick, Gelly, 115–16
Merry Wives of Windsor, The, 27, 45, 61–64
Metonymy (and COR), 200–1
Midlands Revolt, 197–99, 267
Midsummer Night's Dream, A, 18–23; first performance of, 11; maypole in, 26; ROM and, 13; staging of, 12; theme of, 22; TRO and, 130; TNK and, 271, 272
Milton, John, 149
Mirror for Magistrates, A, 42, 260
Money (in Shakespeare's time), 66
Monks: popular contempt for, 147
Monmouth, Robert Carey, first Earl, 135, 249
Montaigne, Michel Eyquem de, 233, 243
Monteagle, William Parker, fourth Baron, 177
Montgomery, Philip Herbert, Earl of, 135–36
Morality plays, 42, 143
More, Thomas, 28; *see also Sir Thomas More, The Book of*
Mortality, as theme, 154, 166; *see also* Disease, as theme; Time, as theme
Mosely, Humphrey, 252
Mother characters (in PER), 221, 222
Mountjoy, Charles Blount, eighth Baron, 115
Mountjoy, Christopher, 146
Mountjoy, Mrs. Christopher, 149
Mountjoy family, 150–51, 217
Mountjoy, Mary, 146–47
Mozart, Wolfgang Amadeus, 75, 221
Much Ado about Nothing, 67–72; AWW and, 155; AYL and, 83, 87; Innogen's silence in, 79–80; Kempe in, 73; TN and, 96
Mulberry tree (Shakespeare's), 59
Munday, Anthony, 40
Music: in AYL, 82; at Blackfriars, 209; in MND, 21; in ADO, 68, 72; in PER, 222; role of, 74; *see also* Opera

Nashe, Thomas, 1, 5, 45
Nash family, 263, 276
Nash, Thomas, 276, 278
Nature: and nurture, 246; as theme, 85, 167
New Place (mansion), 24, 57–60, 247–48
Northern Rebellion, 197
North, Thomas, 110, 191

"Ode to Himself" (Jonson), 127
Oedipus myth, 221, 224
O'Neill, Hugh, second Earl of Tyrone, 115
Opera, 75, 190, 212, 257
Order of St. George, 62
Orlando Furioso (Greene), 78
Orsino, Virginio, Duke of Bracciano, 96
Othello, 140–46; AWW and, 156, 157; Cripplegate plays and, 157–58; LR and, 165, 166; MAC and, 186; MV and, 30; romances and, 223; TRO and, 132; WT and, 233
Ovid (Publius Ovidius Naso), 105, 248
Oxford, and Shakespeare, 188–89

Paris Garden, 90
Parker, William, Lord Monteagle, 177
"Parnassus" plays, 81
Parody (in Shakespeare), 19, 20
Passionate Pilgrim, The, 81
Paulet, William, first Marquis of Winchester, 26–27
Paul's Boys (acting company), 126
Paul, St.: AYL and, 86, 87; on death, 22–23; LR and, 164, 165; MAC and, 186; TMP and, 240; WT and, 236
Peele, George, 4
Pembroke, Mary Herbert, Countess of, 138
Pembroke's Men (acting company), 2, 44–45, 46
Pembroke, William Herbert, Earl of, 136, 140, 206
Pepys, Samuel, 96, 231
Pericles, Prince of Tyre, 216–22, 242, 249

Philaster (Beaumont and Fletcher), 231
Phillips, Augustine, 74, 77, 115, 161
Phoenix and Turtle, The, 101–6; JC and, 108, 110; style of, 274; TRO and, 132–33
Physicians: in TIM, 194; in WT, 233
Pipe Roll, 24
Plague, 2, 46, 137, 161, 204, 208
Plautus, Titus Maccius, 94, 95, 129
Playwrights (compared to Shakespeare), 170–72
Plutarch, 110, 191, 199, 201–2
Poetaster (Jonson), 128
"Poetical Essays" (James I), 147
Poetomachia, 125, 127–28, 131
Pope, Alexander, 142, 147, 190, 252, 253
Pope, Thomas, 76, 77, 161
Popham, John, 116, 148, 177, 239
Poverty, as theme, 167
Prince Henry's Servants (acting company), *see* Admiral's Men (acting company)
Prisons, 93, 148–49; *see also* Bridewell Prison
Privy Council: Essex and, 115, 116; Hayward and, 114; Jonson and, 128; Master of the Revels and, 8; Midlands Revolt and, 198; suppresses plays, 45, 46, 47; in Theater War, 125; Thomas Greene and, 268; William Combe and, 269
Proscenium arch, 174
Prostitution, 92, 148
Prynne, William, 47
Psychomachia, 143, 172, 246, 260
Purcell, Henry, 190
Puritans, 8, 48, 76, 113, 175, 255

Queen's Bench, 61
Quiney family, 266
Quiney, Judith (Shakespeare), 34–35, 265–66, 275, 276
Quiney, Richard: at Bell Tavern, 206; death of, 161; vs. enclosures, 118, 119; as Stratford's spokesman, 29, 65–66
Quiney, Thomas, 265–66

Racine, Jean, 215
Racism, 141, 142; *see also* Xenophobia
Ralegh, Walter, 112, 116, 136
Rape of Lucrece, The, 3
Ravel, Maurice, 224
Recusants, 175, 176, 178, 179, 180, 250
Red Bull (playhouse), 173
Redemption, as theme, 17, 71, 186, 236, 242, 245; *see also* Grace, as theme; Sin, as theme
Replingham, William, 268
Return from Parnassus, The, 128
Revels' Accounts, 7–8, 12
Revels, Master of the, 7–8, 40
Revels Office, 9, 46, 173, 189
Revenge plays, 120
Revenger's Tragedy (Tourneur), 170
Reynolds, Thomas, 180
Reynolds, William, 180, 263, 276
Richard II, 38–44; and Bishopsgate, 27; censorship of, 9; Essex and, 42, 115–16; H8 and, 257; "natural perspectives" in, 49; *Poetaster* and, 128
Richard III: Burbage in, 6; credibility of, 56; Crosby Place and, 24; H8 and, 259; MAC and, 185, 192
Robinson, John, 250, 275
Rogers, Katherine, 160
Rogers, Philip, 60
Rogers, Thomas, 160–61
Roman Catholics, 175, 176, 178, 179, 180, 250
Romeo and Juliet, 13–17; H8 and, 258; humor in, 75; length of, 77; MND and, 18, 20; staging of, 11, 12–13; TRO and, 132
Rookwood, Ambrose, 176
Rosalind (Lodge), 81, 82
Rose (playhouse), 6, 78, 90, 126
Rowe, Nicholas, 126
Royal performances, *see* Court performances
Ruskin, John, 262
Russell, Thomas, 238, 240, 275
Ruth (O.T. character), 85
Rutland, Francis Manners, sixth Earl of, 248, 249, 280
Rutter, Mrs. Margaret, 74

Sadler, Hamnet, 29, 35, 275, 276
Sadler, John, 118
St. Andrew Undershaft (church), 26
St. Anne (church), 206
St. Giles Cripplegate (church), 149
St. Helen's (nunnery), 25
St. John's College (Oxford), 189
St. Martin Outwich (church), 27
St. Mary of Bethlehem (hospital), 26
Salisbury family, 103, 104
Salisbury, Robert Cecil, first Earl of, 112, 116, 175, 177, 180
Salvation, as theme, *see* Redemption, as theme
Samson (O.T. character), 214
Samuel (O.T. book), 35
Savage, Thomas, 93, 251
Schools (in Shakespeare's London), 17
Scurvy, 196
Sea-Venture (ship), 239–40
Sejanus (Jonson), 240
Seneca, Lucius Annaeus, 120
Sexuality, as theme: in HAM, 120; in LR, 166; in MM, 155; in MND, 19–20; in ADO, 68; in OTH, 144; in TRO, 132
Shadwell, Thomas, 190
Shakespeare, Anne, see Hathaway, Anne
Shakespeare Apocrypha, 38
Shakespeare, Edmund, 92, 204–5
Shakespeare, Edward, 204
Shakespeare, Gilbert, 161, 264
Shakespeare, Hamnet, 34, 35, 241
Shakespeare, Henry, 34
Shakespeare, Joan, 118, 264, 275
Shakespeare, John: coat of arms of, 36; death of, 103–4, 117, 179; as defendant, 61; Griffin and, 72–73; Northern Rebellion and, 197; religion of, 179; Shakespeare and, 2, 262; usury of, 24; Wilmcote estate and, 60
Shakespeare, Judith, 34–35, 265–66, 275, 276
Shakespeare, Richard, 264
Shakespeare, Susanna, *see* Hall, Susanna
SHAKESPEARE, WILLIAM: as actor, 78; in Bankside, 151; in Bishopsgate, 23, 24; Burbage's paramour and, 76; character of, 28–29, 277–78; comedies, 20; convention and, 11–12; in Cripplegate, 146–51; death of, 274–75; as director, 79; early career of, 2–6; family of, 34–35, 160–61, 204–5, 254, 264–66; finances of, 48, 263–64, 267; generosity of, 66–67; grain holdings of, 198–99; Gunpowder Plot and, 178; historical philosophy of, 37, 39; history plays, 37–44, 49–57, 195; humorous characters of, 63, 75; James I and, 138–40; Jonson and, 126, 128, 150, 274; Lancastrian plays, 37– 44; language of, 80, 81, 273–74; likenesses of, 278–80; in litigation, 60–61, 151, 263–64; monument to, 279–80; New Place and, 57–60, 247–48; in Oxford, 188–89, 196; real estate acquisitions of, 24, 57–58, 118, 161–62, 249–51; romances, 223–26, 230, 234, 258; in St. Helen's parish, 5; school debates and, 17–18; skepticism of, 37, 85, 153; social rank of, 34, 36–37, 117; sonnets, 223; in Southwark, 91; in Stratford, 196–97, 261–69; tax assessments of, 23–24, 63; theater ownership of, 91, 93, 207, 276; on tour, 138, 161; tragedies, 234; tragicomedies, 230–38; will of, 60, 139–40, 238, 251, 265–66, 275–77; women characters of, 87–88, 145, 182, 193, 203, 214, 241; works credited to, 81; xenophobia of, 27, 226
Shaw, Bernard, 87, 156, 227
Shaw, Julius, 275
Sheep, 267, 269
Sheffield, John, Duke of Buckingham, 189
Shelton, Thomas, 253
Shipwrecks (in TMP), 239–40
Shirley brothers, 94
Sidney, Philip: *Arcadia*, 138, 224, 225; Essex and, 112–13; on Shakespeare's settings; on style, 81; TMP and, 240
Sincler, John, 75, 76
Sin, as theme, 166; *see also* Redemption, as theme
Sir Thomas More, The Book of, 40–41, 44, 56, 79
Skepticism, 37, 85, 153
Sleep, as theme, 22–23, 245

Sly, Stephen, 268
Sly, William, 75, 207
Smith, Rafe, 265
Soer, Dorothy, 61
Somerset House, 139–40
Somerset, Robert Carr, Earl of, 136
Son characters (in Shakespeare), 35, 118
Sons and Lovers (Lawrence), 211
Sophocles, 224
Southampton, Henry Wriothesley, third Earl of: Essex and, 115, 116; James I and, 140; MV and, 29, 30; Rutland and, 249; as Shakespeare's patron, 3, 249; in Spanish War, 67; sweet wines tax and, 136; Virginia and, 93
Southwark district, 91-93
Southwell, Robert, 178, 179, 181, 250
Spanish Tragedy, The (Kyd), 12
Spanish War, 23, 67
Spedding, James, 256
Spencer, Gabriel, 44, 126
Spenser, Edmund, 44, 112, 214
Staging, *see* Theatrical Production
Stanhope, John, 93
Stow, John, 24, 26, 27, 206
Strachey, William, 240
Strange's Men (acting company), 3, 5
Stratford: College, 162; vs. enclosures, 118, 266–67; fires in, 29, 264, 268
Sturley, Abraham, 65, 66, 162
Subsidies (taxation), 23–24
Swan Theater, 44–45
Symons, Thomas, 23
Synecdoche (in LR), 168–69

Tabard Inn, 94
Taming of the Shrew, The, 179, 235
Tarlton, Dick, 73
Tavern (Oxford), 188
Taxation, *see* Subsidies (taxation); Tithes
Tempest, The, 240–46; Anne of Denmark and, 136; at Elizabeth Stuart's wedding, 248; PHT and, 105; as Shakespeare's valedictory, 238, 251
Tennyson, Alfred, 39, 257
Terence (Publius Terentius Afer), 129
Tetrameters (in late Shakespeare), 274
Thames River, 204–5
Theater (Shoreditch playhouse), 5, 6, 77, 88
Theater War, 125–26, 128, 131
Theatrical convention, 11–12, 20–21, 86
Theatrical production, 9–11
Theobald, Lewis, 252, 253, 254
Thrale, Henry, 90
Throckmorton family, 178
Tilney, Edmund, 8–9, 10, 40
Time, as theme, 99, 132, 225, 235, 237; *see also* Cyclical patterns; Mortality, as theme
Timon of Athens, 190–95, 211, 273
'Tis Pity She's a Whore (Ford), 171
Tithes, 162, 163, 263–64, 267
Titus Andronicus, 3, 141
Tooley, Nicholas, 74
Tourneur, Cecil, 164, 170–71, 172
Tragicomedy, 230
Treachery, as theme, 129
Tresham, Francis, 177
Troilus and Cressida, 113, 117, 128–33, 202, 223
Trojan War, 129–30
Twelfth Night, 94-100; generosity theme in, 66; Greek romances and, 224; Jonson and, 127; Malvolio's madness in, 26; music in, 74; PHT and, 102; Sincler in, 75
Twins (in TN), 94–95, 99
Two Gentlemen of Verona, The, 155, 254
Two Noble Kinsmen, The, 223, 241, 254, 269–74
Tyrone, Hugh O'Neill, second Earl of, 115

Ulysses (Joyce), 141
Underhill family, 59-60
Unities, dramatic, 12, 242
Usury, 24, 48

Vautrollier, Thomas, 147
Velasco, John de, 139
Venereal disease (and MM), 148
Venus and Adonis, 3
Vernon, Elizabeth, 29, 30
Virginia Company, 239

Wages, in Shakespeare's England, 66
Wake, Isaac, 188

Wales, Henry Stuart, Prince of, 248
Walker, Henry (mercer), 118
Walker, Henry (minstrel), 250
Walker, William, 241, 275
Walton, Judith, 217
Warwick family, 161
Warwick, Dowager Countess of, 162
"Waste Land, The" (Eliot), 207
Watermen, 205
Wayte, William, 61, 62
Webster, John, 172, 173
Whatcott, Robert, 265, 275
Whately, Anne, 254
Wheeler, Margaret, 265
White Devil, The (Webster), 173
White Peacock, The (Lawrence), 211
"Who Wrote Shakespeare's Henry VIII?" (Spedding), 256
Wilde, Oscar, 97
Wilkins, George, 217–18
Willobie His Avisa, 131, 238
Wilson, Jack, 74
Wilson, Thomas, 263
Wilton House, 138
Winchester House, 26
Winchester, William Paulet, first Marquis of, 26–27
Winter's Tale, The, 231-38; CYM and, 223; John Shakespeare and, 36; Robert Greene and, 4; TMP and, 243; TNK and, 272
Witt, Johannes de, 45, 90
Women: as actresses, 74; as dramatic characters, 87–88, 145, 193, 214, 241, 264; Venetian, 146
Worcester's Men (acting company), 73, 125–26, 139
Wriothesley, Henry, see Southampton, Henry Wriothesley, third Earl of
Wyatt, William, 65

Xenophobia, 27, 40, 226; *see also* Racism